Do The Impossible

My Crash Course on Presidential Politics Inside the Howard Dean Campaign

Kate O'Connor

Do The Impossible
My Crash Course on Presidential Politics
Inside the Howard Dean Campaign

©2011 Kate O'Connor
ISBN Number: 978-1-60571-116-4
Library of Congress Number: 2012901540

SHIRES PRESS

4869 Main Street
P.O. Box 2200
Manchester Center, VT 05255
www.northshire.com/printondemand

NORTHSHIRE BOOKSTORE

Building Community, One Book at a Time
*This book was printed at the Northshire Bookstore, a family-owned,
independent bookstore in Manchester Ctr., Vermont, since 1976.
We are committed to excellence in bookselling. The Northshire Bookstore's
mission is to serve as a resource for information, ideas, and entertainment
while honoring the needs of customers, staff, and community.*

Printed in the United States of America
using an Espresso Book Machine
from On Demand Books

—CONTENTS—

—AUTHOR'S NOTE—

The material in this book, unless otherwise noted, comes from campaign schedules, internal memos, speeches, blog postings, contemporaneous notes, and personal video and audio recordings.

—PROLOGUE—

<u>August 18, 2002</u>

I listened as Howard Dean, standing on a wooden crate in front of an American flag, spoke to a group of New Hampshire Democrats in, of all places, Hermano's Mexican restaurant.

"We are a grassroots campaign. We're probably going to have less money than everybody else, but we're going to make up for that in enthusiasm and volunteers."

The primary election was almost a year and a half away. But it wasn't too early for him to talk about his bid for president of the United States.

The small group of Democrats who came to the Mexican restaurant in Concord, New Hampshire, that Sunday morning may have recognized Howard as the sitting governor of their neighboring state, but they knew little about him as a presidential candidate. He, however, knew exactly why he was running – and how he planned to win the Democratic nomination.

Standing on the box that served as a stage, he outlined his campaign strategy. He would compete in the three states with the earliest votes – Iowa, New Hampshire, and South Carolina – before continuing on to primaries and caucuses in several big states on Super Tuesday. He would build an enormous e-mail list of supporters. And he would appeal to the common sense of the American voter. An American voter, in this case, who may have wondered if a successful presidential campaign could really begin at a Mexican restaurant a few hundred miles south of the Canadian border.

January 19, 2004

I sat in the front row across the aisle from Howard – settled in by the window, as was his custom – as person after person squeezed into our 130-seat charter airplane shortly before midnight.

First came Joe Trippi, the campaign manager who drank a Diet Pepsi, beside Paul Maslin, the campaign's pollster, and Steve McMahon, Howard's media consultant.

Next came the rock singer Joan Jett, an avid supporter and performer at Howard's rallies. Wearing a tight black T-shirt and pants over her tattooed skin, she couldn't have looked more different from her candidate in his business suit and penny loafers.

Next came more than 75 journalists representing newspaper, magazine and television outlets nationwide. Crews from ABC, CBS, CNN, Fox, and MSNBC joined reporters from the *Washington Post, New York Times, Los Angeles Times, Boston Globe*, Associated Press, Reuters, and cameramen from Vermont's major television stations.

Waiting for the plane to take off, campaign staff smiled and chatted – but not because they were happy. Many were trying to put on a brave face while some had yet to fully comprehend what had happened.

Howard had just placed third in the Iowa caucuses.

When the campaign began we would have toasted such an improbable achievement. But instead of celebrating, Howard sat in his seat motionless, not saying a word as people passed by.

He had reached a level of success that no one – Howard included – ever imagined possible. Hundreds of thousands of people had joined his campaign. Tens of thousands had come out to hear him speak. He had led in nationwide polls. He had shattered fundraising records. His face had graced the covers of both *Time* and *Newsweek* magazines when the press had deemed him the front-runner for the Democratic nomination for president of the United States. In a matter of hours, everything had changed.

Flight attendants walked through the airplane offering champagne and shrimp ordered for a celebration. Howard sat with his shoes off, his feet up against the bulkhead. His face was a shade of gray that was slightly lighter than the charcoal suit he was wearing. He was silent. The look of disbelief on his face told the story. The self-proclaimed "greatest grassroots campaign of the modern era" had been cut down.

□ □ □

What happened? How did a man from a small state defy all the odds to draw big crowds, contributions and coverage, only to see it all fall away in a matter of months?

I've read all the explanations by the press, other politicians and pundits. But they weren't working beside Howard in the Mexican restaurant, on the chartered plane or at the countless thousands of campaign stops from Bangor, Maine, to Los Angeles, California.

I was.

Having worked with Howard since he ran for Vermont lieutenant governor in 1990, I worked as his closest advisor through his 11½ years as governor and right to the end of his 2004 presidential campaign.

Many people wonder what really happens inside a presidential campaign. What's the role of the candidate? Consultants? The press and public? What about money? Advertising? The Internet? Their questions aren't simply about the drama (or comedy) of the Dean campaign, but also about the state of U.S. presidential politics in the 21st century.

After traveling two years and more than half a million miles, here's what I saw and heard.

Part 1

—

2000

—NOVEMBER—

"What do you think about me running for president?" That was the question Howard asked me a few weeks after he was re-elected to his fifth term as governor of Vermont in November 2000.

If I didn't know him, I probably would have assumed that he was either joking or delusional. After all, Howard run for president of the United States? But I did know him and no matter how absurd the idea may have sounded, I knew he was serious.

It wasn't the first time he toyed with the idea of running. Howard had been working more hours as a family doctor than as Vermont's part-time lieutenant governor when he became the state's chief executive upon the death of his predecessor in 1991. Howard's wife, Judy, and school-age children Anne and Paul — blasé at best about politics — happily handed him over to us in the office as long as we sent him home on time for dinner and school hockey games. But all that didn't stop Howard from considering the presidency in 1997.

He quickly dismissed the idea after word leaked out to the press and his approval ratings in Vermont plummeted. Vermonters did not want their chief executive officer running the state and running for president at the same time.

But this time Howard was determined to pursue it. He was tired of picking up the newspaper every morning and reading about what the politicians in Washington — both Republicans and Democrats — were talking about. He believed they weren't focused on the real needs of Americans. And he believed he could do something about it.

Part II

—

2001

—JANUARY—

January 29, 2001

Howard took the oath of office and began his tenth year as governor on January 4, 2001. Just a few weeks later he gathered a small group at his home in Burlington, Vermont, to discuss the possibility of him running for president. Howard talked with me, Steve McMahon, and Bob Rogan. Steve was a partner in the Washington, D.C. media firm Trippi, McMahon, and Squier and had been Howard's media consultant for his gubernatorial campaigns since 1992. Bob worked in the governor's office from 1994 to 1998, serving as deputy chief of staff and was now an executive at a Vermont utility company in Rutland.

When Howard said that he was thinking about running for president everyone came to the same conclusion: The idea may sound far-fetched, but why not? Howard had a successful record as governor and, although he had no name recognition, he was no less qualified than any other potential candidate.

After quickly dismissing the question of should he, we turned to how he would do it. The first issue on Howard's mind was who would manage the campaign.

It may sound odd to think about finding a campaign manager before you even know there is going to be a campaign, but Howard always thought ahead. And in this case he may have been premature, but he was realistic.

He wanted to run a serious campaign, which meant having a manager with previous presidential campaign experience. But getting someone to sign on with a governor from a small state who lacked the resources of the better-known candidates was going to be difficult. In addition, Howard was insistent that his campaign would be run out of Vermont, which meant anyone working for him would have to move to the state.

Steve immediately knew the perfect person for the job: Mike Ford, a Maryland political strategist who had worked for Jerry Brown, Dick Gephardt, Ted Kennedy, and Walter Mondale. Steve agreed to call him and see if he was interested.

—APRIL—

April 27, 2001

Howard and I flew to Virginia to meet Mike Ford. Wearing a sweater, khaki pants, and baseball cap, Mike looked more prepared to play golf than meet with a potential candidate for president. It was clear that although Howard was the candidate, Mike knew he would be the one with the presidential campaign experience. That self-confidence allowed him to dominate the meeting. Sitting between Howard and me at a conference room table, he pressed Howard for his positions on issues, presumably in order to get a better understanding of who he was. He wasn't polite and he didn't hesitate to argue with Howard if he disagreed with him.

We didn't discuss any specific strategy nor did Howard ask Mike to run the campaign. We did agree to talk again in six months to give Howard more time to decide if he was really ready to run.

After the two-hour meeting, Howard and I left with the same impression of Mike; he was tough, but he seemed to know what he was doing. We didn't ponder much about the place of the meeting – the Trippi, McMahon, and Squier office in Alexandria, Virginia – or about one of the other people there – Steve's business partner Joe Trippi.

—SEPTEMBER—

September 5, 2001

As Howard plotted out a potential campaign, he struggled with another important decision – whether he was ready to leave the governor's office.

Leaving a job you've enjoyed for more than a decade isn't easy to do, even if you are thinking about running for president. But by fall, after months of going back and forth, Howard was relaxed, upbeat, and clearly comfortable as he told a small crowd of local news media, staff, and other onlookers gathered in front of the Vermont State House that he would not be running for re-election in 2002.

After, we walked back to his office. Howard was happy, but I felt otherwise. Howard asked me why and I told him that it was emotional knowing that something was coming to an end. His response was, "It's not the end, it's just the beginning."

The announcement surprised the press and public. But it didn't take long for people to speculate about what Howard would do in the future.

Howard had done nothing publicly to signal that he might run for president, but that didn't stop the *Rutland Herald*, Vermont's second largest newspaper, from running a front page story headlined "President Dean? Not That Crazy an Idea."

The *Boston Globe* jumped in by editorializing that "should he run for president, Vermont's civil-unions law will take some explaining in less tolerant corners of the land. But a candidate running a campaign based on expanded access to health care, protection of the environment and equal rights would at least have something to talk about."

With the decision not to seek re-election behind him, Howard was free to put his full attention on the potential presidential campaign.

13

Less than one week later, politics would be changed forever by the September 11 terrorist attacks.

—NOVEMBER—

November 3, 2001

North Carolina Senator John Edwards, who many thought would run for president, served as the keynote speaker at a Vermont Democratic Party dinner in Montpelier. As the state's sitting governor, Howard also spoke. And it was his speech that caught the media's attention.

Addressing Democrats in a hotel ballroom in the state's capital city, Howard focused on foreign policy and national issues – issues that had little to do with the agenda of a small state governor. That focus and one line – "I think we have to be very, very careful not to allow the spirit of bipartisanship turn to a spirit of capitulation on the part of our party" – further fueled the speculation that he would run.

November 5, 2001

Exactly two months after Howard announced that he would not seek re-election, we formed a political action committee, Fund for a Healthy America. The committee gave Howard a reason to travel around the country talking about the issues that were important to him, while at the same time meeting people who could be helpful if he did run for president.

Fund for a Healthy America had a message that, like most everything Howard did, was not determined by consultants or polls. Sitting in my office, he pulled out a piece of paper and scribbled down the PAC's purpose. It would assist candidates who supported "the principles of fiscal stability, universal health insurance, better environmental protection and equality for all Americans."

Forming the PAC was as easy as filing a few papers with the Federal Election Commission. But Howard wasn't looking for a PAC in name only. He wanted an active organization that could someday lead to a presidential campaign. To do that, we needed money.

We hadn't run the idea of the PAC by any potential donors, so we didn't know whether anyone would support it enough to make a contribution. Despite this we set a goal of raising $100,000 by the end of the year. That was just eight weeks away.

The amount wasn't based on how much we would need to operate the PAC. We thought a six-figure number would look impressive on the federal finance report we'd have to file in January. It should have been a small sum for someone thinking about running for president, but Howard had spent less than $250,000 on three out of five of his gubernatorial races, so our ability to raise large amounts of money quickly had never been tested.

November 15, 2001

Howard decided to share his plans with Vermont's U.S. senators, Patrick Leahy and Jim Jeffords. He wasn't looking for an endorsement – he wasn't a candidate yet. But a number of U.S. senators, including Joe Biden, Tom Daschle, John Edwards, John Kerry, and Joe Lieberman, were considering a run for president, and Howard wanted his home state senators to know what he was thinking before they endorsed one of their colleagues.

We met with both men in their Washington offices. They were polite when Howard revealed his potential candidacy. Jeffords, who just months earlier had changed the balance of power in Congress when he left the Republican Party and became an Independent, seemed to understand Howard's desire to take on such a challenge. Leahy's chief of staff Luke Albee was skeptical, saying what most people thought, but didn't dare say: "Are you kidding?" He reminded me of the obvious – we had no money or name recognition, which made what we were planning just plain crazy.

—DECEMBER—

December 6, 2001

The West African country of Burkina Faso was a world away from the state of Vermont and seemingly had nothing to do with the presidential election in the United States. But Howard was in the country a month after forming Fund for a Healthy America. The stated purpose of his trip was to attend an International Conference on AIDS. The unspoken reason was to bolster his foreign policy credentials.

During his almost 12 years as governor he shied away from foreign travel, even if it was to recruit businesses to Vermont. However, that changed when he recognized that his foreign policy experience wouldn't measure up when compared to that of a member of Congress.

But Howard enjoyed boasting that he had visited more foreign countries than President Bush. He was intent on adding to the list. He followed up his trip to Africa with visits to Chile, Brazil, and Israel. He also began to brush up on his Spanish, popping tapes into his car's tape deck as he traveled around Vermont, much to the consternation of his state police driver.

December 19, 2001

Iowa and New Hampshire would be the first states to vote in the presidential nominating process and Howard was eager to visit both.

Although Vermont and New Hampshire shared a border, Howard rarely visited the state, as it wasn't necessary in his capacity as governor. Then he was given a reason to cross the border when the Democratic Governors Association asked him to meet with potential gubernatorial candidates.

Getting a chance to meet with the three candidates vying to fill the seat that would be vacated by New Hampshire Governor Jeanne Shaheen was a great opportunity – after all, if one of them were to become governor, they might remember the help Howard gave them and return the favor.

During the trip Howard sat down with the *Concord Monitor* editorial board for his first in-depth interview since the speculation that he would run for president began. He gave the paper a preview of the kind of presidential candidate he planned to be if he ran: "I am who I am. I think America needs the vision of a fiscal conservative and a social progressive. And there's no point in my changing myself to accommodate. I think when this country gets in trouble, it's because they choose people who accommodate their views to whatever people want to hear in order to get elected."

December 29, 2001

With two days to go before the end of the year we were $20,000 short from reaching our self imposed $100,000 fundraising goal. No one knew that we had a goal, so we wouldn't be publicly derided if we failed to reach it, but we would know.

We were spared the blow to our self esteem when the envelope containing the much need last checks arrived. Fund for a Healthy America ended the year with $111,300.

December 30, 2001

Howard spent the last days of the year in Charleston, South Carolina, at Renaissance Weekend, an invitation-only annual event described by organizers as a "private retreat" for "accomplished families of leaders" from the world of business, finance, religion, law, medicine, sports, government, and the arts.

The event gained cachet when Bill and Hillary Clinton made an appearance in the mid-1990s. It was Howard's first time attending and few if any of those gathered were impressed that a potential presidential candidate was among them. For them, money was the measure of a successful candidate and few believed that he would have access to the funds necessary to capture the Democratic nomination. As *Newsweek* magazine columnist and Renaissance Weekend guest Eleanor Clift wrote, Howard's candidacy was greeted that weekend with "extreme skepticism accompanied by eye rolling."

Part III

—

2002

—JANUARY—

The American Prospect, a monthly political magazine, described Fund for a Healthy America: "Compared with the burgeoning and well-oiled machines being assembled by some of his would-be Democratic rivals, Dean's PAC is charmingly modest."

That was an understatement. We began 2002 without an office or a staff other than Howard (the PAC's chairman) and me (the PAC's treasurer). Our only other assets:

1. A little more than $110,000 in the bank.
2. A cardboard box.

When we formed Fund for a Healthy America we didn't have a national database of supporters to draw upon, much less a computer. The closest thing was a well-worn cardboard box filled with hundreds of business cards, letters, and scraps of paper containing the names and contact information of people Howard had met during his political career. He had made many of the contacts through his work as chairman of the National Governors Association and Democratic Governors Association; others had heard him speak at events where he discussed health care, children's issues or civil unions. In 2000, Howard signed the first law in the country granting gay and lesbian couples many of the same rights and benefits as heterosexual couples, which made him a popular speaker at gay and lesbian events nationwide.

It had been close to a decade since Howard had been in touch with many of the individuals whose names were scrawled on the scraps of paper. Finding 50 manila folders – one for each state – I filed the names in alphabetical order and marked each to indicate if the individual had the potential to be a donor or an organizer.

Lack of hard-drives aside, Howard was confident that he had what mattered most – a message he believed in – and he told it to anyone who would listen.

Although he had yet to make a formal announcement, he made a conscious decision to approach everything he did as if he were running. He didn't squander a single opportunity – starting with his annual State of the State speech to the Vermont Legislature. The speech, delivered the first week of January, would set the tone for his presidential campaign:

> America must now take its rightful place as a moral leader, as well as an economic and military leader in the world. We must do so in consultation with other countries and not unilaterally. In our nation's history, isolationism has been a strong and powerful political trend. I hope that isolationism is gone for good; we can never again afford to believe that what happens elsewhere in the world has no effect on Vermont ... Vermont is a small state with a big heart. And this small state has proven that with fiscal caution and caring social policy, Vermont values can serve as a guide for the nation.

In a speech normally reserved for such topics as local land conservation or school lunch programs, Howard's words drew notice. One Vermont newspaper wrote, "The speech offered a tantalizing glimpse of further horizons and the direction Dean's thinking is taking as he considers a campaign for the presidency."

Howard also began to speak out in other states as he recruited candidates on behalf of the Democratic Governors Association.

We never left a state without reaching out to the people he would need to know if he was a candidate. This meant aggressively courting state and local labor leaders, teachers, Democratic activists, elected officials, and the media wherever we went. Most, if not all, had no idea who Howard was and were often confused as to why he wanted to meet with them. Howard's scheduler, a 24-year-old Vermont native named Sarah Buxton, had the unenviable task of convincing people to take time to meet with a man they never heard of. It was not uncommon for her to write notes on the schedule such as "both women are vague about this meeting" to describe the reaction she received when she called.

January 14, 2002

There was often no rhyme or reason to the things we did, and nothing illustrated that better than when we contacted the actor Martin Sheen.

It wasn't long after Howard formed his PAC that several supporters noted that he had a lot in common with the fictional president on the NBC drama *The West Wing*. Martin Sheen played Josiah Bartlet, a former Democratic governor of a New England state who, married to a doctor indifferent to politics, improbably became president of the United States.

Howard had never watched the show, but enough people mentioned the similarities that by mid-January he decided to see if he could meet Sheen. We didn't know the actor and odds were he had never heard of Howard, but we were pulling names out of a cardboard box, so why not try to wrangle a meeting, we figured.

Howard knew one person in Hollywood: Rob Reiner, the actor, producer, and director best known for his portrayal of Archie Bunker's son-in-law, Michael "Meathead" Stivic, on the1970's television hit *All in the Family*. Howard had met Reiner in 1994 as chairman of the National Governors Association. I took a chance and called Reiner's assistant, Chad Griffin. I explained our odd request and asked if he knew how we could get in touch with Sheen.

As luck would have it, Chad was scheduled to take part in an environmental protest with Sheen. He said if I faxed him a letter from Howard, he would pass it along. So I sat down and drafted one of the strangest letters we would ever send. The gist: You play a New England governor turned president on television. I'm looking to do that in real life. Wanna meet?

The letter sounded ridiculous, but I faxed it to Chad. I figured he'd pass it along and that would be the end of it. A few days later, much to my surprise, I received a call from Sheen's publicist. The actor would be happy to meet with Howard.

January 16, 2002

Howard was working hard, but sometimes it was luck that moved us forward. We had been looking for an opportunity to go to Iowa, the state that held the earliest contest in the presidential nominating process. But finding a valid reason for Vermont's departing governor to do so was a challenge. Then we received a letter from Iowa congressional candidate Julie Thomas. Thomas was running to represent the state's 2nd district – home to such population centers as Iowa City and Cedar Rapids – and she wanted to arrange a telephone conversation with Howard in order to get his advice on campaigning.

Howard's potential presidential bid wasn't the reason Thomas contacted him. Thomas, like Howard, was a doctor. Years earlier she had attended an American Academy of Pediatrics conference where Howard, in a keynote speech, encouraged doctors to run for public office. She was answering his call and now seeking his advice.

We knew nothing about Thomas beyond the fact that she was a doctor and she was running for Congress. But the letter was barely out of the envelope when Howard picked up the telephone and called her. All she wanted was to talk to him. But he volunteered to travel to Iowa and campaign for her. Within a month, he'd be there.

January 23, 2002

By the end of January, Howard's name appeared on a list of potential presidential candidates compiled by the ABC News online political journal The Note. No Democrat had officially declared, so the news organization based its list on behind-the-scenes buzz.

Lucky for us they didn't discriminate based on one's chances of actually winning.

The Note rated potential candidates in various categories, including access to money, consultants and policy advisors, and having the drive to run – or what they termed "fire in the belly."

Howard ranked 12 out of 13, followed only by Delaware Senator Joe Biden. He didn't fare well in most categories but received high marks for the heat of his political desire.

Average voters didn't read The Note, so appearing on the list wasn't going to help us connect to people in Iowa and New Hampshire. But political insiders? That's another story.

—FEBRUARY—

February 2, 2002

A candidate travels to Iowa and New Hampshire for votes and to places like Chicago, Los Angeles, and New York for money. With Howard's visit to Iowa confirmed, we set out for California.

Howard had received an invitation to give the keynote address at a West Hollywood dinner sponsored by the California Alliance for Pride and Equality, a gay and lesbian advocacy group.

Wanting to gauge how he and his message of fiscal responsibility, universal health care, and environmental protection would play on the West Coast, he asked a Democratic friend with entertainment connections to gather a small group of industry movers and shakers.

The lunch took place at the Ivy Restaurant in Los Angeles. I had never heard of the place. I opened the menu and discovered that the price of a salad could cover our postage fees for a year. I looked over to make sure that Howard, who was known for his frugality, hadn't passed out.

The restaurant was casual, not fancy, with traditional American fare including salads, sandwiches, and pasta dishes – nothing we couldn't find in Vermont for half the price. It wasn't until later that I discovered we weren't paying for the food, but instead for whom we might see and who might see us. As the Ultimate Hollywood Insider website would tell me, we were eating lunch at "one of LA's leading celebrity hangouts, attracting a virtual who's who in Hollywood stars and moguls . . . there are often paparazzi camped out across the street hoping for photos of arriving celebrities."

We should have gotten a discount – there were no paparazzi waiting out front to snap a picture of Howard.

Twelve people – television and film producers, writers, and actors who were active in causes ranging from environmental protection, civil liberties, and children's issues – attended the lunch. Because most worked behind the scenes, I didn't know who many of them were. But I did recognize one person, the actress Donna Mills. Mills played Abby Cunningham, the manipulating home wrecker, on the primetime soap opera *Knots Landing*, a show I admit watching when I was growing up.

The food may have been pricey, but the lunch was informal. Howard remained seated at the table while he gave his speech. In between bites of salad and sandwiches, the guests asked questions and critiqued his ideas.

In the end there was no doubt that they agreed with his politics. Convincing them to take a risk and support him was something else.

February 6, 2002

It was time for Howard to make his first public appearance in New Hampshire. His trip to the state at the end of the previous year included only private meetings, so this trip marked a coming out of sorts.

Under the auspices of Fund for a Healthy America, he went to campaign for John Kacavas, a Democratic candidate for the state's

Executive Council. (It was an important position. The five council members worked with the governor to administer the affairs of the state.)

Although still relatively unknown, Howard had become a curiosity to the news media – especially those hungry for an excuse to write about an election that was two years away. Kacavas acknowledged in an interview that where a presidential candidate went the press were sure to follow, even if that candidate was one few had heard of. He was right. The trip was covered by the Associated Press, CNN, and a small army of Vermont and New Hampshire newspaper and television reporters.

The full day of campaigning included a tour of a natural gas plant, a stop by a bingo game at a senior center, and lunch with the Democratic mayor of Manchester at the Merrimack Restaurant, a place we later discovered was a popular stop on any presidential campaign tour. The two men also took time to stand on a street corner holding a large Kacavas sign while waving at passing motorists.

The schedule offered Howard the opportunity to shake hands at each stop, even if it caused seniors to lose track of the numbers and letters being shouted out by the bingo announcer.

February 8, 2002

For months Howard had been trying to decide if he wanted Mike Ford to manage the campaign, and after much thought he concluded that he did not. Nothing specific had happened. He just didn't feel that Mike was the right fit. But feeling the pressure of all the work that needed to be done and having no other option (people weren't exactly lining up to work for him), Howard felt he had no choice but to ask Mike to take the job.

The two met for breakfast at the Sheraton Hotel in Burlington, Vermont. Although they sat at the same table, who said what depends on who you talk to. According to Howard, he asked Mike to manage the campaign. According to Mike, he didn't.

Several days after the breakfast meeting, I got a call from Joe Trippi, a partner in the firm Trippi, McMahon, and Squier and a friend of Mike's. He told me that Mike was upset with the way Howard asked – or didn't ask – him to run the campaign. According to Joe, working on a campaign was like entering into a marriage. He used a more crass analogy, but in essence said that Mike expected to be "courted" by Howard before he would say, "I do."

We hadn't been schooled in the Washington ways of dealing with political strategists, so we were taken aback by the notion that Howard was going to have to get down on bended knee before Mike would consent to work for him. We weren't by any means naïve; we knew we needed the help. But we were making a great deal of progress on our own and Howard was more interested in getting work done than pursuing someone he really wasn't sure of to begin with. Joe's call only re-enforced his doubts.

Howard didn't have another conversation with Mike, Joe or Steve, and whether Mike would run the campaign was left up in the air.

February 20, 2002

Two weeks after campaigning for John Kacavas, we made our second trip to New Hampshire – this time on behalf of congressional candidate Martha Fuller Clark.

Howard appreciated the opportunities that candidates like Kacavas and Clark afforded him. That said, because he was campaigning for someone else he was limited in what he could say about himself. Eager to see how he would be received in New Hampshire as a presidential hopeful, he wanted an audience that was focused on him and him alone.

We reached out to former New Hampshire Democratic Party Chair Michael King whose name was in our cardboard box because of a phone call he made to the governor's office years earlier regarding a boat he kept in Vermont. Although King said it was too early for him to commit, he did offer to help us when we visited New Hampshire. He suggested we do a small house party and put me in touch with Carol Appel, the Strafford County Democratic chair who lived in Dover. Carol agreed to invite some of her friends to her home to meet Howard. Like any voter in an early primary state, she made it clear that she was not supporting him; she was helping only as a favor to Michael.

The 10 people who gathered in Carol's living room that Wednesday morning ranged in age from a middle school student who came with her mother to a retired couple.

Howard recognized that although Vermont and New Hampshire shared a border, he was an unfamiliar figure to Granite State residents. But he believed that in a place where candidates were asked to take a "no new taxes" pledge, his fiscal conservatism would be an advantage. He stressed to the group his belief that "social justice can only be accomplished through strong fiscal management" and touted the fact that, during his tenure as governor, he helped erase Vermont's budget deficit and balance spending, all while guaranteeing health coverage to every child up to age 18.

But Howard didn't restrict his focus to policy issues. He told them about his family and the small town medical practice he began with his wife, Judy. He explained how he became the Democratic county chair in Vermont's largest county and how he started in elective office by running for a seat in the Vermont Legislature. He recalled stuffing envelopes for Jimmy Carter in 1980 and being selected to serve as a Carter delegate to the Democratic National Convention. (He drew laughter when confiding he voted with the Carter people by day and partied with the Kennedy supporters at night.) He talked about practicing medicine while at the same time serving as lieutenant governor and how he became governor when the sitting governor died in office. And wanting feedback, he ended his speech with the folksy line, "Now, I'm happy to take questions, comments and, as we say in Vermont, rude remarks."

After, everyone mingled with Howard as they munched on cookies Carol had arranged on her dining room table. People sounded pleased with what they heard and were surprised by all they didn't know about the governor who lived right next door.

One woman was busy running around the room. I assumed she was buzzing about Howard's speech. Making her way over to me, she instead turned out to be a self appointed fashion critic stirring up controversy over his wardrobe. She didn't like his shoes and thought his pants were too short and the collar on his shirt was too tight and frayed. She believed Howard needed a complete makeover and she had polled the room to see how many agreed.

When it was time to go, we thanked Carol for her hospitality and got in the car. Howard was energized. The comments he received after his speech made him feel that those gathered were genuinely interested in him and wanted to know more. He asked me what I had heard. Apparently he was the only one who didn't get the wardrobe report. I repeated the critique of his pants, shoes, and shirt. Howard was wearing his favorite suit – one he bought at JC Penney. He strongly disagreed that his pants were too short. But if they were, he said, he knew how to fix them – he'd let his belt out one notch.

We got good news when we dropped Michael King off at his home in Portsmouth. Howard got out of the car to thank him for his help and when he got back in he had a smile on his face. Michael, despite Howard's short pants, had signed on to the campaign – our first official New Hampshire supporter.

From New Hampshire we drove to New York to attend a fundraiser for Fund for a Healthy America at the city's famed 21

Club. Howard was still thinking about the critical assessment of his pants when he walked by a mirror in the Club's restaurant. He backed up, did an examination, and diagnosed the length as just right.

Howard wasn't the only potential presidential candidate at the 21 Club that evening. A late arriving guest at our reception told Howard that former Vice President Al Gore was having dinner in a private dinning room down the hall. Not wanting to miss the opportunity Howard went to say hello.

February 22, 2002

Two days after our trip to New Hampshire we made our first visit to Iowa. We didn't know much about the Hawkeye State, but we did know this: Since 1972 the Iowa caucuses had held the distinction of being the first contest in the presidential nominating process and many candidates relied on winning there to spring board them to the nomination.

The caucuses would be important for Howard, but if he was unfamiliar to the people of New Hampshire he was even more so to Iowans. His lack of name recognition, however, did not worry him. He believed he could do well because Iowa and Vermont had much in common. Or as he would put it, "If you roll a steamroller over Vermont, you'd have Iowa."

Looking at the numbers, the two states were polar opposites. Vermont had 223 mountains; Iowa was so flat you can see for miles along the horizon. Iowa's 2.9 million people far outnumbered Vermont's 600,000, and Iowa's 55,869 square miles of land made Vermont with its 9,609 square miles seem even smaller than it actually was.

But demographics aside Howard believed the two states had one thing in common that would give him an advantage over his potential rivals: campaigning for president in Iowa was like campaigning for governor in Vermont, something he had done every two years for the past decade.

It's not quite true that Vermont has more cows than people, but it is the second least-populated state in the nation. Vermonters didn't think anything of seeing Howard at the grocery store or cheering his kids on at a high school sporting event. His home telephone number was in the telephone book and people didn't hesitate to use it. When you sent a letter to the governor's office, he read it. And Vermonters expected to be able to shake his hand and give him an earful if necessary. The same was true for Iowans. They were not just used to meeting presidential candidates, but expected to meet them multiple times, either one-on-one or in small settings. And they didn't hesitate to ask questions or express their opinions. It was the kind of campaigning Howard was used to, good at, and enjoyed.

Following so quickly on the heels of his second trip to New Hampshire, the trip to Iowa piqued the Vermont media's interest in Howard's intentions. Vermont had only two television news stations, a CBS affiliate and an NBC affiliate, both located in Burlington, the state's largest city. Neither customarily sent crews far outside the state for news, but in this case a crew from the CBS affiliate, WCAX, accompanied us to Iowa.

Howard, a Vermont state trooper (who was a member of the governor's security detail), and I, along with a reporter and cameraman, boarded a USAir flight that would take us from Burlington to Pittsburgh and on to Cedar Rapids, Iowa.

When we arrived in Cedar Rapids we were greeted by an Iowa state police officer who would spend the day with us. (As a courtesy, governors provided police support to their colleagues who visited their states.) Howard and I and the Vermont state trooper hopped into a marked police car and went to an Iowa City law office to meet Julie Thomas for the first time.

In light of the fact that we knew very little about her we were pleased to find that she was a credible candidate running against the incumbent congressman, Republican Jim Leach.

We found ourselves in Iowa because Thomas wanted to have a simple telephone conversation with Howard. It only took us flying more than 1,000 miles for her to get the advice she was looking for.

□ □ □

The Thomas campaign scheduled events in both Iowa City and Cedar Rapids. It was my first visit to the state and I didn't know what to expect. People associate cows with Vermont and I thought corn when I heard Iowa. But I discovered that Cedar Rapids was a city with a population of just over 120,000 (Vermont's largest city, Burlington, had 38,000 residents), and Iowa City was home to the University of Iowa that boasted a student population of 29,000.

Howard was in Iowa to promote a fellow doctor's candidacy, a fact the Thomas campaign did not want lost, so they arranged a tour of the pediatric ward at Children's Hospital at the University of Iowa Hospital and Clinic in Iowa City. The hospital provided the perfect photo opportunity for both Thomas and Howard. A small army including me, the Vermont state trooper, the Iowa state police officer, the Vermont news crew, and an Iowa news crew, trailed behind the doctor/governor and doctor/candidate as they walked through the facility with several of the hospital's physicians and administrators. It was the first time we would tour a hospital, but not the last, and it always seemed intrusive to me to peer into a patient's room when he or she was most vulnerable. But such visits benefited Howard, so any uneasiness was rationalized away by the fact that he was just a doctor doing what doctors do.

The highlight of the trip was two house parties we attended for Thomas. The parties were Howard's first chance to introduce himself to Iowa voters and he gave the speech he had test driven in New Hampshire two days earlier, putting more emphasis on his and Thomas' physician credentials.

More than 50 people stood shoulder to shoulder in living rooms in both Cedar Rapids and Iowa City listening to Howard extol the virtues of electing a doctor to public office. Access to affordable, quality health care was a major concern and he told his audiences that physicians were the best equipped to address the problems in the health care system because they saw them every day. They treated patients who lacked health insurance and were unable to get the care necessary to prevent and manage illnesses. They experienced it as providers who were faced with cumbersome paperwork and low reimbursement rates, which impacted patient care.

But more generally he talked about how medical training made doctors good in the public policy arena. Doctors were trained to make decisions based on facts, not emotions, a quality Howard thought served him well and obviously the people of Vermont agreed because they had elected him to statewide office eight times.

The people at both events were impressed and, unlike what happened in New Hampshire, no one in the room paid any attention to his shirt, pants, and shoes. This time it was what he had to say – and that he was saying it in Iowa – that made them take notice.

Few if any of the people we met had ever heard of Howard, but Iowans were savvy enough to know that a politician, even the governor of Vermont, didn't visit their state by chance. And after hearing Howard, many speculated that there was more to his visit than just offering a helping hand to Julie Thomas.

Iowa voters weren't lining up behind the first presidential candidate they heard, but his speech did start a small buzz around the living rooms. In the early days we measured the success of a trip by the number of e-mail addresses or telephone numbers we left with. If just one person gave us their contact information we were thrilled. We left Iowa with not one e-mail address but a handful, many from individuals who would later sign on to the campaign.

□ □ □

During the trip we began the practice of staying at private homes. It started because we couldn't afford to stay in hotels, but it quickly became a way to meet potential supporters. I wasn't sold on the idea of staying with total strangers. What if they didn't like us or we didn't like them? But, thankfully, our maiden stay was a positive experience.

The first people who welcomed us into their home were Dan and Marcia Rogers of Cedar Rapids, Iowa. Julie Thomas' campaign asked the couple if they would be willing to host us and they agreed. They had two sons in their early twenties who were no longer living at home leaving two empty bedrooms. The room I slept in was still decorated with posters, photographs, and awards. It resembled other rooms I would stay in around the county – rooms waiting for their former occupants, now grown, to return for a visit.

Dan and Marcia became two of Howard's first Iowa supporters and their home became our home when we were in Cedar Rapids. By the end of the campaign we had stayed there so often that they jokingly renamed their kids' rooms Howard's room and Kate's room.

During 2002 and through the fall of 2003 we stayed with families with young children and teenagers; single parents; older couples whose children were grown and living on their own; and widowed grandmothers. We stayed with people who were financially well off and others with more moderate incomes. I slept on couches, bunk beds, and air mattresses. And if where we stayed was any indication, Democrats preferred cats to dogs.

When asked by *USA Today* to explain his fondness for staying at private homes instead of hotels Howard told the newspaper, "It's more fun. To stay up yakking with somebody until a ridiculous hour when you have to get up at 5 in the morning, that's something I like."

February 23, 2002

When we boarded the airplane to leave Iowa it was clear that Howard was ready to run for president. He had been moving full speed ahead since he formed the PAC and his pace only accelerated. We had been operating without a plan for months, but in the wake of the Iowa trip he began to put the specifics of his would-be campaign into focus.

The reason he wanted to run hadn't changed since he first expressed interest at the end of 2000. He wanted to change what the politicians in Washington – especially the members of his own party – were talking about. To accomplish this he would talk about health care, the federal budget, and foreign policy in a new way. He would emphasize long-term results instead of just "feel good" legislation passed in order to ensure re-election. And he would take on the policies of the Bush administration and challenge Democrats in Congress, who he believed sided too often with the Republican president, to step up and do the same.

He surmised that if he talked about the issues that other Democrats tried to avoid he could set the agenda for the Democratic Party during the primary election campaign. He would tell the *New York Times*, "As long as I'm in the race, everybody has to talk about the issues that I talk about."

But he wasn't going to settle for just influencing the dialogue throughout the primary. He believed there needed to be a fundamental and long-term change in the Democratic Party's policy priorities and he wanted to be at the table when those policies were set. He wanted to be the nominee, but if he wasn't he wanted to be sure that his voice would be heard. He could accomplish this by picking up enough delegates during the primary election season to show strength in numbers at the Democratic National Convention and put the nominee and the party in a position where they could not ignore him. So a key part of his strategy was to pick up delegates wherever he could. And, thankfully, one did not have to win a state to win delegates; they were allotted based on the number of votes a candidate received. All Howard had to do was get enough votes to be awarded delegates in each state and he would either be the nominee or at the very least a player at the convention.

It was one thing for Howard to know why he was running; it was another to actually put a campaign together. He would be competing against a host of better-known candidates and would need an organization if he was going to reach any level of success. But a campaign organization required what we didn't have: money.

Howard's plan for raising money was simple. He would collect $10 million in 2003. The first $2 million would be raised from 2,000 people donating $1,000 each and the rest would come from $15, $25, and $50 contributions. The money he raised in 2003 would be enough for him to receive federal matching funds in 2004. It was a good plan on paper, but it would have been even better if it had come with a list of possible contributors.

Howard never expected to have the resources to hire a large staff and anticipated that a small group of Vermonters would set up and run the organization. But we didn't know the first thing about putting a national campaign together.

In order to learn as much as we could we spent the six months after the trip to Iowa meeting with individuals who had either run for president or had worked on a presidential campaign. Members of former New Jersey Senator Bill Bradley's 2000 presidential campaign staff were the first we reached out to.

Howard wasn't looking for strategic or message advice when we spoke to Gina Glantz, Bradley's former campaign manager. Instead he wanted to know how Bradley set up his organization. During a conference call he quizzed Gina on the timeline of hiring staff, how many people she hired, who she hired, and how much they got paid.

During a trip to Michigan we met with Robert Richmond, Bradley's national field director, who outlined how he put Bradley's field organization together. Much like his conversation with Gina, Howard wanted to know how many people he hired, how much they were paid, and how many states were staffed.

We were learning how to set up an organization, but the reality of how much work was ahead of us didn't set in until we learned about the Iowa caucuses. Howard asked a Democratic activist we met during a visit to Davenport to explain how a caucus worked. She was a bit baffled that a person considering a run for the presidency didn't already know the answer to the question, but in the end she explained the caucus system in detail while I took notes on a yellow legal pad.

We spent months learning as much as we could from anyone willing to take the time to talk to us and not all the advice we received was about organization, some of it was practical and we wouldn't know how true it was until later in the campaign. Former Democratic presidential candidate Gary Hart told us that anyone who runs for president can't be emotionally or physically weak. And the best advice of all came from former Clinton advisor Paul Begala, who recommended that we eat and go to the bathroom whenever the opportunity presented itself.

—MARCH—

March 4, 2002

Howard expanded his efforts into the southern part of the country with visits to Texas, Tennessee, and South Carolina.

South Carolina held the third contest in the delegate selection process after Iowa and New Hampshire and the first in the South. For Howard, South Carolina was as important as Iowa and New

Hampshire. He wanted to prove that he could do well throughout the country and appeal not just to liberal white northerners, but more conservative black southern voters as well.

There were obstacles, however. He was the governor of the second whitest state in the nation who had signed into law a bill establishing civil unions for gay and lesbian couples.

But he did have his conservative side, which he believed would help temper any concern that he was just a liberal from the Northeast. He touted his fiscal conservatism in Iowa and New Hampshire and he did the same in the South, stressing his record of balancing Vermont's budget and erasing the state's deficit. He also talked about his record on an issue that most Democrats wouldn't brag about. Vermont had virtually no gun laws, which earned him an "A" rating from the National Rifle Association during his years as governor. Receiving the support of the NRA would not go over well with Democrats in cities like New York, Los Angeles, and Washington D.C., where gun violence was prevalent, but it would be well received in states like South Carolina and Tennessee, where hunting was a tradition passed on through generations.

We went to South Carolina on the invitation of Democratic Governor Jim Hodges, who asked Howard to speak at a conference he was hosting on the environment.

We stayed at a private home – the governor's mansion – and accomplished our requirement of reaching out to activists by asking Don Fowler, a former chair of the Democratic National Committee, to introduce us to the local movers and shakers. He organized a mid-morning coffee get-together that included elected officials, Democratic Party leaders, and donors.

Howard lived by the motto, "You never get a second chance to make a first impression," and when given the opportunity to introduce himself to South Carolina voters he made it a priority to play up his conservative side. He wasn't subtle when he told a reporter with South Carolina's largest newspaper *The State,* "I'm very conservative with money" and "I have trouble with the liberal wing of my own party."

□ □ □

A few hours before leaving South Carolina we discovered that John Edwards had recorded a telephone message on behalf of a candidate for state senate that would be left on thousands of answering machines in Iowa.

Howard's competitive juices kicked in. He was not going to let Edwards have an advantage over him, so he called the Iowa state senate campaign committee and asked to do the same. Without explanation the staff person said no. But Howard was not going to be refused. He saw no difference between Edwards and himself; they were both potential presidential candidates. If Edwards could record a call, he could too. He persisted and the staff person finally said yes after Howard agreed to make a $5,000 donation to the campaign committee. It felt like extortion, but it was a small price to pay to make sure that John Edwards' voice would not be the only one Iowa voters heard.

The phone calls into Iowa made Howard think of New Hampshire. When he was done dealing with Iowa he called John Kacavas, the candidate for Executive Council, and offered to record a telephone message for him. This time there was no persuading necessary, he agreed without hesitation.

As we sat in the airport in Columbia, Howard wrote the two scripts and practiced while I timed him to make sure the message would fit in the ten to fifteen seconds of time allotted. With only minutes to spare before it was time to board our plane, he sat at a pay telephone and recorded the calls in between the boarding announcements that blared over the airport's loud speakers.

The Iowa caucuses and New Hampshire primary were still two years away, but we were in full campaign mode.

March 5, 2002

Howard was working on a plan for putting the campaign in motion, but whether Mike Ford would be the one managing it was still unresolved. The last time it was discussed, Joe was telling me that Howard had to court Mike, something he was not willing to do. We didn't know what Mike's role was or would be in the future and the lack of clarity was causing tension.

Steve McMahon, Joe Trippi, Mike Ford, Howard's press secretary Sue Allen, scheduler Sarah Buxton, and I had conference calls periodically to discuss how things were going, and during the first week of March our problems bubbled to the surface.

Weeks earlier Mike had suggested that Howard seek the endorsement of the actor Denzel Washington who was starring in the movie *John Q*. The film was about a father who took a hospital emergency room hostage when his insurance wouldn't cover the cost of his son's heart transplant operation. Mike believed the movie would provide Howard with a vehicle to talk about the problems with the health care system in the United States. Howard, with Washington at his side, could travel around the country and appear at special showings of the film.

Howard, Sue, and I didn't like the idea. We believed that Howard's record as governor and the fact that he was a doctor spoke for itself and we didn't need a movie to showcase his record on health care. We didn't say anything, however, because we assumed the idea would go away. When it came up again during the call I decided it was time to be honest, so I told Steve, Joe, and Mike what we thought of the proposal.

Building a campaign continued to be a learning experience. We had discovered that Washington consultants expected to be courted and we were about to find out that it was not polite to tell political strategists that you don't agree with them. Not only did Mike dismiss me, but so did his wife, who told me that I should worry about "my" PAC not "their" presidential campaign. With that the call ended and our working relationship with Mike was not far behind. He would soon send me an e-mail announcing that he was leaving the "Starship Howard."

Joe and Steve saw little hope for the campaign without Mike. They continued their efforts to get Howard to hire him, even trying to pressure him by announcing that the Kerry campaign was talking to Mike about working for the Massachusetts senator.

Mike would not become the campaign manager, a fact that prompted a late night telephone call from Joe. He wanted me to know that losing Mike meant that the only person who would ever agree to run the campaign would be Bozo the Clown.

March 21, 2002

Howard liked to jokingly describe himself as an "asterisk" because his name recognition in national polls was so low he barely warranted a percentage point. Not many people were paying attention to a presidential election two years before it was scheduled to take place, so his lack of name recognition among mainstream Americans was not shocking. But he was getting noticed.

We traveled to Washington, D.C. where Howard had been invited to speak to a group of Democratic attorneys general from around the country, along with Democratic National Committee Chairman Terry McAuliffe. While the two men gave their speeches, I stood in the hallway with a member of the DNC staff. During our conversation he told me that when McAuliffe asked a group of college Democrats who out of the possible presidential candidates they preferred, the majority said Howard.

I'm almost sure that the young staffer was not supposed to pass the information along because McAuliffe never mentioned it to Howard. The national party wasn't taking him seriously and certainly wasn't going to do anything to encourage or help him.

I waited until I was sure McAuliffe had left before sharing the information with Howard. If he didn't want us to know, I didn't want him to know that we did.

Howard had been reaching out to young voters, traveling to Arizona in August of 2001 to attend the Young Democrats of America National Convention and to Washington, D.C. eight months later to speak to the College Democrats of America. But we had no idea that he was making an impression.

March 27, 2002

A request from congressional candidate John Norris brought us back to Iowa for the second time. Norris, who was running against the four-term incumbent Congressman Republican Tom Latham, asked Howard to help him with his fundraising efforts. The campaign wanted help with two groups: the gay and lesbian community and doctors.

The Norris campaign organized an evening fundraising reception at a Des Moines bed and breakfast that catered to a gay and lesbian clientele. Just over 40 people paid between $25 and $100 to hear Howard speak. The owner of the establishment and host of the event was a gay man who had never met Howard before, but was well aware of who he was because he signed the civil unions law.

Many gay and lesbians considered Howard a hero for acknowledging that their relationships were as legitimate as those of heterosexual couples, and what was supposed to be a fundraiser for Norris began with an emotional tribute to Howard. During his introduction, the host broke down in tears when describing what the civil unions law meant to him. His emotion carried into the crowd and Howard ended up comforting the man with a hug.

March 28, 2002

We began our day with John Norris at Mercy Hospital in Des Moines. It was our second visit to an Iowa hospital, but this time we skipped the tour and instead had coffee and bagels with a group of doctors.

Howard and the physicians, who wandered in and out of the boardroom because of their patient schedules, sat around a conference table casually chatting about health care and the federal budget. Howard hadn't treated a patient in more than ten years, but that didn't make him feel any less a doctor. He discussed with his colleagues the challenges of treating patients who were under-insured or had no insurance at all as if he was a practicing physician.

He was a doctor, but he was also a governor and potential presidential candidate who took pride in his willingness to be blunt. And he pulled no punches when he announced that both doctors and patients were going to have to take some responsibility for the rising cost of health care and take a hard look at the costs associated with a procedure before the treatment was carried out.

Despite – or perhaps because of – his honest assessment, we left the hospital with a supporter, a Des Moines surgeon whose family included seven children. Their home would become our home when we were in Des Moines.

After we finished our obligations to Norris we set out on our own to meet the key players in Iowa's political scene. If anyone doubted that Howard was going to run for president, all they had to do was look at his schedule to know that he was serious.

Our first time meeting Iowa State Democratic Party chair Sheila Riggs and incoming chair Gordon Fischer was over cheese and steak soup at a Des Moines restaurant. The Iowa Democratic Party organized the caucuses and knowing the party's leadership could be nothing but helpful to us.

At another restaurant we introduced ourselves over coffee, or hot chocolate in Howard's case, to veteran Iowa political columnist David Yepsen. Yepsen had been covering politics for the *Des Moines Register*, the state's largest newspaper, for more than 30 years. Not only did Iowans read his column, but the national media looked to Yepsen for his insight on the presidential candidates.

We went to the governor's mansion to meet with Governor Tom Vilsack and members of his political team. Howard was the sitting governor of Vermont when we made our visit to the mansion, and although the two men were colleagues there was no talk of an endorsement, it was too early for that. Vilsack and his staff gave us advice about campaigning in Iowa. They listed the key people to meet and the important places to visits. The information was helpful, but the fact that it came from the governor made it more so. We were able to tell the individuals we wanted to meet that the governor suggested we call instead of pretending that we didn't get their names off the Internet.

—APRIL—

April 7, 2002

Finding reasons to go to Iowa and New Hampshire was getting easier. Each appearance Howard made led to another invitation. It was still a challenge, however, to find opportunities in other states. Howard was so eager for exposure that he was quick to accept any invitation that allowed him to travel outside Vermont. In the beginning he wasn't discriminating. If an envelope had an out of state postmark the invitation was accepted. It was a strategy that came with mixed results.

A Greek organization based in Massachusetts invited him to take part in its 8th Greek Independence Day celebration in Boston. He could speak at a brunch and march in a parade that the organizers promised would attract 80,000 people. It was an invitation we would have declined, but in light of a possible campaign he wasn't going to miss it.

The Sunday of the event Howard and I and a Vermont state trooper drove three hours from Burlington to Boston. When we arrived we found an event that did not live up to what had been promised. There were no speeches at the brunch – a brunch that consisted of slightly more than 25 people milling around a ballroom. No one seemed the least bit interested in Howard; they were too busy getting ready to take part in the parade.

Just moments before the parade was set to start, he was handed a blue sash to wear to indicate that he was a dignitary, but he had no sign with his name on it which meant no one watching would know who he was.

The parade participants walked in one big bunch past the onlookers whose numbers had been over estimated by at least one zero, if not two. At the end of the parade route a stage was set up allowing the dignitaries to address the crowd. Howard was invited to speak, but when we heard the others delivering their remarks in Greek we decided it was time to cut our losses and leave.

Without saying good-bye we snuck away. As we were walking behind the stage trying to make our escape unnoticed, the day took a turn for the better, or so we thought. A gentleman in the crowd told Howard he would vote for him. We were happy until he added, "When you run for mayor."

April 13, 2002

Each time we accepted an invitation we took a gamble, and we had better results during a trip to Minnesota.

Howard was invited to give the keynote address at the Minnesota State Democratic-Farmer-Labor Party's annual Humphrey Day dinner, named in honor of the former vice president and Minnesota U.S. senator.

The day we were there Democrats were meeting throughout the state by congressional district to discuss their platform and elect representatives to the party's state committee. We were in Minneapolis, where the 5th Congressional District was holding its convention at a local community center. We hadn't been invited to attend the meeting, but we were in the neighborhood, so we went.

When we arrived the convention organizers told us that Howard couldn't address the crowd, but he was welcome to walk around the room and introduce himself during breaks in the speaking program.

Several hundred people were in the small gymnasium. Some sat in the rows of metal folding chairs that had been set up in the middle of the room, while others stood in the back against the wall. The Minneapolis Democrats were polite as Howard wandered around the room with an outstretched hand, but most didn't know why he was there.

He was in the back of the room when 12-term Congressman Marty Sabo began to address the crowd. When Sabo saw Howard he stopped mid-speech to acknowledge him. He told those gathered to watch Howard because he could be the "next Carter," a reference to former President Jimmy Carter.

—MAY—

May 4, 2002

Massachusetts was the home state of John Kerry, another potential presidential candidate, but that was not going to deter Howard from campaigning there. In fact, it made him want to compete even more.

We erased the Greek Independence Day celebration of a month earlier from our memory and started anew with the help of Steve Grossman, a Democratic candidate for governor. Steve was running in a primary and asked Howard for his help courting the gay and lesbian community.

Steve may have wanted Howard's help, but Howard was eager for his. Not only was Steve a resident of Massachusetts, but he had served as chairman of the Democratic National Committee in 1997 and 1998. The support of a high profile Massachusetts resident would mean a great deal to Howard, but Steve had been a supporter of John Kerry in the past, so it appeared to be an endorsement Howard could only dream of. That was until we received an encouraging telephone call from Steve. He was interested in learning more about our campaign strategy and wondered if Howard and I and the other members of our "brain trust" would be willing to meet with him. There was no question that we would meet, but we had a problem: We didn't have a brain trust. The closest thing we had was Mike Ford, Steve McMahon, and Joe Trippi. But Mike was gone and Joe and Steve were working with their paying clients.

There may not have been a formal group of advisors, but Howard was working hard and making progress. We didn't want Steve to think that the lack of a so-called brain trust made us unprofessional or Howard any less a serious candidate. We didn't want to fool him, but we did want to impress him. We had to find someone to go with us. That's where Bob Rogan came in.

Bob was at the first meeting we had to discuss Howard's potential candidacy, he was a friend, and we could be frank with him about what we needed to do. When Bob heard our plight he agreed to accompany us to Massachusetts to meet with Steve.

The four of us met on a Saturday morning at the Sheraton Hotel in Newton, just outside of Boston. Howard outlined his strategy while Bob and I sat close by holding yellow legal pads – nothing was written on them, but we thought they made us look knowledgeable. We didn't know if we were living up to Steve's expectations, but in the end he asked us to keep him up-to-date as we moved forward. For us it was mission accomplished.

May 11, 2002

Iowa, New Hampshire, and South Carolina received all the attention because they were the first three states to vote, but there were 47 other states, four territories and the District of Columbia that also had delegates.

Traditionally, candidates paid little attention to the states that held contests late in the calendar or had few delegates to award. They relied on early wins to carry them to victory in the later states, giving them the delegates needed to capture the nomination. But Howard wasn't going to rule out any state. He believed that by spending just a little time in the states the other Democrats were sure to ignore he could win enough votes to pick up a few delegates. It was a strategy he began to believe could actually work when he visited Wyoming.

The Wyoming State Democratic Party invited him to be the keynote speaker at its annual convention. Howard was not the party's first choice or even its second or third, but he was the only one who agreed to speak to the group.

The meeting was held at the Western Wyoming Community College in Rock Springs, located in the southwestern corner of the state. We were in Denver for another event and the party offered to fly us to Rock Springs. The state party treasurer was a pilot. He picked us up in Denver in his twin engine Cessna and took Howard and me and the Vermont state trooper to the Rock Springs airport. It was only a one-hour flight, but we were in a small plane and we felt every bump and blast of wind. I wasn't convinced that we were going to make it without crashing. We were, however, flying low enough so in addition to being treated to a wonderful view of the landscape below I was able to figure out in advance how far from civilization we would be if we did crash.

Howard's willingness to attend the meeting, along with what we had to do to get there endeared him to the Democrats long before we got off the plane. And things only got better once we arrived. They liked his message, but they were more pleased to find him approachable. As the guest of honor, they asked him to get his lunch first, but he declined, preferring to wait until the end so he could shake hands with each person as they went through the cafeteria's buffet line. It was a simple gesture, but one that thrilled the Democrats who had been rebuffed so many times they faced having no speaker at their annual convention.

When lunch was over they had all but forgotten that he was not their first choice. They loved Howard and he loved them right back. By the time we boarded the plane to leave, the state party chair had practically joined the campaign and Howard could see lots of Wyoming delegates in his future.

Wyoming's primary wasn't until March 20, putting it two months after Iowa, and there were only 18 delegates up for grabs. But to Howard a delegate was a delegate no matter what day they were chosen or what state they came from, and he left Wyoming feeling good about his strategy.

May 29, 2002

The significant event in Howard's political life turned out to be a non-event. There was no speech, supporters or balloons. It involved only the six pages of bureaucratic paperwork required by the Federal Election Commission – paperwork that officially made Howard a candidate for president of the United States.

There was no press release announcing his entry into the race. Instead we made one telephone call to a Vermont reporter. The news spread to the national media, but it came as a surprise to no one. It was never a question of if he would run, but rather when he would make it official.

There was no magical or strategic reason for choosing the day we did. A week earlier Howard was in Iowa and it was upon his return to Vermont when he made the decision to make it official. The date – May 29 – just happened to be the earliest we could complete the paperwork and have Howard sign it.

There was also no significance to the one thing that would come to symbolize the grassroots nature of the campaign – the committee's name, Dean for America. The treasurer of the Democratic National Committee Andy Tobias suggested it to us. Howard and I decided to use it in part because it was different from the more traditional choice, Dean for President. Our primary reason, however, was that the Federal Election Commission would not accept the papers without a name and we didn't want to delay the filing in order to think of another one. What we didn't learn until months later was that Dean for America was patterned after Bartlet for America, *The West Wing's* fictional president's campaign committee.

—JUNE—

June 1, 2002

Many presidential campaigns get their start in fancy offices in downtown Washington D.C., but not Dean for America. The only thing we had in common with those campaigns was that we also started in a capital city. In our case that city was Montpelier, Vermont.

Montpelier had a population of just over 8,000 and was proud to be the only capital city in the nation without a McDonald's restaurant. And as of the first of June it boasted a national presidential campaign headquarters.

The Dean for America office was located in the downtown, a short three-minute walk from the Vermont State House. We occupied two 12' by 12' rooms on the second floor of a carriage house. Our rent was $400 a month and thanks to the previous tenant we were able to supplement our two card tables and metal folding chairs with a desk and a light blue canvas captain's chair. There was no air conditioning and we shared a bathroom in the hallway with the small apartment next door. We had one single line telephone and an answering machine left over from Howard's gubernatorial campaign. Our office equipment consisted of a used printer and two computers we purchased with the help of the technology director for the Vermont Democratic Party.

And we hired our first staff person to go with our new office, a 22-year-old Vermont native and recent graduate of the University of Vermont who was an intern in the governor's office.

June 20, 2002

We made meeting with the local media a priority and our efforts paid off with the stories that appeared in the local newspapers around the country. With Howard's status as a candidate official, publications that boasted a wider audience began to take notice.

Howard's story made for interesting copy. He was running for president and didn't care that he was being dismissed and even ignored by the Democratic Party and elected officials in Washington. In fact, he made criticizing the policy priorities of his party's leadership a major part of his message to voters. He also reminded many of another small state governor who captured the Democratic Party's nomination and was soon after elected president. But it wasn't *The West Wing's* fictional president; it was Jimmy Carter who came from nowhere to become president in 1976.

The *Baltimore Sun* and the *Chicago Tribune* were the first to write profiles of him. The articles appeared one after the other during the first week of June. But *The New Republic* magazine was the first publication to feature Howard on its cover, or more accurately, not feature Howard on its cover. The piece, which appeared in the July 2002 issue, was a cover story titled "Invisible Man: The Most

Intriguing Presidential Candidate You've Never Seen." Instead of a picture of Howard the cover featured a graphic of a man standing behind a podium. The man's face was left blank.

The day the piece hit the newsstands and the Internet, Howard and I were in Washington, D.C. We were on our way to meet with former Clinton advisor Paul Begala when Sue Allen called from Vermont to tell us about the story. She assured Howard that he would be happy with it. His first reaction, however, was to worry. It wasn't the story's content that concerned him. Instead it was the attention that a cover story might bring. He worried about becoming too visible too early. He needed exposure, but he feared that if he got too much attention, his would-be opponents would begin to view him as a threat and start attacking him before the race even began.

As we were sitting in the car that spring day his concerns seemed misplaced and even laughable. None of the other Democrats were giving him the time of day, much less considering him a serious rival.

June 25, 2002

After spending the month traveling to New Jersey, Michigan, New York, Texas, Oklahoma, Washington State, and Washington, D.C., we found ourselves in Iowa again and this time veteran political reporter David Broder was with us. Broder had covered presidential politics since 1960 and had witnessed the rise and fall of many candidates. He was writing a piece for the *Washington Post* and wanted to gauge which category Howard would find himself in.

He spent a day and a half of our three-day visit with us. It was long before we became selective about what we let the media see and he was given access to everything we did, including fundraising receptions for local candidates, and town and county Democratic Party meetings where Howard spoke to the activists.

It would be a year before Howard hit rock star status and no one was the least bit impressed that someone was writing a story about him for the *Washington Post*. They were more impressed by who was writing the story. Broder was recognized everywhere we went. People wanted to discuss politics with him and some asked him to pose for pictures. When we walked into the office of a local newspaper where Howard was scheduled for an interview, the young reporter's jaw dropped when she saw Broder. Too surprised to care that Howard was there, she nervously answered yes when Broder asked if he could sit in on the interview. Our overnight hosts were so excited to hear that Broder was with us that they almost knocked Howard over on their way to their driveway to say hello before he went off to his hotel.

Broder was with us everywhere, including in the car where he was trapped with us for hours. Because Howard was still a governor, we had a Vermont state trooper and an Iowa state police officer with us, meaning that Howard, Broder, and I had to squeeze into the back seat.

Howard never pretended to know how a national campaign organization worked, even in front of a veteran journalist. He had a question about the media that he had always wanted answered and decided to use the time in the car to pose it to Broder. He knew from watching previous elections that as a campaign progressed media outlets assigned reporters to cover the candidate and those reporters often flew on charter airplanes. Howard was concerned that the campaign would incur huge expenses flying the reporters around and wondered who was responsible for paying for the planes. Broder patiently explained that the members of the media paid for their own seats, an answer that brought much relief to Howard, who always worried about the budget's bottom line.

—JULY—

July 1, 2002

"Paltry" is how one Vermont newspaper described the $35,450 we raised for Dean for America in the first month. Regardless, we were pleased with our efforts.

The money we raised at our first fundraiser, a Sunday brunch on Fire Island, New York, accounted for almost half of our total. The event brought in close to $15,000. The remainder came from many of the same family members, friends, and longtime supporters who helped launch Fund for a Healthy America. The total also included a $5,000 contribution from the PAC.

Despite what anyone else thought, we felt successful because we were accomplishing what we needed to. Our goal for fund-raising in 2002 was to raise only the money necessary to operate the campaign and allow Howard to travel around the country.

There was no doubt that we were going to have to rely on federal campaign matching funds and when we discovered that only money received after January 2003 would be matched by the federal government, it made no sense for us to try to raise more than we needed. Ours was a strategy based on the campaign finance law, but also one grounded in reality. Howard was still unknown nationally and, until he was better known, we weren't going to be able to raise a great deal of money even if we wanted to.

July 7, 2002

The support of labor unions was much sought after by Democratic candidates. With millions of members nationwide, unions could not only deliver votes, but union members could provide the people power to help turn out voters on Election Day. One such union was the Service Employees International Union. The SEIU represented 1.6 million members and was the largest health care union and second largest public employees union in the nation.

Knowing the important role that labor organizations played, we were excited to receive an invitation to dinner from the president of the SEIU, Andy Stern.

Howard and I joined Stern; the union's secretary/treasurer; political director; and a familiar face, Gina Glantz, Bill Bradley's former campaign manager who served as the union's senior advisor, for dinner at a Washington, D.C. restaurant. Stern explained that the SEIU's number one issue was making health care available to all Americans and they would be urging all presidential candidates to make it a central issue of their campaigns. He also hinted that the labor union would look favorably at the candidates who made it a top priority. They wanted Howard to know that his emphasis on health care and his record in Vermont had not gone unnoticed by the union's leadership.

After dinner the two of us stood on the sidewalk in front of the restaurant unsure of what to make of the meeting. With all the better-known candidates who would eventually join the race, we hadn't expected to be in contention for an endorsement and they certainly hadn't promised one. It sounded, however, as if getting the union's support wasn't outside the realm of possibility.

July 12, 2002

Almost two months to the day that we made our first trip to Wyoming we were back, this time to raise money.

Howard's circle of supporters was still limited to gay activists, his friends, and his family, so Wyoming would not normally have been a state we would have targeted for a fundraiser. There were more likely places to go for money, such as Vermont or even California. But Howard wanted to capitalize on the support and good will he received during his appearance at the state convention.

One of the Democrats we met during our first visit organized a late afternoon reception. At the height of the event 10 of us stood in the host's backyard. Howard and I, two Vermont state troopers, a Wyoming state police officer, and Howard's cousin who lived in the area made up the majority of the guests. The state party chair, her husband, and the state party co-chair rounded out our group.

No one likes to be the first to arrive at an event, that's why people show up fashionably late, or so we tried to convince ourselves as we stood there drinking soda and eating crackers and cheese. There's only so much 10 people can say to one another while pretending that a situation is not awkward, but we chatted for a very long hour before we finally acknowledged that no one else was coming. It wasn't a total loss. We did walk away with $800.

July 18, 2002

When the Democratic National Committee set the calendar for the 2004 presidential campaign it shortened the nominating process by scheduling the primaries and caucuses close together. The schedule, described as front loading, meant the contests occurred over a matter of weeks instead of months. A close calendar brought with it less time to campaign and raise money between the caucuses and primaries, giving an advantage to the candidates who had more money and were better known.

The new schedule was seen by many as a problem for Howard, but he was not going to let the schedule deter him. His solution to dealing with it was "persistence."

When asked how he intended to overcome the difficulties posed by the new schedule, he told a group of Democrats in New Hampshire, "I'm very persistent. We'll be on all fifty ballots and we're going to be out there doing a lot of work in Iowa and New Hampshire. . . . It is front loaded and it's difficult . . . but some of it is just persistence."

In mid-July he delivered a similar message to DNC Chair Terry McAuliffe. McAuliffe was in Vermont to attend a Vermont Democratic Party fundraiser when Howard told him that he intended to be in the race to the end.

July 21, 2002

Howard's first nationally televised appearance as a presidential candidate was on NBC's *Meet the Press*.

He was invited to appear on the show because he was the first Democrat in the race. We recognized that it was an amazing opportunity to introduce him to Americans, but we weren't nervous about it. In the beginning we focused on the best outcome, not the worst, something that was easy to do when we had nothing to lose and everything to gain.

It would be the first time Howard would go head-to-head with the show's moderator, Tim Russert, who had a reputation of being tough on his guests. We did little preparation, however. In fact, we spent more time deciding what Howard would wear than discussing what he would say. Howard couldn't be scripted and he wasn't going to start just because he was appearing on national television, so there was no point in trying to get him to memorize answers. Howard, Sue Allen, Joe Trippi, Steve McMahon, and I did discuss one issue, his signing of the civil unions law. At the time it was seen as an obstacle to him winning the nomination, so we knew it was going to come up. It was a short discussion. Howard had his answer: "I signed it and I'd do it again."

□ □ □

Howard, Sue, and I flew to Washington, D.C. the Saturday evening before the Sunday show to have dinner with Steve McMahon at his home in Virginia. Howard arrived carrying a plastic grocery bag filled with every tie he owned. Before dinner he dumped the ties onto the kitchen table so we could decide which one he would wear. Steve, Sue, and I divided them into three piles: good ties, ties that could be worn only in Vermont, and ties that needed to be destroyed. Three ties were deemed good; more than half were sentenced to death.

The network put us up for the evening at the Ritz Carlton and sent a car and driver to pick us up and take us to the studio the next morning. If the hospitality was meant to lull a guest into a false sense of security and make them forget that they were going to be interrogated by Russert, it was a good strategy.

July 22, 2002

Howard arrived at the NBC studio wearing a charcoal gray pinstripe suit and the red tie we had picked out the night before. He was the second guest on the show and while we waited we sat in the green room – which wasn't green – eating the breakfast of bagels, muffins, and fruit provided by the network.

When it was time for Howard to go on, he checked his teeth for any stray poppy seeds from the bagel he was eating and straightened his tie. The minute he left, Sue and I pulled our chairs within two inches of the television as if being closer would make him do better. We held our breath and watched the show.

The twenty-minute interview was similar to a pop quiz, with Russert moving seamlessly from one subject to another making it difficult to anticipate the next question. He asked Howard about the obvious: health care, gun control, tax cuts, and the subject we knew would come up, civil unions. But we never anticipated that Howard would need to know the number of people who died from an adverse reaction after being vaccinated against small pox. Howard's reply to the question? A "small" percentage.

The show ended with a *Meet the Press* minute, a segment that featured a video clip from a 1974 interview with, as described by

Russert, "a governor of a small state, Jimmy Carter of Georgia who went on to win the presidency in 1976."

Howard's appearance on the show was a boon to our database. Hundreds of letters and emails poured in. The responses – almost all positive – came from all over the country from individuals who admitted that they had never heard of Howard before, but liked what he had to say. Many offered their support of his candidacy.

—AUGUST—

August 5, 2002

Two percent. That was the number of Americans who wanted Howard to be the Democratic nominee for president. The nation-wide survey conducted by the polling firm Zogby International asked 393 likely Democratic voters to name their preference if Vice President Al Gore was not in the race.

Joe Lieberman was the first choice of 15 percent of those surveyed. Dick Gephardt and Bill Bradley followed with 11 percent each. Tom Daschle was next with 9 percent. John Kerry and Al Sharpton each polled 6 percent. At the bottom were Joe Biden with 4 percent, John Edwards with 3 percent, and Howard with 2 percent.

We thought it was pretty good for the self-described "asterisk" in the race.

August 23, 2002

Candidates for president do not campaign in Vermont. There is no reason to. By the time the state's primary is held in early March it's clear who the party's nominee will be. If Vermonters want to meet a presidential candidate, they have to cross the border to New Hampshire.

Having lived in Vermont my entire life, I didn't know what it was like to live in a state that had a real say in choosing the party's nominee, until I went to Iowa. Not only do voters get to meet the candidates, but presidential politics is a moneymaking enterprise. Businesses benefit from candidates spending money on advertising, hotel rooms, and food.

In 2002 the Iowa Democratic Party and state and local candidates also reaped the rewards of living in a state that held the first contest in the nation.

When Howard established the political action committee he was identified by the Iowa Democratic Party and every candidate in the state as a potential contributor. And that status was solidified when he officially became a candidate for president. It didn't matter that we didn't have any money.

Iowa Democrats had the upper hand with the presidential candidates and they did what anyone in their position would do; they used it. Howard was the only candidate officially in the race, but that didn't stop the party from pitting the would-be candidates against each other, with the contributions made by one used to get the same or better from another. But we couldn't afford to match the computers John Edwards gave to the party long before he became a candidate.

In August, however, the Iowa Democratic Party came up with a scheme to raise money that we couldn't ignore. It offered its computerized list of registered voters to any presidential candidate, official or potential, who raised $65,000 for the party. The list included the addresses, telephone numbers, and e-mail addresses of every registered voter in Iowa, all important to building a field operation.

The information the list provided was valuable, but the information wasn't what Howard was after. He had something to prove to the media, the other candidates, and the Democrats in Washington: He was a serious candidate. However, convincing them wasn't easy when credibility was measured by money and name recognition. We had raised short of $200,000 for Fund for a Healthy America and Dean for America combined since October 2001 and a nationwide poll showed that his candidacy was favored by just 2 percent of those surveyed.

Buying the voter file would prove his commitment to the race. In addition, he savored the idea of seeing his name listed alongside the better-known and better-funded Democrats such as John Edwards and John Kerry who would surely buy the database.

The party didn't make getting the list easy for a candidate like Howard. They imposed a deadline. If they didn't receive the $65,000 by a date certain the price of the list would go up.

Howard picked up the telephone and convinced his supporters – many of the same individuals who had already financed both the PAC and the presidential committee – to make contributions to the Iowa Democratic Party. He explained why he was asking and, although not everyone understood what he was doing, they made the donations anyway. On the day of the deadline the Iowa Democratic Party was $65,000 richer thanks to Howard.

Who acquired the database and when they got it made Howard's accomplishment even sweeter. John Edwards reached the $65,000 goal first. Howard was second. John Kerry came in third.

—SEPTEMBER—

September 1, 2002

In September we packed up our card tables and metal folding chairs and moved the Dean for America headquarters to Burlington, Vermont. For us the move was significant. We had a website and an expanding database. We were taking contributions online and sending e-mail newsletters to Dean supporters on a weekly basis. And media interest in Howard was at an all time high.

We moved out of our two 12' x 12' rooms and into a 2,500 square foot space in a professional building located in the downtown of Burlington, the state's largest city. Walking into the new space for the first time made the sum total of our work hit home. We were still a small campaign, but we weren't the same organization that was just an idea a year earlier. We now had tangible proof of our progress. An elevator took us to our office, state maps and charts filled the walls, and we looked out windows that faced the city's downtown park.

It didn't take long for the office to fill up. The day we moved our full-time staff tripled from one to three (obviously small by most standards) and we hired a part-time fundraiser. A dozen interns from the city's five colleges, including the University of Vermont, became central to our operation.

We stuck to our frugal roots and filled the space with used furniture. Howard donated an orange couch that had been sitting in his garage for years and an old dining room table the legs of which had been gnawed on by an unknown animal. We bought furniture from the University of Vermont and in November we proved that price trumps party by buying desks, chairs, and wastebaskets from the newly elected Republican governor's campaign. We traded in our one line telephone and invested in a real telephone system, one with multiple lines, voice mail, and even a hold button. We also purchased new computers in order to keep up with the online interest in Howard.

The signs of our progress were all around us, but there was one indication of future success that was hard for us to ignore. The Secret Service, the law enforcement agency that provides protection to the president of the United States, had just moved its offices into the space directly across the hall.

September 3, 2002

It was the lunch hour at Delmonico's restaurant in Manhattan. The restaurant, located in the center of New York's financial district, was decorated in deep browns that complimented the wood paneled walls. The white tablecloths, silver flatware, and china added a touch of elegance. Men, and a few women, in expensive dark business suits who had left their offices on Wall Street for a power lunch, occupied every table in the restaurant.

In a private room off the main dining area Howard and I sat at a table with four executives from the banking and investment firm Goldman Sachs. The executives had asked Howard to come to New York after seeing him on *Meet the Press*. They were impressed with his performance and wanted to discuss how they could help the campaign. They also wanted to introduce him to some potential donors. Howard was not the only candidate they planned to meet with. In a way they were interviewing candidates, but that didn't matter to us. We were glad to be invited to the table.

After lunch they took us on a tour of New York to meet some of the city's most prominent leaders in business, finance, and Democratic Party fundraising. They were known in the political world as heavy hitters, a term that had nothing to do with their batting averages, but everything to do with the size of their bank accounts and Rolodexes. These heavy hitters could make large campaign contributions and, more importantly, had friends who could do the same.

We spent the day in fancy boardrooms, exclusive hotels, and lavish apartments with Howard pitching his ideas in the hope that the would-be donors might be impressed enough to make a contribution in the future. As we sat in one Park Avenue apartment that was decorated in floor to ceiling mirrors, antique furniture, and heavy silk fabric drapes, all I could do was wonder what our hosts would think of our campaign office's hand-me-down decor.

September 7, 2002

Howard's willingness to campaign for any candidate in Iowa was paying off. We had built up a good relationship with the organizers of the state House and Senate campaign committees, as well as the Iowa Democratic Party. We let them know when Howard was going to be visiting the state and they filled his schedule with campaign appearances and fundraisers on behalf of Democratic candidates.

He had become a popular campaigner, and during the month of September he campaigned for fifteen candidates in fifteen different towns. There was no question that we met more people helping other candidates than we did on our own.

One stop brought us to Dallas Center, Iowa, to campaign for a local firefighter who was running for state representative.

Dallas Center was 18 miles from Des Moines and boasted a population of 1,500. There were no sky scrapers or big name chain stores. Instead the small downtown was dotted with brick buildings housing family-owned stores and restaurants. The day we visited the town was having its annual cookout. Residents flocked to the downtown to join in the festivities. Grills were set up in the center of the main street along with long tables that held rolls, ketchup, mustard, chips, and lemonade. It was a hot, sunny day and everyone was dressed in shorts and T-shirts. At first glance no one knew that Howard was the governor of Vermont, much less a candidate for president. All they knew was that he was the guy wearing a dress shirt and a tie to a barbeque.

While Howard attempted to round up votes, the real interest was in the Vermont state trooper who was traveling with us. He was tall with short hair and wore a dark suit and sunglasses. He kept his suit coat on to hide the holster and gun he was wearing. His attempt to remain unseen by standing on the sidewalk away from the crowd and the grills failed miserably. It didn't take long for a circle of children to form around him. There were no policy questions asked that day, just, "Do you have a gun? Can we see it?"

September 18, 2002

He was sitting in the campaign headquarters in Burlington. One minute he was the governor of Vermont receiving a briefing from the Vermont commissioner of education and signing letters to constituents. The next he was a candidate for president of the United States, pretending not to pose as a photographer from Getty Images (a company that distributes photographs worldwide) snapped his picture.

When Howard bought the Iowa database three weeks earlier, he did so in order to be recognized as more than just the governor of Vermont making a fairy tale run for president – and he was accomplishing his goal.

The Vermont school children who wrote to him wanting to know his favorite animal had no idea what the Iowa database was, but the national media did. And the significance of his purchase was finally being noted. Referring to Howard's acquisition of the list, *Newsweek* columnist Howard Fineman wrote: "The big winner in this latest preseason phase isn't Edwards or Kerry, it is Dean, the governor of Vermont. A year ago he wasn't on any pre-presidential radar screen. Now, by sheer dint of hard work – very little of it inside the Beltway – he is on every insider's screen."

September 25, 2002

Former President Jimmy Carter greeted us as we walked into his office at the Carter Center in Atlanta, Georgia. It was obvious why Howard had requested the meeting. When the former president captured the Democratic Party's nomination in 1976 he was the little-known former governor of Georgia. And his win shocked the Democratic Party establishment. Howard was hoping for the same outcome in 2004.

We sat in the sitting area of Carter's office not far from the large window that provided a view of a beautifully landscaped backyard. We had no set agenda. Howard simply wanted the opportunity to talk with the man he admired.

As Carter looked at us it was clear that he remembered when he was in the same place Howard was – unknown, no money, and not wanted by his party. He spent the meeting reminiscing about his own campaign, smiling as he told us stories about the places he went and battles he fought.

We were surprised to learn that Howard was the only candidate or possible candidate to reach out to Carter for advice. For Howard, the former president was an obvious resource, but apparently the other candidates did not need the help like we did.

Before we left, Howard told Carter that in 1980 he served as a delegate for him at the Democratic National Convention and stuffed envelopes as a volunteer in his Vermont campaign office. Carter laughed and said that he would not hold that against him. In 1980 Carter was defeated by Ronald Reagan.

September 29, 2002

Howard made his second appearance on national television on the CBS Sunday morning news program *Face the Nation*.

The day before the interview the United Nations and Iraq had reached an agreement that allowed weapons inspectors into the country. Iraq, however, rejected a request made by the United States that inspectors be allowed into eight presidential palaces.

The Bush administration had been asserting that Saddam Hussein was in possession of weapons of mass destruction that posed a threat to the United States and was using the claim to justify the possibility of military action against Iraq.

The new developments prompted the show's host Bob Schieffer to ask Howard if he thought the United States should invade the country. "You have said at this point that the president has not yet made the case for war. . . . But Iraq now says that it will not accept tougher rules for inspection. Doesn't that make the case now for the administration?"

Many members of Congress – including Dick Gephardt and John Kerry – accepted as fact the Bush administration's declaration that the weapons of mass destruction existed.

Howard, however, bucked conventional wisdom telling Schieffer, "There's no question that Saddam Hussein is a threat to the United States and to our allies. The question is, 'Is he an immediate threat?' The president has not yet made the case for that."

September 30, 2002

Three of us sat at a table for 12 at the Shoney's restaurant in Columbia, South Carolina, waiting for our guests to arrive. One of Howard's first supporters in the state, State Senator David Mack, had invited a small group of African American activists to meet Howard over lunch.

Howard, David, and I sat in the restaurant for 20 minutes, but no one showed up, even for the free food. When it became clear that we would be dining alone, David suggested that we cut our losses and head over to a gathering of African American ministers at a college in nearby Orangeburg. The lunch, sponsored by D.E. Greene Ministries, was taking place at Claflin University, a historically black liberal arts college affiliated with the Methodist Church.

We had not been invited, so it's fair to say that we crashed the event. The organizers were gracious, not only inviting us to lunch, but also allowing Howard to say a few words. Howard, the

Vermont state trooper, and I were the only white people in the audience and we were just a few of the non-ministers in the room.

Howard was used to speaking to groups in Iowa and New Hampshire, so this was different, not only because of race, but because he was speaking to religious leaders for the first time. He did not alter his speech. He gave the same one people in Iowa and New Hampshire had heard numerous times. The audience responded positively. However, instead of the polite applause he was growing accustomed to his remarks were greeted with a chorus of "Amen."

—OCTOBER—

October 1, 2002

Jerry Rafshoon served as Jimmy Carter's media advisor during his 1976 presidential campaign. He was with Carter from the start and knew firsthand the work involved in putting an unlikely campaign together and what happens when it takes off. By pure coincidence he called me when we were in Atlanta on our way to meet with President Carter a week earlier. We had never spoken to Jerry before and he knew nothing about our meeting with his former boss. He was prompted to call because he had been watching Howard, and like many couldn't escape the similarities with the campaign he worked on 24 years earlier.

Howard, Jerry, and I met for the first time at the Willard Hotel in Washington, D.C. We sat in the hotel's restaurant and, like Carter, looking at the two of us made Jerry remember the early days of the 1976 campaign. He told us stories, made suggestions, and gave Howard a piece of advice, "Keep the people you know close by."

<u>October 2, 2002</u>

In what was probably a first in presidential campaign history, we visited the set of a soap opera. One of Howard's supporters in California had a friend who starred on the CBS daytime drama *Guiding Light*. In a twist that could only happen on television, actress Beth Chamberlain was a native Vermonter, having hailed from Danville, population 2,200. Beth and Howard had never met, but she was willing to introduce him to the actors on the show. So we made a visit to the soap opera's New York City set, Howard with his campaign brochures in hand.

The day we visited they were filming the wedding of the show's wealthiest character. The scene was extravagant; everyone was dressed in evening gowns, they had big hair, and lots of make-up. Looking at Howard and me it was clear that if we had been characters on the show we would have played the people who were not invited to the wedding.

Between takes Beth, dressed in a gold sequined floor length gown, introduced Howard to the show's cast and crew. Howard had no idea what the show was about, so when Beth introduced him to her "mother" and "ex-husband" he expressed surprise that her family also worked on the show. We had to explain that they were her television family, not her real one.

Howard gave a brochure to everyone he met and contrary to what one might think about soap opera actors, they were well informed. Several of them had heard an interview he did on National Public Radio and were interested in talking to him about the issues he discussed during the program.

It turned out to be a good visit. Howard left with fewer brochures than he started with and I left with an autographed script.

October 5, 2002

Every year the Iowa Democratic Party holds a fundraising event called the Jefferson-Jackson Day dinner. As a presidential candidate, Howard was invited to speak at the 2002 dinner along with John Edwards and John Kerry, although they had yet to officially declare they were running.

More than 1,000 Democratic activists came out to the Polk County convention center in Des Moines for the event that was a who's who of Iowa Democrats. In addition to activists and donors, every Democratic statewide and federal official was in attendance. It would be the first time many of them would meet Howard or hear him speak. Howard and I arrived armed with 2,000 campaign brochures, determined to make the most of the opportunity.

The dinner was a low-key affair. Howard was the only announced candidate, so it was too early for campaign signs and boisterous supporters.

Iowa's U.S. Senator Tom Harkin was the first to speak during the dinner program. It was his job to make the introductions. Harkin knew Edwards and Kerry because they served together in the Senate, but he didn't know Howard and referred to him as "John Dean." That Dean, no relation to Howard, was the former White House counsel to Richard Nixon and key figure in the Watergate scandal.

Senator Kerry spoke before Howard and his serious speech set the tone for the evening. The dinner marked the first time Howard, Edwards, and Kerry appeared together and Howard used his speech to make the point that he was different from his potential opponents who served in Congress. He had a concrete record of results to point to; they only had votes. A common refrain in his speech was, "I'm a governor and I've done it." He talked about his core issues: health care, early education programs for children, and a balanced budget. Each time he proposed a solution to a problem and reminded the audience, "I'm a governor and I've done it."

During his speech Kerry stressed the need for putting early childhood education programs in place to help young children so they wouldn't end up in jail as adults. It was not lost on Howard that that very issue was part of the stump speech he had been giving for close to a year. He was known to say that any kindergarten teacher could look around the classroom and identify the kids who would end up in trouble. Howard would then describe a program in Vermont that helped support these children before the problems started.

Although he was tempted, it was too early for him to accuse Kerry of stealing his lines. Instead, during his speech he made it clear that it was one thing to talk about helping young children and another thing to have actually done it, telling the crowd and Kerry, "I'm a governor and I've done it."

I had dragged the 2,000 brochures around all evening in two large canvass bags and I had no intention of carrying them back to Vermont. So after dinner while Howard made his way around the room personally introducing himself to the Democrats, I stood by the exit door and handed one to everyone who passed by. They were walking out quickly and I was doing the task by myself. Suddenly I realized that I had handed a brochure to John Edwards. Senator Edwards graciously accepted my apology – and the brochure.

Unlike Edwards and Kerry, Howard and I stayed until the room was empty, the tables had been cleared, and the organizers were ready to turn off the lights.

October 6, 2002

Howard had been searching for a campaign manager since our relationship with Mike Ford ended in March. The closer we got to the end of the year – and to the end of his term in office – the more immediate the need became. When he left the governor's office in January, running for president would be his full-time job and he wanted to have a manager in place. And he thought he found one in Rick Ridder, a political consultant in Denver, Colorado.

Howard and I first met Rick during a visit to Denver in July. He had presidential campaign experience having worked for Gary Hart, Al Gore in 1988, and Clinton and Gore in 1996. He also had a Vermont connection; he had attended Middlebury College.

Howard was making a trip to Denver and would be staying with Rick and his wife Joannie Braden. It would be the perfect time to see if he would be interested in joining the campaign. Rick's answer when Howard asked: He'd consider it.

We saw Rick's interest as a positive development, but not everyone agreed. We had not discussed hiring Rick with Steve McMahon or Joe Trippi, but now that Howard had made the offer we decided that we had better let them know.

When I shared the news with Steve he was not happy that we had made the decision without consulting him first. Furthermore, he believed we had our priorities wrong. Hiring a campaign manager could wait until the beginning of 2003. What we needed immediately was someone to help us raise money. It was a tense conversation, especially when I reminded him that we had been left to fly the "Starship Howard" on our own.

October 17, 2002

By October, Dean for America had brought in just over $135,000 since we formed the committee in May. When we filed our finance report with the Federal Election Commission in July the press described the $35,000 we had raised up until then as "paltry." The press reports about our October total were a little kinder describing our fundraising efforts as being "dwarfed" by the contribution totals of the other would-be candidates.

Because Howard was the only official candidate in the race, he was the only one raising money for a presidential campaign, but that didn't mean the other potential candidates weren't doing fundraising of their own. Some were raising money for political action committees they had set up to fund their political travel and activity. Joe Lieberman had raised more than $2 million for his PAC and John Edwards followed closely behind with $1.5 million.

—NOVEMBER—

November 1, 2002

Election Day was just days away and for the first time in 16 years Howard's name would not appear on the ballot, and for the first time in 11 years Vermonters would elect a new governor.

The upcoming election brought with it the reality that Howard would soon be a full-time candidate for president. We were experiencing a great deal of uncertainty about what would happen in the year ahead, but one thing was finally settled, Howard had a campaign manager. Rick Ridder agreed to take the job and would move to Vermont at the beginning of the new year.

November 11, 2002

Steve Grossman's campaign for governor of Massachusetts ended with the primary election in September; by November he was ready to dive into the national scene. Eight months after the so-called brain trust first met with Steve to lay out our strategy for a winning campaign, Steve endorsed Howard. He was the first high profile Democrat to do so.

Howard was pleased to have the backing of the former chair of the Democratic National Committee and it didn't hurt that we had snatched him away from John Kerry.

November 13, 2002

"If they want a candidate who is not going to say what he thinks, they can find someone else to work for."

It was the first, but certainly not the last time that Howard would utter that line. He made the comment in response to a suggestion that he back away from his opposition to President Bush's No Child Left Behind education initiative. As governor he was an outspoken critic of the law, calling it "terribly flawed." He went so far as to suggest that Vermont give up the $26 million it would receive by complying with the law, an idea that led to a public spat with U.S. Education Secretary Rod Paige. He planned on highlighting his opposition during a speech he was to give at a meeting of the National Coalition of Essential Schools in Washington, D.C.

Howard rarely spoke from a prepared text, but he wanted to use the speech to outline his vision for the Democratic Party, and in order to ensure that he said everything he wanted we wrote the speech in advance. We sent a draft to Steve McMahon and Rick Ridder to get their thoughts and when it came back the reference to NCLB was gone.

When Howard called Steve to find out why the language had been taken out, Steve argued that it was better for Howard to support the law because he predicted that public opinion polls would show that most Americans favored it.

Howard hung up the telephone, vented his frustration, and promptly put the language back in. How could he not when the speech included the line "Democrats cannot put public opinion polls ahead of principled opposition to fundamentally bad policies."

—DECEMBER—

December 15, 2002

Howard was going to run for president regardless of who was in the race, and that included former Vice President Al Gore. He knew it would difficult, if not impossible, to beat Gore, and although he respected the former vice president, he was not going to let his presence in the race deter him.

Howard and I were in New Hampshire the day Gore appeared on CBS's *60 Minutes* to announce that he would not run in 2004. We were leaving a reception for Howard at the Three Sweet Tomatoes restaurant in Lebanon when we heard the news.

Howard saw Gore's leaving the race as an opening for himself and wasted no time trying to capitalize on it. He spent the 90-minute drive back to Vermont on the telephone. After praising Gore for his "tough, courageous decision" in media interviews he began calling Gore supporters, especially those in Iowa, to ask them to consider supporting him now that the former vice president was out of the race. And in order to send a strong message that he was ready to go we immediately announced the hiring of a campaign director in Iowa. Jeani Murray, who we had met in March when she served as the campaign manager for Iowa congressional candidate John Norris, had agreed to take the job just weeks earlier. It was an announcement we hadn't planned on making until the beginning of 2003.

December 16, 2002

The headline "Gore Decides Against '04 Bid" ran across the top of *The Gazette* newspaper in Cedar Rapids. When we set the dates for our three-day visit to Iowa we had no idea that the former vice president would drop out of the race the night before. But as the first candidate to arrive in the state since the unexpected announcement, our timing could not have been better. The state's newspapers were filled with stories speculating as to who would benefit from Gore's decision. There weren't any clear winners, but the Democratic leader in the state legislature did jokingly tell one reporter, "Governor Dean has been here so many times he can vote in Iowa."

December 31, 2002

Howard spent the final days of 2002 the same way he ended 2001—at Renaissance Weekend in Charleston, South Carolina. A year earlier the elite had greeted his potential candidacy with "eye-rolling."

For some that hadn't changed. He was given credit for trying, but little hope of succeeding. The Renaissance guests still believed that money was the key to winning and Howard had raised just shy of $490,000 since they saw him last. He didn't wear designer suits, his label read JC Penney, and much like his taste in clothing, he wasn't going to run a designer-priced campaign.

He was ignoring the skeptics and working hard to build a campaign one step at a time. He had spent 141 days traveling to 31 states and 158 cities and towns. He had made 25 trips to Iowa and 17 to New Hampshire. He had six people on staff and had hired a campaign manager. He had the Iowa voter file and a director for the caucus state. And he had received the endorsement of a former chair of the Democratic National Committee.

He believed in substance over style and, no matter what anyone thought, he ended the year believing he was going to be the Democratic nominee for president of the United States.

Part IV
—
2003

—JANUARY—

January 1, 2003

For Howard the year began with saying good-bye. In a little over a week a new governor would be sworn in and he would leave the office he had held for 11½ years.

He said good-bye to the Vermont Legislature and the Vermont media. He took a farewell tour that brought him to all corners of the state. And he tearfully hugged his staff as they left the office for the last time.

While he was saying good-bye four Democrats were about to join him in the race for president. John Kerry had already formed an exploratory committee and John Edwards, Dick Gephardt, and Joe Lieberman would not be far behind.

January 9, 2003

By 2 p.m. a new governor had been sworn in and Howard was officially the former governor of Vermont and a full-time candidate for president of the United States. Although we had known the day was coming for more than a year, none of us imaged the emotion that would come with leaving the governor's office. And it made for a difficult transition.

As Howard's tenure as governor was ending, Rick Ridder was moving into the campaign office. He had already begun to assemble a staff, hiring a finance director, office manager, policy director, and technology director. He had put together an operating budget for the first year of $6 million, which was realistic, but gave Howard sticker shock any way.

And things were changing. A group designing a bumper sticker was contemplating changing Dean for America to Dean for President and Howard's trademark colors, blue and yellow, to red, white, and blue. I found myself in an office surrounded by people I didn't know, who didn't know how we had gotten to where we were, and who didn't seem to want my input. I thought about leaving. But I wasn't the only one having a difficult time. It was also hard for Steve McMahon and Joe Trippi, who were unsure about what their role in the campaign would be. Steve, Howard, and I had a relationship that went back eleven years. Now Steve found himself having to negotiate a consulting contract with a new face, Rick Ridder. Coping with the changes would not get easier any time soon.

January 11, 2003

Nationally, Howard was dead last in the polls. Most voters were undecided, however, the support he garnered from 2 percent of those surveyed put him behind the leader Joe Lieberman with 11 percent, followed by John Kerry and John Edwards with 9 percent each, Dick Gephardt with 8 percent, and Tom Daschle with 7 percent. Even Al Sharpton, who found support from 3 percent of the people surveyed, was ahead of Howard.

But he fared better in New Hampshire where Al Gore's departure had changed the race. A poll conducted by the American Research Group showed that Howard and John Kerry were the beneficiaries of Gore's decision not to run. The two men topped the survey. Twenty-seven percent of the New Hampshire voters contacted said they'd vote for John Kerry, a gain of 17 points from a poll conducted before Gore's exit. Fifteen percent of those surveyed chose Howard, up 13 points from the previous poll.

January 18, 2003

Howard, Dick Gephardt, and John Kerry all accepted invitations to speak at a banquet hosted by the Linn County Democrats in Marion, Iowa. It marked only the second time Howard was joined by his opponents at an event. The first was at the Iowa Jefferson-

Jackson dinner in October where Howard, Kerry, and John Edwards all spoke. At the time Howard was the only candidate officially in the race. Now Kerry, Gephardt, Edwards, and Joe Lieberman were in and the campaign was off and running (although a poll showed that 82 percent of Iowa voters had no idea who Howard was).

For more than a year Howard had used his speeches and media interviews to criticize the policy priorities of the Democratic Party and his would-be opponents who served in Congress. But he hadn't had the opportunity to directly criticize his fellow Democrats until the joint appearance in Marion.

Before the 300 Democrats who packed the Prairie Hill Pavilion, including Gephardt and Kerry who were seated at separate tables, Howard accused the Democrats in Washington of being too supportive of Republican policies. Rhetorically he asked the crowd, "Do you know why we [Democrats] didn't win the election in 2002?"

Answering his own question he responded, "Because there are too many Democrats that voted for those [President Bush's] tax cuts. Because I'm the only person running for president of the United States on the Democratic ticket that didn't support the president's resolution on Iraq. And I'm the only person running for president of the United States that didn't support the No Teacher Left Standing Bill [No Child Left Behind]." His answer was an indictment of votes made by Gephardt and Kerry.

As the crowd cheered seemingly oblivious to the fact that the very people Howard was criticizing were sitting right next to them he made a plea, "I need your help. I need you to stand up for the Democratic Party. I need a party again where we're proud to talk about Democratic issues, where we don't consult with polls first to find out if it's all right to talk about things like health insurance. If you make me the nominee of this party I will do my best to make you proud to be Democrats again."

January 24, 2003

Martin Sheen invited Howard to visit the set of *The West Wing*. The show was filming in Washington D.C. at the Andrew Mellon Auditorium on Constitution Avenue, within walking distance of the White House.

We walked into the building, over cables, lights, and through racks of clothing until we reached the set. When I saw how it was decorated I stopped and told Howard to look. We were standing next to a white stage with a large sign on the wall that read "Inauguration of the President of the United States." They were filming the inaugural celebration.

When we arrived Sheen was rehearsing a scene with cast mates Bradley Whitford who played deputy chief of staff Josh Lyman and John Spencer who played the chief of staff Leo McGary. Sheen introduced Howard to the actors and then took us to the cafeteria where the cast and crew were having lunch.

After lunch Howard and Sheen walked back to the set together. When the rehearsal resumed, Howard quietly leaned over and told me that Sheen would support him. The endorsement was a surprise and not just because Howard was behind in the polls. We had hoped that Sheen would someday consider endorsing him, but we never expected it so early and we certainly didn't expect it to come so easily. We were learning that most endorsements only happened after multiple meetings and telephone calls.

A writer for *People* magazine was on the set doing a story about the show. Sheen introduced her to Howard and told her that he was his choice for president of the United States. She didn't have a clue as to who Howard was and didn't seem to care. She was more interested in the fictional ex-governor turned president than in the real former governor presidential wannabe standing right next to her.

January 28, 2003

Howard and I put on the camouflage jackets the Marine commander handed us and followed him to the training field. We watched as young men crawled through dirt and mud under the rope-lined obstacle course with their bayonets held close to their chests. Others were dodging bullets to pull their comrades to safety while dozens were running in tight line formation, all the while being yelled at by the drill instructors. We were in Parris Island, South Carolina, at the Marine Corps Recruit Depot. Parris Island was where the Marines trained new recruits. It was boot camp and we were there so Howard could get an inside look at the United States military.

The day of our visit the recruits were taking part in a 54-hour training exercise known as the Crucible. The young men, mostly teenagers, were put through a rigorous series of exercises intended to test their physical and mental strength. They were deprived of sleep, given little food, and forced to perform physical challenges. When we arrived the training was in its final hours.

As we were standing next to the bayonet course a group of recruits arrived back from marching all night. They sat down on the asphalt and by their appearance it was the first time they were allowed to rest in hours. They were hot, dirty, hungry, and tired, but they had survived the challenge.

January 30, 2003

We sat in a booth at the Polo Lounge at the Beverly Hills Hotel in California waiting for Warren Beatty to arrive. Three days earlier we were in South Carolina when Beatty called. He was following the campaign and was interested in meeting with Howard.

Howard didn't go to the movies often, but he had seen Beatty in the movie *Bulworth,* in which he played a politician who said exactly what was on his mind. He enjoyed the movie because, like

Beatty's character, he was known for saying what he thought. After he saw the film, he enjoyed tormenting the governor's office staff with his best *Bulworth* impression.

The green upholstered booth was tucked away in a corner of the restaurant. I was facing the front door, so I was the first to see Beatty walk in followed by his wife, the actress Annette Bening. If you didn't know who they were you would never guess that they were a high-powered Hollywood couple. They were casually dressed and introduced themselves, "Hi, I'm Warren" and "I'm Annette." After a series of introductions, I left the three of them alone to talk.

An hour later Howard emerged from the restaurant and recounted the meeting. He told me that he wasn't sure what Beatty thought of him, but he got the impression that his girlfriend liked him. I stopped and asked him to repeat what he said. Again he said, "I'm not sure about Beatty, but I think his girlfriend liked me." I told him that Bening wasn't Beatty's girlfriend; she was his wife and they had children together. Plus she was an award-winning actress in her own right. He was mortified. He only remembered the stories of Beatty's bachelor days and didn't know that he had settled down. Howard replayed the hour-long conversation over in his head trying to figure out if he had said anything that would indicate that he didn't know who Bening was. He didn't think he had.

—FEBRUARY—

February 13, 2003

Mounds of onion rings and French fries covered the burgers being served at the Beacon Drive-In. It was the lunch hour and the popular Spartanburg, South Carolina, restaurant was filled to capacity. Hungry customers were digging their way to their burgers while others lined up at the counter waiting to order and pick up their food. We sat out on the large glassed-in sun porch having lunch with members of the Mt. Moriah Senior Citizens Bible study group.

It was hard to resist the mouth-watering smell of the fried food and even the seniors couldn't pass up the less than heart-healthy lunch. Four or five seniors took up each of the six tables that had been set aside for us in the corner of the room. As they nibbled on fries and onion rings Howard launched into his stump speech.

Before ending, he added a new line to his remarks, telling the group, "We [the Democratic Party] need to reach out to the white guys who drive pick up trucks with Confederate flag decals in the back and ask them what the Republican Party has done for them." The all African American audience looked up from their plates, set down their knives and forks, and applauded.

February 16, 2003

The map of the United States was highlighted in red and blue to indicate the areas of the country that were part of the National Dean Network or would be in the near future. The network used e-mail addresses to connect Dean supporters around the country. Howard and I first learned about it during a house party in Hollis, New Hampshire, where the network creators explained the system they had set up.

Howard envisioned using e-mail addresses to communicate, but it was communication between the campaign and his supporters. We never imagined direct supporter-to-supporter contact. And it was hard to imagine it that day. Howard listened to the short presentation and left me to learn the details.

I was not web savvy, so I didn't understand how they were putting the network together. It didn't take a technology expert, however, to recognize that the campaign organization that Howard thought he would need to have because of a lack of money – one based on grassroots organizing and e-mail addresses – was building. Only the campaign wasn't building it.

February 19, 2003

"Don't you feel like calling your mother and telling her where we are?" I would have done just what Howard's question suggested if it hadn't been 2 a.m. in Vermont. We were in Beverly Hills, California standing in the living room of Warren Beatty's guesthouse. It was the end of a long day that began in Sacramento and brought us to San Francisco and Los Angeles.

Our last event of the day was supposed to be a fundraising dinner in Santa Monica for U.S. Senator Barbara Boxer. During dinner, however, I received a call from the campaign scheduler, Sarah Buxton. Arianna Huffington, the author, columnist, and liberal activist, had invited Howard to stop by her house for dessert.

Howard and I and our volunteer driver pulled into Huffington's semi-circle driveway in our small two-door hatchback, the kind of car owned by many twenty-somethings. The front door of the house opened and Huffington, dressed in gold colored silk flowing pants and matching blouse, came out to greet us.

We entered into a large marble foyer, which separated the elegant living room and dining room. Sitting around the dining room table were *Seinfeld* co-creator Larry David; actress, songwriter, and former girlfriend of Elvis Presley, Linda Thompson; Court TV host Catherine Crier; Rob Reiner; Barbara Walters; and Warren Beatty.

They were midway through dessert when we arrived, but Huffington was quick to make sure that we were served. Howard schmoozed while I ate the crème brulee that the wait staff, dressed in black and white, handed to me.

An hour later everyone started to leave and it was time for us to go to Beatty's guesthouse, where we were spending the night. I was about to get into the volunteer's car when Howard came out of the house with Beatty. His guesthouse was not on the same property where he lived and he was concerned that we wouldn't know how to get in, so he offered to take us there.

During the drive Beatty asked Howard if he enjoyed the discussion at Huffington's. He had, but when he admitted that he didn't know everyone who was there, Beatty filled him in, sprinkling small pieces of gossip among the biographical information.

When we arrived at the house an automatic gate blocking the driveway opened allowing us to drive in. We walked across a wooden patio to get to the front door. It was a windy night and the outdoor furniture had been blown over. We picked it up and then Beatty showed us around.

It was a modest, yet comfortable house that matched the casualness of the couple we met at the Polo Lounge. After walking around the inside of the house we went back outside. We admired the view of the city lights below while Beatty gave us a lesson about the ecology of the area. When it came time for him to leave, Beatty said good night and left us standing in the living room.

Howard didn't get star struck, primarily because most of the time he didn't know he was talking to a "star," but it wasn't lost on him how out of character for us the evening had been.

February 20, 2003

The automatic gate at Warren Beatty's guesthouse closed behind us. Our stay at Beatty's was over, but our time with Hollywood celebrities wasn't. Howard was about to pick up the endorsement of Rob Reiner who would join Martin Sheen on our list of entertainment industry supporters.

Endorsements from people like Reiner and Sheen were important because they helped us raise money, particularly in California. This wouldn't be the first time Reiner would assist Howard. He had raised money for him during his gubernatorial campaigns.

The two men shared an interest in early childhood education programs, so it was only natural for the endorsement press conference to take place at the Children's Institute International in Los Angeles, a center that served at-risk children. In front of television cameras and still photographers, Howard and Reiner sat in chairs that were low to the ground so they would be level with the children and read books in both English and Spanish. Of course, the 3- and 4-year-olds had no idea who the two men were, but they giggled and followed along with the stories any way.

□ □ □

We sat at a table by the pool at The Beverly Hilton Hotel eating lunch with Merv Griffin, the former talk show host and game show creator best known for *Jeopardy* and *Wheel of Fortune*.

As a longtime friend of Ronald and Nancy Reagan, he was a most unlikely lunch partner. And he was as surprised to be sitting with us as we were to be sitting with him. We weren't supposed to be dining with Griffin. Instead, Howard was scheduled to meet with Aaron Sorkin, the creator of *The West Wing*. Sorkin, however, cancelled at the last minute, leaving us with free time and nowhere to go. Howard decided to use the time to make telephone calls, but with no office in the area our only option was to sit in the car.

We ended up poolside at the suggestion of a member of the campaign's finance staff. The Beverly Hilton, which was owned by Griffin, was nearby. The staff member knew Griffin because he helped him write a book several years earlier, and when we arrived at the hotel he inquired if Griffin was there. We were seated by the pool ready to make telephone calls when he appeared and joined us for lunch.

There weren't very many things that went over Howard's head; he could talk about foreign policy, health care, and the environment. But he was out of touch where television and movies were concerned. In fact, he went without cable at home. So he sat clueless but amused as Griffin and I talked about reality television and *American Idol* host Ryan Seacrest, who Griffin informed us he had discovered.

When Griffin heard that we needed to do some work he arranged for us to use a suite at the hotel. Instead of sitting in a hot car, we ended up on the top floor of The Beverly Hilton looking out at the clear blue Pacific Ocean.

February 21, 2003

We took the red eye from Long Beach, California, to Washington, D.C. to attend the Democratic National Committee's winter meeting. Howard, along with the other presidential candidates, had been invited to speak to the national party's membership.

Our JetBlue flight landed at Dulles airport at 5:35 a.m. By the time we arrived at the Hyatt Hotel on Capitol Hill where the DNC meeting was taking place it was 6:30 a.m. This gave Howard only two hours to rest, shower, and change his clothes before his day began.

It was an important speech, yet Howard arrived in Washington having no idea what he was going to say. Just thirty minutes before he was scheduled to step up to the podium he sat down for the first and only time to discuss his remarks.

Steve McMahon, Rick Ridder, Joe Trippi, Steve Grossman, and I met with Howard in his hotel room. Joe, Steve, and Rick suggested that Howard take on the Democratic Party and its leadership. It didn't take much convincing for him to embrace the idea. He had, after all, been challenging his party on health care, the federal budget, and the impending military action against Iraq for more than a year and it was his displeasure with the status quo that made him enter the presidential race in the first place.

But this time would be different. He would be confronting the party leadership at their own meeting.

Howard found a used envelope and scribbled notes for his speech on the back. He then went down to the ballroom, envelope in hand, ready to address the crowd.

□ □ □

The meeting was the first introduction DNC members had to Howard and his campaign organization, Dean for America. We wanted to show that we were organized, professional, and able to compete against the campaigns of the better-financed and better-known candidates. But at the same time it was important that the Democrats understood that Howard was unique. To accomplish this we played off of his Vermont roots and the fact that he was a doctor.

Staff and volunteers in the Vermont headquarters spent days assembling gift bags. Each clear cellophane bag contained "Dr. Dean's prescription to cure the winter blues": Vermont-made cheese, maple syrup, and chocolates.

As the DNC members filed into the hotel ballroom they were handed a gift bag and a homemade noisemaker – a prescription drug bottle filled with coins. The stickers on the bottles read, "Dr. Dean's prescription for change."

□ □ □

Howard walked across the stage to the podium as the audience applauded politely. The chorus of loud cheers that came from one corner of the room made Howard smile. The rowdy group was his campaign staff.

It was the first time he addressed members of the DNC as a presidential candidate and they didn't know what he was going to say and neither did we. He had notes on the back of an envelope, but exactly what he was going to do with them was a mystery. After a few seconds of silence for dramatic effect he began:

> What I want to know is why in the world is the Democratic Party leadership supporting the president's unilateral attack on Iraq.

What I want to know is why are Democratic Party leaders supporting tax cuts. The question isn't how big a tax cut should be. The question should be can we afford a tax cut at all with the largest deficit in the history of this country.

What I want to know is why we're fighting in Congress about the Patient's Bill of Rights when the Democratic Party ought to be standing up for health care for every single American, man, woman, and child in this country.

What I want to know is why our folks are voting for the president's No Child Left Behind bill that leaves every child behind, every teacher behind, every school board member behind, and every property tax payer behind.

I'm Howard Dean and I'm here to represent the Democratic wing of the Democratic Party!

The DNC members who packed the room went wild. The sound of applause, cheers, and coins rattling swirled around the room.

The crowd was on their feet, which led to a few awkward moments for the DNC officials sitting up on the stage, particularly Chairman Terry McAuliffe. Howard's speech was an indictment of Democratic leaders on a national level and the crowd was enthusiastically supporting him. McAuliffe sat on the stage unsure of what to do. If he joined in the applause he would be agreeing with Howard, but if he didn't he would look out of place among the screaming Democrats. His dilemma was captured by the giant video screens set up on each side of the stage that magnified his image for all those who weren't in the front row to see it. He eventually had no choice but to stand up, his discomfort obvious by the forced smile on his face.

□ □ □

The Howard Dean who addressed the DNC was a Howard Dean no Vermonter had seen before. The excitement of the speech surprised many, but none more than me and the Vermont delegation at the meeting. In Vermont, Howard was not known for his oratory skills. As governor, he gave two formal speeches each year, a budget address and a State of the State address. The dry subject matter combined with his dislike for reading from a prepared text made for a lethal combination.

The new Howard Dean was mobbed as he walked through the hotel lobby. Eager DNC members, who hadn't paid any attention to him before, lined up to shake his hand and have their pictures taken with him.

Before his speech we had feared that only a few of the DNC members would visit the campaign's hospitality suite, preferring instead to spend their time with the better-known candidates. In order to avoid embarrassment, we enlisted the help of two Vermonters who we knew could draw a crowd: Ben & Jerry. We put a sign in the hallway offering free ice cream to anyone who came in to talk to Howard. But after the speech we didn't need the ice cream. Howard Dean trumped Ben & Jerry.

February 23, 2003

Rick Ridder was the campaign manager, but Joe Trippi wanted the job. When the 2002 election was over, Steve and Joe began to focus on the campaign. By the start of 2003, they were concerned that the campaign wasn't going to adequately make use of the grassroots support Howard was garnering around the country. But they believed Joe knew how to do it.

Two days after Howard's successful appearance at the DNC meeting, Steve, Joe, their business partner Mark Squier, and I met with Howard at the Willard Hotel in Washington, D.C. As we sat hidden from public view in a tiny alcove off the main lobby, Steve and Joe made their case as to why Joe should be put in charge of the campaign.

—MARCH—

<u>March 1, 2003</u>

Rick Ridder was still the campaign manager, but Joe joined the staff as the campaign director. The difference between their jobs wasn't clear.

Joe moved to Vermont and not long after, Rick left the campaign. His departure had little to do with what he did or didn't do. It was more about Joe, Steve, and me than anything else. Things were moving fast and we were having a hard time adjusting. For me, the security of almost 12 years in the governor's office was gone. The three of us watched as the campaign office filled up with strangers and we weren't sure how we fit into the organization.

Steve and Joe felt that Joe would be better able to run the campaign. They convinced me of that and then Howard.

Joe had not managed a presidential campaign before, but he brought two things to the organization: an interest in the Internet and experience organizing in Iowa. He worked in the state for Ted Kennedy in 1979, Walter Mondale in 1984, Gary Hart and Dick Gephardt in 1988, and Jerry Brown in 1992.

Although Trippi, McMahon, and Squier had been Howard's media firm for more than 10 years, we had not worked with Joe before; our contact had always been Steve McMahon. In fact, the first time Joe and I met was in April of 2001 in Virginia at the meeting with Mike Ford.

Joe was a character. A profile in the *New York Times* said this about him: "Charitable descriptions liken Mr. Trippi, 47, to an unmade bed; nastier ones compare him with the 'Peanuts' character Pigpen. His wrinkled suit coat inevitably has in its pocket one of the dozen Diet Pepsis he downs a day, while his fingers constantly replenish the cherry Skoal tobacco in his cheek."

When Joe arrived, Howard suggested that the two of us share an office. The space was so small that the only way we could fit was to put our desks together facing each other. Joe's habit of chewing tobacco, eating McDonald's cheeseburgers, and drinking an endless amount of Diet Pepsi drove me crazy. Because I traveled with Howard, I was rarely in Vermont, but when I was I would start the morning off picking up hamburger wrappers and empty soda cans. I would obsessively vacuum the entire area to remove the remains of dried chewing tobacco that covered everything with a layer of cherry smelling dust. We were like the characters in the *Odd Couple*. Joe's habits annoyed me, and I know I had some that annoyed him, but despite our differences we got along quiet well.

But the honeymoon didn't last. Shortly after Joe arrived, we had a disagreement over how the campaign should operate, specifically what Howard's role should be. Joe wanted Howard to do everything he recommended without asking questions and without seeking input from others.

We were sitting face-to-face in our office when he asked me to use my "influence" with Howard to convince him to agree to this approach. I had worked for Howard for 13 years and knew how much he valued the opinion of others. As governor he always took the responsibility for making a decision seriously and never blindly followed anyone. And I didn't think he should start just because he was running for president. It was, after all, his independent nature that was attracting people to his candidacy. Why change that by putting his every move in the hands of a Washington consultant.

When I made my views clear, Joe yelled at me from across the desk.

March 5, 2003

More than 500 people snaked around the sidewalk hoping to get into the New York City nightclub. They weren't there to dance to their favorite band or laugh along with a comedian. It was the first

Wednesday of the month, which meant it was national Dean Meetup night.

The hundreds of people who showed up in New York were joined by thousands of others in bars and restaurants around the country. They were brought together by a mutual interest in Howard and found themselves sharing a beer because of an Internet website known as Meetup.com.

"I wish we were so smart to have figured out the Internet thing, but the fact is, the Internet community found us," Howard would tell *Newsweek* magazine. And he was right. The Dean campaign became synonymous with the Internet, but Howard's supporters were organizing themselves over the web before anyone in the campaign realized it.

Meetup resembled an online dating service connecting people who shared a common interest or hobby. It was easy to participate. All one had to do was log on to the Meetup website and scroll through the dozens of areas of interest that ranged from knitting to Dungeons and Dragons to witches. When they found their interest they could join a group in their area or start their own. Each group picked a regular time and place to meet. For the 5,675 Dean supporters around the country it was the first Wednesday of every month.

March 15, 2003

We began the day in Beverly Hills, California. It was 5 a.m. when our volunteer driver pulled up in front of the stone mansion on Sunset Boulevard where we had spent the night. We hopped in the car and headed to the airport to catch an early morning flight to Sacramento.

When we arrived at the Sacramento convention center, Howard was tired and grumpy. He had gotten less than six hours of sleep the night before and now he had to give a speech at the California

State Democratic Convention. Much like the Democratic National Committee meeting three weeks earlier, he arrived not knowing what he was going to say.

We were ushered to our assigned waiting room. Howard pulled the used envelope with the DNC speech notes on it out of his pocket and started putting his thoughts together.

□ □ □

The half dozen members of the California Teachers Association were polite. It was less than one hour before Howard was scheduled to deliver his speech and they had come to our room to meet with him. He requested the meeting because he hoped to get the union's support. He laid out his positions on issues, emphasizing his opposition to No Child Left Behind. He was the only presidential candidate not to support the initiative, which was also opposed by the teachers.

When he asked the teachers if they planned to make an endorsement their answer was yes. But there was no indication that it might go Howard's way. In fact, they seemed indifferent to his candidacy.

□ □ □

"I want my country back!" Howard roared as the 1,800 Democrats who packed the Sacramento convention center jumped to their feet. When he first walked up to the podium, few in the audience paid any attention to him. They had been listening to speech after speech, so they were more interested in stretching their legs and getting food than listening to another speaker.

Ignoring the activity on the convention floor, he leaned into the microphone, looked directly into the crowd, and began, "What I want to know is what so many Democrats are doing supporting the president's unilateral intervention in Iraq."

I was standing in the front of the room, watching as one by one the Democrats turned to listen to Howard. The more he spoke the more excited the crowd became. It was like watching fans do a wave at a football game. The Democrats were picking up the Dean signs we had passed out earlier and hopping on the seats of their chairs.

Howard fed off the energy of the screaming crowd. "We want our country back!" he proclaimed. "I'm tired of being divided. I don't want to listen to the fundamentalist preachers anymore. I want an America that looks like America. . . . We have a dream. We can only reach the dream if we're all together black and white, gay and straight, men and women, America, the Democratic Party. We're going to win in 2004!" He was yelling so loud that his voice was cracking.

The giant television screen above the stage projected his image to the back of the room. His face turned redder and redder. I was convinced that he was either going to have a heart attack or pass out. But he continued yelling, "Stand up for America! Stand up for America! Stand up for America!"

By the time he left the stage the crowd was in a frenzy. As he walked through the convention hall, people ran up to shake his hand, others just wanted to touch him, reaching out to brush their hands across his JC Penney suit – the same suit that was panned in New Hampshire.

On our way out of the convention center we bumped into a few of the teachers we had met less than two hours earlier. They couldn't contain their excitement. They were jumping up and down and one teacher gave me a big hug. They were indifferent no more.

□ □ □

The speech ended with cheer from the crowd and a note of apology to John Edwards.

Howard had the Democrats on their feet when he announced, "I don't think we can win the White House if we vote for the president's unilateral attack on Iraq in Washington and then come to California and say we're against the war."

The person who did one thing and said another in Howard's scenario was John Edwards. A convention goer had told Howard that in his speech Edwards claimed to oppose the war without ever mentioning that he had voted for it.

But Edwards had made no such claim. In fact, the California Democrats booed him for his vote in favor of the military action.

Howard learned of his mistake as we left the convention center and quickly scribbled a note of apology to his rival.

March 19, 2003

I picked Howard up at his home in Burlington at 5 a.m. and we drove to the city's airport to catch a flight to Columbia, South Carolina. Six hours later we were sitting on a bench in the hallway outside the speaker's office in the South Carolina State Capitol building. Our goal was to meet Democratic members of the House of Representatives.

Between speeches and votes it was difficult to predict the schedule of legislative business, which made it hard to plan meetings with the legislators. But we found a solution. The speaker of the House was a Democrat and his office attracted Democratic members during breaks in the floor action. All we had to do was sit outside the office and wait for the legislators to arrive.

And it worked. State Senator David Mack, a supporter, was with us. He pulled members aside as they went in and out of the speaker's office and introduced them to Howard. Eventually, the speaker invited us in.

Eight hours, eight meetings, and one pig pickin' (a dinner featuring a pig cooked on a spit) later we were ready to wrap up our day.

As we drove to our overnight destination, President Bush was preparing to address the nation. We were staying in Columbia at the home of Bill and Claire Prince. Their house was located on a family-friendly cul-de-sac perfect for raising their two young sons.

When we arrived the kids were getting ready to go to bed and since we had been up since 4 a.m. we weren't far behind. We were shown to our rooms unaware, like the rest of the country, about the impending military action against Iraq.

It was shortly after 9 p.m. in South Carolina, just moments after the air strikes began, when Steve McMahon called to tell me that the United States had begun bombing Iraq and the president would speak from the Oval Office in less than 15 minutes.

I was in one of the kids' rooms surrounded by a large yellow Sponge Bob stuffed toy and an empty hamster cage. I didn't know where Howard was and the house was dark, so I couldn't find my way to the living room to turn the television on. I tried to tune in the clock radio on the nightstand, but to no avail.

It wouldn't be until the next morning that we would talk about the military action that would change the campaign.

March 20, 2003

It had been 12 hours since President Bush announced to the world that a U.S.-led coalition had begun air strikes against Iraq. Addressing the nation from the Oval Office he told Americans, "The people of the United States of America and our friends and allies will not live at the mercy of an outlaw regime that threatens the peace with weapons of mass murder."

Howard was an outspoken critic of the impending war, putting him at odds with John Edwards, Dick Gephardt, John Kerry, and Joe Lieberman all of whom voted in favor of a Congressional resolution passed in October that authorized the president to use force against Iraq if necessary.

The military action would change the campaign, and it would prove to be the start of what Howard would describe as his "frosty" relationship with the national news media.

□ □ □

We left South Carolina early in the morning and flew to Washington, D.C. where Howard spoke at a meeting of the National Newspaper Association. As he walked through the lobby of the Hyatt Hotel he was stopped by Nedra Pickler of the Associated Press and Ron Brownstein of the *Los Angeles Times*. They wanted him to comment on the hours-old war. Howard spoke to the reporters at the same time, but when the stories appeared online later in the evening they were anything but alike.

Brownstein wrote that Howard was "backing away from earlier plans to continue criticizing the war after the fighting began."

In contrast, Pickler's story contained a direct quote from Howard that contradicted what Brownstein had written. "I'm not going to back off my criticism of the president's policy, but I'm certainly going to change the tone. There won't be the kind of red meat remarks that you make in front of partisan Democratic audiences," Pickler quoted Howard as saying.

Howard was annoyed with Brownstein and worried that anyone reading the story would think he was backing away from his opposition to the war. After repeated attempts, all unsuccessful, to get in touch with Brownstein or anyone at the *Los Angeles Times* who could correct the story, Howard decided to take matters into his own hands.

The stories were put side by side on the campaign's website along with a statement that read, "The assertions [in Brownstein's story] are incorrect and the story is incorrect. Dean's view that this is the wrong war at the wrong time is well known and has not changed."

March 26, 2003

It was a three-hour ride from Boston to Burlington. Howard was spending the night in the city, so it was just Joe and I, and Aaron Holmes, one of our field organizers in the car.

The arguing started almost immediately. Three weeks had passed since Joe asked me to convince Howard to listen to him and only him. I was still refusing to have the conversation with Howard and no amount of badgering was going to get me to.

Joe and I had opposite strategies. He yelled at me from the front seat. I remained silent in the back. The more he yelled, the more I refused to speak to him. The more I refused to speak, the more he yelled at me.

Our behavior was more suited for a sandbox than the Oval Office, but the argument was just the first of many in a combative relationship that would get worse as the campaign moved forward.

—APRIL—

April 1, 2003

We spent the first day of the month in New York. Eight fund-raising events were on the schedule. Young professionals, women, Democratic activists, and gay and lesbians were the target audiences. Howard also met with representatives from the publishing house Simon and Shuster. People who run for president need to have a book under their belts we were told. So it was time for Howard to publish one.

As we toured New York, the fundraising totals for the first quarter of the year (January – March) were in. Our take: $2.6 million. It was a far cry from the "paltry" amount we collected in 2002.

While we lagged behind our opponents, who outraised us by almost 3 to 1, the amount of money we raised reflected the momentum Howard saw after his break-out speech at the Democratic National Committee meeting and the activity of the Meetup groups around the country. By the end of the first quarter more than 12,000 individuals had contributed to the campaign and

$750,000 came in over the Internet – $400,000 of that in the last week alone.

April 4, 2003

We were nowhere near New Hampshire, we had flown from Atlanta to Washington, D.C. and hopped a train to New York attending a series of fundraisers along the way, but the Granite State was in the news. Howard had been running second behind Kerry in the state since Al Gore dropped out of the race at the end of the year, but things were changing.

"Kerry, Dean Tied in New Hampshire Poll," read the headline of the Associated Press story. The poll of New Hampshire voters conducted by Franklin Pierce College showed both Howard and Kerry favored by 21 percent of those surveyed.

The poll showed the impact the war in Iraq was having on Howard's candidacy. Ninety percent of those who indicated that Howard was their choice for president opposed the war, while only half of Kerry's support came from war opponents.

April 9, 2003

We were in Washington, D.C. to meet with labor leaders, foreign policy experts, and members of Congress, including then-minority leader Nancy Pelosi, the Hispanic Caucus, and the Black Caucus.

By mid-morning we were sitting in the conference room at The Albright Group, the consulting firm founded by Madeleine Albright, the former secretary of state under President Clinton. Albright hadn't endorsed Howard and we weren't there to ask her to. Instead she had agreed to brief him on foreign policy issues.

Ten minutes into the meeting the fire alarm went off. We were herded down the stairs and out of the building. Albright was ahead of us and by the time we reached the ground floor there was no sign of her.

We stood outside in the pouring rain for 15 minutes before we were allowed back inside. We were ready to continue the meeting, but Albright wasn't there. She had gone to get her hair done.

While we were crisscrossing Washington, there was celebrating half a world away in Baghdad. American troops had taken control of the capital city and jubilant Iraqis had spilled into the streets. It was a military victory for President Bush, one reinforced by the pictures broadcast around the world of American troops and Iraqis toppling a huge statue of Saddam Hussein.

Nineteen days after the first bombs dropped in Baghdad, the fall of the city ignited a new debate among the Democratic candidates for president: What role should the United States play in rebuilding the country?

□ □ □

The nine Democrats running for president sat in the chairs that had been set up in a long line on the stage in a ballroom of a Washington, D.C. hotel. Howard was joined by John Edwards, Dick Gephardt, Bob Graham, John Kerry, Joe Lieberman, Carol Moseley Braun, and Al Sharpton. The event was a forum sponsored by the Children's Defense Fund, a Washington, D.C.-based advocacy group.

The focus of the forum (it was a forum, not a contentious debate the organizers stressed) was supposed to be children's issues, but the military events of the day couldn't be ignored.

"We've gotten rid of him [Saddam Hussein] – I suppose that's a good thing," Howard conceded when responding to a question about the fall of Baghdad. But he warned the audience, "There's going to be a long period when the United States is going to be maintaining Iraq, and that's going to cost this country's taxpayers a lot of money that could be spent on schools and kids."

April 12, 2003

Three days earlier U.S.-led forces captured Baghdad. No one knew whether Saddam Hussein was dead or alive, but it didn't seem to matter. "He's no longer in power," declared President Bush.

While headlines like "U.S. Gains More Control" appeared in newspapers around the country, Howard was in Iowa. Dressed in blue corduroy pants, a blue sweatshirt, and sneakers, he walked down the traffic median that separated the north and south-bound lanes of Highway 61 in Muscatine. On one side of the highway, a 12-foot-tall wooden watermelon slice alerted passersby to the farm stand up ahead. We used the faux melon to mark our progress. The farther away from it we got, the more terrain we had covered.

Piece by piece, Howard filled the orange bag he was carrying with the paper, cigarette butts, and the other random scraps of trash that littered the strip of green grass. It was Earth Day and we had joined 16 members of the Muscatine County Democratic Committee to clean the two-mile stretch of highway the group maintained as part of Iowa's adopt-a-highway program.

One hour and one trash bag later, Howard emerged from a nearby office building dressed in his business suit. He hopped into the mini-van and we continued our day. A day that, with the exception of our foray down the highway, was routine. Interested students gathered at a college campus, activists ate dinner in a hotel ballroom, and even more Democrats gathered for a meal in the community room of a local bank. The venue changed, but the message didn't. At each event the staff instructed Howard to "give your standard stump speech."

April 15, 2003

"U.S.: Fighting Is Over" and "Dean Faces Post-War Tightrope" were the headlines in one Vermont newspaper. They summed up the challenge the campaign was facing.

One day earlier U.S. Major General Stanley McChrystal announced, "I would anticipate that the major combat engagements are over." The announcement came as Saddam Hussein's hometown of Tikrit fell to the U.S.-led forces.

Many people saw Howard as nothing more than an anti-war candidate. The recent poll in New Hampshire that showed most of his supporters also opposed the war seemed to bear that out. Would he be able to continue to build a campaign now that the military action was over?

Howard's answer to the question was yes. "I did not get in this race as the peace candidate. People are turning to my campaign because they want a sense of hope again, they want health insurance, and they want leaders who are not afraid to say what they think."

April 23, 2003

U.S.-led forces had toppled Baghdad, Tikrit, and a statue of Saddam Hussein. They had captured the dictator's half brother. And Congress had approved and President Bush had signed a $79 billion supplemental bill to fund the war. But no amount of success was going to change Howard's mind about the military action.

He was in Vermont when he appeared live via satellite on CNN. "We don't know that yet," he told Wolf Blitzer when the newsman asked if he agreed that the Iraqi people were better off without Saddam Hussein.

Blitzer, who greeted Howard's answer with skepticism – it was, after all, contrary to the prevailing wisdom – followed up, "You think it's possible that whatever emerges in Iraq could be worse than what they have had for decades under Saddam Hussein?"

"I do, I do," was Howard's response.

"We [the United States] have to take a different approach [to diplomacy]. We won't always have the strongest military."

We were flying to California, having just wrapped up a three-day visit to Iowa, when *Time* magazine posted the comment Howard made two weeks earlier on its website. He made the remark during a tour of a yogurt factory in Londonderry, New Hampshire, and it had gone unnoticed – not only by the media, but by our campaign staff as well – until now.

We were in midair when the controversy erupted. By the time we landed the Kerry campaign was in full attack mode. They had already issued a statement asserting that Howard's remarks raised "serious questions about his capacity to serve as commander in chief. No serious candidate for the presidency has ever before suggested that he would compromise or tolerate an erosion of America's military supremacy."

No one on the campaign staff was sure what Howard meant, which forced them to wait until our plane landed in Los Angeles to respond to the Kerry campaign's criticism. Howard didn't deny making the remark, but he did reject Kerry's interpretation of what he said.

Howard explained to Joe that he wasn't questioning the strength of the United States military. Instead he was arguing that the United States shouldn't rely on military action alone to fight the war on terror. There needed to be a diplomatic piece to our foreign policy and national security strategy – something that was lacking under the Bush administration.

With that explanation in hand, Joe issued a statement taking the Kerry campaign to task for its attack. "The statement by Senator John Kerry's campaign is absurd. As Commander in Chief, Howard Dean will never tolerate an erosion of American military power, nor has he ever said such a thing."

□ □ □

The war of words didn't stop us from embarking on the first day of a three-day fundraising blitz that would take us from California to New York.

After meetings with Steven Spielberg and Paramount Picture chairman Sherry Lansing, we headed to the Renaissance Hotel in Hollywood. The hotel was part of the complex that was home to the Kodak Theater, site of the Academy Awards ceremony. The location was far from the Vermont State House where three years earlier Howard signed into law a bill establishing civil unions, which granted same-sex couples in Vermont many of the same rights and benefits as heterosexual couples.

When he signed the first-in-the-nation law, the backlash was so great that he faced losing re-election as governor, and many pundits and members of the media predicted it would create an obstacle for him in a presidential campaign. But none of that had happened and we were in Hollywood using the anniversary to raise money.

Howard moved around the hotel ballroom with 1980s sitcom star Judith Light. The actress, who starred as Angela Bower in the family-oriented show, *Who's the Boss*, was the special guest. Individuals who donated a minimum of $250 were invited to attend a general reception. Those who donated $1,000 or more were invited to a smaller, more exclusive party and treated to a photo with Howard and Light. While guests stood at tall cocktail tables covered with white linen tablecloths nibbling on hors d'oeuvres and sipping champagne, celebrities lined the red carpet on the street below in front of the Kodak Theater for the premiere of the latest *X-Men* movie.

For me the celebrities were down on the red carpet, but for the guests at the fundraiser, who were mainly gay and lesbian, the real stars were Howard and Light, who was known to the crowd for her advocacy of gay rights.

By the time the movie premiere was over we were on our way to San Francisco.

April 29, 2003

We began the day at San Francisco's Glide Memorial United Methodist Church. The reason for our visit to the facility, which provides services for the poor, including health care, drug and alcohol recovery programs, and shelter, was a mystery. Was the visit meant to assuage any guilt the campaign staff felt because of the three-day nonstop fundraising blitz? Who knows, but Howard dutifully toured the center with a reporter from the local CBS affiliate in tow.

After bidding good-bye to the pastor, we sped off to Spago's in Palo Alto. The official start of the second day of our fundraising tour began at the trendy restaurant founded by celebrity chef Wolfgang Puck. The 60 guests who donated $1,000 each included the founder of the Esprit clothing line, the son of the inventor of the birth control pill, an heir to the Estee Lauder cosmetics fortune, and the wives of Apple computer founder Steve Jobs and Google CEO Eric Schmidt.

Next came two receptions at the historic Ferry Building on San Francisco Bay that celebrated the passage of Vermont's civil unions law.

The 75 people who gave $1,000 or more were herded into a curtained-off section of the main room and lined up for a photo with Howard. A note on the schedule from the campaign staff instructed him that because of the tight schedule the "photo line needs to move along very quickly. That means each person with you for less than a minute."

There was no photo line for the 300 general reception guests who donated $250 each. Instead they had to make due with "limited food stations, a couple of cash bars, and some seating."

By 11 p.m. we were settled in for the evening on an American Airlines flight to New York. The seats in the plane would serve as our beds and we'd eat the airline-issued turkey and cheese croissant sandwiches for dinner. In a matter of hours, we'd begin the East Coast leg of our fundraising tour.

April 30, 2003

At 7 a.m. our red-eye flight landed in New York. After a 90-minute rest stop at Howard's mother's Park Avenue apartment, we began our day.

Twelve hours and seven meetings later (including a stop at actress and comedian Whoopi Goldberg's Soho apartment and a meeting with hip hop music producer Russell Simmons on the sidewalk outside) we found ourselves at New York's Hammersmith Ballroom for the final event of our three-day civil unions-themed fundraising celebration.

Like the donors in California who gave $1,000 to the campaign, the New York high-dollar contributors were lined up for a photo with Howard. And once again the staff instructed him to keep the line moving.

The 500 general reception guests mingled around the ballroom and sat at the round white linen-covered tables that dotted the room. Whoopi Goldberg served as the master of ceremonies. The event featured a performance by Joan Jett and her band. Howard and his mother sat in the front row close to the stage and listened as the rock singer entertained the crowd. The room vibrated during the heart-pounding and eardrum-popping show.

The performance by the leather-clad rocker completed our three-day fundraising tour that began with champagne and a television sitcom star. How much did we raise? More than $500,000.

—MAY—

May 1, 2003

The pictures would be broadcast around the globe: President George Bush dressed in a green flight suit exiting the Navy jet moments after it landed on the deck of the aircraft carrier USS Abraham Lincoln. The president stood under a large banner that read "Mission Accomplished," ready to announce to the nation the end of major combat operations in Iraq.

While the president was claiming victory in front of the media cameras, we sat in a conference room at a Burlington, Vermont, law firm preparing Howard for the first presidential debate of the campaign. The nationally televised event sponsored by ABC News was set to take place in two days at the University of South Carolina in Columbia.

A dozen of us sat around a large wooden table. With the exception of me, everyone in the room was a man, including the two Vermont state senators and two Washington D.C.-based political strategists who were there to play the parts of the other candidates.

The table was piled high with policy briefing books and news clips. More than a half dozen notebooks were filled with page after page of information on the voting records, public statements, and personal histories of the other candidates. More books contained information on Howard's record, including facts that his opponents might use against him.

We ran through a mock debate that resembled a real one. Howard was peppered with questions. He responded to those directed at him, as well as rebutted the answers of his rivals. Although we intended to hold our critique until the end of the trial debate, it was impossible and we let no answer pass without offering Howard advice. We analyzed his words, his mannerisms, and even the look on his face. He was offered suggestions on how he should answer a question and precisely what words he should use. He took notes and sometimes disagreed with the assessment offered.

For all the preparing we did, anticipating questions and scripting answers, we knew that much of what would happen was out of our control. Howard had been criticizing his opponents for more than a year, but he hadn't been in a situation before where they could face him and answer back – until now. It had been just days since the war of words began between Howard and the Kerry campaign over his statement that "we won't always have the strongest military." The issue was still very much alive, and with Howard and Kerry sharing the stage for the first time, there was no doubt that the debate moderator, ABC News' George Stephanopoulos, would bring it up. After all, a feud between any of the candidates would make for great television.

At the end of the two hours Howard stretched his arms and sighed. There was nothing more to do. Ready or not, the debate was about to begin.

May 2, 2003

We left for Columbia the day before the debate. We needed to arrive early because the South Carolina Democratic Party had taken advantage of the fact that nine presidential candidates would be in the state and organized a fundraising dinner for the evening before the nationally televised event.

Despite the fact that Howard was on his way to his first debate, the flight from Burlington was not much different from the many we had taken before. Howard, Joe, and I boarded the plane with Howard's presence barely noted by the other passengers. Vermonters were accustomed to seeing him at the airport and nothing had changed because he was running for president. It wasn't until we changed planes at Dulles airport in Washington, D.C. that the impending debate became real. Joining us on the flight – and sitting in the seat directly behind us – was George Stephanopoulos.

When we arrived in Columbia we went directly to the home of Claire and Bill Prince, our regular hosts during our stays in the city, where we waited until it was time to go to the dinner.

After a few hours making telephone calls to the media and potential donors, we left for the state party dinner. On our way we passed a Ben & Jerry's scoop shop and, unable to resist the temptation, we stopped in for a pre-dinner snack. While Howard ate his cone filled with chocolate fudge brownie yogurt, a woman collapsed onto the shop floor. The young workers peered over the counter not knowing what to do. Howard handed his cone to me, knelt down, and talked to her until an ambulance arrived. For a doctor, it was all in a day's work.

□ □ □

It was after 9:30 p.m. when we arrived at the parking garage. It was full, but not with cars. Instead it was packed with people, food, and music. The event was South Carolina Congressman Jim Clyburn's annual fish fry.

More than 1,000 people, including local Democrats and members of the news media, milled around the first floor of the parking structure. Howard took his coat off, removed his tie, rolled up his sleeves, and wandered into the crowd, introducing himself to those who had gathered to eat fish and talk politics. John Edwards, Dick Gephardt, Bob Graham, John Kerry, and Carol Moseley Braun were also there, but Howard attracted the most attention. Not because he was the most well known, he wasn't, but because he dared to dance. He was speaking to a woman in the crowd when she decided she wanted to take a spin around the parking structure. Howard was game and suddenly they were twirling around the concrete floor much to the delight of the other partygoers. The crowd moved back in order to avoid flying limbs and formed a circle around them. As the amused spectators snapped pictures and laughed, no one could deny that Howard would do whatever it took to get elected.

May 3, 2003

The day had arrived. At 9 p.m. Howard would join the other Democratic candidates for president on a stage at the University of South Carolina.

At 3 p.m., after a series of meetings with potential supporters, Howard, Joe Trippi, Steve McMahon, and I met at the home of a supporter in Columbia, where we planned to stay until it was time to go to the debate.

When Howard and I arrived, Joe was ending a telephone conversation with Pat Caddell, a political consultant who once served as Jimmy Carter's pollster. The two had drafted a few lines they wanted to add to the statement Howard planned to give at the end of the debate: "You have the power to rise up and take this country back. You have the power to give this party the backbone to challenge this president, and all of the harm he has done to our country. You have the power to create jobs, balance the budget, and bring us our dream, which Harry Truman put in our platform in 1948 – health care for every American."

Howard wasn't sure that he wanted to use the new language. He had already committed his closing statement to memory and was nervous about changing it, but he scribbled it down anyway.

The time ticked by slowly. We sat in the living room for close to an hour with Howard alternating between studying the new closing statement, answering the questions we lobbed at him, and looking at the clock. The longer he sat, the more anxious and less productive he became. We finally decided the best thing would be for Howard to get his mind off the debate, at least for a while, so we left the house. We had no idea where we were going. Instead Howard, Steve, and I got in the car and asked the local law enforcement officer who had been assigned to accompany us in Columbia to drive us wherever he wanted.

The next thing we knew we were in a Subway sandwich shop. It was after lunch and before dinner and we were the only ones in the shop, which shared its space with a mini mart. We stood at the counter and ordered sandwiches from the teenager on duty. We were sitting in one of the generic yellow booths that could be found in any of the chain's restaurants around the country, when a reporter from the *Washington Post* walked in. Mark Liebovich was in town to cover the debate for the paper and was surprised to see us. It was clear by the look on his face that sitting in a Subway sandwich shop was not what most presidential candidates did before a debate.

Twenty minutes later we were back in the car with still hours to go before the debate. Howard didn't want to go back to the house, so we went to a nearby Holiday Inn where the campaign had rented a room for the staff. Howard relaxed in the empty room upstairs while Steve and I sat next to the pool under a large red patio umbrella.

口 口 口

It was shortly after 7 p.m. when we arrived at Drayton Hall on the University of South Carolina's campus where we were greeted by a group of Dean supporters who lined the sidewalk waving signs and yelling for Howard. He walked through the middle of the crowd shaking hands and thanking everyone for coming before disappearing inside.

As the campaign progressed, debates would become second nature, with each one almost exactly like the one before. The organization sponsoring the debate and the network televising it changed, but not much else. The sets were red, white, and blue. The candidates stood behind podiums and were given thirty seconds to answer how they would bring about world peace. John Kerry would talk about his time in Vietnam and John Edwards would remind everyone that his father worked in a coal mine. And no one was ever quite sure what Howard would say. In a few cases the sponsors tried to spice things up by having the candidates sit on stools instead of standing behind podiums and one tried to appeal to the younger voters by having the candidates take off their suit jackets. The only thing that would change was the food provided backstage to the candidates and staff. And for people who hadn't eaten all day, it was often the thing we were most concerned about. Some sponsors went all out by providing sandwiches and beverages, others just settled for cookies and water, and some were noted for failing to provide anything.

But the South Carolina debate was our first and we didn't know what to expect; when we walked into Drayton Hall we found a world created just for the occasion.

We were ushered into the candidates' waiting area. Elsewhere in the building was a workroom for the media and a room for each campaign. Like traveling to another country, the proper iden-tification was needed in order to move between the three areas. The passport in this case was a laminated card, known as a credential, that all involved were required to wear around their necks. The wearer was identified as either a member of a campaign staff or the media, which also indicated how far one was allowed to roam.

The candidates' area was the most restricted, with only the candidates and two staff members from each campaign given access. When Howard and I arrived we were met by Kelly McMahon, who was helping us with logistics. The three of us were shown to Howard's assigned waiting room, a small room that normally served as a professor's office. The other candidates were in similar offices that lined the hallway.

Outside was a common area where we could indulge in the cookies, fruit, vegetables, soda, and water offered by the network. Behind a curtain a make-up artist worked on the candidates' faces so they wouldn't shine under the hot lights. The space was set up so it was impossible for the candidates not to meet. When they did pass each other, however, there was little or no conversation.

Howard got some food, had powder applied to his face, then returned to the room where he, Kelly and I waited for more than an hour for the debate to start. Howard was too anxious to run through questions. Instead he cleaned out his suit jacket pockets, lint and all.

The knock at the door told us it was time for the debate. In the hallway the staff from ABC lined the nine candidates up in the order they would be seated on stage – Howard, John Edwards, John Kerry, Bob Graham, Joe Lieberman, Dick Gephardt, Dennis Kucinich, Al Sharpton, and Carol Moseley Braun. There was something so unpresidential about the scene. It reminded me of kids in kindergarten lining up to go out for recess.

As soon as Howard took his place in line his demeanor changed – he went from anxious to nervous. The smile was gone, his shoulders stiffened, and his face turned to stone.

When everyone was in place the nine candidates running for the Democratic nomination for president of the United States walked silently in formation down the hallway, into the theater, and onto the stage.

□ □ □

For all the preparation and anticipation, the debate flew by. For 90 minutes the nine candidates sat across a long table in front of the small audience that filled the theater, answering questions posed to them by Stephanopoulos.

Television is all about entertainment, and not wanting a boring show, Stephanopoulos attempted to fan the flames of the argument between Howard and Kerry that started just days earlier. Howard's answer to Stephanopoulos' question about the controversy was short, but pointed: "Everyone respects Senator Kerry's extraordinary, heroic Vietnam record, and I do as well.

However, what I would have preferred – this is 30 years later – I would have preferred if Senator Kerry had some concerns about my fitness to serve, that he speak to me directly about that rather than through his spokesperson."

Kerry's response to a subsequent question was equally pointed: "I really think that anybody who has measured the tests that I think I have performed over the last years on any numbers of fights in the United States Congress, as well as my service in Vietnam, know that I don't need any lectures in courage from Howard Dean."

While the candidates debated on stage, behind the scenes the campaigns engaged in a debate of their own. Each campaign was at the ready to issue press releases calling the media's attention to misstatements made by their rivals, clarifying or expanding on remarks made by their own candidate, and sometimes just adding general information to the mix.

Half a dozen members of our campaign staff sat in a classroom in a building adjacent to the theater. We had an open telephone line to Vermont where the staff had access to Howard's record and that of his opponents. Members of Howard's gubernatorial administration were on call to help answer questions about policies and programs implemented during his tenure as governor. We had a computer and a printer that spit out press releases, which we passed out to the members of the media who sat confined in their room.

"Senator Kerry Misquotes Howard Dean" and "Facts on Dean's Vermont Health Care Record" set out to correct statements made by Kerry. The candidates who supported the Bush tax cuts were taken to task in "Only in Washington is a $350 Billion Tax Cut Not a Tax Cut." And "Dick Gephardt knows that when you find a winning message, steal it!" highlighted the instances when the congressman repeated lines that originated with Howard.

Splitting 90 minutes between nine candidates didn't allow for a substantive discussion on any issue and despite Stephanopoulos' best efforts, besides the early fireworks between Howard and Kerry, the debate was uneventful. A little more than an hour after the first question was asked it was time for closing statements.

Howard looked into the camera and recited the part he had been practicing for days. When it came time for the lines he had seen just hours earlier, he fumbled and tried to recover by reading them. He looked down at his notes, an act so distracting that it was difficult for viewers to focus on what he was saying.

He may have bungled his lines, but it wasn't anything to worry about because his closing statement was in a press release, "Dean Challenges Democrats to Rise Up and Take This Country Back," and in the hands of the media before the debate went off the air.

A press release could correct botched lines or misstatements but it couldn't help Howard's overall performance. The nerves he exhibited back stage didn't go away in front of the camera, and as we sat in the staff room watching the debate on a television monitor we all agreed that he looked tense, cranky, and at times mean. And others felt the same. One press report the next day noted, "Dr. Dean scowled openly as Mr. Kerry spoke." And after watching a tape of the debate Howard himself admitted that he looked "grumpy."

With his first debate over, Howard and I went to the home of Bill and Claire Prince, where I once again found myself sleeping between a Sponge Bob toy and a hamster cage.

May 9, 2003

Our day started at 4:30 a.m. in Kansas City, Missouri. It was a day that would see us in Texas, Arizona, and Iowa. From Kansas City we flew to our first stop: Dallas.

When we walked into the conference room at the University of Texas Southwestern Medical Center, where we were having breakfast with a group of doctors, the first thing that caught our attention was a table set up next to the door. On the table was a sign-up sheet for those interested in joining the campaign and a stack of red, white, and blue bumper stickers with the words "Texans for Dean" written over an outline of the state.

Howard said hello to the gentleman standing behind the table. In turn, the man introduced himself as the Dean for America Texas state coordinator. He went on to tell us that a campaign office would soon be opening in the state.

We thought it was odd that no one in Burlington had mentioned it to us, so I called the headquarters to find out what was going on. But the staff in Burlington was surprised by the news. They hadn't hired any staff in Texas and had no plans to open an office.

It turned out that the Texan had taken it upon himself to begin organizing the state. And he was just the first of many supporters who planted the seeds of our grassroots effort.

May 13, 2003

It was 6:30 a.m. and Howard and I were sitting in a dressing room at the ABC studios in New York City. Howard was going to appear on the network's early morning show *Good Morning America* to preview the health care plan he would unveil a few hours later. He sat in a make-up chair as one of the show's make-up artists put powder on his face and covered up the circles under his eyes that naturally occurred because of late nights and early mornings.

He would be interviewed by co-host Diane Sawyer for five minutes at 7:10 a.m. When he went on the set I prepared to watch the show on the monitor that hung from the wall. But first I looked out the window and saw Howard's name in lights. The scrolling marquee on the Reuters news service building in Times Square read, "Democrat Dean will announce health care plan."

The health care plan was the first major policy initiative developed by the campaign and it would be the first policy speech

Howard would deliver. His anti-war stance was getting most of the media attention, but providing health care to all Americans was one of the reasons he decided to run for president, and the plan he would unveil was the product of more than a year's worth of work.

For the doctor-turned-governor who had made providing access to health care for virtually every child in Vermont a priority, and for the presidential candidate who had taken his opponents to task for not getting the job done in Washington, this was a big day.

He would unveil the plan at Columbia University, a fitting location given the fact that he had taken night courses at the school in order to fulfill the science course credits needed to get into medical school.

Regardless of the event's importance to the campaign, we didn't take a car or cab to get there. Howard didn't want to spend the money or waste time sitting in traffic, so we took the subway. We pushed our way through the station and onto the train with hundreds of other New Yorkers. When we came up from underground we weren't sure where we were, but with the help of some passersby we were pointed in the direction of the university's School of International and Public Affairs. We walked across the campus looking for the right building, and thanks to a young man holding a "Columbia loves Dean" sign, we knew when we had reached our destination.

A half dozen television cameras lined the back of the room while the print reporters sat to the side. Howard stood in the front facing more than 100 friendly faces, including his mother's, and delivered his speech. He read from the prepared text that sat in front of him on the podium. The lights in the room were dimmed so an overhead projector could beam the major points of the plan onto a screen set up behind him.

Before he outlined the specifics of the plan he tried to set himself apart from the other candidates. He never used their names, but the implication of his words was clear. He was the only one who could truly understand the problems with the health care system because he was a doctor.

He sprinkled his medical credentials over four pages. He had volunteered in a New York City emergency room, an experience that led him to attend medical school. He moved to Vermont to complete his residency and later set up a private practice with his wife, Judy. And he told a story no one could ever top. He was in the middle of giving a patient a physical exam when he learned that the governor had died and suddenly he, as lieutenant governor, was the governor of Vermont. And despite the news, he finished the exam before leaving to take the oath of office.

His health care plan was built on the work he had done as governor. In Vermont, he made sure that virtually every child under the age of 18 had access to health care. As a presidential candidate he wanted to expand the existing federal program to cover all Americans up to age 25. He would also offer health insurance to individuals and small businesses in a program similar to what was offered to federal employees. The total cost was $88 billion and could be raised by eliminating President Bush's tax cuts. Howard was a pragmatist, and in his speech he described the plan as "ambitious" but "also realistic, targeted, and affordable."

When the speech was over we walked back across the campus, down the stairs to the subway, and caught a train that would take us to our next appointment.

May 14, 2003

When we arrived in Seattle we had no reason to believe that it would be anything but an ordinary day on the campaign trail. We had no paid staff in the state, so the local volunteers were left to plan the schedule. They set up the standard appointments: meetings with environmentalists and elected officials, along with media interviews. But they added an event in the evening they billed as a rally – a first for the campaign. They were anticipating

500 people to attend. Howard was skeptical. The visit marked only his second trip to the state, his first was in June of 2002 when he was the guest speaker at a local Democratic Party dinner. How could a governor from the other side of the country attract a crowd that size?

The rally was set to take place at Seattle's historic Town Hall. The building was formerly a church and Howard would be speaking in the sanctuary, a room that seated 1,200. If we were lucky half the seats would be occupied.

We peeked through a curtain in the back of the stage, watching the crowd arrive. By the time Howard walked on stage the room was filled to capacity. The 1,200 people sitting shoulder-to-shoulder in the pews erupted in cheers when Howard and former Governor Booth Gardner held their hands high in the air.

Speaking in front of a large crowd wasn't new to Howard. He had given speeches at the Democratic National Committee meeting and California Democratic Party state convention, but this was different. He was the main attraction. Energized by the size and enthusiasm of the crowd, he stretched his arms out to the audience like a preacher drawing his followers into his sermon. Dry subjects like health care, tax cuts, and the federal budget brought them to their feet.

It felt like a turning point in the campaign, one I needed to share with the staff back in Vermont. When I called Joe he thought I was kidding or at the very least exaggerating the number of people in the room. To prove otherwise I held my cell phone in the air so he could hear the roar of the crowd.

May 16, 2003

Howard wasn't considered a contender yet, but the energy he was generating was enough to make some Democrats nervous.

One group, the Washington, D.C.-based Democratic Leadership Council, sent a memo to its members warning about the dismal outcome of the general election if the party nominated Howard. Calling Howard and his supporters "elitist," the group's founder and CEO, Al From, and president Bruce Reed wrote, "What activists like Dean call the Democratic wing of the Democratic Party is an aberration: The McGovern-Mondale wing, defined principally by weakness abroad and elitist interest-group liberalism at home." The Democratic Party nominated George McGovern in 1972 and Walter Mondale in 1984. Both men lost in landslides to the Republican incumbent.

From's sudden interest in Howard's candidacy was a far cry from the attention he gave it the first time the two men met. In January 2002 Howard and I paid a visit to the DLC offices in Washington, D.C., where Howard told From that he was seriously considering running for president. From wasn't impressed; in fact he showed little interest in Howard. Instead he handed us some brochures on the DLC and sent us on our way.

From and Reed's memo elicited a public response from Vermonters who defended Howard's positions and record as governor. Howard didn't immediately respond publicly, choosing to leave that to others, but privately he felt that Democratic Party Chairman Terry McAuliffe needed to step in and tell the group to tone down its rhetoric. Looking ahead to the general election, Howard knew that if he won the nomination there would need to be a united Democratic Party and he believed that the DLC's actions could make that difficult. They could also lead to consequences for From, whose attacks would make him persona non grata among Dean supporters.

May 17, 2003

We left Davenport, Iowa, at 3:30 p.m. and arrived back eight hours later, having attended Democratic state party dinners in two states. Flying between time zones allowed us to accept invitations from the Democrats in both Ohio and Indiana. We lost an hour when we flew from Iowa to Columbus, Ohio, for the first event, but we arrived as the guests were being seated for dinner. We gained the hour back when we flew to Indianapolis and arrived in time to enjoy our second meal of the night.

Joe and I used the time changes to do battle in two states.

A young couple in their early 20s was dispatched to pick Joe and me up at the airport in Columbus. It didn't matter to them that Howard was riding in another car. They had the campaign manager and their candidate's longtime aide with them – they couldn't have been happier. They were still giddy over their recent marriage and while the honeymoon wasn't over for them, Joe and I argued like a couple on the verge of a divorce.

I was still fuming over a fight Joe and I had the night before regarding a phone call between Howard and Al Gore. When I wasn't able to tell Joe the exact words Gore used he called me incompetent. It didn't matter that I could only hear Howard's end of the conversation and was relaying Gore's side as told to me by Howard. When Joe yelled at me I told him to call Howard directly then abruptly hung up.

Joe and I were sitting side by side in the backseat when the newlyweds excitedly asked us how we were. Joe responded with a mixture of contempt and sarcasm, "I don't know because Kate's not talking to me." He was right; I wasn't and had no plans to.

May 26, 2003

Howard was in fourth place in Iowa (Gephardt 25 percent; Kerry 13 percent; Lieberman 9 percent; Dean 6 percent) and slightly behind Kerry in New Hampshire (Kerry 25 percent; Dean 22 percent), but his online support was growing, and as May ended the campaign reached some important milestones. The number of people signing up to join Dean groups on Meetup had swelled to 25,000, up from the nearly 5,000 members when Howard attended his first Meetup meeting in New York just two months earlier. The amount of money the campaign raised over the Internet also grew. Howard became the first candidate to collect more than $1 million online.

May 31, 2003

"We don't need Dean-lite" was Howard's response to a speech John Kerry gave to a group of Democrats from upstate New York. Howard, Kerry, Dennis Kucinich, and Al Sharpton all accepted invitations from the New York Democratic Rural Conference to speak at the group's presidential forum.

When we arrived at the Olympic Center in Lake Placid, John Kerry was on stage. I went into the auditorium to listen to his speech and was struck by the similarities it had with the one Howard had been giving. Not only did he talk about Howard's pet project as governor, helping young children, but he also appropriated the line "Take two tax cuts and call me in the morning."

When Kerry first talked about young children at the Iowa Jefferson-Jackson Day dinner in October 2002, Howard let it go. But he had no intention of doing so this time. He was known to describe his opponents as "Bush-lite," meaning their support of the president's policies made them just a paler version of the real thing. When he got up on stage his first order of business was to address the fact that Kerry's speech sounded a lot like his own. He told the New York Democrats that he was flattered that Kerry had copied his speech, but they didn't need "Dean-lite" when they could have the real thing. The line was a hit with the crowd and didn't go unnoticed by the media covering the convention. When asked about Kerry's speech, Howard told a CNN reporter, "John Kerry did a great job giving my speech. Imitation is the biggest form of flattery."

□ □ □

We were standing in the hallway outside the Olympic Center's auditorium when Howard was approached by a gentleman who wanted to shake his hand. The man's face was recognizable, but his appearance in the hallway was unexpected. It was George McGovern. Howard and McGovern shook hands and exchanged pleasantries. It was a photograph that many would have loved to snap (including the Democratic Leadership Council's Al From who two weeks early compared Howard to the unsuccessful presidential candidate). But the impromptu meeting took place in a curtained area that was off limits to the public and the prying eyes of the media.

—JUNE—

June 1, 2003

We walked through the crowd of sign-waving supporters and went into the lobby of the Sheraton Gateway Hotel in Los Angeles. The half dozen women who greeted us at the door were giddy. Their favorite presidential candidate had arrived.

We were at the California Teachers Association annual convention. When Howard first met the union's leadership in February, they were indifferent to his candidacy, but that changed after his speech at the California State Democratic convention. It was a speech that inspired and energized them and the months that had passed since had not tempered their emotions.

When Howard walked into the ballroom, a quiet murmur began and slowly spread throughout the room. Most of the teachers had never heard him speak before, but had taken the word of their colleagues and greeted him like an old friend. The crowd, which numbered close to 1,000, jumped to their feet and cheered when he was introduced. The union had not formally endorsed a candidate, but Howard was the only one invited to speak at the convention, a sign that an endorsement was likely coming his way. He moved one step closer to sealing the deal when he told them why he could never be a teacher. He recounted his short stint as a student teacher and how he realized then that he didn't have a long-term career in the field because he "couldn't spend five hours standing without going to the bathroom." The teachers cheered with delight.

June 4, 2003

The actors Paul Newman and Joanne Woodward were the first Hollywood celebrities to host a fundraiser for Howard. The reception was held at the New York City apartment of the couple's publicist in an upscale neighborhood near the Lincoln Center for the Performing Arts.

Howard and I made our way to the event after he gave the commencement address at his alma mater, Albert Einstein College of Medicine. When the two and a half hour ceremony was over, we left the Bronx campus and wandered out into the pouring rain in search of the nearest subway station. It was still raining and, because it was after 8 p.m., very dark when we came up from underground. We walked for more than 15 minutes before we reached our destination. The one umbrella we shared left each of us soaked on one side, and when we walked into the swanky apartment building we looked like drowned rats.

Newman and Woodward were mingling with their guests in the living room. The two actors became stars when being a celebrity didn't mean having your picture splashed all over gossip magazines or the Internet. Because of this there was regal air about them. Yet at the same time they were down to earth, and, except for Newman's beard, looked just like I imagined they would.

Howard stood on a chair so he could be seen by all the guests, including the actor Alec Baldwin and filmmaker Michael Moore, who were just a few of the well-known faces in the mostly non-celebrity audience. After roughly 45 minutes he hopped down. Just then the smell of fresh baked cookies filled the apartment. I hadn't eaten all day, so I made my way over to the table for my dinner – an oatmeal raisin cookie. I was munching away when the gentleman standing next to me remarked how good the cookies were. When I turned to agree, I found that I was conversing about cookies with none other than the Oscar, Tony, Golden Globe, and Emmy award-winning music composer Marvin Hamlisch. (Hamlisch would later compose a song about Howard, which he would perform at a fundraiser in New York City.)

June 9, 2003

Our self-appointed Texas state coordinator agreed to organize a rally in Austin. Howard enjoyed visiting Texas because he relished the chance to take on President Bush in his home state.

It was close to 9 p.m. when we parked our minivan on the street less than a block away from the site of the rally, the Plaza Saltillo, a traditional outdoor Mexican marketplace.

The Plaza had a large open courtyard surrounded on two sides by small shop fronts and anchored on one end by the main entrance and the other by a small gazebo. We walked up onto the gazebo and saw an incredible sight – 3,200 people. The courtyard was packed and the sea of faces – young and old – stretched from the people who were seated on the ground beneath the gazebo to those who looked like dots standing in the back by the entrance.

Howard stood behind the podium that had been set up on the gazebo. The warm weather forced him to strip off his suit coat and roll up his shirt sleeves. He grabbed the microphone out of its stand and moved in front of the podium; he needed to be closer to his enthusiastic supporters. The Texas Democrats greeted his stump speech with loud cheers. Health care for everyone? Yes! Bush tax cuts? No! And when Howard mentioned the federal budget he had the crowd on their feet.

It was the largest gathering of Dean supporters yet and proving the power of the web, the rally was organized almost exclusively over the Internet.

June 11, 2003

The subject line on the memo read "Definitional Moment." In the nine-page document, Joe outlined for Howard his belief that the campaign that started out focused on issues was no longer about issues at all. Instead it was about empowering people. He argued that Howard had a choice: He could be a transactional leader, one who talked about issues, or a transformational leader who "rises to the historical moment, and leads a movement to save and restore America's ideals." Joe maintained that circumstances were calling Howard to follow in the footsteps of former presidents Andrew Jackson, Abraham Lincoln, Teddy Roosevelt, Woodrow Wilson, and Franklin Roosevelt.

Joe had spent a great deal of time on the memo, but Howard paid little attention to it.

He was a practical person who wanted to know in fifty words or less how he was going to win the Democratic nomination. He was not interested in a conceptual memo that read in part, "This is not Sgt. Pepper's Magical Mystery Tour – This is Howard Dean's Magical History Tour of the Greatest Nation on this Earth." Plus he was, at his core, Joe's definition of a transactional leader. As a governor, he cared about finding solutions to problems, whether it was the size of the signs on the interstate highways, balancing the state budget or providing health care to Vermonters, and that's what he wanted to do as president.

June 13, 2003

The Kerry campaign had a way of making us feel like the kids in high school who weren't allowed to sit at the lunch table with the football team and cheerleaders. You know, the nerds who were supposed to be grateful when the cheerleader said hello.

I was sitting on a bench outside an art gallery in Milwaukee, Wisconsin, waiting for Howard to make his way out of a reception for local Democrats, when John Kerry came out surrounded by a handful of men in business suits. One of them looked over at me, smiled, waved, and said, "Hi, Kate." It was Jim Margolis, Kerry's media advisor. I knew Margolis because he worked for Howard for a short time in 1992. At that moment I was the kid who wasn't quite good enough and they were the football players and star quarterback allowing me into their world, but only for a split second.

We were in Milwaukee for the Wisconsin Democratic State Convention. John Kerry, Dennis Kucinich, and Howard accepted invitations to speak during the after-dinner program.

After the successes in Seattle and Austin, rallies became a normal part of the schedule. The rally in Milwaukee took place in the parking lot of the high school next door to the Sheraton Hotel, the site of the convention. More than 400 people showed up on the sunny Saturday afternoon. A small riser and a podium were set up in one corner of the parking lot. Howard rolled up his sleeves and launched into his stump speech. He was growing comfortable with the fiery delivery style he exhibited in both Seattle and Austin – and from the response he received he knew the crowd liked it too.

Those who attended the rally weren't fazed by the fact that they were standing in a parking lot. They cheered, clapped, and waved homemade signs that included "I want my country back" and "Green Bay 4 Dean." When his speech was over, Howard turned and pulled the American flag set up behind him out of its stand and, in a move resembling a fan at a European soccer match, waved it high over his head.

By dinnertime, Howard had traded the parking lot for a hotel ballroom, but other than wearing his suit coat, he gave the same speech he had delivered to his supporters a few hours earlier. Most of the convention goers were undecided voters, but their response mirrored that of his supporters. The more than 800 Democrats who packed the ballroom were on their feet as Howard spoke. During one outburst of applause, I spied Jim Margolis standing in the back of the room. If I had been closer I would have waved and said hello.

By the end of the evening we had our first electoral victory of the campaign when Howard won the straw poll of the Democrats who attended the convention. It was early in the process and so few people voted that the poll was considered meaningless. And we probably would have shared that opinion had it not been for the fact that we won. Howard received 126 votes compared to Kerry's 33 and Kucinich's 16.

June 18, 2003

When our plane arrived in Santa Barbara, California, from Des Moines, we traded town hall meetings at union halls for fundraisers at a private club and a celebrity home.

More than 200 people paid $150 to eat hors d'oeuvres at the Rockwood Women's Club. Thirty contributed a minimum of $1,000 to eat a finely-prepared chicken lunch (and take home specially made toffee) at a private home overlooking the Pacific Ocean in Santa Barbara. Another 150 paid $2,000 to eat hors d'oeuvres and sip champagne under a white tent at the Los Angeles home of Rob and Michele Reiner.

Our route from Santa Barbara to the Reiner home brought us down the 405 Freeway. Our volunteer driver maneuvered down the busy stretch of highway while Howard made phone calls in the front seat and I did the same in the back. We all had our eyes on the road when we spotted a blue and yellow bumper sticker affixed to the back of a passing car. It took us a few seconds to realize that it was a bumper sticker with Howard's name on it, the first we had seen on a car not parked at the headquarters in Burlington. Our driver accelerated and pulled even with the car. Howard waved to the occupants in an attempt to get their attention. They may have had a Dean sticker but they didn't notice that the crazy man waving at them was the candidate himself. They pulled ahead without responding.

June 22, 2003

Howard had been a candidate for president for more than a year, but he had yet to make a formal announcement. That would change in one day when he would officially kick off his campaign at an afternoon rally in Burlington, Vermont.

In conjunction with the announcement, he was invited to appear on the NBC Sunday morning show *Meet the Press*. He first appeared on the program in July 2002 and the interview was by all accounts a success. Back then, however, he was more interesting than viable. He wasn't seen as a candidate with a serious chance of winning the nomination and received little scrutiny.

But now the long shot candidate was attracting large crowds and the media had turned their attention to him. And at the end of the hour-long interview the reviews were not kind. The media panned his performance describing it as "faltering," "shifting," and "evasive."

Howard was roundly criticized in articles and columns for not knowing the number of American military personnel stationed around the world and for justifying it by saying that as a candidate in a primary contest he didn't need to know the information. He was also taken to task for not knowing how he felt about a constitutional amendment calling for a balanced budget or whether he supported a prescription drug plan backed by the Bush administration.

The media were critical, but Howard's supporters saw nothing wrong with his performance. They defended him on the campaign's blog and congratulated him for doing a great job under the circumstances. Circumstances they viewed as being brought about by the show's moderator, Tim Russert. They accused Russert of making it "his mission to bring down a presidential campaign in an hour-long interview." They called the interview "hostile" and described Russert as "aggressive" and trying "hard for a 'gotcha' moment." And they demonstrated their unwavering support of Howard by making $93,000 worth of Internet donations the day the show aired.

When the Sunday morning show was over, Howard and I, along with Steve McMahon, left Washington and flew to Chicago where Howard was going to take part in a forum sponsored by the Rainbow/PUSH Coalition, the organization founded by the Rev. Jesse Jackson.

The announcement rally was just a day away. There would be supporters and signs, but the most important part for Howard was the speech he would deliver. It was sure to receive more media attention than any speech he had given before. In fact, some cable news outlets planned to cover it live. It would set the tone for the campaign and he wanted it to be perfect.

He had several free hours before the forum and used the time to review the speech before sending the final version to Burlington. He wanted it to reflect his thoughts and voice and made numerous edits including moving paragraphs and completely removing others from the text. (Gone, for example, was: "Our founders declared that America was to be built on a foundation of Democratic Capitalism where the undeniable power of capitalism would be subservient to democracy and not the master.")

During the forum, I sat in the back of the hotel ballroom and e-mailed the changes to Burlington. Soon after, Steve came in and told me we had a problem. Joe and the campaign's communications director Tricia Enright had given some of the speech to Associated Press reporter Ron Fournier, including the sections Howard had taken out during his most recent edits. They didn't tell Howard that they planned to give the speech to Fournier and now they found themselves in a bind. Fournier had a copy of a speech that Howard was not going to give. Because they didn't want to ask Fournier for the speech back, their solution was to have Howard give it as originally drafted. They needed him to put the deleted sections back in. After the forum, Steve and I talked to Howard. When he learned that Fournier had the speech he was not happy with Joe and Tricia. His response to the news: "They are supposed to cover my butt. I'm not supposed to cover theirs."

When we boarded our charter flight to Burlington at 9:00 p.m., Howard had yet to speak to either Joe or Tricia. It had been more than four hours since he learned about the problem with the speech and he still hadn't decided what he was going to do. When our plane took off they were left with the possibility that they wouldn't find out what he was going to say until he stood on the stage the next day.

During the flight home Howard looked at the speech again. While the other four passengers – including Steve – slept, I opened my lap-top computer and typed the changes as he made them. He didn't want to put the portions he deleted back in. He had taken them out for a reason and he was still upset that the speech had been released without his approval. But in the end he reluctantly restored some – but not all – of the text he removed. He worried that the deletions would not go unnoticed by Fournier, which might lead to questions that could distract from the rest of the speech. (Back in: "The history of our nation is clear: at every turn when there has been an imbalance of power, the truth questioned or our beliefs and values distorted, the change required to restore our nation has always come from the bottom up – from our people.")

We landed in Burlington at midnight and by 12:30 a.m. I had e-mailed Howard's latest version to Joe and Tricia.

June 23, 2003

Burlington, Vermont, is Howard's hometown. He raised his family there, he did his medical internship at the city's hospital and it was where he began his political career by representing a section of the city in the state Legislature. And there was never a doubt that it would be where he would make his campaign for the presidency official.

The last time Church Street, Burlington's pedestrian market place, was shut down for a political event was in 1995 when President Bill Clinton took a stroll down the street. Then, Vermonters, standing behind barricades set up by the Secret Service, lined the street hoping for a glimpse of the sitting president. Now, more than 5,000 people from all around the country swarmed the street waiting anxiously to hear their candidate for president of the United States make his campaign official.

New supporters joined with Howard's earliest to celebrate the announcement. My parents, who helped Howard in 1986 when he first ran for lieutenant governor and who gave us the money to buy our first roll of stamps for Fund for a Healthy America in 2001, stood alongside new supporters from places like Washington, D.C., Michigan, and New Hampshire.

For the new supporters, the Howard Dean who energized and inspired them with his fiery speeches was the only Howard they knew. But for Vermonters like my family, it was a side of him they had never seen before. They knew him as the man who hated to give speeches, who wore his cheapness on his sleeve, literally when he wore his JC Penney suit, and who was known for blurting out whatever he was thinking, no matter the consequences. Now they stood alongside thousands of people who saw Howard as the hope for the future of the country.

Standing under the clear blue sky as a slight breeze blew over the market place, the crowd began celebrating long before Howard took the stage. They listened to the music that blared from speakers and enjoyed a special treat made just for the day by Vermont's famous ice cream makers Ben & Jerry. The "Maple Powered Howard" ice cream sundae was made out of vanilla ice cream, maple-flavored whipped cream, maple syrup, and walnuts. They cheered as Vermont senators Jim Jeffords and Patrick Leahy talked about why they supported Howard. Things had come a long way since the two men listened politely as he first told them of his plans to run for president a year and a half earlier.

The announcement was short on glitz. A stage was set up in the middle of the street, but there was no manufactured backdrop, no blue curtain, no signs advertising the campaign's website or 1-800 number, and no risers holding cheering supporters. Instead all that could be seen was the simple brick church that anchored one end of the street.

□ □ □

Howard took the stage to the thunderous applause of his supporters. The woman in the red suit standing next to him was unknown to most in the crowd. She was his wife, Judy, and when she joined him on the stage it marked her first appearance at a campaign event – ever.

Vermont doesn't have a governor's mansion and when Howard held the state's top job there was no expectation that a spouse would give up his or her life to serve the state in any capacity. Judy was a practicing physician and hadn't traded the title of doctor for first lady. She made one public appearance each year. In even numbered years she'd attend the election night celebration and during odd numbered years she'd hold the Bible at Howard's inauguration. Now she found herself standing on a stage watching more than 5,000 people cheer her husband on as he announced that he was running for the nation's highest office – a position that would make her the country's first lady.

Howard stood behind the podium and read from the text I had e-mailed to the office just hours earlier. He looked relaxed and casual in his red tie and pale blue shirt with its sleeves rolled up. The crowd cheered and he grinned in response when he stated what his supporters were eager to hear, "Today I announce that I am running for president of the United States of America."

The thousands who packed the street hung on his every word. The supporters who pressed up to the bicycle racks that held them back in the front row stared up at him, appearing mesmerized by his presence. Those who couldn't find a space on the street leaned out of open windows three stories up. For his part Howard looked out at the sea of blue campaign signs and smiled in delight.

While he talked about health care and a balanced budget, the speech was more about inspiration as he told the crowd, "This is a campaign to unite and empower people everywhere. It is a call to every American, regardless of party, to join together in common purpose and for the common good to save and restore all that it means to be an American."

The thirty-minute speech was interrupted by applause, cheers, and chants of "We want Dean!" from the crowd who, along with campaign signs, waved small American flags high in the air.

He ended his speech with a call to action. With fire in his eyes he pointed to the screaming crowd and told them, "You have the power to take this country back! You have the power! You have the power! We're going to take our country back! You have the power!"

<u>June 24, 2003</u>

When Howard announced his candidacy he was standing in front of 5,000 people, but he was not leading in the polls. (He was slightly behind Kerry in New Hampshire, and trailed Gephardt in Iowa and Lieberman nationally.) He still had a long way to go with the general public, but he had caught the attention of late night talk show host David Letterman. The media – and even the other campaigns – marveled at Howard's ability to attract large crowds and were amazed by the fierce loyalty he inspired in his supporters – who had appropriately been dubbed "Deaniacs."

Letterman took the opportunity to poke fun at Howard and his followers during his popular "Top Ten" segment when he listed the "Top Ten Signs You're in Love with Democratic Presidential Candidate Howard Dean." The list:

10. You've actually heard of him

9. Whenever he discusses plans to revitalize the economy, you get goose bumps

8. Named your cats "Howard," "Dean" and "Six-Term Governor Howard Dean"

7. You'll only watch movies featuring Ron Howard or Harry Dean Stanton

6. When you hear a report on the radio about a highway accident, you murmur, "Please, god, don't let Howard Dean be involved"

5. Constantly complain rival candidate Dennis Kucinich isn't "Howardly" enough

4. Changed outfit four times before watching appearance on *Meet the Press*

3. You stand by him despite the fact his infidelities embarrassed you in front of the entire . . . oh wait, wrong Democrat

2. When he announced his candidacy, you didn't laugh your ass off

And the number one reason:

You're actually considering wasting a vote on him

June 27, 2003

"I had a 21-hour day and I'm not rushing," Howard told the young man who was tasked with shuttling us to the breakfast fundraiser. We were in La Jolla, California, sitting at the kitchen table enjoying the continental breakfast of toast, muffins, and fruit that had been prepared by our overnight hostess.

Twenty-one hours wasn't an exaggeration. The day before began at 6:30 a.m. in Washington, D.C. After boarding a plane we made stops in Denver, Los Angeles, and Riverside, California — each time for a fundraiser (when the day was over we had netted close to $75,000). By the time we arrived at our overnight location in La Jolla it was after midnight on the West Coast, 3 a.m. on the East.

Howard's pronouncement came after the volunteer driver insisted that we leave 15 minutes earlier than scheduled. The schedule was a sore point for Howard, who complained to no avail to the staff in Burlington that the days were too long. By standing firm on the departure time he was exerting the only control he appeared to have over how he spent his time. After exactly 15 minutes we bid our hostess good-bye and headed out for a relatively short 15-hour day that included fundraisers and rallies in San Diego, Beverly Hills, and Los Angeles.

The news of the day was Howard's first place finish in an online poll conducted by the web-based advocacy group MoveOn.org. More than 317,000 of the organization's 1.4 million members voted in the online poll that the organization dubbed a primary. Howard received 44 percent or 139,360 votes. (His pitch to the MoveOn members: "If you are as tired and angered as I am by the manipulation and lies [of the Bush administration] then please join my campaign.") Dennis Kucinich came in second with 24 percent, followed by Kerry with 16 percent.

"We're ecstatic about the 44 percent," Joe told the media in response to the results. He went on to call the vote, "An historic event in American politics. It's a primary where hundreds of thousands of people got together early on and said this is who we support right now. Hundreds of thousands of Americans participated in their democracy today."

June 28, 2003

We left Los Angeles in the morning and after a stop for a fundraiser in Phoenix, Arizona, our plane landed in Santa Fe, New Mexico. It was our first visit to the city and we were there for a rally.

A local volunteer picked us up at the airport and drove us downtown. He parked his car on a street lined with an array of small shops. It was a beautiful Saturday evening and hundreds of people were milling around in a small park across the street. Howard looked on wondering if he should walk over and shake some hands at what appeared to be a fair, but we were late for the rally, so any extracurricular campaigning would have to wait. "Where's the rally?" we asked our driver. He pointed across the street to the park. The crowd that we had envied – more than 2,500 people – was there to see Howard.

We hadn't quite grasped Howard's popularity and it was hard to explain the level of enthusiasm with which people greeted him to anyone who hadn't experienced it firsthand. When the speech was over we walked down the stairs set up on the side of the stage. The crowd surged forward hoping to shake Howard's hand, forcing the volunteer organizers to form a human barrier to keep them back. They were able to hold on long enough for Howard and me to run to the car that was waiting for us behind the stage. The doors were barely closed when the supporters broke free and began tapping on the windows. Our driver accelerated just in time to get the car out before we were surrounded.

From Santa Fe we flew to Las Vegas where we were going to take the red eye to Boston. Our flight left at midnight and we spent the hour and a half before the flight sitting in the terminal. The Las Vegas airport was like no other. The gift shops were stocked with giant fuzzy dice and slot machines were interspersed among the seats at the gates.

We arrived at our gate carrying our suitcases and two large trash bags. During the stop in Santa Fe we were given gifts – three framed photographs, two large bags of campaign buttons made by a local supporter, and two jars of jam – none of which fit into our suitcases. We borrowed the trash bags from the airport and loaded our presents into them.

As we waited for our flight, Howard put quarters into the slot machines hoping not for a big payday, but for one of the quarters minted in the state series by the U.S. Treasury. Two quarters were minted for each state, one in Denver and the other in Philadelphia. Howard collected the quarters and used the opportunity on the West Coast to find one of the Denver-minted coins.

Meanwhile, I logged on to the campaign's website to update our supporters on our travels. There I found a baseball bat that was being used like a thermometer to track contributions. It was less than two days before the end of the three-month fundraising quarter that began in April and the campaign was encouraging people to give or in baseball terms to "hit one for Howard." As the contributions came in the bat was filled in as a way of tracking the fundraising progress. The goal at the top of the bat read $6.5 million – an amount that seemed unimaginable given we had raised just $2.6 million during the first quarter.

June 30, 2003

Howard's fashion sense, or lack of it, had become an issue. Calls for a makeover dated back to his first visit to New Hampshire in early 2002. But his solution then – letting his belt out one notch – was no longer acceptable. His supporters who didn't share his appreciation for his JC Penney suit were clamoring to take him shopping.

But he was not willing to shop with a group of people who had expensive tastes, so in order to avoid the entourage of well-meaning fashionistas we arranged for a secret shopping trip during a visit to New York. Steve McMahon and I were tasked with making sure he shopped 'til he dropped, or at the very least until he found one new suit.

The three of us set out on foot. Our first stop was the men's store Kenneth Cole, named after the designer. The price tag that came with the label was enough to send Howard into shock and we left the store not long after we arrived without making a purchase.

Next was the men's department at Saks Fifth Avenue. The suits were less expensive and there were more of them to choose from, but Howard rejected every suit Steve and I and the salesman pulled off the racks. Although the men's department was a bust, we found success in the cosmetics department. As we were walking through the main floor, I noticed the women behind the cosmetics counter whispering to each other and pointing in our direction. I turned to see if Brad Pitt was behind us, but there was no one there; they were pointing at Howard. When he walked over to say hello they greeted him with "President Dean! President Dean!" Bolstered by the women's enthusiasm we headed to one last store: Paul Stuart. Howard happened to be wearing a Paul Stuart suit, one he liked almost as much as the suit he bought at JC Penney. The store offered us our best – and last – chance to declare mission accomplished.

□ □ □

As we walked the busy city streets in pursuit of the perfect suit we were unaware that the campaign's website had become the talk of political circles. It was the last day to raise money in the fundraising quarter and the campaign was making a final appeal to supporters, urging them to give as much as they could. In order to generate excitement, the contribution-tracking baseball bat on the blog was updated every half hour, and as the contribution total rose, so too did the excitement level. The bat was averaging $25,000 every thirty minutes and was climbing at such a fast pace that people couldn't help but give more in order to watch the total rise.

For Howard, Steve, and I the day's success came in the form of not one, but two, new suits. We were still in the dark about the online fundraising frenzy when we walked triumphantly out of the Paul Stuart store with a charcoal gray suit, along with a similar one in navy blue.

Two meetings and two fundraisers later we arrived at the Roxy nightclub in New York City where 1,000 people were waiting inside. It was close to 8:30 p.m. and, unbeknownst to us, two hours earlier the campaign had broken its online fundraising record for a single day – which stood at $514,000 – by raising just over $519,000.

What we also didn't know, until informed by a member of the media as we were entering the back door of the club, was that the campaign had raised more than $7 million for the quarter. The amount came as a surprise. The last time we'd had an update was in the Las Vegas airport two days earlier when the push was on to raise $6.5 million (an amount Howard wasn't sure we could reach).

Shortly after 9:30 p.m. we got in the car and headed to Vermont. It was a six-hour drive made longer by rain and road construction.

Just after midnight the staff in Burlington called with the final fundraising numbers and it proved to be Howard's best quarter yet. During the three months, he raised close to $7.5 million, three times the $2.6 million he collected in the previous quarter. And the money raised on-line proved to be impressive. More than $800,000 came in over the Internet during the day, which brought the web total for the quarter to $3 million.

The candidate, whose bank account had once been described as paltry by the media, had raised more money than all of his opponents. His final total trumped Kerry's $5.9 million, Lieberman's $5.1 million, Edwards' $4.5 million, and Gephardt's $3.8 million.

Around 2 a.m. we stopped at a Mobil gas station and mini mart not far from the New York-Vermont border. Howard and I and the staff member from Vermont who was driving us were the only customers in the store. We used the bathroom, I bought a granola bar from the young clerk behind the counter, who gave no indication that he recognized Howard, and then we hopped back into the car and continued the journey home.

—JULY—

July 2, 2003

"We could win Iowa." Howard said the words with caution as if saying them out loud would change the outcome. We were flying from Burlington, Vermont, to Dubuque, Iowa, when he expressed optimism in his chances.

He had never said the words before, not because he didn't believe them, but because he was careful. It was better to be safe and work hard than to assume a win was inevitable. It was the way he approached a 30-point lead over his nearest opponent when he ran for governor, and it was the way he would run for president. The record crowds and successful fundraising, however, were exciting and for one moment he soaked in his success. The words passed quickly and just as suddenly he was back sifting through his bag of paperwork.

July 4, 2003

For Howard, the celebration of our nation's birthday started off with breakfast at a restaurant in Amherst, New Hampshire. He sat at the counter with some of his supporters and filled up on pancakes. He was appropriately attired in blue, but not by design. The light blue dress shirt and dark blue pants just happened to be what he was wearing the day before.

The first parade was in Amherst and the sun was shining when we arrived at the local school to find our place in line. Whether they used poll numbers to decide I'm not sure, but we were positioned between John Kerry and Joe Lieberman.

It was a beautiful day and there was a sense of camaraderie among the people who would take part in the parade. Howard chatted with kids dressed in oversized top hats to look like Uncle Sam, talked small cars with a group of Shriners, and played the kazoo with a kazoo band. He did, however, decline an offer to take a spin on a Segway. With all the cameras around he didn't want to risk losing his balance on the two-wheeled motorized contraption. John Kerry walked around as well, consciously steering clear of Howard. When it came time to line up, the two men found themselves standing just a few feet apart. They shook hands and smiled for the cameras and the on-lookers who had been waiting for the unavoidable encounter.

The Dean entry featured a makeshift float. The mid-sized flat bed truck was decorated on all sides with "Dean for America" signs. Two large American flags and a white and blue balloon arch rounded out the decorations. Dozens of supporters dressed in shorts and white campaign T-shirts walked with Howard down the parade route. They carried signs and, like fans at a football game, followed the cheers called out by the staff person with the bullhorn.

"I say Howard, you say Dean."

"Howard!"

"Dean!"

"Howard!"

"Dean!"

Before the parade began, campaign volunteers had walked down the route passing out lapel stickers to anyone willing to wear one. Kids who were too young to vote and had no idea who the candidates were, but liked stickers, advertised multiple candidates on their chests. Howard walked down the side of the road shaking hands with the crowd. Although he didn't discriminate, he did make an effort to reach out to those wearing one of his stickers. When he began to fall behind he was admonished by the parade organizers for holding up the parade, which resulted in him having to run to keep up.

By the time the parade was over his blue shirt was wet. But there was no time to stop. We hopped in a minivan and drove to Merrimack for our second parade. We arrived just as the parade was about to begin. Before starting his second run of the day, Howard bought a cup of lemonade from a group of siblings who had set up a stand in front of their house. The media cameras were there to capture the event. They documented the money changing hands and Howard's reaction to his first sip of the cold beverage. Despite all of the attention, he didn't make the purchase for public relations reasons. He did so because he was, of all things, thirsty.

The second parade was a repeat of the first. Float, balloons, supporters, cheers, and signs. This time, however, we were in front of John Kerry, a position we liked better. And Howard had learned a lesson in Amherst and started off in a trot so as not to hold up the parade.

July 8, 2003

The meeting at the Burlington hotel was the first and would turn out to be the only gathering of all the senior staff and consultants.

In light of Howard's growing popularity and unexpected fundraising success, it was time for the campaign to regroup.

Jeani Murray flew in from Iowa. New Hampshire state director Karen Hicks came across the border. Steve McMahon and Mark Squier were also there. Representatives from the finance, field, research, scheduling, political, and press offices sat around the table. Missing was Joe Trippi, who spent the better part of the day with *Washington Post* reporter Dan Balz and *Newsweek* columnist Howard Fineman, who were in Burlington.

Although we met for hours we accomplished very little. Most of the discussion revolved around two points of contention within the campaign: Howard's schedule and campaign leadership.

Howard was exhausted and for months he had been requesting that we slow down his schedule. He was on the road six days a week, working on average 18 hours a day. The finance, field, press, and political departments were all competing for his time. There was a scheduling team but no leader, so all the players were left to fight things out among themselves. This led to impasses that either resulted in a delay in putting the schedule together or ended with everyone getting the meetings they requested, which led to even longer days for Howard.

The problem with the schedule was a direct result of the second issue we discussed – campaign leadership. There was a growing feeling among the staff that some of the problems we were having could be avoided if Joe, as the campaign manager, helped to solve them. However, he showed little interest in doing so and his decision to spend time with the press, instead of the staff, didn't help matters.

While we were meeting at the hotel, Howard was at the campaign office meeting with Howard Fineman, who was interviewing him for a piece he was writing for *Newsweek*.

During our meeting, we learned from a member of the campaign staff who sat in on the interview that Howard cried during the questioning. It happened when Fineman asked him about his brother, Charlie. Charlie Dean went missing in Laos 30 years earlier and the Dean family had been searching for an answer to what happened to him ever since. Howard was very private and rarely talked publicly about his brother, but when he did he was controlled. So I was surprised by his uncharacteristic show of emotion.

Joe had joined us at the hotel when the call came in and his response to the news confused me. I couldn't see how Howard's crying could be good for the campaign, but when Joe and Steve heard about his reaction, they smiled at each other and went out to the lobby. I suspected that they had something to do with Fineman asking Howard about his brother. I followed them and asked Joe why he would prompt Fineman to ask about something so personal to Howard and his family without asking or preparing Howard in advance. Joe took offense to my accusation and denied having anything to do with it.

Not long after, Howard arrived at the staff meeting. He recounted the interview to the dozen of us seated around the table. He also talked about Charlie's disappearance. It was the first time most of the staff had heard the story. It was also the first time Howard revealed that he had sought counseling after Charlie went missing. Later that day, Fineman called with one last question for Howard: Had he ever sought professional counseling after Charlie's disappearance?

July 12, 2003

Howard and I were at the Arizona Democratic Party dinner in Phoenix when I called Joe in Vermont. It was our third visit to an Arizona city that the day. The first stop was at a picnic at a state park in Flagstaff, hosted by a local Democratic Party county committee. Howard, dressed in his dress shirt, tie, and suit pants, spoke to the T-shirt and shorts clad crowd made up of more than 300 Democrats who had come out to enjoy the sunny Saturday afternoon.

From Flagstaff we hopped a plane to Tucson where local supporters had organized a rally. Two thousand people stood shoulder to shoulder in a ballroom at the Marriott Hotel at the University of Arizona. The number of people who showed up exceeded expectations and the hotel was forced to deny access to the room to many because of fire code restrictions.

Now we were sitting in a banquet hall in Phoenix, watching the state Democrats honor their own at their annual volunteer recognition dinner. But instead of listening to the acceptance speeches, I sneaked out of the room and called Joe.

It was the night before Howard Fineman's piece was scheduled to appear on *Newsweek* magazine's website. And in light of the fact that Howard had cried during the interview and acknowledged that he had sought counseling after the disappearance of his brother, the piece would unquestionably be more personal than policy-related.

Articles about Howard were routinely put on the campaign's website often along with editorial comments by the staff. Because of the potential personal nature of the piece, I wanted to make sure that Howard would have the chance to read the story before it was put on the website. I thought it was important that if any editorializing was done, it was in line with Howard's opinion of the piece. Joe agreed.

July 13, 2003

"His features collapse, his eyes and his face turn red. He raises a hand to his brow as tears stream down his cheeks and he sobs quietly."

It was 4:30 a.m. in Arizona when I received a call from Vermont telling me the *Newsweek* piece was online. They were ready to post it on the campaign blog but wanted to make sure that Howard had seen it first. He wasn't awake so I told them they would have to wait.

Several hours later I showed Howard the story. He read it, but never said a word. It was an hour later when we were standing in the security line at the airport when he commented on the piece for the first time. He didn't like it. He had been thinking about Fineman's questions and was beginning to believe that Fineman knew exactly what he was doing. The questions he asked were intended to elicit an emotional reaction. Howard felt like he had been set up.

It wasn't until we arrived in Houston, Texas, at noon that I had my first chance to call Vermont. They were eager to put the article on the website and correct what Joe believed was an inaccurate description of Howard. The last line in the piece read, "Not knowing everything [about what happened to his brother] is a form of powerlessness Howard Dean cannot stand."

Equating Howard Dean, the candidate who ended his speeches by telling his supporters, "You've got the power" with powerlessness did not sit well with Joe and he wanted to put a statement on the website clarifying that Howard was not powerless. I saw no reason for a statement. There was no connection between the campaign and the disappearance of Howard's brother, and in light of Howard's negative reaction to the story I suggested that we stay away from any editorializing and simply put a link to the story on our website.

Joe felt strongly that a statement was necessary. When I continued to argue against it he became frustrated and the next thing I heard was a crash, followed by silence. He had thrown the telephone – and me with it – across the room. I called back and said that I'd have Howard call Joe so the two could work it out directly. Howard called, but Joe never mentioned the statement. In the end, only a link to the story was posted on the campaign blog.

□ □ □

The going rate at the two Houston fundraisers was $150 or $1,000 depending on how much time one wanted to spend with Howard. After mingling with both groups of donors we boarded a plane and headed for Love Field in Dallas.

When we touched down we repeated the two tier fundraisers, but this time we didn't leave the city before attending a rally. More than 1,000 people gathered in the plaza in front of Dallas City Hall for the free event. Howard stood on a stage decorated with a large American flag and columns of red, white, and blue balloons. As he spoke, a Texas flag waved high in the cloudy sky from a pole next to City Hall. Standing in front of the large crowd he couldn't hide his satisfaction. He had visited two cities in the president's home state – and the day wasn't over. After the rally we boarded a plane and headed for Austin.

July 18, 2003

I hopped out of my bunk bed and went downstairs to the kitchen. Howard was already sitting at the table big enough to seat the two adults and seven kids who made the house their home.

The McGuire family first welcomed us into their Des Moines home in October 2002 when Howard was a little-known candidate. We stayed with them whenever we were in Des Moines and they had watched the campaign grow. But this morning they were unusually excited. The man sitting in their kitchen eating cereal alongside three young children was now, as they put it, a "rock star." It wasn't the money or the crowds that earned him that status. It was his mention in the comic strip *Doonesbury*. The popular politically-themed cartoon was running a series of strips that followed the exploits of the fictional Alex Doonesbury and her friends as they worked in support of Howard's candidacy.

□ □ □

It was close to 1 a.m. and Howard was standing in front of the terminal at New York's LaGuardia airport offering rides into the city to the passengers who walked by. His goal was to find ten people willing to share the Super Shuttle van.

Our flight from Des Moines through Chicago arrived almost two hours late and, judging by the number of people waiting for a taxi, we weren't alone in experiencing a delay. Howard didn't want to wait for a cab, so when he spotted the blue Super Shuttle van he asked the driver if he would give us a ride into the city. The driver was off duty, but agreed to help us under one condition: Howard needed to find enough riders to fill the twelve-passenger van. So the candidate for president stood in front of the terminal. If anyone recognized him, they didn't admit it. And luckily, it didn't take him long to round up ten people.

In a matter of hours Howard would be meeting CBS News anchor Dan Rather for breakfast. Because of the early morning start, he was anxious to get to his mother's Park Avenue apartment and offered the driver directions that would allow him to be dropped off first. When he began reciting the directions for a second time the driver turned on the CD player and a song by the singer Madonna blasted through the van. I burst out laughing and couldn't stop. Howard didn't see the humor in the situation, but when I explained that I couldn't imagine John Kerry surviving the adventure he smiled and laughed.

Howard was the eleventh person dropped off. I was the twelfth and final passenger to exit the van, arriving at my hotel shortly before 2:30 a.m.

July 19, 2003

After breakfast with Dan Rather, we hopped into a car sent by *Time* magazine to ferry us to a photo shoot. The magazine had chosen Howard to grace its cover.

Technically, *Time* wouldn't be the first publication to feature Howard on its cover. That distinction went to *The New Republic,* with a piece a year earlier. That cover, however, featured a man with a blank face, symbolizing an unknown Howard Dean. This time Howard would be front and center.

The photo shoot had the air of a covert spy operation. When we expressed our disbelief that Howard was going to grace the cover of a national magazine, our driver reprimanded us for talking about it. He instructed us not to speak to anyone about what we were doing at the warehouse, including the photographer and his staff. His orders seemed odd because it was clear that everyone at the photo shoot knew exactly where their photograph was going to end up. But we did what we were told and never mentioned "the cover" again.

The photographer greeted us when we entered the warehouse. His first words to Howard were, "Is that the tie you're going to wear?" He was sporting a maroon tie dotted with small mallard ducks. Taking the hint, Howard went out to the car and retrieved his suitcase. He put it up on the table next to the muffins, fruit, and juice and rummaged through it as the photographer (whose face screamed, "This guy wants to be president?") looked on. He halfheartedly approved the best tie Howard pulled out of the suitcase: a red silk number adorned with small dark diamond shapes.

Soon, what was supposed to be a one-hour shoot had turned into three. Howard posed in front of a white backdrop that covered both the wall and the floor. Under the photographer's direction he stood and he sat. He wore his coat and his tie. He wore no coat. He wore no tie. He smiled and he was serious. And at the end he posed for a picture with the entire crew.

July 22, 2003

"It's a victory for the Iraqi people . . . but it doesn't have any effect on whether we should or shouldn't have had a war," Howard told a group of reporters after a tour of a hospital in Manchester, New Hampshire. His remarks were in response to the death of two of Saddam Hussein's sons who were killed by U.S. forces during a raid on a villa in Iraq.

Despite the action that some claimed was a victory for the president's war on terror, Howard remained firm in his opposition to the military action in Iraq. He continued to criticize his opponents who voted in favor of the war, and he also began to call into question what he saw as their attempts to have it both ways – voting to go to war, but criticizing it at the same time.

John Kerry had become increasingly critical of President Bush's handling of the situation since Saddam had been removed from power. He had asserted just days earlier that he had "urged the president to seek international support before going to war." Howard saw Kerry's comments as a way to connect to the voters in Iowa and New Hampshire where anti-war sentiment was strong.

July 24, 2003

Iowa has 99 counties and we were almost halfway to reaching our goal of visiting each one. It was a quest that we began a year and a half earlier when we made our first visit to the state.

For the summer, we embarked on the "Get on Board with Dean" tour. It was a driving tour that would take us to all four corners of the state. To mark the start of the tour we traded in our minivan for a Winnebago Sports Van. It carried the Winnebago name, but it wasn't what most people associate with the brand-name camper. There was no kitchen, bathroom, bed or bug screen. Instead the ten-passenger vehicle featured wood paneling and two green upholstered swivel chairs. Its back door locked from the outside putting passengers at the mercy of the person with the key. And when traveling at speeds over 40 mph it shook, which necessitated us tying ourselves down along with anything we had with us.

The Iowa license plate read "McFun" and people thought it was cute that we were publicly exclaiming the good times we were having on the campaign trail. They were only slightly disappointed when we explained that the name had nothing to do with our travels, but instead came from the McGuires, the Des Moines family that loaned us the vehicle.

□ □ □

A handful of people were outside the Copper Lantern Restaurant in the city of Sigourney when we pulled up. It was our first visit to Keokuk County. The county, known for having one of the largest pheasant populations in the country, was the 48th we would visit.

While Howard was drawing crowds of supporters that numbered into the thousands in large cities across the country, the focus was different in Iowa. He was reaching out to undecided voters and he had to earn their support – one voter at a time.

Just over thirty Democrats were waiting inside the restaurant. Although Sigourney was deemed a city, its population was barely more than 2,200. Nevertheless, the people who gathered at the Cooper Lantern weren't impressed by fundraising totals or crowds that rivaled their own city's population. They were focused on the issues that were important to them: health care, jobs, and putting their kids through college. There was no fiery rhetoric from Howard and no standing ovation from the crowd. Instead his call for "questions, comments, and rude remarks" was answered by the hands that popped up in front of him.

July 25, 2003

At 7:30 a.m. Howard donned his borrowed blue helmet, jumped on his matching borrowed blue bicycle, and began an 11.2-mile ride from Bloomfield, Iowa, to Troy, Iowa. He was taking part in RAGBRAI, the *Des Moines Register*'s Annual Great Bike Ride Across Iowa. The seven-day, 450-mile trek attracted 10,000 riders and was known for being the longest, largest, and oldest bicycle-touring event in the world.

In his aqua cotton shorts, gray socks, and oversized T-shirt Howard was in no danger of being mistaken for Lance Armstrong. The tour attracted men and women of all ages and skill levels and despite his obvious status as a recreational cyclist, he was welcomed by his spandex-wearing counterparts.

As Howard peddled alongside the small group of supporters who joined him in making the journey, Jeani Murray and I followed behind in our newly acquired Winnebago.

Two hours later, Howard was showered, dressed, and standing in the Skean Block Restaurant in Albia, Iowa, taking questions from those who had gathered at the first "Get on Board with Dean" event of the day.

□ □ □

At 11:15 p.m. the baseball bat appeared on the campaign's website for the first time since its introduction at the end of June. The Friday evening announcement that the off-beat contribution tracker was back came in response to a fundraiser that Vice President Dick Cheney was scheduled to attend in South Carolina three days later. The $2,000 a plate luncheon was expected to raise $250,000 for the Bush/Cheney ticket.

In response, the campaign challenged Howard's supporters to match the amount the vice president would raise. But instead of handing over big checks and sitting in a fancy restaurant, the plan was to raise the money through small contributions over the

Internet. The baseball bat set the goal: $250,000 by midnight on Monday – three days away.

July 26, 2003

Howard issued an ultimatum: Slow the schedule down or you won't have a candidate.

We knew it wasn't going to be a good day when the clerk at the United Airlines ticket counter in Des Moines informed us that we did not have seats on the 8:50 a.m. flight to Chicago. Although the flight times and numbers were typed on our daily schedule, the campaign had forgotten to purchase the tickets. We had to be in Provincetown, Massachusetts, by 4 p.m. and to make it there on time we had to make our connections in Chicago and Boston, but the United Airlines flight was full. We ended up walking from airline counter to airline counter looking for any flight that could get us to Boston in time to catch the plane to Provincetown. American Airlines had a flight to St. Louis and a connecting flight to Boston. It would be tight, but we had no other option.

When we arrived in Boston six hours later Howard was exhausted. It had been a long day and we still weren't at our final destination. We were making the seven-hour trip to Provincetown to attend a fundraising dinner and reception.

The long hours were typical. We were working up to 18 hours a day, six days a week and traveling to multiple cities and states each day. And it finally caught up with Howard.

We were standing in our third ticket line of the day when he decided to issue the order. I was on a conference call with Joe, Steve McMahon, Paul Maslin, Mark Squier, and Bob Rogan discussing an upcoming television commercial, when I handed the phone to Howard.

He told them that he was exhausted and desperately in need of rest. If they didn't fix the schedule their services would no longer be needed because without a candidate there would be no campaign. To make his point clear he canceled the filming of a television commercial that was scheduled to take place in Burlington the next day.

July 28, 2003

While Dick Cheney was in South Carolina dining with his wealthy contributors, Howard was sitting at a desk in his Burlington, Vermont, headquarters taking the plastic wrap off a turkey sandwich.

A picture of Howard eating the $3 sandwich was posted on the campaign's website. Although it was safe to assume that the vice president wasn't sharing a sandwich with his supporters, the photo wasn't simply meant to call attention to the two men's culinary preferences. Instead, it served to encourage people to give money towards the Cheney luncheon challenge. There were just 12 hours left to reach the campaign's goal of matching the $250,000 Cheney was expected to raise.

By midnight the contribution tracking bat was broken. For little more than the cost of a turkey sandwich, the campaign doubled the amount of money raised by Dick Cheney. The web challenge brought in more than $500,000 from close to 9,500 contributors.

July 30, 2003

Howard believed that "social justice can only be accomplished through strong fiscal management." In practice, he supported eliminating all of President Bush's tax cuts and putting the money towards balancing the federal budget and providing health care to all Americans.

Some in the campaign believed that Howard needed to soften his position. They wanted him to support keeping in place the tax cuts that benefited middle class Americans.

Howard was scheduled to give a speech on jobs and the economy in front of members of the Plumbers and Steamfitters Union in Des Moines, Iowa. A few hours before the speech, John Kerry released a speech of his own in which he chastised Howard for wanting to roll back the tax cuts and in the process increase taxes for the middle class.

As we were pulling up in front of the union hall Steve McMahon called. We all knew the press would ask Howard for his reaction to Kerry's comments and Steve wanted him to leave the door open to keeping the middle class tax cuts.

This had been an issue for weeks, and each time it came up Howard made it clear that he wasn't going to change his position until he was given numbers that proved that it was possible to keep the cuts and still balance the budget and provide health care for all Americans. Once again he asked for the numbers, and once again no one had them.

As expected, the media asked him to respond to Kerry. Much to the chagrin of some on the staff, he didn't temper his remarks, telling reporters, "Real Democrats don't make promises they can't keep. Working Americans have a choice: They can have the president's tax cuts or they can have health care that can't be taken away. They can't have both."

July 31, 2003

Surprise! You're going to appear on the cover of *Newsweek* magazine. I first learned of the impending cover story on Howard when I received an e-mail from the campaign scheduler telling me that a session with a *Newsweek* photographer had been scheduled for the next day.

I had heard nothing about a *Newsweek* story and assumed there had been a misunderstanding. Howard was going to appear on *Time* magazine's cover and I thought that the scheduler had mixed up the names. I called Steve McMahon to find out, but there had been no mistake. Howard was indeed going to be featured on the cover of *Newsweek* – the same week he was going to appear on *Time's* cover. The reason no one discussed the *Newsweek* piece with him? They wanted it to be a surprise.

As far back as 2002 when he appeared on the cover of *The New Republic*, Howard worried about peaking too soon and the *Time* piece alone had reignited that concern. Now, like it or not, he was going to grace the cover of *Newsweek*, as well as *Time*.

—AUGUST—

August 1, 2003

The photo shoot for the *Newsweek* magazine cover took place at a private hangar at Washington, D.C.'s Dulles airport. The site was chosen not because of its unique scenery. Instead, it was the result of the magazine's deadline. The photograph was needed immediately and the only free time Howard had was the 30 minutes before we had to board a private plane to Bangor, Maine.

Because the shoot was planned at the last minute it had none of the flair of the *Time* shoot. A makeshift black curtain backdrop was set up just outside the hangar. The photographer took no interest in what Howard was wearing and there was no chair, leaving him no choice but to stand.

The photographer was a character and his presence made for a comical photo session. He was dressed in slim black pants and a black shirt. He rounded out his outfit with white shoes. He directed Howard to turn his head to the right than to the left, point his fingers in the air, and pretend that he was giving a speech. As Howard played his role the photographer ran around him, bending, kneeling, and swinging his arms in order to get the perfect picture. It had the feel of a high fashion photo shoot and it was all I could do not to laugh.

We were surprised when Joe arrived, not only because we didn't expect him, but also because he was dressed in something he didn't wear often, a neatly pressed suit jacket. The photographer began taking shots of him alone and with Howard.

When all the pictures had been taken we left Joe behind and hopped aboard the small plane that would take us from Washington to Bangor.

□ □ □

The chair of the Maine Democratic Party was there to greet Howard and introduce him to the crowd that had gathered in the function room at the Bangor Motor Inn. She told the story of the last time a presidential candidate had visited the Bangor motel. In was October of 1991 and the candidate was Bill Clinton. Thirty people came out to hear him speak. As she told the story the more than 300 people who made up the standing-room-only crowd cheered and laughed with delight.

By 9 p.m. we were back on the plane, but now we were sitting on the tarmac at a small airport in Owls Head, Maine. It was raining and the fog was thick. The airport was not staffed, so the pilots were left to call Nashua, New Hampshire, themselves to find out the weather conditions at the airport that was our destination. The cell phone service was limited, however, which left us stranded on the tarmac.

Before boarding the plane we received a fax outlining the next day's schedule. Howard looked it over as we waited for the plane to take off and discovered that the next day started in a matter of hours.

Despite his most recent pleadings, the schedule was still out of control. He jokingly, yet a little seriously, suggested that we go on strike and skip some of the events on the schedule. He thought that it might be the only way to send a message to the staff in Burlington.

August 2, 2003

As our small charter plane bound for Islip, New York taxied down the runway, my Blackberry buzzed. It was an e-mail from a member of the media telling me that he had heard that Joe – not Howard – was going to be featured on the cover of *Newsweek* for a story titled "Joe Trippi: Howard Dean's Puppet Master." We didn't know whether the e-mail was accurate or just a joke, but it didn't matter because Howard was not happy with the prospect of it being true.

For Howard, it was the straw that broke the camel's back. He was frustrated by what he saw as Joe's constant self-promotion. (He once asked Joe why he had a can of shaving cream and a suit coat in the office. Joe's response that he needed to be prepared to go on television on short notice left Howard asking if he shouldn't be the one on television.)

Howard sat on the plane determined to end what had been bothering him for months. He came to the conclusion that he needed a new communications director. He believed that the current occupant of the job catered too much to Joe. It was time that he had someone who understood that the candidate, not the campaign manager, was the priority. He decided that when the plane touched down he would issue the order that he wanted a change at the top of the communications team.

And while he was at it he would demand that the campaign hire a scheduling director. His schedule was out of control and he was tired of his concerns being ignored. He wanted someone to be accountable for making sure that his time was managed wisely.

When the wheels of the plane hit the runway, Howard called Steve. He had until October 1 to make the hires.

□ □ □

Time and *Newsweek* were just two of the three national magazines to run feature stories about Howard. The third was *U.S. News and World Report.*

The magazine ran its piece at the same time as *Time* and *Newsweek.* It wasn't given as much attention as the two competing magazines because of where Howard's photograph was placed on the cover. The small one-inch picture in the top left corner of the page was lost in the shadow of an image of a space satellite being launched into the sky for a story on America's spy satellite program.

The story had been printed off and was waiting for us when we arrived in Islip. Howard was by nature cautious, so he was not happy with what he read. The reporter recounted a visit to the headquarters in Burlington where Joe demonstrated a trick he had taught his dog. When asked if he would rather work for George Bush or be dead the dog flopped onto the ground. Until recently, Joe had used John Kerry's name.

The message that the campaign had moved its sights from Kerry and the primary campaign to Bush and the general election did not sit well with Howard. It was a sense of inevitability that he did not share and did not want the campaign to adopt.

August 3, 2003

Raising money brought us to Martha's Vineyard, the popular vacation destination in Massachusetts. We had arrived the evening before and spent the night at the home of a supporter. It was a Sunday morning and in deference to church-goers, our money raising events had to wait until after church services were over.

As our host family buzzed around the kitchen making coffee and getting ready to take us to the fundraiser, Howard sat at a computer set up in the corner of the room. Ignoring the activity around him, he stared at the screen, reading the online versions of the *Time* and *Newsweek* stories that put him on the magazines' covers.

The *Time* cover read, "The Dean Factor: A feisty ex-Governor of Vermont is setting the pace in the race against Bush. Does Dean's renegade campaign stand a chance?" *Newsweek* posed the question, "Howard Dean: Destiny or Disaster?"

Both stories documented his rise from an unknown small state governor to popular outsider. They pointed out his weaknesses (he was angry and brusque) and his strengths (he was raising cash in impressive amounts). They quoted his friends ("Washington Democrats have a failed strategy on dealing with President Bush. Howard Dean is going to draw the line.") and his foes ("A Dean nomination could again mean Democrats lose 49 out of 50 states").

But in the end, the articles weren't all bad. *Time* summed up its piece with, "Dean may not be a maverick, but he may be something better: a real contender."

When Howard finally got up and made his way over to the breakfast table his only reaction was the smile on his face.

□ □ □

The clouds in the sky didn't dampen the spirits of the guests who mingled on the lawn during the Sunday morning brunch. The Martha's Vineyard oceanfront home was owned by Diane English, best known as the creator of the television sitcom *Murphy Brown*.

The guests were attracted to the event by the entertainment industry insiders whose names appeared on the invitation. The most recognizable were the actors Jake Gyllenhaal, Kirsten Dunst, Mary Steenburgen, Ted Danson, and Rob Reiner. It didn't matter that they weren't there.

While the guests stood in the backyard sipping juice out of champagne glasses and listening to Howard's stump speech, I sat in English's living room scribbling down the results of a poll of Iowa voters conducted by the *Des Moines Register*.

A staffer in Burlington had called with the news – for the first time Howard was leading in the caucus state. The poll showed him favored by 23 percent of those surveyed, giving him a slight lead over the presumed favorite Dick Gephardt, who polled 21 percent. John Kerry came in third with 14 percent followed by Lieberman with 10 percent, and Edwards trailing with 5 percent.

After a hop to the island of Nantucket for one last fundraiser, we were back in Vermont. By the time I dropped Howard off at his Burlington home the significance of the events of the day had set in.

He was featured on the covers of three national magazines, the latest poll showed him ahead in Iowa, and all eyes were on him. He was seen as an inspiration to his supporters (who totaled a record setting 68,000 on Meetup along with the 227,000 who had signed up on the campaign's website) and a threat to his rivals – and that made him in his words "afraid."

August 5, 2003

Dozens of magazine titles with subjects ranging from travel to fashion to business filled the racks at the gift shop at Chicago's O'Hare airport.

Rolling Stone profiled *American Idol* winner Ruben Studdard. *People* magazine paid tribute to the recently deceased comedian Bob Hope. *Backpacker* exposed "The Secrets of Yosemite" and *Forbes* magazine's "power issue" featured Bill Gates and Warren Buffet. Sandwiched in between was Howard.

We had read the *Time* and *Newsweek* pieces online, but had not seen the actual magazines, so our first stop after landing was at the airport gift shop.

It wasn't hard to find Howard. *Time* magazine featured a close up picture of his face that took up the entire cover. A picture of a waist up Howard with his sleeves rolled up and fingers pointing in the air graced *Newsweek*. And his face could be seen tucked into the corner of *U.S. News and World Report*.

Howard stood in front of the racks holding a copy of *Time* while I took a picture of him for the campaign blog. A few feet away a confused shopper looked on. The gentleman didn't recognize Howard as the face on the cover of the magazine. He peered over the top of the magazine he was reading hoping to go unnoticed as he tried to figure out what we were doing.

August 11, 2003

"Yo, Philadelphia!" Howard did his best Rocky impersonation as he greeted the crowd. Bad weather in Washington, D.C. almost made us miss the rally in the city whose residents take as much pride at being the home of the fictional movie character as they do in serving as the keeper of nation's most famous bell.

The outdoor rally organized by the volunteer members of the Philly4Dean group took place in a park just two blocks from the Liberty Bell. When we were dropped off at the street corner a short half block from the stage, Howard was surrounded by his supporters despite the best efforts of the bicycle racks to keep them at bay.

It was the largest crowd yet. More than 3,500 people packed the plaza. White haired grandmothers, young children, and all ages in between, many dressed in Dean for America T-shirts, stood under the overcast skies and cheered Howard on. He stood behind a podium. With his shirtsleeves rolled up high he energized the crowd that stood spellbound, ignoring the threat of rain from above.

When his speech was over he was handed a gift: a Philadelphia Phillies jersey which, to the roar of the crowd, he proudly put over his pale blue dress shirt – the jersey's red stripes perfectly matching his red tie.

August 14, 2003

A gaggle of reporters watched Howard take a ten-dollar bill out of his wallet and hand it to the cashier. In return he got $2.00 and a ticket to the Iowa State Fair.

Vermont had fairs, but they paled in comparison to the Iowa State Fair, which was spread over 400 acres in Des Moines and attracted more than 1 million people each year – almost twice the population of Vermont.

When we passed through the main gate it was clear why the fair was a must-do event for a presidential candidate. The photo opportunities were endless and the thousands of people who roamed the grounds were prime targets for a candidate looking for hands to shake.

The fairgoers knew exactly why Howard was there, but that didn't stop him from pretending he just wanted to have fun. With an entourage of print journalists, still photographers, and television cameras following closely behind, he admired the blue ribbon-winning vegetables, cooed over the cute baby rabbits, and watched the cow-judging contest in the dirt-floored arena.

He donned an apron and heavy gloves to cook pork chops over an open fire, sampled pork on a stick, and then made a visit to Pepperoni, the world's largest pig, who viewed him warily.

He walked by the concession stands that popped up every few feet selling everything from nachos to deep friend Twinkies. He stopped once to buy a $2.50 cup of "old fashioned" lemonade from a woman in a trailer who was completely unfazed by the cameras pointed in her direction.

On a dare he ate a deep fried Oreo. He reluctantly took a bite of the batter-dipped cookie after challenging me to eat one first, a challenge he probably would have reneged on if it hadn't been witnessed by the media. After all, he couldn't be seen as flip-flopping.

He ended the two and half hour visit with a meeting with the Butter Cow lady famous for her creation of the same name. The life-sized cow, sculpted out of 600 pounds of butter, had been one of the fair's most popular attractions since 1911. And Howard did what few others could; he went into the display case that housed the cow for a close up look. The long line of people who waited to get a glimpse of the cow seemed more impressed that he was in the display case than by the fact that he was running for president.

□ □ □

The call was over as soon as it began.

The poll numbers were rising, the money was coming in fast, and the media were paying attention. There was no denying that the campaign was a success. Sustaining the success until the Iowa caucuses (5 months away) was important, and Howard wanted to know how it was going to be done. At his request a conference call to discuss the strategy was scheduled.

The senior staff and consultants were gathered in Vermont while Howard, Jeani Murray, and I were in Des Moines. The staff in Burlington went around the room identifying themselves so Howard would know who was on the call. Joe Trippi, Steve McMahon, Bob Rogan . . . Peter Goldman. Howard stiffened when he heard the name. Goldman was part of a team of *Newsweek* reporters writing a book about the presidential election.

Howard was not going to discuss strategy with Goldman in the room. I called Vermont, yet despite Howard's wishes Joe would not ask him to leave. So Howard ended the call and it was never rescheduled.

□ □ □

Bill Clinton had the saxophone. Howard had the guitar and harmonica. As governor, Howard shied away from revealing his musical skills to the masses, only playing his guitar once during his almost 12 years in office. But Jeani Murray convinced him to share his talent at a blues club in Iowa.

She arranged for him to "jam" with Iowa blues artist Hawkeye Herman at the Blues on Grand club in downtown Des Moines. The campaign billed the musical showcase as an event to "Help Howard Give Bush the Blues" and promised that he would deliver "a searing set of classic blues."

The club was small, stuffy, and despite the fact that the sun was shining outside, dark. Howard sat on a stool next to Hawkeye's and bobbed his head and swayed his shoulders to the music. He could have passed for a real musician if it weren't for his dress shirt, suit pants, and penny loafers.

The highlight of the show came at the end when Hawkeye premiered "It's Dean for America," a song he wrote for the campaign. "He's a man with a positive plan. He's on my mind because I've been left behind," Hawkeye belted out while Howard accompanied him on the harmonica. The crowd made up of Dean supporters, not music aficionados, roared with delight.

August 16, 2003

We were exceeding our fundraising expectations. In addition to raising more money than the other campaigns, we had brought in a staggering $5 million over the Internet. And with the number of supporters signing up online growing each day – we had close to 300,000 – the amount we could raise appeared to be endless.

Our success prompted some on the staff to discuss opting out of the federal campaign finance system. Under the system a candidate was limited to spending $45 million during the primary election, but would in return receive close to $19 million from the federal government. In the general election a campaign's overall spending would be limited to $74 million with the full amount coming from the federal government.

Rejecting the federal money was an option that Howard did not want discussed by anyone in the campaign – even privately.

Not taking the federal money meant the campaign would not be subject to the spending limits, but opting out only made sense if we were confident that we could raise more than the amount of money we would receive from the federal government, which between the primary and general elections totaled nearly $94 million.

Howard believed it was premature to discuss opting out. There was no guarantee that the fundraising would continue at its current pace. But word of the staff's discussions was leaked to the media and the Associated Press reported that Howard was backing "away from his pledge to adhere to spending limits."

He was forced to address an issue he didn't want to discuss. "We're not looking at that [rejecting the federal money] as an option, although there are those in our campaign that insist on thinking privately that they want to look at it as an option," he told the media.

August 20, 2003

We were in Vermont when the headline appeared, "Poll: Dean Grabs Lead in New Hampshire." A poll conducted by the American Research Group showed that for the first time Howard was ahead of his opponents in the Granite State. The results of the survey had Howard at 28 percent to Kerry's 21 percent and Gephardt's 10 percent.

After spending the morning and early afternoon in Vermont, Howard and I boarded a private plane and flew to New Hampshire. By dinnertime we had arrived at the first event of the day, a meeting with members of the local AFL-CIO at the Plumbers and Pipefitters Hall in Hooksett. When the meeting was over, Howard mingled with the union members over pizza and beer provided by the campaign.

When our final event of the night – a house party with teachers – was over, we headed to our overnight location in Manchester, the home of Esther Fishman, or "Goodie" as she was known to her friends.

Goodie was an 80-something grandmother who wasn't star struck or intimidated by the presidential candidate in her midst. To the contrary, she treated us like we were her grandchildren. (Her house was warm and cozy and my twin bed was comfortable, as was her bathroom which had dozens of towels hanging from hooks on the walls.) We stayed with her often and it didn't matter how late we were scheduled to arrive, she was always waiting up for us – and she always had a cake for us to eat before we went to bed.

It was after 9 p.m. when we pulled up to her house. As soon as we walked through the front door she instructed us to sit down at the dining room table where a chocolate cake was waiting.

August 22, 2003

Howard greeted the singers David Crosby and Graham Nash as they hopped out of the large tour bus. The two men were passing through Manchester, New Hampshire, and took a detour to cheer on the Dean campaign's softball team during a tournament that pitted the Democratic campaigns against each other.

Crosby, with his long white hair flowing out from underneath the blue baseball cap perched on his head, and Graham, sporting a Dean sticker on his black T-shirt, joined Howard along the fence that served as the Dean team's bullpen.

After cheering on several batters – and autographing one guitar – they went on their way, leaving Howard to take his turn on the field. The news cameras watched as he, dressed in his uniform – dress shirt, tie, suit pants, and loafers – wandered out to first base. Instead of a mitt, he held a cup of vanilla ice cream in his hands. Standing several feet from the base, which was being guarded under the watchful eye of the first baseman, he ate his ice cream and cheered on his team.

In the end, Dean topped Gephardt, but was defeated by Kerry.

August 23, 2003

More than 4,000 people packed the back lawn at the Cherry Hill Farms in Falls Church, Virginia, waiting for Howard to arrive.

It was the first rally in a four day, 10 city coast-to-coast journey, dubbed the "Sleepless Summer Tour" by the campaign. The trip was scheduled to coincide with President Bush's month long vacation and was intended to highlight that while Bush was sleeping soundly on his ranch in Crawford, Texas, Americans were losing sleep worrying about their future.

When Howard walked on stage and gave the crowd two thumbs up his supporters roared in response. He stood with his sleeves rolled up and gave a speech packed with fiery rhetoric:

On the Iraq war

"As commander in chief of the U.S. military it's my job to send our troops wherever I have to send them in the world to defend America. But as commander in chief of the U.S. military it's also my job never to send our sons and daughters, brothers and sisters to a foreign country to fight without telling the truth about why they're going there."

On health care for all Americans

"If we can have health insurance in the small state of Vermont than surely the most powerful and wealthy society on the face of the earth can join the British, French, Germans, Irish, Italians, Israelis, Canadians, Dutch, and even the Costa Ricans have health insurance!"

On a balanced federal budget

"No Republican president has balanced the budget in 34 years. If you want someone to trust with your money you had better elect a Democrat because Republicans cannot manage money."

"When it comes to defense the president is, as they say in Texas, all hat and no cattle."

He closed his remarks with a rallying cry for change:

The power to change this country is in your hands not mine. Abraham Lincoln said that a government of the people, by the people, and for the people shall not perish from this earth. You have the power to take back the Democratic Party and make it stand for something again and together we have the power to take back the White House and that's exactly what we're going to do!

The words that he had bungled during the debate in South Carolina were now an inspiration to his supporters who roared with delight when he exclaimed, "You have the power!"

Thirty minutes after the first thumbs up, the speech ended with a wave and the debut of the campaign's theme song. After an exhaustive search Joe had settled on the song "We Can" from the soundtrack of the movie *Legally Blonde* starring Reese Witherspoon. It wasn't Howard's choice (he preferred "Let the River Run" by Carly Simon), but Joe thought the lyrics matched the spirit of the campaign:

They'll try to stop the dream we're dreamin'
But they can't stop us from believing
They will fill your head with doubt
But that won't stop us now
So let them say we can't do it
Put up a road block
We'll just run right through it 'cause . . .

We can, do the impossible
We have the power in our hands
And we won't stop 'cause we've got to make a difference in this life
With our one voice, one heart, two hands, we can

As the song blasted throughout the usually tranquil farm, Howard jumped off the stage and into the crowd. After warning his eager supporters not to "squish each other" he posed for pictures, signed autographs, and shook hands, even climbing over the bicycle racks set up to keep his supporters back, in order to reach more of them.

□ □ □

For the coast-to-coast tour we traded in our boarding passes for a charter airplane dubbed the "Grassroots Express." Seventy-five passengers including supporters, media, and staff made the trip. Joe Trippi, Steve McMahon, Mark Squier, and Paul Maslin joined in the journey.

The inside of the plane was decorated with large pieces of plastic grass that were tucked between the tops of each seat and "Sleepless Summer Tour" signs lined the front and back walls of the cabin – just in case we forgot what we were doing.

As we took off for our next destination – Milwaukee, Wisconsin – the flight attendants passed out a special treat – Ben & Jerry's ice cream bars. The wrappers weren't off the ice cream before Joe and I had a disagreement. I refused a CNN producer's request to clip a microphone to my clothing. Joe had agreed to allow the cable network to follow the two of us around for a behind the scenes documentary on the campaign, but he hadn't asked me first.

I was always with Howard, so if a camera followed me, it followed him. I didn't think that was fair. And in any case the documentary wasn't scheduled to air until after the campaign, which made the piece of no value to our current efforts.

Joe worried that the cable network would nix the project without my participation, so he enlisted Steve to plead his case. Steve sat next to me during the first leg of the flight, and as Joe looked on from several rows back, tried to convince me to consent to the filming. But I didn't change my mind.

□ □ □

176

Howard stood behind the blue curtain listening to the crowd chant, "We want Dean! We want Dean!"

It was after 10:00 p.m. and close to 800 people packed inside the small airport hangar at the private airfield in Milwaukee. Joe summed up the activity on the other side of the curtain, "This is crazy man." Out of sight of the crowd, Howard pursed his lips and smiled, looking embarrassed by all the attention.

With the introduction "I give you the next president of the United States," the curtain parted and he sprang up four stairs and onto the stage. As "We Can" played he waved to the crowd and shook hands with the supporters who stood behind him on the stage. He then turned to the crowd and exclaimed, "We're going to win!"

August 24, 2003

We boarded the plane for Portland, Oregon, at 7:30 a.m. It was only the second day of the tour, so there were no groans when the pilot announced the 3 hour and 6 minute flight time.

Not long after the plane took off some on board were lulled into a sound sleep. Howard decided to teach them that it was not smart to fall asleep on the Sleepless Summer Tour. He quietly sat down next to the sleeping beauties and posed for pictures, which we posted on the campaign's website.

But it wasn't all fun and games. Dr. Dean was called into service when one of the flight attendants complained of a swollen ankle. The reason for the swelling was a mystery and Howard offered to take a look. Readying himself for the exam he took off his suit coat to the cheers of the passengers who treated the action as if Clark Kent was turning into Superman. After almost opening the cabin door thinking it was a seat, he knelt down in front of the flight attendant, now being photographed by the media, which couldn't resist a shot of the candidate being a doctor. As the group watched she described the pain that was shooting through her right ankle. Howard poked and prodded, wondering out loud if it might be a blood clot. The plane landed before the doctor could make a clear diagnosis.

▫ ▫ ▫

The "spud drop" in Boise was a surprise to Howard and the media. What was billed as a refueling stop was actually a rally named after the state's most famous crop. Idaho, like Wyoming, was part of Howard's early strategy to win delegates by focusing on the states that the other Democrats would ignore. Despite his success, he still operated by that strategy and his yearlong affection for Idaho had become a running joke in the campaign.

More than 400 people lined the tarmac at the private airport waiting to greet him. But they'd have to wait. He couldn't exit the aircraft until the scene was set. The press, staff, and supporters walked off the plane first. The staff and supporters joined the crowd while the photographers waited at the bottom of the stairs to get a photo of Howard as he descended.

When he got the go-ahead to leave by a member of the campaign staff, he stood in the doorway of the airplane and gave a thumbs up to the crowd.

As "We Can" played he made his way down the stairs and across the tarmac to the stage. With the plane in the shadows he launched into his speech.

By the time we reached our fourth destination, Portland, Oregon, the rallies had fallen into a rhythm and so had Howard.

The events were planned right down to the eager supporters who stood behind the podium next to a banner that advertised the campaign's website and toll free number, all perfectly positioned to be captured by the cameras covering the event.

Howard played his part. He'd walk on stage as "We Can" blared from the sound system and acknowledge the crowd's reaction with two thumbs up and a wave before starting his speech.

The production was the same in each city, but the crowds were growing larger. When he took the stage in the outdoor courtyard at Portland State University he surveyed the crowd and exclaimed, "Holy Cow! This is unbelievable." He was overwhelmed by the more than 5,000 people who stood in front of him and on the rooftops of the four-story brick buildings that surrounded the courtyard.

The first thumbs up was repeated again thirty minutes later and after one last chorus of "You've got the power," Howard joined hands with the others on stage and held them high in the air. As "We Can" played he hopped off the stage and walked along the barriers that had been set up, shaking hands, posing for pictures, and signing autographs.

The sights and sounds of the rallies were posted on the campaign's website, along with first person accounts of what it was like to be in the crowd. The campaign wanted the crowds to grow, so a challenge was issued to Howard's supporters to make each event bigger and louder than the one that came before.

The next stop was Seattle, where Dr. Dean hoped to find out what was wrong with the flight attendant's ankle. Before our plane took off he called his cousin who lived in the city. She was a doctor and he asked for her help.

The examination took place at Seattle's Westin Hotel away from the prying eyes of the media. His cousin made a preliminary diagnosis, wrote a prescription, and recommended that the flight attendant see a doctor when she got home. Problem solved.

For the second time in one day came "Holy Cow! You are unbelievable. This is unbelievable." This time Howard was standing in downtown Seattle's Westlake Park.

The crowd, which stretched from the stage to a Starbuck's restaurant across from the park, was the largest the campaign had ever seen – topping 10,000 – and required the city to close down some of the streets surrounding the event.

When the speech was over, Howard talked to the local press while several feet away Joe held a handmade sign high in the air that read "You Gotta Believe."

August 25, 2003

Coat or no coat? That was the question.

At 7:30 a.m. the Grassroots Express took off for Spokane, Washington. Instead of a rally, the campaign planned a town hall meeting dubbed "Speak Up Spokane." The event was a chance for Howard to discuss jobs and the economy with local citizens.

Standing in a small room at the West Central Community Center, Howard debated the appropriateness of wearing his suit coat or taking it off. After discussing each option, the decision was made. The gathering was meant to have the air of a casual discussion between friends with Howard sitting on a stool – so no coat.

Close to 900 people showed up for the town hall meeting that took place in a room that held 200. Two overflow rooms were set up and the sound was piped in by speakers.

After visiting one of the overflow rooms he went into the main room. The event wasn't a rally, but when he walked in the crowd stood and cheered, "We want Dean!" which prompted Howard to wave and give two thumbs up.

From Spokane we flew south to San Antonio, Texas, to a fundraiser that netted the campaign more than $50,000. We then boarded three buses for a 90-minute ride to Austin. Two buses carried supporters who were willing to pay the campaign's $125 fare for the close-up ride with Howard.

In order to allow for equal time, halfway through the trip we stopped on the side of the road so he could switch buses. He stood in the aisle steadying himself by holding on to the luggage racks as the bus swayed back and forth. He chatted casually and took questions from the people who peered over their seats to see him.

At the request of one passenger he reluctantly entertained the riders with a harmonica solo. The woman had brought the instrument with her just for the occasion. He launched into his own rendition of a Bob Dylan tune. When he announced that he could have done better if he had a harmonica in the key of G, the woman reached into her bag and produced one.

By 9:30 p.m. he was in Austin standing on a stage in front of more than 3,000 people wearing a large black Sombrero and dancing with Flamenco dancers.

□ □ □

It had been two weeks since the media reported that we were considering rejecting federal money to finance the campaign, and the issue came up again when Howard took questions from the press after the Austin rally.

With Joe Trippi, Steve McMahon, and communications director Tricia Enright looking on, Howard responded when asked by *Los Angeles Times* reporter Ron Brownstein if he planned to opt out of the federal program, "I can't answer your question because we really haven't discussed it. The staff has. They shot off their mouths to the press and I told them not to, but they did any way. We are going to consider that but we won't consider that until the end of January reporting period. We'll see where we are at the end of January."

August 26, 2003

The fourth and final day of our summer tour began at 5:00 a.m. in San Antonio, where a group of bleary-eyed passengers waited to board the "Grassroots Express" to Chicago.

People were slumped in chairs and lying motionless on the floor in the airport terminal waiting for the signal that it was time to pass through security. A few feet away, Howard stood reading a newspaper surrounded by photographers documenting the mundane action that most Americans did each morning.

When it was time to leave Howard lifted his arms in the air so the security personnel could wand him and then he took off his shoes for inspection.

□ □ □

"Holy shit!" was Howard's reaction to the news that more than 3,500 people were waiting for him on the rooftop.

It was hot and sunny in Chicago, the perfect day for a rally on top of a building at the city's Navy Pier. The landmark boasted a spectacular view of Lake Michigan and the Chicago skyline.

Before the rally we sat in a small room eating sandwiches and French fries. Howard guzzled a bottle of water as the organizers ran through the timeline for the event. It was the seventh rally of the tour and it was choreographed like a Broadway production.

The plan: Small white towels would be passed out to each person as they arrived. To create an air of excitement the crowd would wave the towels in the air and chant "We want Dean!" as they waited for Howard to appear. As "We Can" played, Howard would walk across the rooftop and onto the stage where he would shake hands with the supporters positioned behind him. When the speech was over, he would wave his towel in the air, prompting the crowd to do the same. After a short pause "We Can" would play, the crowd would chant "We want Dean!" and he would work his way down the rope line and exit the rooftop the same way he came in.

Howard listened to the instructions and assured the staff that he understood the plan.

The water below rippled in sync with the song "We Can" that signaled Howard's arrival. All the elements – hand wave, thumbs up, fiery rhetoric – were there to make for a perfectly executed rally.

And it would have been if Howard hadn't forgotten to wave his towel when his speech was over.

From Chicago we flew to New York City for the final rally of the four-day cross-country tour. The plastic grass that once stood tall between the seats was long gone and with it the energy we had when we first took off four days earlier. People sat quietly or napped during the 90-minute flight. Our clothes were rumpled and newspapers, blankets, jackets, and empty soda cans were strewn around the once orderly plane.

□ □ □

"Thank you, New York!" A slightly hoarse Howard yelled in response to the "Howard! Howard! Howard!" chants from the more than 10,000 people who stood in Bryant Park. When we arrived in midtown Manhattan it was after 10:00 p.m., but the hour did not temper the crowd's enthusiasm.

Moments after he arrived on stage Howard was handed a baseball bat and the tune "Take Me Out to the Ballgame" blasted out over the sound system. The song meant it was time to announce how much money the campaign raised online during the four-day tour. On the first day of the tour the contribution counting bat was put on the website and the goal was set at one million dollars.

As Howard swung the bat in the air a large screen set up to the left of the stage projected the image of the bat on the website. The final result: $1,003,620 from 17,115 contributors.

When the speech was over, "We Can" played one last time as Howard hopped off the stage and walked along the bicycle racks that were set up to keep the crowd a safe distance away. He shook hands, posed for pictures, and signed autographs. The crowd was so thick and, although they were held back by the racks, people were grabbing him. The only way he could get free was to count to ten then turn and run until he got behind the stage.

While Howard was making his mad dash, Joe and I got caught up in the excitement and before we realized it we were hugging.

One hour later the only sign that a rally had taken place at the site were the bicycle racks that still lined the empty grounds. Howard and I got in a car and drove to a private airfield outside the city to catch a flight back to Vermont.

The tour had been a success. More that 30,000 people had come out to hear Howard speak and the campaign had raised $1 million.

As we were driving along the dark streets, Howard sat in the back of the car munching on a Krispy Kreme donut from a box that was given to us by one of the rally goers. When we arrived in Vermont after 1 a.m. we hopped in my car that was parked at the airport. I dropped Howard off at his house than drove to my own.

August 29, 2003

Success did not bring peace between Joe and me. We rarely spoke to each other and when we were together it usually ended in yelling, although most of the time I had no idea what we were fighting about (and I don't think Joe did either).

The excitement of the Sleepless Summer Tour hadn't dimmed when Joe and I had a fight in the office that resulted in him throwing his computer across the room and storming out of the building when I refused his order to leave. (The reason for the fight was a mystery to me, so I told him that if anyone was going to leave, it would be him.)

Unfortunately, we weren't alone and the scene was witnessed by the members of the staff who filled the cubicles and desks just outside the office Joe and I shared. It was normally a busy place, but had turned so quiet that you could hear a pin drop. When I apologized for our behavior a single head slowly popped up from behind one of the cubicle walls and scanned the room to make sure it was safe to come out.

August 30, 2003

"Guess what? This is your life for the next year and a half," Howard remarked to New Hampshire state director Karen Hicks as we tried to drive away from the crowd that was following our car.

It was chaos as we left the backyard party at the home of a state representative in Walpole, New Hampshire. The Saturday morning event took place on the heels of the Sleepless Summer Tour and two days after newspaper headlines screamed, "Dean Surges Ahead in New Hampshire," announcing the results of a newly released poll that showed Howard with a "commanding" 21-point lead over Kerry in the Granite State.

More than 1,000 people had gathered to listen to Howard speak from a small stage that was framed by miles of green mountains and blue sky. The New Hampshire town was just 20 miles from Vermont's eastern boarder, an easy drive for Vermonters who wanted to see the man they called governor long before the rest of the nation even knew his name.

The speech was over, but the enthusiastic crowd wanted more. Howard was surrounded when he tried to make his way through the house and out to the driveway. When he disappeared into the car, his supporters weren't ready to say good-bye. They swarmed around the car hoping for one last look at their candidate.

—SEPTEMBER—

September 1, 2003

It would be a "September to Remember" according to the campaign. We boasted that the monthlong event – during which Dean supporters would be challenged to complete a different action each day in support of Howard's candidacy – would "change forever the way politics is practiced in America" and "demonstrate the power of the grassroots."

Howard began the September we would never forget in Iowa.

"Hey! Hey! Ho! Ho! Howard Dean is on the go!" It was Labor Day and we had flown from Burlington to Des Moines to take part in the city's celebration.

The Dean contingent – several dozen strong – cheered their candidate on as he walked in the annual parade. It was warm and sunny and Howard, surrounded by his supporters dressed in shorts and campaign T-shirts, sprinted down the route in his penny loafers and suit trousers. He zigzagged from one side of the street to the other shaking as many hands as possible. The spectators sitting in lawn chairs and on the curb politely accepted his hand. News photographers ran ahead looking for the perfect shot.

Kids knelt and stood close to the road, plastic grocery bags in hand, waiting to scoop up the candy that was thrown by each parade participant. Candy was a requirement, not an option. It reminded me of Halloween when homeowners are judged by the quality of the goodies given out. Dean supporters carried orange buckets and made sure not to miss even one child – especially those sitting with a possible caucus goer.

"Well, that was a good work out," Howard announced when he arrived at the Iowa State fairgrounds, the official end of the parade, 90 minutes after it began.

One supporter asked him why he hadn't traded his loafers for sneakers during the walk that had turned into a run. He responded, "People don't know me as well around here so I feel I have to be much more formal."

As Howard bid good-bye to the people who marched with him, John Kerry's supporters who walked on behalf of the missing candidate spotted their rival and broke out in a loud chorus of "Kerry! Kerry! Kerry!"

September 3, 2003

There were just enough seats on the small charter airplane to accommodate the seven of us flying from Burlington to Santa Fe, New Mexico. Howard and I, along with Joe Trippi, Steve McMahon, Bob Rogan, deputy campaign manager Andi Pringle, and policy director Jeremy Ben-Ami, packed into the plane. Because I was the smallest I had to squeeze into the narrow space between Joe and Steve. It was the first time Joe and I were seeing each other since our fight five days earlier and I didn't greet the pilot's announcement that the ride would take 4 hours and 50 minutes with much delight.

We were making the long and uncomfortable journey to attend a debate scheduled to take place in Albuquerque the next day. It was the first time Howard would meet his opponents on stage since the debate in South Carolina in May and the first time since he had taken on the status of front-runner – something that was sure to make him the target of his rivals.

□ □ □

Howard, Bob, and I sat in the living room waiting for the others to join us. When we arrived in Santa Fe the seven of us had driven to the home of a supporter where we planned to spend time preparing for the debate.

Sitting with us in the room was a man we had never met before. He didn't get up from his chair or say anything to us when we walked in. It was so strange that we didn't say anything to him either. The four of us sat in silence, as Howard grew increasingly frustrated with Joe and Steve, who chose to make phone calls on the patio instead of joining him in the living room.

It wasn't until Howard demanded their presence did we find out the identity of the mystery man. His name was Joe Costello and he had worked with Joe Trippi on former California Governor Jerry

Brown's 1972 presidential campaign. Joe had hired him to develop Howard's campaign message.

▫ ▫ ▫

It was the first Wednesday of the month – the campaign's designated Meetup day – which meant Dean supporters were gathering around the country.

Howard joined the Santa Fe Meetup group at Tribes Coffee House. When we arrived dozens of people had filled the walkway leading into the restaurant hoping to shake his hand. Inside more than 200 people packed into the small space. They stood side by side, sat on tables and on the floor – anywhere they could to hear him speak. The media – representing national and local outlets – lined the back of the room.

The number of people signing up around the country to be a member of a Dean Meetup group had grown at an unbelievable rate. We had just topped 100,000 members. To mark the milestone, the Colorado woman who was the 100,000[th] person to sign up was flown to Santa Fe to meet Howard and take part in a celebration at the coffee house.

"Now, I'm happy to take questions, comments, and rude remarks," Howard announced to the friendly crowd when he finished his stump speech.

One woman asked him how he would approach the discord in the Middle East. He responded that the United States should not "take sides" in the conflict between Israel and the Palestinians.

For decades the policy of the United States had been to support Israel. The words Howard chose to use to answer the question put his position at odds with the long-standing policy. None of his supporters took issue with what he said, or even seemed to notice, but his answer was not lost on the media in the room.

September 4, 2003

The time had arrived. The debate was set to begin in a matter of minutes. After spending most of the day attending fundraisers and doing press interviews, we had made our way to the candidates' holding area in Popejoy Hall at the University of New Mexico.

Howard declined to sit behind the blue curtain that was set up to serve as his private waiting area. Instead, he stood eyeing the cookies that had been arranged on the table in the hallway. As he was deciding which sugary treat would serve as his dinner before the 6 p.m. debate, he was interrupted by Democratic National Committee Chairman Terry McAuliffe. He took his eye off his prize and said hello to the party chair.

After making small talk with McAuliffe he went back to the cookie platter, only to be interrupted by John Edwards who had made his way backstage. The two rivals were all smiles, greeting each other with a handshake.

But Howard's attention remained trained on the cookies. His third and final attempt to nab one was scuttled by the arrival of Bob Graham who, along with his wife, came in search of his waiting area. Soon after, he made his way to the stage hungry, but exhibiting none of the nerves that were so obvious during the first debate in May.

While the candidates stood next to each other on the stage, members of each campaign staff were ushered into a small theater to watch the debate together.

Having all of the campaigns in the same room for a confrontational event like a debate proved to be awkward. One of the advantages of having separate rooms was that we could verbally – and if necessary physically – react to the action on the stage. But the shared space meant that nothing more than whispers could be heard when the larger than life images of the candidates appeared on the television screen. No one wanted to give away their strategy or acknowledge that another candidate had scored a point against their own.

Steve McMahon, Bob Rogan, Paul Maslin, Tricia Enright, Andi Pringle, and I sat braced for a fight. The media and pundits had high expectations for the debate. Many were looking for Dick Gephardt and John Kerry to take aim at Howard, who was leading in Iowa and New Hampshire. But the debate proved to be anything but feisty. With the exception of Joe Lieberman, Howard's opponents left him alone.

When the 90-minute debate was over we made our way across the campus to the student union where Dean supporters had gathered to watch the debate. A smile crossed Howard's face when he heard that cake was being served.

September 6, 2003

It was listed as a "family breakfast" on Howard's schedule. The deception was necessary to keep the staff from knowing the true purpose of the meeting – breakfast with Wesley Clark. Clark was thinking about running for president and Howard wanted to find out if he intended to get into the race.

The secret rendezvous was set for the Sheraton Four Points Hotel in Los Angeles. We were in the city and in the hotel to assist California Governor Gray Davis. The Democrat was facing a recall election, and Howard, who believed that a Democrat running for president would have an easier time in California if the state's chief executive was a Democrat, agreed to publicly support the embattled governor.

The media – both national and state – swarmed the hotel in anticipation of Howard's appearance, which made it challenging to keep the "family meeting" a secret. But we had what we thought was the perfect plan. The two men would meet in Howard's room. They would dial "5" on the phone to place their breakfast order with room service, which had been instructed to put a rush on the order.

We were all set to go when Howard decided that his room was no place to meet the retired general – it was too small and the furniture was unattractive.

We scrabbled and with the hotel's help found a small conference room located on the lobby level. The furniture was better, but the location – around the corner from where the Davis press conference would take place – wasn't. The timing had to be perfect if both men were going to get into the room unseen. Clark entered the hotel through a back entrance. Howard took an elevator down to the lobby that opened directly across from the conference room. The hustle and bustle worked in our favor. No one noticed.

A waiter took their order and then Joe, who had flown in for the meeting, left the room, leaving the two men alone to meet. One hour later Clark exited the same way he came in and Howard walked across the lobby and joined Davis, the media none the wiser.

September 7, 2003

It was Sunday, but that mattered little. For us it was just another day on the campaign trail and we began the day like we ended the night before, at a private retreat for high dollar donors. The two-day get together intended to stroke the largest contributors (Joe was there to give the group a PowerPoint presentation on how we were going to win) took place at a rustic camp in Nicasio, California, 40 miles outside of San Francisco.

There were no tents at this camp, however. Instead, the property came right out of the pages of *House and Garden Magazine*. The main house, made of large finished logs, was rustic yet elegant. It was decorated in deep browns and every detail had its place right down to the blankets slung over the couch and the large wood-carved bear that greeted guests at the front door. Howard and I, along with our hosts, stayed in the main house while the rest of the guests slept in small cabins – also elegantly decorated – that sat among the trees that were so tall and dense they kept the sky hidden.

The guests at the morning breakfast were dressed in what seemed like costumes to fit the occasion – blue jeans and boots. Howard and I sat at the long wooden tables in the same clothes we wore at the dinner under the stars the night before – a business suit for him and a pantsuit for me.

From the mountain retreat we headed to San Jose to raise money, but not before stopping at a Baptist Church in San Francisco. We stayed just long enough for the pastor to introduce Howard to the congregation before we sneaked out the back door.

□ □ □

The people who mingled inside the home in San Jose had contributed a minimum of $1,000 to attend the reception. As Howard made small talk with the donors reality intruded. President Bush went on national television to announce that he would ask Congress for $87 billion in emergency spending for military operations and reconstruction in Iraq and Afghanistan.

As soon as the president finished his remarks, Howard slipped into a small den where he dialed into a conference call arranged by the campaign to share his reaction with the media – and it was a response he had been eager to use. He told the reporters that President Bush "is beginning to remind me of what was happening with Lyndon Johnson and Dick Nixon during the Vietnam War. The government begins to feed misinformation to the American people in order to justify an enormous commitment of American troops, which turned out to be a tremendous mistake."

Within minutes he was back at the fundraiser. The guests were too busy chatting and eating to even notice that he had left.

When his appointed time with the high dollar donors expired, Howard moved out onto the deck and marveled at the 1,200 people who were barely contained in the walled backyard. He stood on the steps that led to the patio and preached his message to the converted, all of whom had donated $100 (enough to get them a spot in the backyard, but not inside). At the end of the speech, all decorum was lost and as the Motown hit "Heard It Through the Grapevine" blared throughout the yard – and the neighborhood – the crowd pushed its way forward to shake Howard's hand. In less than two hours we had raised more than $175,000.

□ □ □

A small group of people stood around the food court whispering and pointing in our direction. It was after 9 p.m. and we were sitting in the boarding area at the airport in Oakland, California, waiting to board our plane to Washington, D.C.

Howard, sitting slumped in a chair, opened a newspaper and held it in front of his face. The open paper had become the sign – conscious on his part or not – that he did not want to talk to anyone.

Where he was once able to move around unnoticed, he was now recognized almost everywhere he went. It didn't matter the size of the town or the city. He was noticed when he walked down a crowded street, stood on a subway car in New York or went through security at some of the country's busiest airports. Our only strategy to deal with his new-found fame was to have me sit in the middle seat on airplanes so he wouldn't be bothered by the person sitting next to him and registering him under a different name when we stayed at a hotel. And now he had adopted the newspaper strategy.

Joe marveled at the attention Howard was getting from the people at the food court and wanted him to go over and say hello to his fans. But Howard wasn't in the mood to be the object of anyone's affection. Not wanting to disappoint the group, Joe went over and said hello.

September 8, 2003

Our plane landed at Dulles airport in Washington, D.C. at 5:54 a.m. just in time for Howard to appear on ABC's *Good Morning America*, CBS's *Early Show,* and the *Today Show* on NBC. The production crews for the early morning shows were waiting for us at a nearby hotel and so were the morning newspapers.

It had been five days since Howard told a group of supporters that the United States should not "take sides" in the Middle East. And for five days, Joe Lieberman had been pounding Howard for the remark.

The papers carried another attack by Lieberman: "It's hard to say if this is a well thought out position. If it is, it is a major break in a half century of American foreign policy. If it's not, as a candidate for president, you've really got to think before you talk."

□ □ □

K Street wasn't just a street in Washington, D.C. famous for the numerous lobbying firms that made the street their home; it was also a television show on the cable channel HBO. The show that boasted the actor George Clooney as an executive producer was part reality and part fiction. Working mostly without a script, actors and non-actors, including Democratic strategist James Carville and Republican strategist Mary Matalin, carried out story lines that sought to tell the tale of what goes on behind the scenes in the world of politics.

The producers asked Howard to appear on the first episode. It was a request that caused real drama that wasn't caught on tape.

For days Steve McMahon and I had debated whether Howard should appear on the show. Steve thought he should. I disagreed. The filming was set to take place on a day that was already overbooked. We had agreed that keeping Howard's schedule under control was a priority, which would mean saying no. But Steve didn't want to say no to his colleague and friend, Democratic strategist Paul Begala, who made the request. Howard left it up to us to make the decision and in the end I left it up to Steve.

The scene was shot in a small ballroom at the St. Regis Hotel in Washington. The plot had James Carville, Paul Begala, and an actor playing a third political strategist helping Howard prepare for an upcoming debate – an actual debate in Baltimore hosted by the Congressional Black Caucus.

Howard stood behind a podium in front of the two strategists and the actor. It took him a few tries before he understood that he wasn't supposed to act. Instead he needed to treat the filming like a real debate preparation session. It was made to look like a meeting between four men, but in reality dozens of people wandered in and out of the room trying to make the picture and sound perfect.

Almost unnoticed was George Clooney, who knelt on the floor filming the scene using a hand held camera. Thinking that meeting Clooney would change my mind about the filming, Steve made sure I was introduced to the movie star. But I refused to melt under the actor's charm.

□ □ □

By the time the mayor of Baltimore – the seventh and final speaker – made his way to the podium the crowd was weary. Filming *K Street* made us 30 minutes late in arriving for the rally at the University of Maryland.

When word spread through the crowd – numbering close to 3,500 – that Howard had arrived on campus, the mayor was interrupted by a chorus of "We want Dean! We want Dean!" The mayor responded quickly, ending his speech and welcoming Howard on stage as "We Can" played on cue.

The rally saw the introduction of a new chant from the crowd. As Howard talked about the failure to find the administration's promised weapons of mass destruction in Iraq, the crowd called out, "No more lies!"

By the time the sky was dark, Howard was yelling, "You have the power!" He held hands with the people on the stage, hopped down to the ground, and walked along the bicycle racks shaking hands, and posing for pictures.

□ □ □

It had been two days since Howard had slept and there was just one more event between his head and a pillow – a fundraiser for young professionals at the Bohemian Caverns nightclub in Washington, D.C.

Joe, with the CNN camerawoman who had been following him since the Sleepless Summer Tour in tow, joined me in the backseat of the car for the drive over. The presence of the camera and the microphone that Joe wore clipped to his lapel had become a source of friction. Howard didn't want the camera around – even if it wasn't rolling. But Joe would go nowhere without it. When they hopped in the car, he assured us that his microphone was turned off. Regardless, Howard sat in the front, barely speaking during the 30-minute ride.

September 9, 2003

The passengers waiting in Washington's Union Station to board the Metroliner train to Philadelphia couldn't help but stare at the commotion a few feet away. Howard was standing surrounded by a group of photographers. He wasn't doing anything remarkable; regardless, the news cameras remained pointed in his direction. They didn't want to miss the opportunity to capture the front-runner coughing, hiccupping or smiling.

When we boarded the train Mike Ford took the seat next to Howard. The last time we heard from Mike he announced that he was leaving the "Starship Howard." Now, a year and a half later, Joe wanted Mike to join the campaign.

For months I watched people who hadn't given Howard the time of a day a year earlier reach out to him like they were long lost friends. It was amazing what high poll numbers and money did for his popularity.

I was getting used to it, but the scene on the train still annoyed me. It seemed ridiculous to bring Mike into the campaign since the first time he was given the chance to work for Howard he left because he thought we were hopeless. Not to mention that Howard did not pursue Mike because he was uncomfortable with him.

Now Howard was the front-runner and could hire anyone he wanted, yet he was sitting on a train listening to Joe explain why he should hire Mike. Rounding out the scene was the CNN camerawoman who, with Joe's blessing, sat across from me pointing her camera in his direction. There was video of the meeting, but no audio. I insisted that Joe turn his microphone off so his conversation with Howard would not be picked up.

□ □ □

After attending a fundraiser in Philadelphia, Howard, and I – we had parted ways with Mike and Joe when we first reached the city – took the train back to Baltimore where Howard was going to take part in a debate sponsored by the Congressional Black Caucus.

As we drove up to the Fine Arts Building at Baltimore's Morgan State University, Howard rolled down his window and waved to the crowd of people holding signs. The sign holders were there to show their support for their candidates. The public display of affection had little or no impact on the debate – the only people who saw it were the candidates and a small group of partisans who had tickets to the event. Instead it was a psychological war played out between the campaigns, the winner being the one with more signs and louder voices.

First in the line that spanned the driveway were supporters of Lyndon LaRouche, who beat out the competition by using a bullhorn. Next came the Dean supporters who cheered with delight when Howard yelled hello. We continued on past the Kerry, Kucinich, and Edwards supporters, Howard politely waving to each group.

The debate was a combination of conflict, comedy, and controversy – with Howard involved in each exchange.

Steve McMahon, Tricia Enright, Andi Pringle, policy advisors Ron Weich and Jeremy Ben-Ami, research director Brent Colburn, Joe, and I watched the debate in the classroom assigned to us by the debate organizers. Soda and sandwiches – which Joe nibbled under the watchful eye of his constant companion, the CNN camera – served as our dinner. We held our breaths waiting for Howard's rivals to attack, but like the debate in New Mexico the week before, the attacks were rare.

When Joe Lieberman tried to score a point by confronting Howard about the Middle East, Howard would have none of it, quickly dismissing him with, "It doesn't help . . . to demagogue the issue."

Conflict turned into comedy when Howard answered a question posed to him by one of the journalists on the debate panel. When asked how he – the former governor of the second whitest state in the nation – could relate to African Americans he responded, "If the percentage of minorities who are in your state has anything to do with how connected you are with African-American voters, then Trent Lott would be Martin Luther King."

The response elicited a laugh from the audience – and from the staff gathered in the classroom. What only a few people knew was that the answer originated with James Carville, who offered it to Howard the day before during the debate prep session staged for *K Street*. (Some in the campaign, not knowing where the quote came from, told the media that Howard had made it up, causing the

Kerry campaign to accuse us of lying when Howard revealed the true origin of the quote.)

Howard caused a minor furor on stage – and gave his opponents and the media something else to add to the list of his so-called "gaffes" – when he announced that he was the only candidate talking to white audiences about race. His opponents took exception to the claim, especially John Edwards, who hailed from North Carolina and said he'd been doing it for most of his life.

When the debate was over Howard, Steve, Joe, and I boarded a small private plane and flew to Burlington. Howard wouldn't allow the CNN camerawoman on the flight, so she was forced to fly commercial – and in the process miss an hour of Joe's day.

Howard had lost his patience with the constant presence of the CNN camera and took the opportunity to set down some ground rules. The camera was not to be around during his private time and Joe, instead of just turning off his microphone, was to take it off and leave it outside any room Howard was in.

September 12, 2003

After spending a day in Burlington – a day during which Howard denied media speculation that he had offered Wes Clark the vice presidency during their now not-so-secret meeting in Los Angeles five days earlier – we drove to New Hampshire. It was our first visit to the state in two weeks. (September marked the last month in the third quarter fundraising period and we were spending the majority of the time raising money around the country.)

Our first stop was at Dartmouth Hitchcock Medical Center in Lebanon, where Howard unveiled his mental health care plan. Addressing a crowd that included hospital leadership, staff, medical students, and leaders in the mental health community, he outlined his plan that, like the health care plan he unveiled in May, was based on his experience in Vermont.

It took 45 minutes to roll out the plan and answer questions from the audience. When the time was up we were in the car and off to our next stop: Plymouth, New Hampshire.

□ □ □

Howard made his way through the Main Street Diner. The popular restaurant was located across the street from Plymouth State University where he was going to meet with undecided voters. It was the lunch hour in the busy restaurant, making it the perfect time for a quick stop.

As he tried to suck a thick strawberry shake topped with whipped cream through a straw, he wandered from table to table and down the lunch counter, introducing himself to the patrons most of whom needed no introduction – they recognized him.

He finished his quick loop around the diner before the milk shake was gone. The owner of the restaurant came to his aid, pouring the remaining contents of the glass into a paper cup. He sprinted across the street and up the driveway that led to the college. Abandoning the straw, he finished guzzling the rest of the ice cream beverage just as he reached a group of waiting supporters.

□ □ □

"It's a sad end for Dick Gephardt," Howard announced to the small contingent of press standing outside Heritage Commons at Plymouth State University after the meeting with undecided voters.

Howard had been on the defensive for weeks. His own words – or as characterized by some as gaffes and misstatement – had been getting him into trouble. Now he was responding to what marked the first direct – and harshest – attack by one of his opponents.

With polls showing Gephardt trailing Howard in Iowa, the congressman decided to turn up the heat. Citing events that occurred in 1995, Gephardt accused Howard of supporting Republican efforts to cut billions of dollars from Medicare, the federal program that provides health care to seniors.

While Howard was in Plymouth, Gephardt was telling union members in Des Moines, Iowa, "Howard Dean actually agreed with the Gingrich Republicans. . . . Howard Dean, as chairman of the National Governors Association, was supporting Republican efforts to scale back Medicare." Medicare was an important issue in Iowa, a state that ranked fourth in the nation in the number of residents over 65 – beneficiaries of the federal program.

Howard was blindsided by the attack, only learning of it when confronted by the media in Plymouth. So when he proclaimed a "sad end" for Dick Gephardt, he did so without thinking his comments through. (Although there was no evidence to suggest that waiting to respond would have produced a different answer.) Shortly after he spoke to the media, a formal statement was released from the headquarters in Burlington. "Sad end" had been changed to "sad day." We didn't want Howard to appear arrogant by proclaiming Gephardt's campaign over.

When Howard got into the minivan in Plymouth he had just been attacked by Dick Gephardt; by the time he arrived in Concord 40 minutes later he was responding to criticism lobbed at him by John Kerry.

Kerry had released a statement taking Howard to task for the word he used to describe members of the Palestinian terrorist organization Hamas. Howard had appeared on CNN the day before to defend his position on the Middle East in light of Joe Lieberman's continued criticism. During the course of the interview he described the members of the terrorist group as "soldiers."

Kerry took exception to Howard calling known terrorists soldiers, telling reporters, "Hamas militants are not soldiers in a war – they are terrorists who need to be stopped." And he joined Lieberman in calling Howard's knowledge of the Middle East into question.

When we arrived in Concord Howard had already been on the phone with reporters explaining what he meant. "Obviously I oppose terrorism. Obviously Hamas are terrorists. The reason I answered the way I did is because it was a way of saying the assassination policy against Hamas is justified."

□ □ □

People called out his name and beckoned him over to say hello. Women, old enough to be his grandmother, greeted him with an affectionate hug and kiss on the cheek. Those who had not seen him, but knew he was in the building, peered around hoping for a glimpse of him.

As Howard walked through the Greek Festival in Manchester, New Hampshire, he encountered the same reaction and same question from everyone he met, "Where's George?" The George in question was George Stephanopoulos, who was following Howard for a profile piece he was putting together for his Sunday morning talk show, *This Week*.

The men cooking lamb and women selling Greek pastries politely accepted Howard's hand, but all the while they had one eye on the famous Greek who was a few steps behind. For his part, Stephanopoulos did his best not to steal the limelight, but both men quickly realized that it wasn't going to work. Howard happily facilitated the introductions while Stephanopoulos graciously said hello.

With Stephanopoulos in tow, Howard made his way through the community center at St. George's church. He chatted with the women selling homemade crafts, licked the batter off of a spoon after helping to make loukamades (Greek donuts), and shook hands with people eating dinner under the food tent. The only sore point of the evening came when he was reprimanded by a woman standing in the line to purchase loukamades. He was unaware that he had stepped in front of her and quickly apologized when she pointed the fact out to him. He put his wallet in his pocket and told the woman selling the treats that he'd be back later.

By the time Howard reached the dance floor, Stephanopoulos and his camera crew had left – a good thing for them, otherwise they would have been recruited by Howard to dance. As a band played he held hands with four of his supporters on the empty dance floor. A small group of onlookers watched as they kicked up their legs and moved around in a circle – bumping into each other when they got confused which way they were going. The crowd applauded when the song ended, but Howard was not ready to stop. When the band started up again he grabbed his fellow dancers' hands and kicked up his feet. When the second song ended the bandleader paused and announced, "Let's have another big round of applause for the next president."

September 13, 2003

"O-K-L-A-H-O-M-A!" Howard stood in the Des Moines head-quarters and listened to a group from the state of Oklahoma belt out the classic Rogers and Hammerstein song. When the tune was over they proudly informed him that they had made a nine hour bus ride to see him.

We were back in Iowa for the first time since Labor Day and, like us, they had come to Iowa to attend a steak fry hosted by Iowa U.S. Senator Tom Harkin. The annual event attracted thousands of Iowa caucus goers – and this year hundreds of Dean supporters from around the country.

The Oklahomans may have thought their bus riding days were over, but the campaign had arranged for Dean supporters to ride to the event together in a caravan of school buses. Howard's bus was filled with 40 undecided caucus goers. His goal during the 30-minute ride was to get them to support him. He stood in the front of the bus, made his case, and then opened the floor – or the aisle – up for questions.

Time was up when the bus pulled into Pickard Park in Indianola for a pre-steak fry rally for Dean supporters. It was cold and pouring rain, but that didn't stop more than 500 people from squeezing under the picnic shelter. Wearing clear plastic rain slickers over their orange T-shirts that read, "Hey Harkin These Steaks are DEAN-licious!" the crowd cheered Howard on as he ran through the rain and up onto the top of a picnic table where he stood to address the crowd. Upon proclaiming those present, "My crowd! My people!" he launched into what he promised would be a "fun speech."

□ □ □

Large white tents dotted the muddy field providing protection from the rain to the Democrats who came out to the steak fry. The candidates for president shook hands with those who waited, hungry and wet, in the long lines that stretched to the grills.

Howard's supporters, in their telltale orange T-shirts, wandered around the field while those who couldn't be there in person enjoyed the event via the live reports that were posted on the campaign blog.

The speaking program began with the arrival of the special guest, former President Bill Clinton. Tom Harkin and John Edwards greeted Clinton, dressed in cowboy boots, blue jeans, and a matching shirt. When Howard walked over to say hello, he was stopped by two members of the former president's security detail who informed him he would have to wait for Clinton back by the stage.

Howard, Edwards, Bob Graham, John Kerry, Dennis Kucinich, and Carol Moseley Braun joined Harkin and Clinton on the stage. The large American flag, bales of hay, cornhusks, and apples that decorated the platform were arranged with the precision of Martha Stewart. One by one the candidates – with the exception of Dick Gephardt who had already left – approached the podium and addressed the crowd. Howard, sporting a red and black jacket he borrowed from a member of the staff – he came unprepared for the elements – was introduced to a smattering of cheers from his supporters, who had taken their place along the fence that separated the crowd from the stage.

The theme of Howard's five-minute speech was supposed to be "I believe." His supporters had been instructed to shout, "I believe!" when he posed the question, "Do you believe in (insert subject). But Howard forgot the theme, so his supporters were left with no cheer to chant.

The song "We Are Family" signaled the end of the speaking program. The six candidates along with Clinton and Harkin clapped and swayed to the music. By the time the music started most of those in attendance, with the exception of Howard's supporters who lined the fence waiting to shake his hand, had left to find shelter from the drizzling rain.

September 14, 2003

The summer's so-called "Get on Board with Dean" tour of Iowa was over, only to be replaced with "activist meetings." There was no difference between the two except for the name. Howard was still trying to win support from caucus goers and reach his goal of visiting all 99 counties.

We were 22 counties away when we stopped in the town of Dennison in Crawford County. The town was the home of the actress Donna Reed and had adopted as its slogan, "It's a Wonderful Life," after the movie she starred in of the same name.

The sun was shining when we arrived at Yellow Smoke Park. It was the first time the small group of Democrats who had gathered under the picnic shelter had met Howard, and they had no idea that the scene they were taking part in had been repeated dozens of times over the last few months.

Howard went through the motions. He got out of the van and shook hands with the local Democratic officials who had been lined up by the campaign in front of the shelter. He had his picture taken with each one before joining the rest of the crowd. While he gave his speech the pictures were printed off on a small printer that traveled with us. Before we left he autographed the photos and we left them behind as a reminder of his visit.

Our next stop was at the Clay County Fair in Spencer. The fair was the second largest in the state, behind the Iowa State Fair. We walked around the grounds past the concession stands. Howard stopped to get a glass of root beer and while he waited in line he introduced himself to the two young women in front of him. "I'm Howard Dean and I'm running for president." He summed up the encounter – and the hundreds like it – by explaining to the small group of local Democratic officials with him, "I pounce on unsuspecting citizens to talk about the caucuses."

While people walked by in search of the popcorn vendor, Howard held court at the Democratic Party booth located nearby. He stood on a chair and preached to the people who stopped to listen – both Democrats who knew he would be at the booth and the others who had no choice but to stop because of the crowd blocking their way.

□ □ □

A week after Howard sat next to Mike Ford on an Amtrak train and reluctantly welcomed him back to the campaign, Steve McMahon proposed adding another one of Joe's friends to the campaign staff. We were in Sioux City, Iowa, where we had stopped at a local television station so Howard could appear on the 11 p.m. news broadcast, when Steve called to explain his idea.

Things weren't working and Howard wasn't happy. He was waiting for a new communications director, his schedule was still out of control, and there was no scheduling director in sight. He and Joe had an awkward relationship at best. The two men rarely spoke. And there was confusion in the office brought on by Joe's obsession with the Internet.

Howard was growing tired and it was clear that if things continued as they were there would be major changes. But Joe was reluctant to let anyone help. He was insecure and worried that he was going to be replaced and saw anyone coming into the office as a threat to his position. So Steve proposed bringing in John Haber, a friend of Joe's who was working as a lobbyist in Washington and had worked on the presidential campaigns of Ted Kennedy, Walter Mondale, Dick Gephardt in 1988, and Bill Clinton in 1992. Steve rationalized that Joe would feel comfortable enough with John to let him (along with Mike) manage some of the day-to-day operations.

I liked the idea of bringing someone in, but I didn't think John Haber was the answer. We already had Steve, Paul Maslin, and Mark Squier spending most of their time in the office and Joe wouldn't let them help, so why would John – or Mike Ford for that matter – be any different. Steve explained that John would be coming to Vermont to meet the staff and "observe the operation."

September 15, 2003

Our first stop was in Alabama, a state that didn't hold its primary until June 1. But the primary was secondary to Howard's true purpose for the visit, which was to demonstrate his commitment to the South.

To that end, the campaign planned a town hall meeting at Alabama A & M University, a historically black college in Huntsville. When we walked into the university's multipurpose room we found an audience of several hundred; however, it was mostly white (about two-thirds) and whether it was a function of when people arrived, most of the African Americans were standing toward the back of the room.

Next we flew to Atlanta where before speaking to the more than 1,000 people waiting for him in a downtown city park, Howard launched "Generation Dean." The official youth outreach organization of the campaign had more than 600 groups and 6,000 members nationally. Howard credited the Generation Dean set, 18-to-24-year-olds, with much of the campaign's success. They were one of the first groups to organize over the Internet and on the grassroots level.

The event to officially launch the organization took place at Georgia State University. The stage was set with a group of young people sitting on risers, and handmade signs that read "Dean Rocks" were taped to the walls. Several hundred young people greeted Howard with thunderous applause when he walked into the school's recital hall. When he gave two thumbs up, they cheered louder which seemed to embarrass him because he smiled and turned a light shade of red.

Howard wasn't stodgy, but no one had ever described him as being cool or trendy. He was the 54-year-old father of two Generation Dean-age kids. He knew very little if anything about pop culture and his favorite drink was ginger ale. (He confessed to the MTV camera crew following him that he didn't have cable television and his kids had to visit friends in order to watch the music channel.) Despite this, or perhaps because he never tried to present himself as something he wasn't, the young people in the recital hall – and around the country – embraced him as cool and current.

September 20, 2003

"Dean's imploding" and "his bubble is bursting a bit," John Kerry told a local television station in New York. Whether the comments were the truth, wishful thinking or just frustration on Kerry's part (he trailed in New Hampshire, in Iowa, and in fundraising), the senator predicted that Howard's growing list of "gaffes" (including his most recent "slip" about rolling back the tax cuts) would result in a decline in his poll numbers.

Kerry's comments came as we were making a full-day fundraising swing through the state. We stopped at events in Albany and Hudson, attracting more than 1,250 people. One reception was hosted at the Katonah, New York, home of billionaire George Soros, the global financier and one of *Forbes* magazine's "100 Wealthiest in the World."

Our final event was a glitzy evening fundraiser at a nightclub in New York City. The young man guarding the green door just east of 6th Avenue was fully outfitted with a headset, walkie-talkie, clipboard, and badge that identified him as a member of the Dean campaign staff. He sternly informed us that if we wanted to gain entry into the event we would have to go around to the main entrance and have our names verified on the guest list. Despite all of his equipment, he did not recognize the man standing in front of him as the candidate he was working for. He continued to rebuff our attempts to get in until Howard finally announced, "But, I'm Howard Dean."

Behind the green door was the back stage of the Avalon, an old church turned nightclub. The main room featured a stage, dance floor, and theater seating. When we arrived, Whoopi Goldberg was on stage entertaining the 1,000 people who packed the dance floor and sat in the balcony. Waiting in the wings were the comedian Al Franken, comedian and actress Janeane Garofalo, and the singers Phoebe Snow and Gloria Gaynor.

When Goldberg introduced Howard, the audience of mostly twenty-somethings exploded. He walked on stage and gave Goldberg a hug, his rolled up sleeves and suit pants looking decidedly unhip next to Goldberg in her jeans, dark brown leather jacket, and dark glasses.

Howard stood on the stage perfectly framed by the spotlight that left the rest of the room dark and addressed the crowd. They cheered as he talked health care, taxes, and the war in Iraq. By the time he announced, "You've got the power!" the roar of the crowd was deafening.

He waved to the crowd, but the show was not over. 1970s disco queen Gloria Gaynor joined him on stage. Wearing a floor length red and blue sequin gown she belted out her hit "I Will Survive," while Howard stood alone behind her awkwardly clapping to the beat of the music. He relaxed when Goldberg, Franken, Snow, and Garofalo emerged from the darkness and lined up next to him. He quickly got in the spirit of the event, grabbing the hands of a surprised Goldberg and twirling her around the stage as Gaynor sang. Much to Goldberg's relief the show – and the dancing – ended when the celebrities joined hands with Howard and bowed in unison.

September 23, 2003

It was the shot heard round the world – or at least from Burlington to Boston. After reading a few paragraphs of the speech, Howard folded it in half and stuffed it into the back pocket of his pants. The more than 4,000 people gathered before him in Copley Square in Boston didn't notice the action, but hundreds of miles away in Burlington the campaign staff was reeling.

It all began a few hours earlier when Howard emerged from his Burlington home wearing his JC Penney suit. The weather forecast was predicting rain in the Northeast and he explained that he made the decision to wear it because it repelled water and wouldn't wrinkle. Seeing that he would be taking part in an outdoor rally the decision was a practical one.

We were on our way to the airport to catch a flight to Boston for the rally planned as part of the campaign's month long September to Remember event. The "Democracy Freedom Action" rally would feature what the campaign called a "major address," during which Howard would "lay out what is at stake for Americans in this election."

The music blared as Howard ran through the crowd slapping the hands of his screaming supporters. The threat of rain did nothing to dampen their enthusiasm. Howard was in John Kerry's home state and the crowd was relishing the moment. Dressed in raincoats, they waved their campaign signs high in the air. "Red Sox '03, Dean '04" and "Beantown is Dean town" stood out in the sea of blue and yellow preprinted campaign signs.

Standing before a backdrop that read "Democracy Freedom Action," he placed the speech on the podium. After greeting the crowd with a wave he looked down at the papers and began to read the text:

> Two hundred and thirty years ago, right here in Boston, fifty dedicated patriots known as the Sons of Liberty boarded three ships in Boston Harbor to protest a government more concerned with moneyed interests than its own people. The fifty patriots believed that they had the power and the duty to change their government. What they did that night became known as the Boston Tea Party. It marked the beginning of the first great grassroots campaign in our history. Their action – which they took together – set this country on the path to freedom and democracy. And a King – named George – who had forgotten his own people in favor of special interests, was replaced by a government of, by and for the people.

He was noticeably tentative and a little awkward, stumbling over the words. He faced his supporters knowing they expected to be energized, but he couldn't excite or inspire with a speech he didn't know or one he wasn't sure he even liked.

He had only been given the final draft of the speech a few hours earlier when he boarded the plane in Vermont. The 22-minute flight to Boston wasn't enough time from him to feel adequately prepared, so as the staff in Burlington watched via the live streaming video available on the campaign website he put the speech away and launched into his stump speech – a speech that he knew never failed to excite a crowd.

After one last "You have the power!" he hopped off the stage. In the drizzling rain he walked along the bicycle racks, shaking hands, posing for pictures, and signing autographs – he was in no rush in his weather-resistant suit.

To the supporters gathered, it was an exciting and successful event. But back in Burlington the staff was anything but happy. For them, what had been billed as a "major address" was suddenly no different from the dozens of speeches that had come before. Joe and the others who organized the rally sat fuming in the headquarters, trying to figure out why Howard hadn't delivered the speech they had written, and the only explanation they could come up with was that I had told him not to.

But the reason was simple. He made the decision not to give the speech because they hadn't given him the text in time for him to prepare.

By the time the rally was over everyone was angry and no one was communicating. Howard was tired of the staff in the headquarters not listening to him, so he didn't bother to call them to explain his actions. And no one in Vermont called him. Instead they posted the speech they had drafted – not the one he gave – on the campaign's website. Howard was giving the speech whether he liked it or not.

September 25, 2003

It was time for another debate. The event at New York's Pace University was sponsored by the *Wall Street Journal* and the cable network CNBC. We arrived in New York City just hours before the debate, having flown in after attending a labor breakfast in Michigan. But there was no time for any debate preparation - Howard had a rally to go to.

The rally took place at a small park across the street from the university. Howard stood on a small riser under the sunny sky in his debate attire – a crisp white shirt and pale blue tie. With stop and go traffic moving slowly down the busy street nearby, he spoke to several hundred people, many holding handmade signs.

After shaking hands and posing for pictures, he made his way back to the university only to be followed by the hoard of supporters who had broken free from the bicycle racks that held them a safe distance from the stage. It was only after New York City police arrived that he was able to make his way across the street, and the angry drivers who were forced to stop because of the crowd were allowed to continue down the road.

Once back in the building he waited in a classroom for the debate to start, eating a brownie he picked out of a gift bag stuffed with potato chips, Pellegrino water, Kit Kats, Hershey candy bars, and nuts.

□ □ □

There was one extra podium on the stage. Wes Clark had jumped into the race a week earlier and his appearance at Pace marked his first debate. Many pundits and media types speculated that Howard and Clark would be the targets. Howard because of his front-runner status and Clark because he was seen by many as the candidate that voters unsure of Howard would coalesce around. (Or as *Newsweek* magazine put it, he was one of the candidates who could end up being the "Un-Dean.")

Clark did take some hits for past statements he made supporting George Bush and Ronald Regan and because of his apparent changing position on the war in Iraq. But for the most part he was left alone.

Howard was not so lucky. Dick Gephardt continued to assert that he had joined Newt Gingrich in wanting to cut funding for Medicare. When asked about the accusation during a telephone interview earlier in the day with *USA Today*, Howard called

Gephardt's comments "pathetic, really sad, and plain false." And he continued to dispute them during the debate.

The New York Times described the scene. "Dr. Dean's face reddened and he flashed a look in Mr. Gephardt's direction." Howard answered the charges, "I'm ashamed that you would compare me with Newt Gingrich. I've done more for health insurance, Dick Gephardt, frankly, than you ever have."

September 29, 2003

In 48 hours the time to raise money in the third quarter fundraising period would be over. We were in a race to reach our goal of $15 million. It was a goal Howard wasn't sure we were going to meet, "How the hell are we going to get $2 million in the last day?" To that end we made an early morning exit from Iowa and flew to California.

□ □ □

The 50 people who paid $2,000 each waited for Howard in a private room at the Regency Club in Los Angeles. A campaign memo alerted him to the guests, including a family whose net worth was estimated to be between $10 and $15 billion who could "raise us a lot of money"; a woman who was "very interested in traveling and collecting modern art"; a money manager who would not stop raising money until "you are elected"; and Vidal Sassoon, the founder of the hair products company of the same name.

From the Regency we headed to the home of a legal aid attorney and his wife. The couple, along with an estimated 10,000 other Dean supporters, were taking part in "Dr. Dean's House Call," which, according to the campaign, would be the "largest telephone conference call in history."

We liked to boast about our ability to set records, whether it was for the size of a crowd, the number of people signing up online or the amount of money we raised over the Internet. So it was only natural that we'd take our record setting to the ultimate authority: the *Guinness Book of World Records.*

Howard sat on the couch flanked on each side by the homeowners and dialed into the call. While the dozens of reporters who had packed into the modest living room looked on, Howard and his supporters listened to the singer Melissa Etheridge welcome them to the call and urge them to log on to the campaign's website and make a contribution.

I watched from a few feet away, but I listened on my cell phone. I had dialed in to add my phone line to our record-breaking quest. In the end, the more than 10,000 people who called in from 1,400 separate lines put the Dean campaign in the record books.

□ □ □

"The goal, of course, is to have fun, but it's really to get the hell out of here." We were pulling up to Les Deux Café in Los Angeles for a fundraiser when a member of the campaign's California staff told Howard what he needed to do at the reception. The comment reflected the urgency of our mission to raise money. We had back-to-back fundraising events and if we were going to reach $15 million we had to keep on schedule.

We spent one hour at the reception for "major players" in the entertainment industry hosted by the actress Beth Broderick (best known for her role as Aunt Zelda in the late '90s television show *Sabrina the Teenage Witch*) before moving on to the final event of the night – a reception at a private home for 50 "affluent" people who each paid $2,000 to meet Howard.

September 30, 2003

Howard stood on the sidewalk in Burbank, California, strumming his guitar. Two hand lettered signs were propped up next to him, "Will Strum for the Presidency" and "Your Change for Real

Change." His guitar case was open, ready to accept any spare coins the passersby were willing to throw his way.

It was the last day in the third quarter fundraising period and the campaign had put on a final push to bring in last minute donations. And although Howard would have gladly accepted any money the pedestrians donated, his true purpose for standing on the sidewalk was to tape a skit for NBC's *Tonight Show with Jay Leno*. The show's producers and a camera crew stood a few feet away directing the action. It was Howard's first foray into acting and to make sure he got it right we enlisted the help of actor, writer, producer, and Dean supporter Rob Reiner.

The taping went off without a hitch. Howard strummed the blues, bobbing his head, while two actors walked by on cue, ignoring him. The third passerby stopped, read the signs, and threw a dollar bill into the guitar case – it was Rob Reiner making a cameo appearance. Howard said, "Thank you," and continued strumming.

When the taping was complete we said good-bye to the people who lined the sidewalk waiting to become part of the studio audience and went inside where we were escorted to a small waiting room that held a couch, chair, television, and a fruit platter.

While Howard waited for the late afternoon taping to begin he decided to say hello to the other guest appearing on the show, the actress Catherine Zeta-Jones, who was in the room next to his. With her flawless hair and makeup and skintight black cocktail dress, she looked ready to walk down a red carpet. Howard rarely went to the movies, so he had no idea who she was, a fact he didn't admit to her. But she knew him, a fact that delighted him.

It would be Howard's first appearance on the *Tonight Show* or any late night show for that matter. Although the show had an interview format, it was a comedy show at heart and he worried that he wouldn't be funny enough. But Leno and his staff weren't going to let him fail – having an entertaining show was in their best interests. A few days before the taping, I received a call from one of the producers. He was looking for interesting or funny things about Howard that Leno could talk to him about. With the producer's help I came up with a list.

I sat backstage with Rob Reiner and watched Howard walk across the stage and sit in the chair next to Leno's desk. After inquiring about the presidential race, the comedian asked Howard about his JC Penney suit, one of the topics I had passed on to the show's producer.

He grinned as he told Leno about his favorite suit, a suit he explained that he was no longer allowed to wear outside of Vermont because so many people complained that the pants were too short. He reminisced about the day he put the dry clean-only suit in the washing machine and how it came out of the dryer clean and wrinkle free – a testament to the fact that it was of a higher quality than the pricier designer labels he was now forced to wear.

□ □ □

The confetti cannon sent small pieces of paper raining down on the crowd. It was the end of the fundraising period and the event at Union Station in Los Angeles was a celebration of the campaign's fundraising success.

A large image of the contribution counting bat was projected onto a screen in the front of the room. Like the ball that drops in Times Square on New Year's Eve, the bat was ready to flash the final fundraising total at exactly 12 a.m. Eastern Time.

The anticipation in the room was high. Hundreds of people were waiting for Howard to take the stage and announce the final number. Timing was everything. He needed to be on stage one minute before midnight – no earlier and no later – in order to make the announcement when the clock struck midnight.

We waited backstage, and along with the crowd watched a slide show of motivational quotes, listened to a comedian make a fundraising phone call, and took part in an interactive "spoken word performance." (A first for me.)

At 8:55 p.m. California time (11:55 p.m. on the East Coast), the countdown was on. Howard took his position at the bottom of the stairs that led up to the stage. One minute later "We Can" played and he made his way up. He waved to the cheering crowd and right on time – and synchronized with the bat – announced the final fundraising total while confetti flew into the air.

The number $15 million flashed on the screen and it made Howard the undisputed money-raising leader. He had crushed his opponents in fundraising during the third quarter. In fact, added together Kerry's $4 million, Gephardt's $3.8 million, Lieberman's $3.6 million, Clark's $3.5 million, and Edwards' $2.6 million barely topped the total amount Howard had raised.

Added to the previous two fundraising quarters, the $15 million brought Howard's year to date total to $25 million, surpassing the $20 million raised during the same time period by John Kerry. Our campaign also boasted a record setting $14 million in Internet contributions for the first nine months of the year.

—OCTOBER—

October 1, 2003

Howard's supporters were still celebrating when we left Los Angeles on an airplane bound for Vermont. And it was on the small private plane that we would welcome in the first day of October, the deadline Howard had imposed for hiring a new communications director and a scheduling director.

Before we reached Burlington, our final destination, we made a stop in Chicago. Howard was scheduled to tout his fundraising success on the early morning television shows, but we wouldn't arrive in Vermont in time so the quick stop was necessary. It was 4:30 a.m. when we arrived at an empty terminal at Chicago's O'Hare airport.

It was now a requirement, one imposed by Howard, that he be given at least one hour each day of "down time," or time that was not scheduled – allowing him to relax or do what he wanted. That day he was free to live it up between 4:30 a.m. and 5:30 a.m. We passed the time sitting in a small airport conference room eating the left over popcorn we found in the terminal and chatting with the production crew that would facilitate Howard's appearance via satellite on the five morning shows – ABC, CBS, CNN, Fox, and NBC.

By the time the sun came up, Howard learned that he had neither a new communications director nor a scheduling director. No effort had been made to find someone to oversee the schedule and instead of a new communications director he had a new press secretary. He had no problem with adding a press secretary to the staff and was happy with who was hired (Jay Carson served as a spokesperson for U.S. Senator Tom Daschle), but it didn't address the problem he was trying to fix – Joe's presence in the news.

October 3, 2003

The new month brought changes to the way we moved around the country. For close to two years Howard and I had stood in long lines at airport gates and bunked at private homes. Over the month of September we had begun to shift to charter airplanes and hotel stays. By October it was our regular way of life.

Our comfort wasn't the reason we were flying on private planes or staying in hotels. In fact, the first planes we flew on were anything but comfortable. They were small and cramped, seating at most eight passengers. The two pilots who made up the crew would point out the basket of candy and cooler of soda that served as our in-flight refreshments and recite the safety instructions before climbing into the open cockpit just a few feet away from our seats.

The changes allowed us to spend more hours in a day campaigning. We weren't at the mercy of commercial airline schedules and we didn't have to worry about keeping our hosts up waiting for us to arrive.

Our use of private planes didn't sit well with Howard's supporters, who feared losing their candidate in a plane crash. They posted comments by the dozens on the campaign's blog urging us to stop the practice and go back to flying commercial.

Our entourage also grew. I had been the only staff person regularly traveling with Howard, but we finally acknowledged the challenges that came with his growing popularity and increased the traveling staff from one to two. Mike O'Mary, a member of the New Hampshire staff, joined us on the road.

We were also joined by members of the news media, who became our constant companions. Representatives from ABC, CBS, Fox, MSNBC, and the *New York Times* were traveling with us on a regular basis. And David Broder was right, they made it possible for us to afford the airplane.

□ □ □

In our rented plane and with our new entourage in tow, we ventured out on another orchestrated cross-country excursion. The "Raise the Roots Tour" – patterned after our successful Sleepless Summer Tour in August – took Howard to college campuses from one coast to the other and in between. The tour wasn't as grand as the summer tour, but its purpose was the same: motivate the masses and prove the overwhelming support Howard was receiving from the grassroots, in this case 18- to 24-year-olds, also known as "Generation Dean."

The four-day, six-city tour began at Howard University in Washington, D.C. The school wasn't picked solely because it shared the same name with the candidate – although that didn't hurt – it also happened to be a predominately black university.

While the tour featured our trademark rallies, the event at Howard University was different. It was structured to educate more than motivate and reflected Howard's continuing efforts to make his case to African American voters.

There was no rally. In its place was a town hall-style meeting in a lecture hall at the university's business school. Standing in front of the more than 100 people who sat ready to listen, the only clue that Howard wasn't a professor teaching a class was the large campaign banner that hung behind him. He didn't remove his suit coat or roll up his sleeves; instead, he delivered a muted version of his stump speech that was more befitting the academic setting. In the end, the student-teacher relationship was reversed with Howard talking questions from the audience.

When the event was over, Howard, Joe, and I left the press behind and made a covert visit to a town house on Capitol Hill.

Conflicting news reports the day before had Bob Graham either dropping out of the race or continuing on. If he was planning to end his campaign, Howard wanted his support. Like Howard, Graham opposed the war, a fact he thought worked in his favor.

Howard and Joe met with Graham and his wife for 30 minutes. They emerged from the meeting with no promise of an endorsement, but Howard had something to think about. Would he make Graham his running mate?

□ □ □

It was late afternoon by the time our plane landed in Charleston, South Carolina. The sun was going down when Howard reached the stage set up in an outdoor courtyard at the College of Charleston. Standing next to him – in front of the mostly white audience – was Illinois congressman Jesse Jackson, Jr. who had accompanied Howard to the southern state in an effort to attract African American support.

It was a typical Dean rally, replete with a boisterous sign-waving crowd and the familiar "You have the power!" chant by Howard. It ended like all the others with our anthem "We Can" playing while Howard signed autographs and posed for pictures.

When the rally was over, we left the fresh air of the college courtyard and went to a nearby bar for a Generation Dean "social." The lights were dim and the cloud of cigarette smoke that hung in the air made it hard to distinguish the college students from the regular patrons. The only clearly identifiable Dean supporters were the handful of young people who wore white T-shirts adorned with the words "Generation Dean."

Dozens of people sat at the tables that were scattered around the room, others were propped up on the stools next to the bar. Howard, unsure of what to do, walked around the room shaking hands and introducing himself, "Hi, I'm Howard Dean." The regular patrons had no idea who he was or why he was being so friendly. In his business suit, the ginger ale-drinking, non-smoker looked like a fish out of water.

When it came time for him to speak, the young people crowded around the small stage while the regulars looked on confused by the scene. As the lights of the disco ball hanging over his head swirled around him, he yelled a few words over the music. But he quickly gave up when he realized that no one could hear him.

October 4, 2003

We were off to Norman, Oklahoma. Howard sat in the back of the plane, looking disheveled in his suit coat and open shirt collar, yawning and stretching as Generation Dean leader Ginny Hunt briefed him on the day's activities.

More than 1,000 young people had gathered in the Sharp Concert Hall at the University of Oklahoma waiting for what the *Norman (OK) Transcript* described as a "high-energy rap session" with Howard.

On the stage, 30 young people dressed in identical white Generation Dean T-shirts were arranged on three rows of risers.

They would serve as the backdrop for the event. Howard sat in the front row between two students and listened as a young woman introduced him. His light blue shirt, red tie, and touch of gray in his hair were dead giveaways that he was not a member of the Dean generation. Despite the fact that he was old enough to be their father, the young people treated him like a contemporary.

His declaration that he didn't know what a blog was before the campaign was greeted with delight instead of the eye rolling a parent would receive by such an admission. They listened intently as he referenced growing up in the 1960s – a decade that was as foreign to them as life without cell phones. He gave them a lesson in history with references to John F. Kennedy and Martin Luther King, Jr. And he had them hooting when he joked that he hadn't checked out the bar scene in Norman, so he didn't know if being a 20-year-old in 2003 was like being twenty in the '60s.

By the time he announced, "You have the power!" the crowd was on their feet. When "We Can" began to play Howard ran off the stage and into the crowd to sign autographs and pose for pictures.

From Oklahoma we flew to Seattle with the knowledge that the scene would repeat itself. The monotony of the never changing rallies was matched by the boredom of sitting on an airplane for hours.

Each leg of the journey was a continuation of the one before. Candy, soda, and sandwich wraps awaited us. We swapped seats, but the plane was so small that we'd end up sitting next to the same people. Joe sat in the back of the plane reciting his history in politics. He never missed a beat, always picking up where he left off. His storytelling prompted one reporter to exclaim, "Oh, God. We're only on 1988!"

We were settling in for the flight to Seattle when the flight attendant produced a deck of cards. Howard and the press had an adversarial relationship, but when the cards came out their differences were forgotten. Who would have guessed that boredom would be a unifier?

The spirited game of hearts that ensued between Howard, Eric Saltzman of CBS, Marc Ambinder of ABC, and Jodi Wilgoren of the *New York Times* would become – along with the basket of candy – a tradition.

□ □ □

When we arrived in Seattle the position of scheduling director was still not filled. Howard had made it clear that filling the position was a top priority, along with finding a new communications director. He fell short of making a change in the communications office, but it was progress compared to finding a scheduling director where little effort had been made.

During the trip Howard took it upon himself to offer the job to Todd Dennett. We first met Todd during the Sleepless Summer Tour and now he was helping with the Seattle leg of the Raise the Roots Tour. Howard didn't consult with Joe, despite the fact that he was with us in Seattle. Instead, he informed Joe of the hire only after Todd agreed to take the job.

October 5, 2003

At 7:30 a.m. the Raise the Roots Express left Seattle. By 1:30 p.m. Howard was standing in the hallway outside a ballroom at the University of Iowa in Cedar Rapids listening to the more than 900 people gathered inside chant, "We want Dean!"

The scene was familiar. On a stage, young people dressed in Dean T-shirts were arranged on risers behind a podium. A large campaign banner hung from above. Howard played his part by bounding up the stairs, shaking hands with the students, and launching into his speech: health care, balancing the budget, rolling back the Bush tax cuts, and the bar scene in Cedar Rapids.

The only indication that we weren't living the same day over and over were the adjustments Howard made to his speech to reflect current events. Two days earlier the U.S. Justice Department announced that investigators would begin interviewing Bush administration officials in an effort to find out who leaked the name of CIA operative Valerie Plame to the media.

Howard tried to make news and rally the young people by comparing the actions of the Bush administration in regards to Plame with events that occurred under the presidency of Richard Nixon. (He had made a similar argument a month earlier when he compared Bush's handling of the Iraq war with Nixon and the Vietnam War.) He told the crowd, "Richard Nixon's presidency came to an end because they lied about a third rate burglary . . . and they covered it up. In this presidency the administration has lied and covered up the exposure of a CIA agent. This presidency reminds me more and more every day of the presidency of Richard Milhous Nixon."

The crowd applauded, but not with the same fervor as when Howard expressed his opposition to the Iraq war. It seemed the Nixon analogy was better suited for the parents of those gathered.

From Iowa we flew to Madison, Wisconsin. When we arrived at the University of Wisconsin, the campaign's state director briefed Howard on the important issues facing the state: The Green Bay Packers and the Badgers, the University of Wisconsin's football team, had won their most recent games.

The more than 5,000 people who were held back from the stage by a sea of bicycle racks greeted him with a roar when he hopped on stage, waved, and announced, "Good gracious! This is an amazing crowd. You might have thought the Badgers won yesterday and the Packers won today."

He tried the Nixon analogy again, but got the same muted response he received a few hours earlier in Iowa. In fact, the crowd's reaction paled in comparison to the cheers he received when he referenced the two football teams.

Nevertheless, he gave a fiery speech that left the crowd wanting more. After he had worked his way down the line of bicycle racks, reaching in ten people deep to shake every hand he could, he ran back on stage and gave his supporters one last thumbs up – and they gave him one last roar.

October 6, 2003

It was after midnight when our flight from Wisconsin arrived in Lebanon, New Hampshire, for the last day of the Raise the Roots Tour.

After a few hours of sleep at a local hotel, we headed out to visit the first of two college campuses. But before making our way to Keene State College, we took a detour from our purpose and stopped at the Earl Borden Senior Center in Claremont. The center was on the way to Keene and was a convenient place for a meeting with seniors, the AARP kind.

Before he walked into the meeting, Howard asked me to call Bob Rogan and have him call Bob Graham's chief of staff. Graham was still in the race, but by all indications not for long. Howard had made a decision about whether he would choose Graham as his running mate if he won the nomination. He wanted the chief of staff to know what he had decided so Graham wouldn't be surprised when the two men spoke later in the day.

□ □ □

The smell of waffles wafted through the student center at Keene State College. The Kerry campaign was serving up the breakfast treat to the students, many of whom were on their way to the rally for Howard.

Kerry was using the waffles to symbolize what he claimed were Howard's changing positions on issues. We weren't bothered by the gimmick. To the contrary, Dean supporters and campaign workers happily indulged in the free food provided courtesy of the Kerry campaign.

After rallying the troops who filled the lawn outside the student center, Howard went into an empty classroom and placed a call to Bob Graham. He respected the senator, but couldn't promise him a place on the ticket. He would put Graham on his list of potential running mates, however, should he secure the nomination.

By the time we reached the University of New Hampshire in Durham for the last rally of the tour the Kerry campaign had reached a high point in creativity – a human waffle was waiting for us.

Sandwiched in between two pieces of painted yellow cardboard was a college-age man. His arms, legs, and head popped out through the holes that had been cut in the larger than life waffle. While we preferred the edible kind, the cardboard waffle was amusing and flattering. Forget the poll numbers, magazine covers, and money, being followed around by a person wearing a costume was the true sign that a candidate had made it. (Although I thought we were deserving of a waffle made of foam not cardboard – it would have been more realistic.)

□ □ □

The Raise the Roots Tour was over, but the day wasn't. At 9 p.m. Howard was playing pool at the Ten Pin Lanes in Manchester, New Hampshire. We were at the combination bar and bowling alley for an off-the-record bonding session with the media covering the campaign.

While we were playing pool and eating greasy bar food, Bob Graham was preparing to appear on CNN's *Larry King Live* to announce that he was ending his campaign.

But the changing face of the presidential campaign was not on the minds of anyone in the bar. The televisions were tuned to a playoff game between the Boston Red Sox, the hometown team, and the Oakland A's. And it seemed that it wasn't a top priority for King either, who relegated Graham to the last 10 minutes of the show. The senator was forced to wait while King interviewed Roy Horn, the Las Vegas performer who had been mauled by a tiger.

October 9, 2003

We were in Phoenix, Arizona, for a debate sponsored by CNN. By now, taking time to prepare for a debate rarely happened. The time was set aside on the schedule, but we used it to do anything but prepare.

We sat in a small conference room on the ground floor of the Wyndham Park Hotel. There were no windows, just four white walls. Outside, the sun was shining brightly in the afternoon sky, but for us it could easily have been the middle of the night.

Joe Costello was tapping on his computer, writing something that Howard would never take the time to read. (Joe Trippi had hired Costello a month earlier to develop the campaign message, but Howard didn't like Costello's writing style and refused to give any speech he wrote. That didn't stop the campaign, however, from using his ideas on the website or in literature.) Joe Trippi was checking the activity on the Internet while trading barbs with me. (They were nothing significant. We just couldn't be in the same room without fighting.) Meanwhile, Howard sat next to us making phone calls and writing thank you notes, ignoring what was going on around him.

The debate at the Phoenix's Orpheum Theater was the second time Wes Clark appeared with his rivals and he, along with Howard, was a target.

The Democrats had mostly ignored Clark during the debate at Pace University two weeks earlier. But since then he had vaulted to the top of some national polls and had raised close to $3.5 million. His instant success necessitated action from his rivals. And although he was blessed with success, he was also cursed with the same problem faced by many newcomers to politics – statements he had made in the past.

Howard took Clark to task for apparently changing his position on the war in Iraq. Upon entering the race, the retired general expressed his opposition to the war, yet Howard reminded him that a year earlier he had counseled a congressional candidate in New Hampshire to support the military action. Clark was also questioned about his loyalty to the Democratic Party. Why had he expressed support for President Bush and Vice President Cheney and why had he voted for Ronald Reagan?

Howard didn't leave the 90-minute debate unscathed. He was ahead in New Hampshire, in a dead heat with Dick Gephardt in Iowa, and he was the top fundraiser – making him still the one to beat. Gephardt, looking towards Iowa, once again compared his record on Medicare to that of Newt Gingrich. Howard (avoiding the red face of the Pace debate) answered by joking that he had been compared to the liberal former senator and presidential candidate George McGovern (the Democratic Leadership Council had made the accusation because of this anti-war stance) and now he was being compared to the conservative former House speaker. Which one is it? he asked his rivals.

□ □ □

After the debate, Howard, Joe Trippi, Tricia Enright, and I drove to the private airfield in Phoenix where our plane was waiting. It was close to 9 p.m. and we were tired and hungry, so it felt like we had won the lottery when the airport staff told us that food had been put on our plane.

We said hello and good-bye to Wes Clark, who had just arrived to catch his own plane, and boarded our small jet, eager to get home and ready for food. We looked around, but all we could find was the almost empty basket containing the candy that we didn't like enough to eat on the flight out the day before. It turned out that the food the airport staff told us about was for Clark, not us.

We were asleep – or as asleep as one could be sitting up in a cramped airplane – when the wheels of the plane hit the runway at 4:30 a.m. We were home, or so we thought, until the pilot emerged from the cockpit and announced that we were in Allentown, Pennsylvania. He explained that because of construction on the airport runway in Vermont we had to delay our landing by 45 minutes and for lack of a better place they stopped in Allentown.

The pilots turned the lights on in the dark and empty Allentown airport as we looked around for a place to pass the time. Howard decided to take a nap on a small love seat in the waiting area. Joe, Tricia, and I settled into the recliners in the pilots' lounge and watched infomercials on the television while eating Pop-Tarts we bought out of the vending machine with the spare change we pooled together. Whether it was due to exhaustion or the fruit-filled toaster pastries, Joe and I were able to sit in the same room without fighting.

Forty-five minutes later, Howard was up and analyzing the weather radar with the pilots. Now it was rain and wind that would delay our landing in Burlington. The pilots were content to wait until the weather cleared (which could have been several hours), but Howard wasn't. He wanted to get home. So he came up with a new plan. We would fly to Plattsburgh, New York, a city just 80 miles from Burlington.

Two hours had passed since our scheduled arrival in Vermont and we hadn't received any telephone calls from the headquarters asking where we were. A staff person was supposed to meet us at the Burlington airport at 5 a.m., but we clearly weren't there. The candidate was missing, yet no one was looking for him.

Once the pilots agreed to fly us to Plattsburgh we called Chris Canning, who worked in the scheduling office, and asked him to pick us up in New York. If he left Burlington as soon as he hung up he could make it to Plattsburgh at almost the same time we would.

The small airport in Plattsburg was eerily quite. Joe, Tricia, and I sat inside listening to a ringing phone go unanswered. Howard, too anxious to sit, walked in circles in the parking lot waiting for Chris to arrive.

"What a f - - - - - - nightmare," Howard declared when we got into Chris's car just after 8:20 a.m. He was right and so was Joe when he responded, "It's not over yet."

Plattsburgh, New York, may have been closer to Vermont than Allentown, but we were still an hour away from home. And if we were going to get from New York to Vermont we had to cross Lake Champlain, which meant taking the ferry across the lake that separated the two states.

The other riders on the ferry did a double take when they saw Howard, but no one was more surprised than the ferry operators, who had watched the debate in Phoenix the night before and couldn't figure out how we landed on their ferry boat. When they heard our sad tale they invited us up to the top of the boat to meet the captain. They also offered us the free sticky buns and plastic coffee mugs they were giving away in celebration of customer appreciation day. We skimmed across the lake arriving in Vermont in 12 minutes.

We hopped back into the car for the final leg of the journey, but we were soon stopping at the Island Beverage and Redemption Center in South Hero, Vermont, (population 1,800) so Joe could get his daily fix of Diet Pepsi.

The 10-hour journey ended when we pulled into Howard's driveway. We laughed with relief at finally making it to Burlington. Howard bid us good-bye and with his suitcase in hand wearily walked into his house.

October 14, 2003

It was our first day in Iowa since the Raise the Roots rally at the University of Iowa, more than a week earlier. And it felt like we were back to real campaigning. The screaming crowds of young fans were replaced by small groups of undecided voters – voters who weren't clinging to every word Howard said, instead, ones who expected him to earn their support.

We spent the day in nine small towns. The first stop was in Sidney, Iowa, a town with a population of 1,300.

Howard pointed up to the "soda fountain" sign hanging in the window. It had been a long time since he had seen one of those. When we walked into the drugstore we found the sign wasn't just something left over from bygone days, there actually was a soda fountain.

It was clear that the pharmacy wasn't just a place to shop; it was the gathering place for the town's residents. Howard went to work, introducing himself to the people enjoying their morning coffee at the counter (probably in the same seats they occupied every day). He made his way over to the set of booths that sat between the shelves holding drugs, gifts, and other knick-knacks. With an outstretched hand, he announced, "Hi, I'm Howard Dean."

He could have been mistaken for a friendly neighbor had it not been for the handful of reporters and media cameras trained on his every move.

□ □ □

It felt like we had driven onto a movie set. The streets, lined in red brick, were dotted with family businesses. The large brick courthouse was surrounded by immaculately groomed green grass. A dome of cloudless blue sky hovered above. The town of Mount Ayr, Iowa, (population 1,800) was perfect.

Howard posed for pictures outside the courthouse with the local Democratic officials who had been lined up in advance by the campaign staff.

Inside, he was greeted politely by the group of three dozen Democrats who sat in the rows of wooden seats in the courthouse's community room. As he would all day, he kept his suit coat on instead of removing it and rolling up his sleeves like his fans were accustomed to him doing. The respectful gesture was made in recognition of the fact that he wasn't speaking to the converted.

The group contained very few from the Generation Dean set. Instead most in the room were sixty or older and Howard had to introduce himself to those gathered, something he never had to do at rallies. He began his speech with a summary of his personal and political history, the same one he recited for the first time during a visit to New Hampshire a year and a half earlier: family, medical practice, Carter delegate, lieutenant governor, and finally governor.

He launched into his speech leaving out the yelling and screaming and the "You have the power" ending. He dutifully answered questions for the inquisitive crowd after asking for "questions, comments, and rude remarks."

The scene would be replayed for the rest of the day in a small wood paneled community room at a local library, in a hotel lobby decorated in colorful country prints, and at the Get To Gather Room where Tupperware containers filled with homemade cookies and brownies lined the long wooden bar – a treat for those who made it to the end of Howard's speech.

October 15, 2003

It was one day, but seemed like two. We began with pizza and beer and ended with wine and cheese.

It was mid-morning when we arrived at George's Pizza Steak House in Keosauqua, Iowa. The colorful neon signs in the restaurant's window advertised some of what the family-owned establishment had to offer: Budweiser, Bud Lite, and pizza. Two dozen of the town's undecided voters sat inside listening to Howard explain why they should support him.

When the event was over they streamed out onto the sidewalk shaking hands and getting in one last question. Before Howard hopped into the van he posed for a picture under the red neon pizza sign with the restaurant's owners and employees, all dressed in T-shirts and wrapped in white aprons.

Our next stop was at a senior center in Knoxville, Iowa. The seniors listened intently as Howard told them that he was a doctor and the former governor of Vermont. They followed him through his days a delegate for Jimmy Carter and his decision to run for president.

Many wanted to ask him a question; others just wanted him to leave. While he was speaking to one group of seniors, a handful of others sat at one of the large round tables scattered throughout the room. They had no interest in listening to a presidential candidate (even if it was the front-runner). They were there to play cards and in what could only be described as an act of rebellion, they openly continued their game even after Howard had launched into the substance of his speech.

By the time the sun had gone down we were walking into a swanky loft apartment in Kansas City, Missouri. The white walls were covered with modern artwork and expensive sculptures stood around the open space. Close to 100 people – dressed to be elegant, yet casual at the same time – had paid for what the card-playing seniors just wanted to ignore. A contribution of between $500 and $1,000 got them 45 minutes with Howard plus wine and cheese and a buffet dinner, which was over by the time we arrived.

After the reception we headed to the Uptown Theater where more than 750 people were waiting. They were at the cheaper but rowdier event – tickets were just $50. Howard gave the same speech he gave in Iowa earlier in the day – minus the dissertation of his history and his suit coat – there were no undecided voters here.

October 19, 2003

John Edwards didn't know what to say. Edwards, along with Howard, was speaking at the Institute of Politics at St. Anselm's College in Manchester, New Hampshire. He had finished his speech and was getting into his car when Howard hopped off the back of the box truck that had just driven into the parking lot. Howard greeted his rival, "Hi, John," then walked into the building as if arriving on the back of a truck was standard procedure.

The incident began a few minutes earlier when Howard was greeting supporters who were standing at the top of the driveway that led to the school building. As he was chatting with them a red box truck carrying sound equipment drove in and stopped. As a joke on his staff who were standing on the other side of the driveway and couldn't see him, he stepped up onto the back of the truck. The driver didn't know he was there and proceeded down the driveway.

The supporters who had seen him hop up began to laugh as the truck drove away and that's when the rest of us saw him. The step he was standing on was at most a foot wide. He was stretched out flat against the back door of the truck holding on for dear life.

He jumped off in front of the stunned Edwards and members of his own staff, who reminded him that such daredevil tricks from a presidential candidate didn't set a good example for the youth of America.

October 20, 2003

Howard was putting his suit coat on when he emerged from the van in front of Lally's Restaurant in the town of La Mars, Iowa. (A town that according to the sign we passed on the drive there was just 8.5 miles from Pumpkin Land.) It was the beginning of a three-day tour of the state and our goal was to complete our task of visiting each of the state's 99 counties. We had 13 to go.

We began the journey on the western side of the state where Iowa bordered Nebraska, and over the three days we traveled eastward through the state's most northern counties until we reached Wisconsin.

The scene in front of Lally's was a familiar one. Howard said hello and then posed for pictures with the handful of local Democratic leaders the campaign had assembled. When the pleasantries were completed, he walked into the family-owned restaurant and into the back section where a group of close to 50 undecided voters were waiting. They sat at tables in the wood paneled room eating the lunch they had ordered off the menu.

Howard approached each table and either by force of habit or to make sure there was no confusion that he was the man they had all come to see, he extended his hand to each guest and greeted them with an upbeat, "Hi, I'm Howard Dean."

Most in the room were older voters – meaning 50 or older – and they were truly undecided. They listened, but rarely offered any reaction to his words – until the end when they grilled him on subjects ranging from the war in Iraq to prescription drug prices.

Forty-five minutes after arriving, Howard was back out on the sidewalk. It was a picture- perfect scene. His suit coat was slung over his shoulder and a group of interested voters was standing with him in a circle. They bobbed their heads in nods of approval as he outlined his position on prescription drug prices and health care. Howard was winning them over.

As he was moving to another subject, Steve McMahon interrupted and asked him to move over a few inches, he needed to get another camera angle. The perfect scene was being shot for a television commercial. The half dozen people surrounding Howard weren't actors, but they weren't undecided voters either. They were die-hard Dean supporters who had to be reminded to peel off their campaign stickers before the cameras began to roll.

□ □ □

"My goal is to get 17-year-olds to caucus," Howard told the principal of the Central Lyon High School in Rock Rapids. (Seventeen-year-olds are allowed to caucus in Iowa as long as they will be eighteen on Election Day.) It was 3:15 p.m. and students were still milling around the locker-lined hallways as Howard made his way to the school's library.

When he walked in he found two dozen older voters (no seventeen-year-olds were in sight) sitting in the chairs that had been lined up in between the stacks of books. Steve McMahon was standing in front of the group explaining that the camera and large fuzzy microphone dangling from above were there to tape Howard for a television commercial and he hoped they wouldn't mind.

When the speech was over, Howard shook hands with the seniors who were enjoying the cookies, brownies, and punch made just for the occasion. As he was eyeing the snack table, he was pulled away by Jeani Murray who explained that there was no time for food – we were late.

After stops at two public library community rooms, we reached the site of the final event of the night: Iowa Lakes Community College in Estherville. When Howard walked into the small lecture hall he received the most enthusiastic greeting of the day. The crowd stood, clapped, and waved their Dean signs. They were all seniors, but not the college kind.

By the time we pulled up to the Suburban Motel in Emmetsburg, we had traveled north, east, south, and north again and were six counties closer to visiting every county in the caucus state.

<u>October 21, 2003</u>

The day was similar to the one before.

The glass counters at McNally's Bakery in Emmetsburg displayed the muffins, fritters, donuts, bread, and cookies made fresh in the kitchen a few feet away. Whether the dozens of people gathered at the restaurant were drawn there by Howard or the freshly made treats was up for debate.

The ceiling fans whirled overhead at the Chrome Truck Stop in Algona as Howard described to the small group of people sitting at the faux wood covered tables how he was tired of Dick Gephardt misrepresenting his position on Medicare.

The young children squirmed in their seats during the all school assembly in the Lake Mills High School Auditorium. Howard had failed the impossible task of making his speech interesting to the five-year-olds who were forced to listen along with the high school students.

A woman in Joice, Iowa, cut pepperoni and arranged it on a plate along with cheese and crackers as Howard stood in her living room making his pitch to her neighbors who had gathered to meet him.

Along the way he posed for pictures, answered questions, and Steve continued to collect footage for a television commercial.

The day did bring one change. Howard had made an addition to his speech. He recounted meeting the parents of his daughter's college roommate for the first time in 2002. The young woman's mother asked him what he was going to do when he left the governor's office. When he told the Connecticut woman that he was going to run for president she began to laugh, only stopping when she realized he was serious. After the crowd stopped giggling, he explained the moral of the story: While others found the prospects of him running for president funny, Iowans always took the news seriously because they knew they got to choose the party's nominee.

October 22, 2003

Howard, dressed in blue jeans, a white polo shirt, boots, and a black windbreaker he borrowed from a staffer, listened as the farmer talked about the difference in the smell of liquid manure versus the dry base variety. Just a few feet away the source of the smell roamed around their pens.

We began the day at a family farm in Clear Lake, Iowa, hearing firsthand the impact that large hog lots had on smaller family farms in the state.

The big hogs chose to focus on eating the feed corn that lined the ground while the small pigs ran around like excited children when Howard greeted them with, "Hi, guys." The farmer had taken us behind his barn so we could get a look at his hogs. In his jeans and boots, Howard looked at home, but the same could not be said for the writer from *Vogue* magazine who stepped gingerly, trying not to soil her black patent leather shoes and white knee length coat.

A photograph of a candidate with a cuddly animal is almost as good as one of a candidate kissing a baby and Howard readily posed for a picture with the pigs, joking with the press photographers, "Don't I have to get around a cute one?"

After the tutorial on large factory farms, Howard changed into his suit and boarded the bus that would take us, along with two dozen supporters and members of the media, through the final counties that would lead us to our goal of visiting all 99.

By the time our bus pulled up in front of the home of a supporter in the town of Waukon, we had driven down miles of straight roads, past farms, silos and water towers, eaten BLTs and peanut butter sandwiches, and sung multiple choruses of "The Wheels on the Bus."

We were visiting Allamakee County for the first time. This made the northeastern county, which bordered Minnesota and Wisconsin, our 98th.

Two dozen undecided voters sat in mismatched chairs that clearly came from all over the house and had been set up in the living room. The people who couldn't fit in the living room stood shoulder to shoulder on the sun porch and strained to hear Howard as the family pet, a black and white cat, playfully walked in circles around their feet.

During the question time one person was concerned that Howard didn't smile enough. To which he grinned and conceded that he could smile more.

□ □ □

The 99th county was fittingly Howard County, picked to be last for the obvious reason.

When our bus rolled into the town of Cresco we stopped at the county courthouse. Howard posed for pictures with his supporters under the Howard County Courthouse sign that hung from the building's brick façade. He was decked out for the occasion in a red, white, and blue shirt emblazoned with "Howard" on the front that we was given during his visit to Washington, D.C.'s Howard University. It seemed as good a time as any to bring out the shirt. He took the opportunity to pose for a picture with the media traveling with us. Although they had just recently joined us on the trail, he felt they had been around long enough to share in the milestone.

The main event took place at Crestwood High School. The people sitting in the metal folding chairs stood and cheered when Howard made his way into the school's student center. The yellow and blue balloons that decorated the room made the event feel more like a celebration than the introduction to undecided caucus goers that it was intended to be.

Ever sensitive to what he was wearing (he rarely met Iowa voters without his suit coat), he explained to those gathered that a "Howard" shirt was not his normal attire, but given where he was he thought it would be okay to wear it.

Keeping the Howard theme going he stood in front of the Howard County flag and some in the crowd wore white T-shirts with "H3" written on the front. The meaning of the mysterious symbol was spelled out on the back: "Howard-Powered Howard in Howard" (whatever that meant).

After his traditional stump speech and questions from those gathered, he took out a lime green marker and made his way over to a map of Iowa that was hanging on the wall. The map was colored green expect for one white spot – Howard County. To chart our progress (and give us hope that the end was near) we had taped the map to the ceiling of our van and colored in the counties as we visited them. Howard did the honors of coloring in Howard County, completing the map and making him the first candidate to visit all 99 counties.

While Howard was in the front of the room celebrating his achievement, the members of the press were huddled in the back trying to confirm a rumor that he had called Dick Gephardt a "blow hard." They were hungry for a good story and name calling would do the trick.

I couldn't remember Howard saying it, but given his history of speaking his mind it wasn't outside the realm of possibility. We recorded everything he said, just for times like this, and when I listened to the interview in question I found that Howard hadn't called Gephardt a blow hard – close, but not quite. He had called Gephardt's characterization of his Medicare position "Washington hot air." News of the less than compelling language was received by the small press contingent with genuine sadness.

October 25, 2003

The flight from Burlington, Vermont, to Whitefield, New Hampshire, took less than 30 minutes, but it seemed like we had left October behind and landed smack in the middle of January.

The ground was covered with snow when Howard, new scheduling director Todd Dennett, and I arrived at the small airport located near the White Mountains in northern New Hampshire. The winter scene continued when we walked into the lobby at the Mountain View Hotel and found the fireplace in full use.

Dennis Kucinich was hovering, clearly waiting for Howard to finish the conversation he was having in the corner of the lobby. When the gentleman Howard was chatting with left, Kucinich walked up to him. Their interaction was short and to the point. Kucinich was upset that Howard claimed in his speeches and in a television ad that he was the only candidate to oppose the war, when in fact Kucinich voted against it.

Shortly after his talk with Kucinich, Howard spoke to members of the AFL-CIO and went out of his way to point out that Kucinich opposed the war. (Although in subsequent speeches Howard referred to himself as the only "top tier" candidate to oppose the military action.)

□ □ □

The season went from winter to fall as we drove from Whitefield to the city of Keene in the southern part of the state. The city was hosting its annual Pumpkin Festival, an event that brought out more than 60,000 people. There was no snow to be found under the sunny sky, just close to 25,000 pumpkins.

People moved slowly, almost shoulder to shoulder, down the main street admiring the star attraction. Pumpkins of all shapes and sizes, carved with happy smiles and scary faces sat on tables that lined the streets and on large metal shelves that spanned from the ground to the sky.

Howard waded into the crowd. Following along was a group of his New Hampshire supporters, dressed for the occasion in T-shirts adorned with both the words "Pumpkin-Powered Howard" and a picture of Howard's face superimposed on a pumpkin.

It was a slow walk. People crowded around him looking for a picture, a handshake or an answer to a question. The news photographers were delighted when he posed with a two-year-old child in a pumpkin costume and then stopped to pat the head of a small white dog that had been dressed as a pumpkin by its owners.

The sight of all the pumpkins made Howard hungry for what else but pumpkin pie. While he kept one eye on the voters, the other was on the look out for a place to pick up a piece. When he spotted a table full of pies, he darted through the crowd and bought himself a piece with a heaping helping of whipped cream on top. He pierced his slice with the plastic fork and enjoyed the dessert while he walked and talked with a voter.

As he walked, talked, and ate pie, a young woman who worked for the Kerry campaign was close by with a small tape recorder. She held the recorder as near to Howard as she could – it was often in his face – taping his every word (and every chew). We were used to having opposing campaign staff at events like town hall meetings, but it was the first time someone was sent to capture even private conversations.

Before leaving Keene we stopped at a ham and bean supper sponsored by the local Unitarian Church. When Howard walked into the community room, an elderly gentleman sitting at the piano broke into a spirited version of "Hail to the Chief." Howard grabbed a cup of tea and his second piece of pumpkin pie and sat down at one of the tables to talk and eat.

This time he wasn't followed by the tape recorder-carrying Kerry staffer. We got rid of her by telling the people at the front door that she was not with us, so they should be sure to ask her for the dinner fee if she wanted to come in. They did, but paying to record Howard eating a piece of pie wasn't in the Kerry campaign's budget.

October 26, 2003

Howard sat in the lobby of the Hampton Inn in Madison Heights, Michigan, (a suburb of Detroit) reading the paper and finishing the free continental breakfast offered by the hotel. Joe sat alone two tables away dressed in a suit and tie sipping a Diet Pepsi. Tricia Enright wandered around in a T-shirt and shorts.

We had flown to Michigan the night before after the pumpkin festival, and now a power outage had drawn us, along with most of the other hotel guests, to the lobby where the emergency lights gave off the only light available in the hotel.

In the evening Howard would take part in a debate sponsored by the Congressional Black Caucus and the Democratic National Committee, but we were up and dressed in our Sunday best to attend mass at two Detroit churches with African American congregations.

We parked our car on the street in front of the Fellowship Chapel and went inside the foyer to look for Congressman John Conyers. Conyers, who had represented Detroit for 38 years, had agreed to take Howard to the churches and introduce him to the churchgoers. We were excited that the popular African American congressman was willing to appear publicly with Howard and we took it as a sign that he might be moving in the direction of endorsing him. People were starting to arrive, but there was no sign of Conyers.

We stood and watched as the church filled up. People noticed Howard, but only because he and I and the Michigan campaign director were the only white people there. They didn't know that he was running for president and, because we were at a church, he didn't want to appear crass by introducing himself as they walked in. We needed Conyers (who was known by the congregants) to make the introductions.

As the church doors were closing Conyers pulled up. He was late because he had been at another church with Dick Gephardt.

October 28, 2003

Dick Gephardt was on the attack again. For a month he had been accusing Howard of supporting efforts by Newt Gingrich to make cuts to the Medicare program in the mid-1990s. Now he was comparing Howard to George Bush.

Gephardt made his remarks in Iowa the day after Howard was in the state to pick up the support of the United Painters and Allied Trade union, his first labor union endorsement. Gephardt countered Howard's visit with a speech to a group of seniors in Des Moines. He told the seniors that "on all these Medicare issues, there is very little difference between George Bush and Howard Dean."

Meanwhile, we had moved on to Boulder, Colorado. The more than 2,500 people who lined the grounds and the roofs of the brick buildings at the University of Colorado would normally have been the highlight of our day. It was, however, Howard's declaration to the several hundred people who attended an early morning fundraising breakfast that he was a "metrosexual" that took the spotlight. He made the announcement for no particular reason; in fact, he didn't even know what a metrosexual was. It was only after he hopped in the car that he learned that a metrosexual was someone who prides himself on his appearance, a description that was not normally bestowed upon him.

When we left Boulder, we made stops in Denver and Las Vegas before arriving in San Francisco. Along the way Howard responded to Gephardt's contention that he was no better than George Bush on the issue of Medicare. In separate interviews he conjured up images of the Wild West when he told the press that Gephardt needed to "put his gun back into his holster" and "pull his horns in on this stuff."

October 30, 2003

Before Howard left his room at Rickey's Hyatt in Palo Alto, California, for the first event of the day he had made a decision – he would call Vermont and demand a day off. He hadn't had a break in seven days and he still had two days to go before he would get one. He was supposed to fly to Iowa to film a television commercial, but he would cancel the trip. He was tired and wanted an extra day off to get some rest.

We headed to the headquarters of the web search engine Google. Howard was trying to woo the employees and the company's chairman and CEO Eric Schmidt. We wanted their money and their technology expertise.

Schmidt led us through the company's campus and into a large conference room where Howard spoke to a group of about 50 employees. The work environment was very relaxed and casual, which may have played a part in Howard's answer to one of the questions he was asked.

One employee asked him to list some of President Bush's negatives. His response: "He's a Republican, so he probably doesn't have much of a sex life."

The room filled with laughter, most likely due to the fact that they couldn't believe what he had just said. Thankfully, the meeting was closed to the media and, surprisingly, the comment never made its way to the general public, which everything seemed to do.

From Palo Alto we flew to Seattle for a town hall meeting before heading to Boise, Idaho. Idaho was a priority for Howard, but not for anyone else on the campaign. When he got invited to give the keynote address at the Ada County Democratic Party dinner, there was no question in his mind that he would go – and he ignored anyone who suggested otherwise.

The several hundred Democrats who packed the ballroom at the Boise Airport Holiday Inn interrupted Howard with cheers and were on their feet during most of the speech.

He believed more than ever that he could win Idaho and he wanted to spend a little money to hire staff to organize the state. When I told him that the staff in Vermont wouldn't like the idea, he didn't care and his frustration with the campaign was reflected in his response. "If they can spend $8,000 a month on Joe's friends, I can put money into Idaho."

Our day that began with Howard wanting more rest ended at 3:30 a.m. when our plane landed in Portsmouth, New Hampshire.

—NOVEMBER—

November 3, 2003

The banner behind Howard read, "A New Day is Coming: Healthcare for All Americans." Howard was at Grandview College in Des Moines, Iowa, to talk about his health care plan to a group of 200 health care professionals. The campaign had organized the event so he could "take ownership of the health care issue."

Dick Gephardt continued to call Howard's commitment to Medicare into question. In September he accused him of wanting to cut the program and he was still making the charge. And it was a charge that drove Howard crazy. He was not only a doctor, but he had a record of expanding health care as governor and he was frustrated that, given his record, he had to keep answering to Gephardt.

Explaining that he had no intention of cutting the program for seniors had become a constant refrain when he met with Iowa voters, and when he arrived at Grandview, he had his own plan on how to "take ownership of the health care issue."

As he listed off Gephardt's charges he reached into his suit coat pocket. He was standing behind a podium, so the audience did not know what he was doing until he held his hand high in the air. He was holding a stethoscope.

The dramatic and picture perfect gesture was followed by Howard telling those gathered, "I've spent 13 years of my life with this. And senior citizens, as president of the United States I can promise you that Medicare won't be cut. Every senior will have health care. No senior needs to fear."

November 4, 2003

We started the day in Florida with events in Jacksonville and Tallahassee. By the time we arrived in Boston it was 4:30 p.m. and Howard was tired.

It was his second day back on the road after taking a day off – he had canceled filming a television commercial because he was exhausted and needed rest. But his day of rest was negated by a two-day schedule that included visits to four states and 18-hour days. Now, in a matter of hours, he would be meeting his opponents for a debate televised nationally on MTV. He had neither the time nor the energy to prepare.

His head was back and his eyes were closed as he sat on the couch in the hotel room that served as the pre-debate holding area. His nap lasted only a few minutes before he was interrupted by a make-up artist who arrived to pat his face with powder and cover up the dark circles under his eyes. Soon after, a member of the debate organizing staff arrived at the door; it was time to make the 15-block car ride to Faneuil Hall, the site of the debate.

When we arrived at Faneuil Hall, we were greeted by a mob of supporters from each campaign, held back by the Boston police and a line of bicycle racks. The Dean people shrieked when Howard emerged from the car, which made their rivals' supporters yell even louder. Howard was escorted to the set, while Joe and I were taken to another building where the staffs and media would watch the debate.

It was an informal affair. There were no podiums in sight, just stools for the candidates to sit on. Wes Clark wore a black turtleneck, while the other men countered by removing their suit coats. The questions would be asked by the young people who filled the audience, and it began like one would expect a debate on the music television station would. Have you ever smoked marijuana? Yes. Who is your favorite musician? Wyclef John.

But the debate took a serious turn when a young African American man stood up and directed a comment to Howard. He was offended that Howard would suggest courting voters who embraced the Confederate flag, a symbol of slavery and racism to many. His question stemmed from an idea Howard often discussed on the campaign trail. Specifically, he had told voters, "I'm going to go to the South and say to white guys who drive pickup trucks with Confederate flag decals in the back 'We want your vote, too.'"

Howard slipped off the stool and answered the young man, "We have had white Southern working people voting Republican for 30 years, and they've got nothing to show for it. . . . I think we need to talk to white Southern workers about how they vote, because when white people and black people and brown people vote together in this country, that's the only time that we make social progress, and they need to come back to the Democratic Party."

His answer caused a firestorm and brought Al Sharpton and John Edwards to their feet, both critical of Howard's use of the racist symbol.

SHARPTON: I don't think you're a bigot, but I think that [invoking the Confederate flag] is insensitive, and I think you ought to apologize to people for that. When Bill Clinton was found to be a member of a white-only country club, he apologized. You are not a bigot, but you appear to be too arrogant to say 'I'm wrong' and go on.

EDWARDS: Were you wrong [to use the flag] Howard? Were you wrong to say that?

DEAN: No, I wasn't, John Edwards, because people who vote who fly the Confederate flag, I think they are wrong because I think the Confederate flag is a racist symbol. But I think there are a lot of poor people who fly that flag because the Republicans have been dividing us by race since 1968 with their Southern race strategy.

EDWARDS: The last thing we need in the South is somebody like you coming down and telling us what we need to do.

After the debate Howard faced the media. A dozen journalists with microphones, tape recorders and cameras surrounded him and they were only interested in talking about the Confederate flag. He tried to downplay the interaction during the debate telling the media gathered, "I think those guys [my opponents] are worried because they're not doing well and I think they are making a mistake by trying to make a big deal out of something that isn't a big deal."

A short time later Howard, Joe Trippi, Mike O'Mary, and I boarded a plane for New York. We knew that despite Howard's efforts to convince the media otherwise his use of the Confederate flag had turned into a big deal. It was too early for us to know how it would play out. Howard, however, was concerned, not only about how the exchange would impact the campaign, but more than anything it bothered him that it had been implied that he was something he wasn't: racist.

What made our situation frustrating was the fact that Howard had used the Confederate flag imagery in public settings before and had never been taken to task for it by anyone – not an audience member, not the media, and not one of his opponents.

He first made the comment in January during a meeting with African American senior citizens in South Carolina. He used it again a month later at the Democratic National Committee meeting in front of the media, the members of the national party, and a national audience watching on C-SPAN. And it came up a third time in front of more than 1,800 Democrats at the California state party convention. On each occasion his words were received with applause. The only difference was back then he was not considered a threat to his rivals.

Howard felt he needed to address the issue, but what he would say and when he would say it was the question. We discussed our options.

The next day he was scheduled to give a speech about his campaign finances in the Great Hall at the Cooper Union in New York City. The setting was significant because it was where, in 1860, Abraham Lincoln gave a speech affirming his belief that slavery was wrong. It was a speech that many believed put Lincoln on the path to the presidency. The Great Hall's historic relevance made it the perfect venue for Howard to answer his critics and put the issue behind him right away. On the other hand, it might be better to wait a day to assess the fall out and address the issue on its own at a separate event if necessary.

When we arrived in New York the only decision we had made was to think about it overnight and decide in the morning.

November 5, 2003

It was early in the morning and Joe and I were standing on the sidewalk outside the hotel waiting for a member of the New York campaign staff to pick us up. The Confederate flag issue hadn't gone away with the start of a new day. To the contrary, we were facing a potential crisis for the campaign. But that didn't matter; the two of us started arguing almost immediately.

If we had been in Vermont our exchange would have caught the attention of passersby, but it didn't faze the New Yorkers who appeared to accept our yelling at each other as a normal part of city living. (The high point came when Joe proclaimed that "lily white" people like Howard and me would never be able to understand the problems that Howard's comments would mean for the campaign. I didn't know why Joe was any more qualified to understand than we were, but I decided that is was best not to ask.)

Howard was waiting for us in front of his mother's Park Avenue apartment. When he hopped into the van he announced that he would address his use of the Confederate flag during the speech he would deliver at Cooper Union – a speech that would take place in just a matter of hours.

Although he was concerned about the political fallout from his comments, the implication that he was somehow racist weighed heavily on him.

He called Jeani Murray in Iowa and Karen Hicks in New Hampshire to see what they were hearing. They hadn't heard anything from supporters, it was still early in the morning, but stories about the debate were in the local newspapers.

He called Vermont and spoke to Mike Ford (he had arrived in Burlington just days earlier) to see what the consultants and senior staff thought about him speaking to the issue at Cooper Union. They were divided. Some agreed that he needed to confront the matter right away. Others who didn't want to distract from the real purpose of the speech – an announcement on campaign finance – argued that it would be best to save the Confederate flag discussion for another day.

Howard's first meeting was with the New York Times editorial board. We pulled up to the newspaper offices and parked on the street. Before going in Howard called Jimmy Carter. He reached out to the former president because he was from the South and he knew what it was like to be under media scrutiny. When Howard hung up he was confident that talking about the Confederate flag during his speech at Cooper Union was the right thing to do.

While Howard settled into the large paneled boardroom to meet with the editorial board, I called Mike Ford to let him know about Howard's decision.

We arrived at Cooper Union two hours later. (It was an entertaining drive over. Joe muttered, "F--- you, Kate" from the back of the van while Howard worked on his speech). Howard and

I headed to the holding room behind the stage while Joe went into the main theater to talk to the media.

Howard began his speech by denouncing the Confederate flag, but he never backed away from his belief that all Americans, regardless of race and political affiliation, needed to unite:

> The issue of the Confederate flag has become an issue in the presidential race. Let me be clear. I believe that we have one flag in this country, the flag of the United States of America. I believe the flag of the Confederate States of America is a painful symbol and reminder of racial injustice and slavery and I don't condone the use of the flag of the Confederate States of America. . . . I do believe that this country needs to engage in a serious discussion about race and that everyone must engage in that discussion. I started this discussion in a clumsy way. This discussion will be painful and I regret the pain that I may have caused either African Americans or Southern white voters in the beginning of this discussion, but we need to have this discussion.

November 8, 2003

Howard stood on a stage at the University of Vermont in Burlington and did the unimaginable. No one – including Howard himself – ever thought he'd be in the position to make such an announcement. It was a decision that no candidate looking to be the Democratic nominee had ever made before.

A great deal had changed during the two years since he decided to enter the race. He had gone from an asterisk to the front-runner and from the candidate who was sure to be outspent to the one setting the fundraising records. Nevertheless, it was still unbelievable that Howard would be opting out of the federal campaign finance program. The candidate with the "paltry" bank account would be the first Democrat in history to turn away the federal money.

Rejecting the money was an idea Howard had resisted. When some on the campaign started talking about it after his fundraising success in June, he ordered them to stop. He was cautious and not ready to assume that he would be able to maintain his fundraising advantage.

But the staff continued to pursue it, confident that Howard could raise whatever money he would lose by rejecting the federal funds – and more. After months of trying to convince him that he should opt out he finally agreed. Yet even after getting his approval they didn't move forward immediately.

A decision to spurn the federal money might be unacceptable to his supporters who believed in what campaign finance reform was all about and what he preached on the campaign trail: limiting big money and special interests in politics.

Joe proposed a solution that would blunt the criticism. Let Howard's supporters decide if he should reject the federal money by conducting an online vote. How could they criticize a decision they made?

For Joe, the vote was more than a strategy for buy-in – it was in the spirit of our grassroots campaign and followed his bottom-up management style. He was driven by the ideas and opinions of the grassroots. He monitored not only the campaign blog, but other blogs as well and he was known to tell Howard's online community that he wasn't managing the campaign, they were.

Howard was concerned about leaving a major decision that could impact his chances of winning the nomination to a group of supporters. Regardless, we put it up for a vote – a vote that began when he announced it during his speech at the Cooper Union three days earlier.

Of course, we didn't leave the outcome completely up to chance. A compelling argument for opting out was posted on the website – and it was one that we had used successfully before. It was the "us" versus "them" strategy. If the campaign accepted the federal matching funds, we would be limiting the amount of money we could spend to $45 million – an amount that would be dwarfed by the $200 million that President Bush would use against us. We needed to opt out if we were going to have a chance of beating the establishment, our argument went.

In addition, opting out wouldn't be a rejection of campaign finance reform. To the contrary, it would be campaign finance reform. Campaign finance reform was intended to get big money out of politics. What would prove that was possible more than a campaign that didn't rely on $2,000 contributions, but instead on two million people making $100 contributions?

And that's how Howard ended up on a stage at the University of Vermont. Joined by six supporters from around the country he announced that as a result of the online vote he would reject federal money.

Making the announcement at the University of Vermont was not Joe's first choice. He had a grander vision. He wanted to stage the event in Philadelphia where the Declaration of Independence was signed in 1776. Dean supporters were declaring their "independence from special interests," so where better to do it than in Philadelphia.

But Howard said no. He was scheduled to take the morning off and he didn't want to change his plans in order to fly to Pennsylvania. So Joe had to settle for UVM where Howard and his supporters put their John Hancock's on "A Declaration of Independence by the People of Dean for America." The document – right down to the language, script, and faux parchment paper – was made to resemble the nation's first Declaration. It read in part:

> WE, therefore, the architects and builders of Dean for America, appealing to the Wise Judgment of the American people on our Intentions, do, in the Name, and by Authority of the good People of these United States, solemnly Publish and Declare, the People of these United States are, and of Right ought to be, FREE AND INDEPENDENT OF SPECIAL INTERESTS and that as FREE AND INDEPENDENT CITIZENS, they have full Power to participate, deliberate, pursue the common good, protect their own interest from corruption, and to do all other Acts and Things which

INDEPENDENT CITIZENS may of right do. And for the support of this Declaration, we mutually pledge to each other to write letters, knock on doors, organize our neighbors, self-fund this effort, and vote.

After making the historic announcement we hopped on a plane and flew to Portland, Maine, for the state party's annual fundraising dinner.

By the time we arrived, Howard's opponents were criticizing his decision to forgo public financing. Senator Kerry had issued a statement, but his campaign took the added step of bringing out the heavy artillery. A giant waffle, along with two dozen of the senator's supporters, greeted us at the restaurant. Howard's announcement had given new life to the oversized breakfast food, which now represented Howard's changing position on campaign finance reform.

Instead of stepping aside and letting Howard through, the waffle and its compatriots surrounded us. As one of them used a bullhorn to lead the others in chanting "JK all the way!" we put our heads down and pushed our way through. It was a chaotic scene and I ended up losing my cell phone and Blackberry in the scuffle with the giant waffle.

November 11, 2003

John Kerry's campaign had stalled. Polls showed the once front-runner and presumptive nominee lagging behind Howard in New Hampshire and Iowa. In addition, Kerry was falling behind in fundraising.

In an effort to re-energize his campaign, he fired his campaign manager, Jim Jordan, and replaced him with Mary Beth Cahill, Ted Kennedy's chief of staff.

Jordan's departure was followed by Kerry's press secretary and deputy finance director, both of whom quit because they were upset with the way Kerry had treated Jordan. Press stories detailed the divisions within the campaign, which was described as being divided into three factions, "his Washington team, paid consultants and friends and family from Boston."

Many on our campaign celebrated Jordan's demise. They saw the turmoil as proof of our power and inevitability, ignoring the fact that behind the scenes our campaign was in as much trouble as Kerry's.

November 12, 2003

Howard's public stock was rising and the crowd in the ballroom at the Mayflower Hotel in Washington, D.C. knew it.

The men and women dressed in purple and green roared when Howard entered the room. He looked like a prizefighter making his way to the center of the ring to acknowledge his victory. Dressed in a green T-shirt and purple jacket he smiled broadly as he shook hands on his way to the podium.

The hundreds of people who packed the room and spilled out into the hallway were members of two of the country's largest labor unions, the Service Employees International Union and the Association of Federal State and Municipal Employees. (It had been a year and a half since Howard and I first met with the SEIU and left with a glimmer of hope that the union would give a long shot candidate a chance.) The two groups had come together sporting their union colors at the joint press event to announce their endorsement of Howard.

With the endorsements came the people power of millions of union members around the country, along with the millions of dollars the organizations would invest in the campaign. For Howard, the large number of African Americans and Hispanics who were members of the two unions added much needed racial diversity to his campaign.

The unions throwing their support behind Howard was a blow to the other Democrats, especially Dick Gephardt, who had already gained the support of 20 labor unions around the country.

The energy in the room was electric and the union members who were there to rally for Howard were so excited that it was impossible for him to get out of the room. We were forced to escape the crowd through a service entrance.

November 13, 2003

Dean supporters lined the hallway that led to the Secretary of State's office in the New Hampshire State House in Concord. Howard was there to file the papers that would place his name on the state's primary ballot and hundreds of people where there to witness it.

He smiled and shook hands with his supporters who stood on both sides of the hallway chanting, "Howard! Howard!" as he walked by.

When he made it to the Secretary of State's office he was met by dozens of news cameras and reporters. At their request he signed the official paperwork slowly so they could get the right camera angle.

Howard told those who had squeezed into the room, "This is something of a milestone in the campaign. If you asked me three years ago if I could have imagined this – something like this – the answer would have been no. This is not about running for president. This is about all of us taking back our country. This whole campaign is about empowering voters to stand up for what they believe is right."

November 14, 2003

We spent the day driving around Iowa on a bus. We were joined by college-age supporters who were on board to help Howard kick off our "Commit for Change: Caucus for Dean" program at a series of rallies at college campuses around the state. The "C4C" program encouraged people to show their commitment to supporting Howard by signing a pledge card that read, "Today, by signing this card, I commit to change the direction of my country by caucusing for Governor Howard Dean at my local precinct on Monday, January 19, 2004."

Nine days had past since the MTV debate and during that time Howard had apologized for and explained his comment about the Confederate flag. We had weathered the worst of the storm and put the controversy behind us (although his rivals and the media added the flag comment to the list of what they termed "gaffes" – including the strength of the U.S. military, the Middle East, and Hamas – that they repeated often). The flag flap, however, wasn't over. Confederate flags began appearing around us.

A young man carrying a flag had shown up at an event in New Hampshire the day before, but we figured it was a one-day, one-state, one-person thing. But the effort proved to be coordinated – by whom we didn't know – when more showed up in Iowa.

Two young men holding "Confederates for Dean" signs appeared at the second rally of the day. They stood in the back of the room waving their signs that were printed on the image of a Confederate flag. However, because they were in the back Howard didn't see them and neither did most of his supporters.

But at the final event of the day, they became more brazen, moving closer to the stage. Howard couldn't miss them and neither could the people in the crowd. When one man began to heckle Howard, the crowd drowned out his voice by chanting, "Dean, Dean, Dean" and swallowed up his flag by waving their symbol of support for Howard: foam fingers. The blue and white novelty items, seen mostly at sporting events, emblazoned with "Dean's #1," had been passed out to the crowd before the event. We never imagined that they would be used as a weapon against our detractors. I couldn't wait for the confrontation with the Kerry campaign waffle.

November 15, 2003

Howard, Steve McMahon, Joe Trippi, Jeani Murray, and I sat in front of the television that had been wheeled into Howard's suite at the Hotel Fort Des Moines and watched the final cut of our latest television ad.

When Steve pushed the play button on the VCR, a photograph of Dick Gephardt standing in the Rose Garden with President Bush appeared. A narrator outlined Gephardt's efforts in 2002 to draft the resolution that authorized the use of force in Iraq and his vote in favor of the president's request for an additional $87 billion to support the war.

Pollster Paul Maslin had tested the language in the 30-second ad on Iowa caucus goers. The results showed a significant number of voters would shift their support to Howard when they learned that the congressman supported the war – a shift large enough to put Howard firmly in first place.

While the poll results indicated a gain for Howard, there was a risk to running the ad. It would be the first ad aired during the campaign in which one candidate used the name of another and could be viewed by some as an attack ad.

Howard approved the ad that night, but insisted that one change be made before it aired. The photograph of Gephardt with Bush that Steve used was not from the Rose Garden ceremony announcing the war resolution. Howard wanted the picture from the actual ceremony used so the accuracy of the 30-second spot could not be challenged.

□ □ □

When the 47 yellow school buses arrived at the Polk County Convention Center in downtown Des Moines for the Jefferson-Jackson Day dinner, the crowd went wild.

When Howard and I attended our first Iowa Jefferson-Jackson Day dinner in 2002, it was just the two of us toting 2,000 brochures, and Howard's name was so unfamiliar that Senator Tom Harkin referred to him as "John Dean." Much had changed in a year. Now, a line of yellow school buses filled with hundreds of Dean supporters was being greeted by a sea of blue signs – all with Howard's name on them.

After approving the ad against Gephardt, Howard joined several hundred supporters on the ten-minute bus ride that took them through the downtown and to the convention center. He got out once to wave at the news cameras the campaign had strategically placed on an overpass, where they could photograph the long line of buses from above.

When he arrived at the convention center, hundreds of his supporters were waiting outside.

Standing on both sides of the bicycle rack-lined sidewalk that led to the main entrance, they waited for Howard to emerge from the bus and make his way up to the building.

Even with the barricades to hold people back, the scene was chaotic. Hundreds of excited supporters were lined five deep on each side, reaching their hands out to touch Howard's. He slowly made his way up the sidewalk, moving quickly from one side to the other. In front of him a dozen news photographers walked backwards in an effort to get the perfect picture.

The dinner was held in the sports arena. More than 7,000 people packed into the arena to hear the candidates. Despite appearances to the contrary, Howard wasn't the only candidate there. John Edwards, Dick Gephardt, John Kerry, Dennis Kucinich, and Carol Moseley Braun were in attendance, along with Hillary Clinton, who served as the master of ceremonies.

Individuals who made large donations to the state party were seated at linen covered round tables on the arena floor, while those who couldn't afford the ticket price were seated high in the bleacher seats in the balcony. They didn't get the chicken dinner served below, but they could dine on the beer and French fries sold in the concession stands in the hallways – and of course they could hear the candidates.

Our campaign had purchased 2,000 tickets for our supporters to sit in the bleachers. The Dean supporters, who came from all over the country, far outnumbered those of our rivals and created an overwhelming presence in the room.

□ □ □

Howard was missing. Iowa State Party chair Gordon Fischer stood on the large stage that had been set up in the middle of the arena floor and introduced each candidate. One by one they walked onto the stage, waved to the crowd, and walked off. The scene was broadcast on a large JumboTron that hung directly above the stage.

When Fischer called Howard's name, he didn't appear. A soft murmur floated throughout the room as people looked around wondering where he was. Suddenly, the crowd in the balcony began to roar. The people sitting on the main floor didn't know what was happening, but they assumed by the noise coming from the Dean supporters that Howard was in the arena, but they still couldn't see him.

The operator of the JumboTron was the first to spot him and the rest of the crowd quickly followed when Howard's larger than life image appeared on the screen. He was in the bleachers with his supporters, both arms high in the air giving the crowd below two thumbs up. The gesture was a greeting to the crowd, but it could just as well have been an acknowledgement of our success in pulling off the stunt.

Our campaign hadn't told anyone – including the organizers of the event – that Howard would be in the bleachers instead of on the stage. We knew if we did they would not have allowed us to do it. And it was worth breaking the rules. His surprise entrance electrified the crowd and projected the image of a winner. (Not to mention the fact that it annoyed the other campaigns.)

The production didn't stop there. Throughout the dinner and in between speeches, the Dean supporters put on a show with their signs and cheers. Dean staffers armed with walkie-talkies told the crowd when to wave their signs. When Howard was in the bleachers it was: "Howard Dean: A New Day for Democrats." When he delivered his speech: "Win With Dean." And they told them what cheers to chant: "We say Howard, you say Dean."

At the end of Howard's speech, the crowd in the bleachers unfurled three large banners. The 50 foot signs spelled out "Win With Dean."

When all the speeches had been given, the candidates joined Hillary Clinton on the stage. Smiling through their irritation with Howard, they clapped, waved, and pumped their fists in the air to the beat of the song "We Are Family" as confetti dropped from the ceiling – and the Dean supporters roared from the rafters.

November 17, 2003

While the ad targeting Gephardt began running in Iowa, Howard was on the East Coast celebrating his birthday – and he had much to celebrate. Newly released polls showed him with a 22-point lead over Kerry in New Hampshire and Granite State voters had deemed him the candidate with the best chance of beating George Bush.

A year earlier the self-proclaimed "asterisk" celebrated his birthday in relative obscurity eating cake with his staff in the governor's office in Vermont. Now his 55th birthday was being treated like a national holiday in Dean nation and the campaign was using – or exploiting – the occasion to fill the campaign coffers.

Trick candles, cakes, and songs were the highlights of the elaborate and well-attended birthday parties.

We raised $100,000 during a lunch in Baltimore where Howard laughed when the candles he blew out lit again, where he lamented the fact that he wasn't wearing his JC Penney suit when he got frosting on his lapel, and where he cut the birthday cake with such force that there would have been cause for concern if he was trained as a surgeon.

More than 500 people paid $1,000 to watch the actress Sally Kellerman, who starred as "Hot Lips" Houlihan in the 1970 movie *M*A*S*H**, dressed in a hot pink pant suit, serenade Howard with her own rendition of "Happy Birthday" at the National Museum of Women in the Arts in Washington, D.C. We had to leave before the cake topped with white frosting, chocolate sprinkles, and strawberries was served, but we did stay long enough for Howard to throw caution to the wind and entertain the crowd with a tune on the harmonica.

The official celebration ended at the Capitol Brewing Company just blocks from the U.S. Capitol. We collected more than $25,000 from the 500 Generation Deaners who packed into the restaurant. Howard smiled and acted as if it was the first time he heard the song when the crowd (which included Congressmen Jesse Jackson, Jr. and John Lewis) broke into "Happy Birthday." He blew out the candles and, while holding the knife high in the air, announced to the crowd, "You all know what that wish was!"

Howard's official obligations were over, but there was still one hour left in his birthday when we boarded a plane for Manchester. Before the fourth cake of the day was served Howard's traveling media entourage presented him with a pair of socks. They explained that the gift was meant to correct a fashion faux pas that irritated them. They complained that Howard's socks were too short, a flaw they noted (and were forced to look at) when he was sitting down.

264

November 21, 2003

When Howard walked up the back stairs of the Opera House in Rochester, New Hampshire, to meet with undecided voters, he was greeted by a familiar face: his own.

He wasn't looking in a mirror; he was standing in front of a life-size cardboard cut out of himself. Smiling in a blue suit and red and white-striped tie, the faux Howard was made from a color photograph of the real one. It looked so real – right down to the ever present wrinkled suit coat pocket where Howard stuffed his cell phone or papers – that it was hard to distinguish the real from the fake or, as the cardboard version was aptly named, Flat Howard.

Somewhere along the way Howard had become more than a candidate, he had become a rock star. His supporters couldn't get enough of him. Some were attracted to his message while others were just attracted to him. On the website Crushies for Dean, supporters expounded on his "outright sex appeal" and swooned over his teeth and eyes in comments they posted on the site.

And Howard Dean merchandise had sprung up everywhere. There were the usual T-shirts, buttons, posters, and bumper stickers that all campaigns had. But Howard's supporters – and others looking to make a buck – went beyond the norm.

His name and image appeared on playing cards, mouse pads, magnetic calendars and, of course, foam fingers. His name could be found on fortune cookies, candy bars, tote bags, and flags that attached to car windows. There were the "Deanie Baby for America" beanbag toys and teddy bears for kids. The fashion conscious could choose from jewelry, silk scarves, and hats adorned with the Dean name. Cardboard fans came in handy in the summer, ice scrappers helped in the winter, and tongue depressors and prescription drug bottles served as reminders of his profession. And it wouldn't take long for a make your own Flat Howard kit to become available online.

□ □ □

Howard picked up the copy of the *New York Times* and threw it on the floor of the airplane vowing to never again read the paper he read religiously every day.

It was after 9:30 p.m. and we were flying from New Hampshire to Detroit. As we were taxing down the runway my Blackberry buzzed, signaling the arrival of a message in my inbox. It was a *New York Times* story about Howard's Vietnam draft status – a story that prompted Howard's aggressive move against the paper. The story, written by reporter Rick Lyman, had been posted on the paper's website and was set to be published in the print edition the next day.

A news story about the military draft seemed to be a prerequisite for every presidential election. In 1992 it was Bill Clinton, in 2000 it was George Bush. Now it was Howard.

The *Times* piece misquoted Howard and implied that he had intentionally avoided the draft.

Howard wanted the story corrected immediately. He knew if it wasn't fixed right away it would be repeated over and over and the fiction would quickly become fact. He picked up the phone on the airplane (we usually didn't have such a luxury) and called the staff in Vermont. But the staffers he spoke to, including Steve McMahon and Tricia Enright, were hesitant to call the paper. They didn't believe Howard's assertion that he had been misquoted. (I was at the interview and knew for a fact that the story, as written, was incorrect.) The staff's reluctance to call the *Times* aggravated Howard almost as much as the story did.

He called Vermont two more times during the 2 hour and 20 minute flight and was frustrated to learn each time that no call had been made to the paper.

The minute the plane's wheels hit the tarmac he called Vermont again. This time they reported that they had been in touch with the editor, who reviewed Lyman's notes and found that Howard was right, he had indeed been misquoted. The online version was corrected, but it was too late to fix the print edition.

November 23, 2003

I sat in the balcony with the news media and watched Howard in the pews below. We were attending Sunday mass at a predominantly African American church in New York City. It was clear that the church was in transition and struggling on how to keep the old, but attract the new.

Sitting not far from me in the balcony in the back of the church was a choir. The dozen members were dressed in long black robes with blue trim. They stood and sang traditional songs, using nothing to amplify their voices except their own energy. Set up below in the front of the church was another choir – or more accurately a band. A drummer, guitar player, and a singer belted out high energy songs on the church's new sound system (a sound system we thanked God for during the mass). The two groups took turns singing, a compromise that allowed each to be a part of the service. But if the new sound system was any indication, the traditional choir was in serious jeopardy.

While we sat in the church that the minister described as "the home of peace, happiness, and contentment," hundreds of miles away in Iowa our feud with Dick Gephardt was escalating. Gephardt had responded to our ad – which David Yepsen of the *Des Moines Register* described as "sleaze" – with one of his own. In the ad he accused Howard of supporting the additional $87 billion to fund the war in Iraq that President Bush proposed in September – a position Howard attacked Gephardt for taking in his ad.

□ □ □

"This makes me look like Lyndon LaRouche," Howard announced to Joe Costello when he read the text of the brochure Costello planned to distribute under Howard's name. (LaRouche was the

267

perennial presidential candidate who had been described as the leader of "one of the strangest political groups in America.")

It was the beginning of an argument that had been brewing for months and harkened back to Joe's memo of June – should Howard be a transactional leader or a transitional leader or, in other words, was our purpose to elect Howard president or build a movement. Howard was moving between both worlds tailoring his message to his audience.

When he met with small groups of undecided voters in senior centers, VFW halls or school libraries, he remained fixed on the issues, talking about everything from property taxes to health care reform. He portrayed a serious image by leaving his suit coat on and answering questions from the voters.

When he met with his diehard supporters at venues that held thousands, he talked about the same issues, but he became a fighter, rolling up his sleeves and adding the rhetoric – "Take the country back" and "You've got the power" – that fired them up.

But the message coming out of Burlington wasn't issue-driven and left out the undecided voters; instead it was targeted at the loyal supporters who came to the rallies and those who spent their time on the Internet.

We had adopted a war mentality – it was Dean supporters versus everyone else. When Howard was attacked by his opponents or the media, our response to our supporters was, "They're not trying to stop Howard; they're trying to stop you." When we opted out of the federal campaign finance program, we drafted our own "Declaration of Independence." And the campaign had adopted the motto, "The tea is in the harbor" in reference to the Boston Tea Party, the protest that was a precursor to the Revolutionary War.

And now Joe Costello had written "Common Sense for a New Century." The piece was described as a "call to action for a new generation of American patriots." The name and idea for the document was adapted from a pamphlet written in 1776 by Thomas Paine that challenged the authority of the British government.

I insisted that Costello show the document to Howard before it was printed. The extreme language alarmed me and along with the fact that it was devoid of any references to the issues that were important to the voters Howard was courting in places like Iowa and New Hampshire.

Howard saw the document for the first time when he, Costello, and I were sitting in a minivan on our way to the airport in New Jersey. Howard agreed with my assessment of the piece and told Costello that it would not be printed until he had a time to make changes. I was sitting next to Costello, who immediately called Joe Trippi and told him what I had done.

November 24, 2003

The Common Sense document pitted Joe Trippi and me squarely against each other. I'm not sure what angered him more, the fact that Howard wanted to edit the piece or that I was the one who had made an issue of it.

During a tense meeting at Iowa's Hotel Fort Des Moines, Joe urged Howard to print the document as written. The purpose of the meeting was to prepare for an afternoon debate sponsored by the DNC and MSNBC, but it soon devolved into an argument about the document and, by extension, the campaign message.

The lines were clearly drawn. Joe sat alongside Joe Costello on the floor on one side of the room. I was in a chair on the other. Howard sat on the couch between us. (Paul Maslin and Jeani Murray were on the sidelines staying out of the fray.)

Howard asked each of us to state our case. By now Joe and I could barely look at each other. Joe explained that the document and its message were important to energizing the base. I acknowledged that we needed to energize our core supporters, but I thought we were neglecting the issues that were important to a wider audience. I also thought the message was getting so extreme that we ran the risk of alienating undecided voters.

Howard agreed with me. The document would not go out until he had time to look at it. Joe was furious and if looks could kill, I would have been dead on the spot. (Paul Maslin would later write about Joe's reaction, "Trippi blamed Kate O'Connor, Dean's closest aide, for the holdup; he left the candidate's suite, threw his cell phone down the corridor, and screamed, 'That bitch!'")

After the discussion, Joe Trippi, Joe Costello, and Paul left the room. A short time later, Paul returned with a new draft of the document. Joe had sent him in as an emissary. Howard had moved on (he had other things to do), but Joe hadn't and he forced Howard to deal with it before he wanted to.

Finally, Howard had become so tired of having to look at the draft that he approved a copy that wasn't perfect, but was better than the original. I thought it still missed the mark.

Over two hundred years ago, Thomas Paine wrote a pamphlet that would light the fire that forged our nation. He called it 'Common Sense.' Passed from hand to hand, patriot to patriot, it was a call to action for those Americans who believed their government had to change. It spelled out the values of a new republic. And King George III – who had forgotten his own people in favor of special interests – was replaced by a government of, by and for the people. America was born.

A year ago, the Dean campaign began as a traditional candidacy for the presidency. We hoped to talk about health care for all, and fiscal responsibility that would benefit everyone. But this campaign has grown above and beyond the discussion of the important issues that concern us. It has become a movement that is allowing the American people to reclaim their political process.

□ □ □

The debate moved from the Hotel Fort Des Moines to the Polk County Convention Center. But instead of mediating a dispute, Howard found himself in the crosshairs. He and Dick Gephardt were in a dead heat in the caucus state with John Kerry trailing in third place. And the animosity between Howard and Gephardt had escalated with the ads that each man was running against the other.

Howard was the center of attention during the two-hour debate moderated by NBC's Tom Brokaw. Gephardt accused him of cutting social programs for the most vulnerable as governor of Vermont (a claim he denied) and Kerry questioned his unwillingness to pledge not to cut the rate of growth in the Medicare program as president. (Kerry argued that a cut in the rate of growth would equal a cut to the program that provided health care to seniors.)

Press reports described the activity on the stage as "sometimes raucous, slightly bizarre" and described Howard as "appearing exasperated" with Kerry and "arching his eyebrows in a show of irritation."

While Howard took a beating on the stage, Joe and I sat in the campaign's staff room watching the debate on television. Joe was still seething over the Common Sense document and the tension in the room matched the mood on the stage. A reporter from the *New York Times* joined us and watched as Joe snipped at me and yelled at the television when Howard gave an answer he didn't like.

But at least one person liked Howard's performance. David Yepsen the *Des Moines Register* columnist who days earlier called the ad against Gephardt "sleaze" declared Howard the winner of the debate. He wrote that he "stayed above the fray" and answered the criticisms with "respect and courtesy."

November 25, 2003

There were still two days to campaign before Thanksgiving, but Howard left Iowa and headed for Hawaii. A week earlier he had been notified by the U.S. military that the remains of his brother Charlie had been found in Laos. Howard, his mother, and two brothers boarded a private plane and made the 18-hour flight to Hawaii to reclaim them.

It was a personal trip for the Dean family (no staff or media were making the trip), one that ended a 30-year search, but nonetheless Joe and Tricia Enright proposed allowing *Newsweek* columnist Howard Fineman to fly with the family. (Fineman elicited tears from Howard for his first story about Charlie.) They told Howard that in exchange for a seat on the plane *Newsweek* would put him on the magazine's cover. Howard said no.

—DECEMBER—

December 1, 2003

"I'll unseal mine, if he'll unseal his" was Howard's response to the question posed to him by Charles Gibson during a live interview from Burlington on ABC's *Good Morning America.*

Gibson had asked Howard about the latest controversy to hit the campaign. When Howard left the governor's office in 2003, he did what was common practice for Vermont governors. Citing "executive privilege," he sealed some – not all – of his official papers from the public's view.

Chances were no one would have been interested in the documents, but now that he had been deemed the front-runner for the Democratic nomination, the media and his opponents were eager to examine them. When they learned some of the documents were off limits they protested and called on Howard to release them.

The "he" Howard was referring to in his answer to Gibson was President Bush. As a former governor himself, some of Bush's documents had been sealed from the public. Howard thought putting the ball in Bush's court would help quell the controversy.

While Howard was appearing on the early morning show, Steve McMahon, Paul Maslin, and I sat in the Burlington headquarters discussing the status of our efforts in Iowa.

Public polls showed Howard leading Gephardt in the caucus state by 4 percentage points, but according to our own polling Howard's numbers were slipping. Steve and Paul said it was nothing that running more television ads in the state couldn't fix.

I didn't think that airing more ads was enough, especially since our strategy to capture the nomination hinged on a strong showing for Howard in the state. I suggested that Joe go to Iowa in order to get a firsthand look at what was going on. It was a suggestion that was received with resistance by Steve and Paul, who told me that I was overreacting – there was no reason for Joe to go to Iowa.

The idea didn't seem radical to me. After all, when Howard and I first met with Mike, Joe, and Steve in 2001, they told us that Joe was an expert at organizing Iowa and regaled us with countless war stories to prove it. I didn't understand what harm there was in having Joe do what we were told he did best.

I wasn't willing to settle for a no from Steve and Paul. Howard would be in the office later in the morning for a meeting to prepare for his appearance on MSNBC's *Hardball* later that evening. It would be the perfect time to discuss our options.

When Howard arrived in the campaign headquarters shortly after noon, a small group of senior staff and consultants gathered in the office Joe and I shared. The one person missing from the meeting was Joe. He would later say that he didn't know about the *Hardball* prep session – a meeting that turned into a discussion about what to do in Iowa. We didn't intend to have the discussion without Joe, but Howard went ahead because he was rarely in Vermont and with the caucuses just seven weeks away any decision had to be made sooner rather than later.

I repeated my recommendation that Joe go to Iowa to check things out. Howard wanted to know what the others thought so he polled the room. Almost everyone – including Steve and Paul – told Howard that Joe should make the trip. Mike Ford came in halfway through the conversation and said he needed time to think about it.

Howard agreed that Joe should go to Iowa and told the group that he would ask him to do so.

By the time Howard and I arrived at Harvard University in Boston where he would appear on *Hardball*, his rivals and the media were calling attention to the fact that contrary to Howard's assertion on *Good Morning America*, President Bush's gubernatorial records weren't sealed (the Texas attorney general had ordered them to be released years earlier) and they wanted him to make good on his promise to "unseal mine, if he'll unseal his."

And by the time our plane landed in Iowa later in the evening, word had spread throughout the campaign office that Howard wanted Joe to go to Iowa and Joe was convinced that the idea was just a ploy on my part to oust him as campaign manager.

December 2, 2003

In the span of a day, the controversy over the sealed documents had become a distraction. As Howard tried to convince undecided caucus goers in Cedar Rapids, Iowa, to support him, his rivals continued to imply that he was hiding something, and the Washington D.C. watchdog organization Judicial Watch had joined the chorus by announcing that it was considering filing a lawsuit to force him to unseal the records.

Making matters worse was how the campaign was dealing with the matter. During the meeting in Vermont the day before, Howard had asked the staff to come up with a solution to the problem.

We were headed to a meeting with undecided voters when I received a message from Steve. The staff had decided that the campaign would issue a statement by the end of the day calling for the release of the documents. Howard wasn't to tell the media that we were going to call for the release of the records, but he could tell them that a statement would be forthcoming. He was being hounded by the reporters traveling with him, so having a promise of a response came as a relief.

Howard did what he was told and informed the press about the impending statement, but several hours later Steve called again. The plan had changed. No statement would be issued by the campaign.

No statement from Burlington only put more pressure on Howard. Unlike the staff in Vermont, who could forward press inquiries to voice mail, Howard couldn't avoid the media. They were sitting on the plane with him and they were upset by the lack of the promised statement.

So in the midst of the confusion that reigned in the campaign, Howard could do little more than give an answer that left the subject unresolved for another day. "We're talking about trying to be accommodating. We think that transparency is important. But executive privilege is a serious issue, and there are private things in there that can't be let out. We are kind of having that internal discussion."

December 3, 2003

When Howard told the press the day before that we were "kind of having that internal discussion" about releasing his gubernatorial records he was stretching it. It took us three days after the controversy began to sit down as a group and have a serious conversation about what to do.

We were back in Vermont for the day, and when we gathered around the conference room table in the Burlington headquarters we were divided.

Howard, Bob Rogan, and I were the only ones in the room who had worked in the governor's office and were, therefore, the only ones who knew the kind of documents that flowed through the office. None of us knew exactly what documents were in the sealed boxes. Bob had left the governor's office in 1996 and neither Howard nor I had reviewed the documents before they were sealed – that was left up to the governor's legal counsel – but I had a general idea of what we were talking about.

Paul Maslin and Joe Costello were adamant that the documents needed to be released, after all the campaign was built on transparency. We held nothing back from our supporters. In fact, we made them part of the decision-making process. Paul paced the room passionately arguing that withholding the information would go against what the campaign was all about – and make Howard just another politician.

For them it was about showing the supporters that we had nothing to hide, but I thought they were forgetting that Howard was not new to politics. The almost 12 years worth of papers documented his thoughts and opinions. I knew of no smoking gun, but I thought the risk of being surprised by something in the boxes was too great.

It came down to a vote. Paul and Joe Costello wanted the documents released. I thought they should remain sealed. Mike Ford agreed and so did Howard. A decision had been made, we would not call for the documents to be released, but we wouldn't announce it – at least not yet.

We decided to wait until Judicial Watch made its decision about whether to file a lawsuit against Howard. We realized that a lawsuit could work in our favor. By putting the fate of the documents in the court's hands, Howard would be able to say that the legal process would sort out the matter and he would never have to announce that he opposed their release. So we'd let the controversy ride for a few more days and hold off responding until Judicial Watch decided what it was going to do.

With the decision on the documents made, Howard asked Joe to go to Iowa. Joe's response to the request was no. He told Howard that he was running a fifty state campaign and needed to focus on the states after Iowa. But more importantly, Joe contended that if he left Vermont the Internet component of the campaign would collapse.

December 5, 2003

We arrived in Iowa ready to spend the day converting undecided voters at a series of Caucus for Change events.

After attending our first event at a public library in Mason City, we stopped at a Maid Rite sandwich shop. The popular Iowa restaurant chain was known for its loose meat sandwiches. It was the lunch rush hour and every table was occupied. Howard turned heads when he entered the shop, but it had less to do with him – presidential candidates were a dime a dozen in Iowa – and more to do with the twenty people who came with him – half of whom were carrying cameras pointed in his direction.

Howard stood at the counter waiting his turn to order lunch all the while ignoring the fact that the simple act had turned into an event worthy of being documented. When it was his turn he ordered a pork sandwich and strawberry milk shake, which prompted him to ask a couple sitting at a nearby table whether Iowans preferred the term frappe to milk shake. (The couple revealed they called the ice cream drink a milk shake, but gave no hint as to their choice of presidential candidate).

When he opened his wallet and handed his money to the waitress the cameras zoomed in for a close up.

No voters were converted during the visit, but Howard left with lunch and the reporters had their "presidential candidate being a normal person" story of the day.

As Howard sipped his shake he hopped in the van and we headed to an RSVP Center in Webster City for another C4C event.

Color cutouts of Santa Claus were taped to the walls alongside a handmade food pyramid chart. Howard stood under one of the many oversized paper Christmas ornaments that dangled from the ceiling and addressed the dozens of senior citizens who sat in folding metal chairs in the center's small community room.

After similar events in Fort Dodge and Boone, our final stop of the day was at the elementary school in Perry. Although it was a campaign event, the Iowa staff opted not to hang a Dean banner on the wall behind Howard. Instead, the school's motto seemed appropriate, "Perry Elementary School will display a good attitude and reach our goals."

□ □ □

It was close to 9 p.m. when we pulled up to the Hotel Fort Des Moines where we would spend the night. The van was coming to a stop at the curb when Howard's cell phone rang. It was Al Gore. The call was not a surprise. It was one in a series scheduled between the two men. Howard had been reaching out to Gore for advice, and of course, hoping for his support.

Howard was on the telephone for less than five minutes and he didn't say much beyond a couple of yeses and one, "That's great." When he hung up he didn't act overly excited and made no comment about what was said during the call.

To me his behavior was strange. For him to say almost nothing during a call and not report what was said after was unheard of. He was too quiet, which I read as meaning only one thing: Gore had told him that he was ready to endorse him.

We stopped at the front desk for our room keys, then left everyone else in the lobby and got on the elevator. I told Howard that despite his efforts to act like nothing had happened I knew what Gore had said to him.

Our rooms were on the same floor and when we got off the elevator every door was open. Teenage girls were sitting up and down the hallway talking and listening to the radios and televisions that were blaring from their rooms. They were students participating in a high school cheerleading competition and it appeared that the only two rooms not occupied by schoolgirls were Howard's and mine. We stepped over legs until we got to Howard's suite. He was eager to begin planning the endorsement announcement.

It had been just minutes since he hung up with Gore and the idea that the endorsement was real hadn't sunk in. We sat in disbelief. When Howard began the journey two years earlier he was prepared to go against the odds and challenge the former vice president, now he was getting his support. It was something we never imagined would happen. Howard was the Washington outsider, a status many believed made him unelectable, but Gore's endorsement was the stamp of approval from a Democratic Party heavyweight. And it was the endorsement that above all others made us feel legitimate.

Howard did not want anyone to know about the endorsement, including Joe. He believed that the more people who knew about it, the more likely it would be that the news would get out prematurely. And although Joe was the campaign manager, Howard did not trust that he would be able to keep Gore's decision to himself and worried that he would spill the beans to the media. (How can anyone keep a secret with a CNN camera around?) Gore had the same concerns about the news getting out and planned to share his decision with only one person, Rick Jacobs, a mutual friend who would help with the arrangements on his behalf. Rick, who lived in California, knew Gore from Tennessee and was one of the first people to help Howard in 2002.

Gore had given Howard two dates that worked best for him. One of them was December 9, four days away. Howard was set to attend a breakfast in Harlem that morning and then go to Pennsylvania. He wasn't scheduled to be in Iowa, but he wanted one of his first appearances with Gore to be in the caucus state, so we decided to change the schedule. Our plan was to have the two men make the announcement in front of African American leaders in Harlem and then travel to Iowa to repeat it.

We called Rick, who was as excited as we were, with the date and waited for Gore's approval.

December 6, 2003

Howard greeted his would-be supporters with, "What'll it be?" Wrapped in a green apron, he stood behind the cafeteria line (and in front of the media cameras) at Drake University in Des Moines, dolling out pancakes and taking requests for scrambled eggs and sausage.

Hundreds of people turned out to hear him speak, but before he tried to sell them on his policy positions he tempted them with food. Some people acted as if it was normal to be served by a presidential candidate (it was in Iowa), others laughed, while one squealed with delight. A two-year-old boy whose parents were Dean junkies pointed and yelled, "Howard Dean!" as if he had come face-to-face with Barney or Elmo.

Howard took the job of pancake distributor seriously, telling anyone who had a question that the answer would have to wait until he was off duty, otherwise the line would back up.

After breakfast we left Des Moines and flew to Orlando, Florida, for the Florida Democratic Party State Convention. The meeting of the state's Democrats was held at a Mexican themed resort at Walt Disney World.

When we arrived at the Magic Kingdom I received a call from Rick Jacobs – the plan for December 9 sounded good to Gore.

We continued to keep the endorsement a secret, even from Joe, who joined us in Florida. We went about the day trying to act normal, while planning for the major announcement. Our most pressing need was two airplanes to take us from New York to Iowa. I enlisted the help of Todd Dennett, the scheduling director. I didn't tell him the reason for the planes and I asked him not to share my request with anyone.

In between our whispered conversations, Howard spoke at the convention. While we waited for him to be introduced, we debated whether or not he should wear his suit coat. When to wear the coat, while not the most important decision we made each day, did reflect the evolution of the campaign.

In the early days, he never went without it. But as the campaign grew and the crowds got larger and his speeches took on a fiery tone he took the coat off and rolled up his sleeves. It was a relaxed look that mirrored the youthfulness of his audience. Now he was the front-runner, the potential Democratic nominee for president. Should he reflect his status in the polls with a serious look or take the coat off to portray the image of a fighter?

As the upbeat tune "Walking on Sunshine" played, Howard entered the ballroom packed with more than 3,000 Florida Democrats. He had left his suit coat in a room across the hall. We came to the decision after peeking into the convention hall and witnessing the hooting and hollering of the audience. The relaxed look seemed appropriate.

Members of the Painters Union – dressed in their black and gold T-shirts and carrying matching signs – were on hand to escort him to the stage. But their efforts were hindered by his supporters, who filled the aisle and swept him to the front of the room by the sheer force of their numbers.

Close to 100 of Howard's supporters clustered around him while he spoke. It wasn't a Dean rally, but the Deaniacs who yelled and waved their signs when his face appeared on the two large screens in the front of the room overwhelmed the non-believers.

The scene when he entered the room was repeated when he finished his speech. His supporters standing with him on the stage pulled at him from all sides. Some had a firm grip on his hands, while others held him in a tight bear hug. The Painters – many of whom were built like wrestlers – came to his rescue, prying him away from his overzealous fans.

December 7, 2003

We began the day in Columbia, South Carolina, after flying in at midnight the evening before. Howard's first public appearance was on the Fox News channel's Sunday morning show.

The calls for him to release his sealed gubernatorial papers were stronger than ever. Four days had passed since we met in Burlington and decided that Howard would hold off making a public statement until Judicial Watch decided if it was going to file a lawsuit.

We saw a lawsuit as the best scenario and luckily, the group decided it would go to court to force the release of the records. Howard used his appearance on Fox to announce that he thought the best course of action would be to let the lawsuit play out and have a judge decide if the documents should be unsealed.

□ □ □

The former governor of the second whitest state in the nation was still trying to prove that he could appeal to African American voters. To that end, he attended a Sunday morning church service at the Community CME Church, an African American church in Columbia.

After the service he headed to the Clarion Town House Hotel to deliver a speech on "Race and Community Relations." The campaign had gathered a half dozen prominent African American elected officials from South Carolina to stand with him during his speech to the African American audience. Joining them was

Congressman Jesse Jackson, Jr. who had flown in from Chicago to offer his support. When Howard entered the hotel ballroom, the cheers of the enthusiastic – but all white – audience greeted him.

We left South Carolina on an airplane bound for New York City, but on the way we touched down in Virginia. It was a quick visit – just one hour – however, it was an important one. The hundreds of people who packed into the tiny ballroom at the Holiday Inn in Virginia Beach were there to watch Virginia Congressman Bobby Scott throw his support behind Howard. Scott held the distinction of being the first African American elected to Congress from Virginia since Reconstruction.

By 10:30 p.m. we were in New York City and things were out of control in Vermont. I received an e-mail from a staffer in Burlington informing me that Joe had learned about a rally being planned in Iowa. (Earlier in the day I had asked Jeani Murray to organize an event in Cedar Rapids on December 9, but I didn't tell her why.) He had confronted the scheduling staff demanding to know what was going on, but they couldn't answer because they didn't know. He then angrily announced that he was going to call Howard.

A short time later, I got a call from Howard. Joe had called him, but Howard didn't tell Joe about Gore's endorsement. Instead he told Joe that he couldn't tell him what was going on, but he should plan to be in New York on December 9.

December 8, 2003

It was going to be a long day, one that began at 9 a.m. and wouldn't end until midnight.

Joe flew to New York early in the morning and by then Howard knew he needed to tell him about Gore's endorsement. Although he told Joe, he told no one else. There was only one day left before the announcement and he was going to do everything possible to ensure that it was a surprise. (He went so far as to never refer to Gore by name; instead we called him the "special guest.")

We still had work to do, namely alerting the press that Howard's schedule had been changed to include a trip to Iowa. Joe took to the phone, calling the reporters who covered the campaign to tell them that Howard would be going to the caucus state for an event they wouldn't want to miss.

Our appointments were all over the city, which meant we spent a great deal of time in the car, Joe calling the press and Howard worrying that news of Gore's endorsement would leak out.

As more members of the media learned about the trip to Iowa, the speculation as to the reason grew and solving the mystery became an obsession.

During an afternoon press conference, Howard received the support of New York City Council Speaker Gifford Miller and 20 city councilors. The endorsement was a big deal, but all the media wanted to know was what was going happen in Iowa the next day. First they thought that Iowa U.S. Senator Tom Harkin was going to throw his support behind Howard. But when they realized that Howard was going to attend a breakfast in Harlem before flying to Iowa, they began to suspect that he was going to be endorsed by Bill Clinton who had an office in the area.

For much of the day we played a version of the kids' game hot or cold. The media would take a guess and ask if they were getting closer to solving the mystery. By the afternoon our secret was still safe. No one had guessed that Al Gore was the answer to the puzzle.

By 4 p.m. we had made it through a press conference, an interview on CNN, and two fundraisers out of the eight we had scheduled (one that attracted 2,500 people and raised $1 million) without anyone uncovering our secret. But our luck was about to end.

Two dozen people mingled around the sparsely furnished New York apartment – the minimalist look was not due to a lack of funds, to the contrary the well-healed owner probably over-paid an interior decorator to accomplish the effect. The wine and cheese and a private chat with Howard cost each person $500. The event had the air of exclusivity, but as special as those in the room thought they were, they didn't know that Al Gore would be endorsing Howard the next morning.

I was engaged in idle chitchat when I received a call from Burlington. MSNBC was reporting that Gore was set to endorse Howard the next day. It was disappointing because we had been able to keep the secret for three days and had less than one to go. CBS and the *Los Angeles Times* followed, reporting that the story had come from inside the campaign. Reporters for the news organizations said that Joe was the source, something he denied.

It didn't matter, however, because the story was out. And what began as a secret among four people turned into a full-blown feeding frenzy. Howard's supporters celebrated the news by posting thousands of comments on the campaign blog. Their responses ranged from "Oh, gosh, I just scared the cat by screaming with delight!" to "This means he's for sure going to win!"

Meanwhile, Howard ignored all the excitement, remaining steadfast in his desire to make it a surprise. He refused to confirm the story for the press – or the campaign staff. We continued to use the term "special guest" and because the staff had no official confirmation, Gore's name never appeared on the schedule they prepared for December 9. "Special guest" was used in its place.

December 9, 2003

"Howard don't get too excited, they're not here for you." Howard's mother made the pronouncement when he expressed his amazement at the sight of the eleven satellite trucks that lined the streets around the National Black Theater's Institute of Action Art.

And she was right, because for all of Howard's popularity and front-runner status it was the largest congregation of media we had seen – and they had come out to the Institute in Harlem to watch Al Gore endorse Howard.

If you hadn't heard the news you might not have known that the event was special. It began like all the others. The song "We Can" blared and the crowd cheered. Howard walked on stage, waved, stood in front of a large Dean banner, and clasped hands with the man standing next to him.

But when more than 50 cameras clicked, flashed, and taped the entrance it was clear that it wasn't just an ordinary event. The 200 people in the room, who were expecting to attend a simple breakfast meeting before news of the endorsement broke, sensed they were witnessing a turning point in the campaign and reacted with loud cheers.

Howard took to the podium first and introduced Gore. He hadn't uttered the former vice president's name in four days and seemed to forget that it was now safe to do so when he thanked his "special guest" for being there.

When Gore announced that he was "very proud and honored to endorse Howard Dean to be the next president of the United States of America," the crowd roared and Howard waved as the cameras captured the moment. (There was one camera in the room that missed the action on the stage. The CNN camerawoman had her camera trained on Joe.)

When Gore was done complementing Howard and Howard was finished complementing Gore, the two men left the stage the way they arrived – hands in the air and then down the stairs to the beat of "We Can."

We left the building through a back door. Gore walked quickly through a small group of waiting reporters and hopped into the car followed by Howard.

From New York we flew to Cedar Rapids, Iowa. Gore, Howard, Rick Jacobs, and I, along with traveling press secretary Doug Thornell and one of the vice president's assistants, boarded one plane while the 23 members of the press boarded another. Joe chose to ride with the media so he could brief them on how the endorsement came about.

During the two and a half-hour flight we chatted, ate box lunches, and Gore offered Howard advice. He was surprised to learn that our schedule included six days a week on the road and 18 hour days. He knew the result of such a relentless schedule – something we had discovered the hard way and couldn't seem to fix – that all the hours take their toll. He recommended that Howard slow down.

He also suggested that Howard spend more time studying policy issues, picking one issue and becoming an expert on it. Gore practiced what he preached. During the flight he took out his laptop computer, set it on one of the airplane's small pullout tables, and asked us to close our window shades. He then launched into a 30-minute presentation on global warming. His presentation was both passionate and interesting, but I had the flu and was operating on three hours of sleep, so it was all I could do to stay awake in the darkness of the plane.

For his part, Howard pondered aloud what Gore's endorsement could mean for the campaign organization. Many accomplished individuals (some of whom had worked for Bill Clinton and Gore) had offered their services to the campaign, but for the most part they were shut out by Joe and some of the consultants. Howard wanted them involved and Gore could provide the cover necessary to get them on the campaign staff. He reasoned that if he told Joe that the former vice president wanted them involved their help couldn't be refused.

We entered the Five Seasons Hotel in Cedar Rapids through the kitchen, where a dozen former Gore and current Dean supporters were lined up waiting to get their pictures taken with the two men. There were celebratory hugs all around as Howard and Gore posed in front of a backdrop of stainless steel kitchen appliances.

The hundreds of people who filled the hotel ballroom cheered at the sight of Howard and Gore walking up the stairs that led to the stage. By the time we arrived in Iowa pictures from the morning event were appearing online. The identity of the "special guest" that had been advertised on the campaign flyers for the rally had been confirmed. But it didn't lessen the excitement in the room.

When the two men acknowledged the crowd by holding their hands high in the air, the lyrics from the campaign theme song – "we can do the impossible" – took on a ring of truth.

After the rally, Howard, Mike O'Mary, Doug Thornell, and I flew to Portsmouth, New Hampshire. The Iowa staff had stocked the plane with pork chops and twice baked potatoes. It was as close to a celebration as we would have, because in four hours Howard would be joining his fellow Democrats at a debate in New Hampshire sponsored by ABC News.

□ □ □

When we arrived on the campus of the University of New Hampshire we were greeted by a crush of supporters who swarmed Howard when he emerged from the car. The supporters – along with the bright lights of the television cameras that illuminated our path – wanted to share in the celebration of Gore's endorsement and formed a tight circle around him, forcing us to inch our way to the building.

We made our way to the Johnson Theater and slipped through a back door, leaving the supporters on the other side. A member of the ABC staff escorted us to the small office where we would wait for the debate to start.

The backstage area of the theater was calm and quiet. Howard and I sat in the office, leaving only once to walk down the hall where a make-up artist was waiting to put powder on his face. A few people who worked for ABC News milled around, but none of his rivals were in sight.

Howard needed to put the excitement of the endorsement aside and focus on the debate.

He sat at the desk by the window and concentrated on reviewing his notes. Suddenly, the silence was broken by the pounding on the window followed by the chants of "JK all the way!" A dozen Kerry supporters were standing in the darkness outside. They had walked around the building peering into windows looking for Howard.

If their goal was to rattle him they succeeded. Security from the university chased them away, but it was time for Howard to go on stage. It had become the norm for Kerry supporters to harass us (we had been attacked by the giant waffle in Maine), but they had crossed the line this time. As Howard walked down the hallway to the theater he talked about confronting Kerry during the debate about the actions of his supporters. He changed his mind when reminded that in light of the Gore endorsement his complaining could look petty.

□ □ □

"Raise your hand if you believe that Governor Dean can beat George Bush," Ted Koppel from ABC News asked the nine Democrats who lined the stage at the University of New Hampshire.

Polls showed Howard leading his rivals nationally, in Iowa, and in New Hampshire and it had been just hours since he picked up the endorsement of Al Gore. It wasn't a surprise that Howard's hand was the only one to go up.

The final debate of the year became a debate about Gore and the significance of his endorsement. The candidates asserted that it would make no difference to voters and they even attacked Gore for throwing his support behind a candidate.

The man who Democrats rallied around in 2000 after he lost the election to George Bush was assailed for trying to have a "coronation" and for being disloyal to his former running mate Joe Lieberman. John Edwards told the audience, "Republicans have coronations. We have campaigns, we have elections." John Kerry questioned why Gore would endorse Howard with Lieberman in the race, while Lieberman asserted that the endorsement would actually help him. He was being contacted by many voters who were angry with the way Gore was treating him.

By the end of the debate, Howard was defending Gore, "If you guys are upset about Al Gore's endorsement, you attack me, don't attack Al Gore. Al Gore worked too hard in 2000 and I don't think he deserves to be attacked by anybody up here."

December 11, 2003

Poll numbers, fundraising totals, and endorsements led many pundits, our supporters, and some on staff to predict that Howard was headed toward capturing the nomination. However, despite our success – or perhaps because of it – we were falling apart internally.

A week before Gore's endorsement, the *Washington Post* published a story about Howard's "trusted inner circle." It portrayed us as a tight knit group of people working together with the common goal of getting Howard elected. It recounted about the daily phone calls between Howard and Joe and lovingly described the office Joe and I shared.

But nothing could have been further from the truth. In reality, Howard and Joe rarely spoke, all Joe and I did was fight, and as a group we spent most of our time questioning each other's motives. And the problems only grew with Howard's success and took a turn for the worse with Gore's endorsement.

Unbeknownst to Joe, Mike Ford and Steve McMahon had decided that Mike would take over as campaign manager after

Howard won the New Hampshire primary, and they had been lobbying Bob and me, hoping that we'd agree to convince Howard to make the change. Besides the fact that we hadn't won anything yet, neither of us was sold on the idea. But the strategizing had become so distracting that we asked Howard to meet with Mike.

Howard had just finished a photo shoot for *Newsweek* magazine at a private home in downtown Burlington. It was one of his rare days in Vermont and all he wanted to do was go home. He was tired and not interested in having the discussion, but he stayed and listened to Mike outlined his plan: Mike would leave Vermont immediately and go back to his home in Maryland where he would work on the strategy for the general election and nominating convention. He would return in February – after the New Hampshire primary – as the campaign manager. (The same job he rejected almost two years earlier.)

Howard's response was a quick and decisive, "No." Mike was hired because he was Joe's friend and because of the promise that Joe would let him help with the daily operations of the office. If Mike wanted to work on the campaign he needed to stay in Vermont and do just that.

December 12, 2003

The vintage clothing, telephone operator's switchboard, radios, television sets, and knick knacks that filled the stuffy back room at the Historical Society in Winterset, Iowa, were from another era. One that seemed much simpler than the one we were living in. Al Gore's endorsement, while exciting to our supporters, had intensified the efforts of Howard's rivals to knock him out of the race.

While we waited for the undecided caucus goers to settle into the metal folding chairs in the next room, the museum's curator gave us a tour. The town of Winterset was located in Madison County, the setting for the book-turned-major motion picture

Bridges of Madison County, starring Meryl Streep and Clint Eastwood. When Howard cheerfully inquired whether any of the museum's collection was used in the film, the outside world seemed far away.

His rivals had seized on a *Boston Globe* story that claimed that as governor he had given tax breaks to large corporations including Enron. Howard was a constant critic of "Ken Lay (Enron CEO) and the boys," which prompted Dick Gephardt to launch a new round of attacks accusing him of "gross hypocrisy" for "attacking President Bush's special treatment of Enron" while he "turned Vermont into a tax shelter for that very same corporate criminal."

At the same time, a group calling itself "Americans for Jobs, Health Care and Progressive Values" was running a television ad against him in South Carolina and New Hampshire. The commercial opened with a picture of Osama bin Laden. As the camera lens focused on bin Laden the words "Dangerous World," "Destroy Us," "Dangers Ahead," and "No Experience" appeared on the screen. Along with the images a narrator read from a script, "Americans want a president who can face the dangers ahead. But Howard Dean has no military or foreign policy experience. And Howard Dean just cannot compete with George Bush on foreign policy. It's time for Democrats to think about that – and think about it now."

The ad was harsh and frightening – and to Howard, over the top and unfair. He didn't like the message, but what upset him more was that according to the law, Americans for Jobs, Health Care and Progressive Values did not have to disclose the names of the individuals who funded the ad.

Refuting the claims of his named critics was hard enough (his pronouncement that "we did not give tax breaks to Enron," was treated by the media as just another denial), but fighting a faceless person or persons frustrated him.

December 14, 2003

Howard stood behind the podium set up in the driveway outside of the Holiday Inn Hotel in West Palm Beach, Florida. More than a dozen reporters listened while a handful of curious hotel guests dressed in shorts and T-shirts looked on and snapped pictures. We hadn't planned on holding a press conference that sunny Sunday morning, but we hadn't expected the capture of Saddam Hussein either.

An early morning phone call from Burlington alerted us to the news of the Iraqi leader's capture by U.S. forces. We were in Palm Beach getting ready to attend a round of morning fundraisers when the news came in.

We were as delighted and excited as every American, but the shocking news was also disheartening. Saddam's capture was obviously a significant – and positive – development in world affairs, but as the country celebrated we were left to wonder if Howard's front-runner status would be affected by the success of the military action that he opposed from the beginning – a position that many credited for his surge in the polls.

Howard sat on the edge of the bed in his hotel room. While images of a bearded Hussein flashed on the television screen, he was on the phone trying to figure out how to react to the news. His first call was to Al Gore; followed by Senator Hillary Clinton, a member of the Senate Armed Services Committee; and Delaware Senator Joe Biden, chair of the Senate Foreign Relations Committee.

While the capture of Saddam was a victory for the U.S. military, Howard's opposition to the war hadn't changed – the end didn't justify the means. But in the face of celebration he couldn't be defiant – at least not yet. After a quick conversation with the campaign staff and foreign policy advisors, he decided to keep his response tame and focused. He would congratulate the troops, but concede nothing.

As he stood behind the light green podium set up not far from a group of orange traffic cones that kept the cars away, he told the media, "This is a great day of pride in the American military, a great day for the Iraqis, a great day for the American people and, frankly, a great day for the administration. This is a day to celebrate the fact that Saddam's been caught. We'll have to see what happens to the campaign later."

□ □ □

Saddam Hussein was in custody and what that meant for the campaign was anyone's guess, but we couldn't let the events of the day slow us down. We had money to raise.

After two fundraising receptions in Florida, we hopped on a plane and flew to California. More than six hours later we walked into the backstage area of the Masonic Auditorium in San Francisco for the first in a series of money raising events dubbed "All I Want For The Holidays Is My Country Back." On stage the singer Bonnie Raitt was performing for the crowd that topped 2,500. The actor Sean Penn and singer David Crosby were mingling in one of the small rooms that housed food and drinks for the performers.

Howard said hello, thanked them for coming, and then headed on stage to speak to the crowd. He walked through the drums, guitars, microphone stands, and amplifiers that had been left by the musicians. His sleeves were rolled up and he held a microphone in one hand. The crowd that filled the main floor and the balcony stood and cheered as Howard gave them a thumb's up.

While we were flying from Florida to California Howard's opponents had been responding to the news of Saddam's capture, and the speculation as to the future of our campaign had begun in earnest. The Democrats who voted in favor of the military action in Iraq saw the capture as a vindication of their position and more proof that Howard lacked the foreign policy experience to be the commander-in-chief.

Howard used the occasion in front of his supporters to respond to his critics. He began his remarks by congratulating the troops, but told the cheering crowd, "You should know that my views on Iraq have not changed one bit." To those who deemed his campaign in trouble he fiercely declared, "You know, some people have said, 'Oh, Saddam Hussein is captured, this campaign is going away.' I don't think so."

December 15, 2003

The gold-trimmed chairs were lined up in rows in the ballroom at the St. Regis Hotel in Los Angeles. Matching gold and red carpeting complemented the striped gold wallpaper. A small riser in the front of the room held a podium and four American flags that dangled lifeless from their stands. Men and women dressed in business suits sat silently, their perfect posture courtesy of the straight-backed chairs. The scene was devoid of campaign signs and T-shirt-wearing supporters. Instead, it was serious setting for a serious event. Howard was set to give his first major address on national security and his audience was the Pacific World Affairs Council.

The speech had been planned long before Saddam Hussein was captured, but in light of the developments in Iraq his remarks had taken on new significance – a fact made clear by the more than 50 members of the media who had assembled in the back of the room.

As the council members took their seats in the main ballroom, Howard waited in a small room next door. He stood and reviewed the speech one last time. It had been in the works for weeks but had been hastily revised the night before to address the capture of the Iraqi leader.

Warren Christopher, the former Secretary of State under President Clinton, introduced Howard who walked on the stage to the polite applause of the gathered guests. He placed the text of the speech on the podium and thanked the audience for the kind welcome.

His script was in front of him and all the staff in Burlington wanted him to do was read it. He began with the new text that addressed the capture of Saddam Hussein. In keeping with the serious event, he showed little emotion when he told the staid audience what he so proudly announced to Sean Penn, Bonnie Raitt, and his 2,500 screaming supporters the night before, "Let me be clear. My position on the Iraq war has not changed."

He continued to read what was typed on the pages. His recitation was exact until he reached the third page, when he declared, "The capture of Saddam has not made America safer." The line appeared on exactly one copy of the speech – his own. He had scribbled it down just before he walked on stage.

There was no reaction from the audience, but within seconds my Blackberry and cell phone were buzzing. It was the staff in Burlington. They were listening to the speech and wanted to know how I could let Howard make such a stupid remark. But short of leaping over Warren Christopher to tackle him, there wasn't much I or anyone could have done to stop him.

We knew that Saddam's capture threatened to overshadow the broader national security message in the speech, but it turned out that it was Howard's own comment that stole the spotlight.

His rivals and critics quickly seized on his declaration that the United States was no safer, using it to further bolster their claim that he lacked the foreign policy experience necessary to be president.

When he stepped off the stage the campaign was fully engulfed in another controversy. But Howard rebuffed anyone (staff included) who called his comment a gaffe, a blunder or just naïve.

He wasn't going to apologize or explain his remark because he firmly believed in what he said.

While Howard's critics hoped otherwise, his supporters didn't think the capture of Saddam would change the campaign's fortunes, nor did they rebuke his assertion that the United States was no safer with the dictator in jail.

Hours after his speech to the Pacific World Affairs Council, we were at a fundraiser at the House of Blues in Los Angeles. The 1,000-person capacity crowd stood shoulder to shoulder singing along with the 1980s all girl band the Bangels as they waited for Howard to appear.

When Rob Reiner introduced him, he emerged from the wings to the roar of the crowd. The spotlights washed over the audience to the barely audible beat of "We Can." Two dozen photographers stood in front of the stage jockeying for a picture while fighting to stay upright as they were pushed forward by Howard's eager supporters.

The room exploded when he announced that his position on the war hadn't changed because of the capture of Saddam Hussein, and there was no hesitation when he asserted that the United States was "no safer." The crowd cheered and clapped their hands high in the air in agreement.

By the end of the speech the noise in the room was deafening as the crowd joined Howard in chanting, "We have the power!" He leaned over the stage, barely avoiding being pulled in by his supporters, as he shook hands, signed autographs, and posed for pictures. He finally pried himself free and with two thumbs up thanked the crowd and hustled back to the wings.

December 16, 2003

It was a hot and sunny day in Arizona, and for Vermonters who were used to measuring time by the amount of snow on the ground it didn't feel like Christmas was just a little over a week away. If it hadn't been for the strands of tiny white lights that dangled from the ceiling at a senior center or for the barely newborn baby dressed in a tiny red Santa suit, we could have easily forgotten about the holiday.

As we arrived in the state a newly released poll showed that Howard was, as one Arizona newspaper put it, "breaking away from the pack." The survey of Arizona voters showed him leading his closest competitor Wes Clark 22 percent to 12 percent.

He was all smiles in front of the seniors who packed the Sundial Recreation Center in Sun City to watch him pick up the endorsement of the state's former U.S. Senator and Clinton Natural Resources Secretary Bruce Babbitt. He was unfazed – and unscathed – when the rush of the crowd resulted in him nearly being run over by an eager supporter in a wheel chair.

He was delighted by the hundreds of supporters who filled the ballroom at the Ramada Inn in Yuma. The light pink sign in front of the hotel not only boasted that the establishment was AAA approved, but giant black block letters had been arranged to read "Welcome to Yuma Howard Dean."

He was thrilled by the roar of the crowd that greeted him at the small airplane hangar in Sierra Vista and equally delighted by the platters of fresh-baked cookies presented to him upon his arrival.

But behind the smiles, cheers, and handshakes, he was seething over the ad being run by Americans for Jobs, Health Care and Progressive Values and had become obsessed with finding out who funded it.

There was no legal requirement for the organization to make its donors public, which left Howard to speculate, and by the time we landed in Arizona his prime suspect was multi-millionaire movie producer Steve Bing. There no was evidence linking Bing to the group, but he had donated hundreds of thousands of dollars to Howard's opponents in the past and, as a millionaire, had easy access to funds, which was enough to put him in Howard's sights.

Howard had shared his suspicions with enough people that it didn't take long for word to get back to Bing, who was furious at being accused of doing such a thing. Bing called Rob Reiner and asked him to relay a message to Howard: Stop saying that I funded the ad or I *will* run ads against you. Before our plane left Arizona Howard called Bing and apologized.

December 19, 2003

For four days Howard defended himself against the attacks of his rivals, who condemned his assertion that the country was no safer after the capture of Saddam Hussein. He pushed back hard, dubbing his fellow Democrats the "Washington politics-as-usual club" and faulting them for failing to question the president. "Instead of standing up for what was right, these Democrats backed away from the fight."

With the success of the military mission, his rivals and many pundits waited for him to take a hit in public opinion polls. But it didn't happen. Despite the sharp attacks from his rivals, his polls numbers remained steady. A poll taken after Saddam's capture showed Howard maintaining a 29-point lead over John Kerry in New Hampshire.

Kerry needed to do something. It had been a month since he had replaced his campaign manager, but Howard was still leading in both Iowa and New Hampshire. And the once presumed top money raiser was running short on cash.

In an effort to revive his campaign, Kerry wrote a personal check for $850,000 and was set to mortgage his Boston home. He also shifted his resources to Iowa, betting that a good showing in the caucus state would give him the momentum going into New Hampshire.

While Kerry was regrouping, I was sitting in a restaurant at the Marriott Hotel in Trenton, New Jersey, with Joe's friend, John Haber. Howard was set to receive the endorsement of the state's

Democratic Governor Jim McGreevy and Haber was set on taking a leading role in the campaign.

Three months had passed since he first traveled to Vermont at the behest of Steve McMahon to discuss joining the campaign. He didn't come on board then, but was intent on doing so now.

It had been a week since Howard rejected Mike Ford's proposal to take over as the campaign manager. As cheery elevator music played in the background, it became clear that Haber was under the impression that he was going to be running the organization. (An impression he didn't get from Howard who barely knew him.) I almost choked on my toast when he told me that his first order of business when he arrived in Burlington would be to send Joe into exile traveling around the country far from the office and the rest of the staff. The announcement surprised me. Not only because Haber thought he was going to be running the show, but because the reason Steve recommended him in the first place was because he was Joe's friend, which Steve contended would make Joe more apt to trust him.

First it was Mike Ford. Now it was John Haber angling for the top job. One needed a score card to keep track of what was going on, and it would have been entertaining but for the fact that Howard was running for president of the United States.

December 20, 2003

The lobby of the Country Inn & Suites hotel in Clinton, Iowa, was decked out for the holidays. Green garland flowed down the banister on the stairs that led to the upper floors. Small white lights twinkled on the Christmas tree and on the string of lights that outlined the reception desk. Hand knit stockings hung over the fireplace. The hotel had worked hard to live up to its motto, "A Cozy Stay at a Comfortable Price."

Among all the trimmings, members of the media and a handful of campaign staffers sat slumped over, sleepy from our late night arrival in the caucus state. Dressed in our winter coats and hats, we waited to board the bus that would carry us around Iowa for the day. As we checked our e-mail and cell phones, a young girl wrapped in an oversized towel, hair dripping wet, walked through the lobby on her way to her room after an early morning dip in the hotel pool. She was a reminder of a world that seemed far away.

□ □ □

Row after row of cafeteria tables lined the Washington Middle School gymnasium in Clinton. The muffled sounds of the more than 300 people who had crowded in filled the room, the conversations interrupted ever so briefly when Howard made his entrance.

Wearing a green apron and holding a large stainless steel spatula, he made his way to the griddle. Yvonne, a short, stout, white-haired woman known to us as the pancake lady, dispensed batter onto the hot surface, as Howard stood ready to flip the pancakes over. It was only his second pancake breakfast of the campaign, yet he was feeling confident about his flipping abilities. He threw the pancakes high over his head and tossed them – rotating them multiple times in the air – across the griddle onto the Styrofoam plates being held by his would-be supporters.

As he watched the pancakes float through the air, his broad smile masked his frustration with his opponents. He was growing increasingly tired of their relentless attacks – attacks that were only getting harsher and coming faster as his poll numbers remained strong and the first contests got closer.

They were criticizing his public statements, questioning his competence, and scrutinizing his record as governor. They continued to hammer on his contention that the United States was no safer after the capture of Saddam Hussein. They accused him of giving tax breaks to Enron, holding secret meetings to set

Vermont's energy policy, and ignoring safety concerns at Vermont's nuclear power plant. They questioned his integrity, citing his refusal to unseal his gubernatorial records. They accused him of supporting policies that would raise taxes on the middle class and threaten the health care security of the nation's seniors. And they described him as quick tempered and angry.

By the time he arrived at a reception in Dubuque that featured the smooth sounds of a high school jazz band, his frustration was beginning to show. He issued a rebuke of his rivals' methods telling the press, "This campaign needs a little character transplant. It's not necessary to tear down the other opponents."

December 21, 2003

It had been three weeks since Joe said no to Howard's request that he go to Iowa. With the caucuses just a month away, Howard decided to prevail upon him again.

We were in New Hampshire, having flown in from Iowa the night before. It was the first day of a three-day tour of the state that included town hall meetings and time set aside to shoot a television commercial far from public view.

The commercial brought Joe, along with Steve McMahon and Mark Squier, to New Hampshire. The shoot took place at the home of a supporter in Concord. The house was decorated for the holidays with a wreath on the door and a tree inside. Camera equipment filled the living room, but it didn't take away from the festive feel.

In between takes, Howard and Joe moved to a small den where Howard made his case. This time he enlisted the help of Mike Ford. He hoped that because of the two men's long-running friendship, Mike could convince Joe that going to Iowa was necessary.

Not more than 15 minutes later Joe emerged from the room alone. Unaware that I was in the next room, he stood in front of the glimmering Christmas tree and defiantly announced to Steve and Mark that regardless of what Howard wanted he was not going to Iowa.

December 23, 2003

If Iowa and New Hampshire voters had been willing to turn their Christmas dinner into a Dean house party, we would have been there bearing gifts. The last thing anyone wanted to see, however, was a presidential candidate sitting under their tree, so we were about to be forced off the campaign trail, but not before we spent one last day in New Hampshire.

It may have been two days before a religious holiday, but there was no cease-fire between the campaigns. The other Democrats greeted Howard's comment that the campaign needed a "character transplant" with disbelief and sarcasm. They saw his criticism of their tactics as hypocritical. They shot back, claiming they were doing nothing that he hadn't done to them. For nearly two years, Howard had been openly critical of their support of Bush policies such as the war in Iraq and No Child Left Behind, even describing his opponents as Bush-lite.

They may have been competing against each other, but now more than ever the rivals were unified behind one cause: defeating Howard. Echoing the sentiments of all the Democrats, Dick Gephardt told reporters, "I think he's been lobbing attacks on the other Democrats in the race for about a year. He only sees negative campaigning when it isn't him."

They used his complaints against them as proof that he would not be the best candidate to go face-to-face with Bush. Almost in unison they described him as thinned-skinned and weak. If he couldn't take the heat now, he would surely whither under the attacks from the Republicans during the general election.

Howard was upset with his opponents, but he was equally frustrated with the media for reporting the attacks and claims that were made against him. He couldn't understand why they would so easily believe what his opponents were saying and often repeat charges that would later prove to be baseless.

For more than three months our small media entourage had been traveling with us on a regular basis. We spent almost every minute of every day together. There is a natural tension that occurs between the press and a politician. For Howard, however, it had turned to animosity that was made awkward by the fact that the people we were sharing our lives with were often the ones reporting the charges that he deemed unfair.

After our last event of the day – a tour of a manufacturing plant in Seabrook – we were ready to hop in the car and make the three-hour drive to Burlington. But before Howard and I headed home we bid good-bye to the media with handshakes and hugs. For all the tension between us, the idea of being separated – even for just a few days – was oddly unsettling.

December 27, 2003

The red awning above the door announced that we were entering Morg's, a family restaurant in Waterloo, Iowa. It was our first day back on the campaign trail after a three-day break for the Christmas holiday. Howard walked into the restaurant followed by the media. As he made his way to the booth that had been reserved for him, he stopped and introduced himself to the patrons who sat on swivel stools at the counter or in booths along the wall.

After the handshakes, he slid into a green vinyl upholstered booth. Waiting for him was a hamburger and French fries. As the photographers circled around, he squirted ketchup on the burger and added two slices of tomato.

The other lunch goers looked on, puzzled as to why eating a hamburger was worthy of such attention. But there was a point to the seemingly normal action. Howard was going to eat the hamburger to prove that there was no health risk to eating beef. A Mad Cow disease scare had left the Iowa beef industry vulnerable, and Howard decided he could help restore confidence in the industry by eating a hamburger.

After asking the photographers if they were ready, he took a big bite out of the burger. The flashbulbs shined on his suit like a disco ball as he held the hamburger in the air showing off the bite mark.

The stunt didn't take long. Ten minutes after arriving, we were heading out the door. As Howard was leaving, a woman sitting in one of the booths stopped him. It wasn't clear whether it was the death defying act that made her stop him, but in any case she asked him which political party he belonged to. When he answered Democrat she held out her hand to shake his.

Feeling no ill effects from the hamburger, we set out to meet with undecided voters. Would-be caucus goers in five towns assembled at community centers and at a YMCA to hear Howard speak.

Christmas was just a memory and with the remnants of the holiday still hanging on the walls, Howard picked up where he left off. He espoused his opposition to the war in Iraq, talked of his support for universal health care, characterized Republicans as "borrow and spend radicals," and told his audiences that it was time to take the American flag back from people like Rush Limbaugh and Jerry Falwell.

And despite telling a reporter during an interview earlier in the day, "I think the person who wins the caucuses in Iowa is going to be the person who ends up being the most positive. I'm going to try to concentrate on bringing the Democratic Party together so we can beat George Bush," he continued to take his fellow Democrats to task for supporting Bush policies, using the line he repeated often, "We're not going to beat George Bush by being Bush-lite."

But Howard wasn't the only one who picked up where he left off; his opponents did as well. They remained critical, particularly John Kerry, who came back from the holiday swinging. He had set up shop in Iowa and although behind by double digits had not given up on New Hampshire. He was positioning himself as the alternative to Howard and on his first day back on the campaign trail delivered a speech described by one newspaper as a "withering attack" on Howard. Highlighting Howard's belief that the capture of Saddam Hussein had not made the United States any safer, Kerry portrayed him as lacking the competence and temperament to be president.

Adding fodder for Kerry was a comment published in the *Concord Monitor* the day before. Howard had told the paper that he didn't want to prejudge Osama bin Laden's guilt. His opponents immediately responded that a person who didn't see that bin Laden was guilty of masterminding the September 11 attacks should not be president.

Howard clarified the comment explaining that bin Laden was "exactly the kind of case the death penalty is made for." Despite the clarification, however, his opponents had already condemned the remark and added it to their running list of ill-conceived statements made by Howard.

December 28, 2003

The news coming out of the press conference was supposed to be Howard's response to the Mad Cow scare. He had eaten a hamburger the day before but had waited for the scheduled press conference to make a formal statement.

He sat in a metal folding chair in the Des Moines headquarters. Facing him in matching metal chairs were seven members of the media. Sitting slumped back with his legs crossed and hands in his pockets he read from the press release on his lap.

In the context of a heated presidential campaign, a health scare even with an impressive scientific name like Bovine Spongiform Encephalopathy was boring. The gathered media listened, but they had other questions for Howard and it didn't take long for the topic to turn from Mad Cow to mad candidate. When he finished reading his statement he was asked about the war of words with his opponents. He sat back and let his frustration flow.

For five days he had been calling on them to end their attacks on him – a request they ignored and even ridiculed. He had become consumed by the attacks that seemed never-ending. He had had enough and lashed out, but his target was not his opponents, it was Democratic Party Chair Terry McAuliffe. Howard was critical of McAuliffe, believing that the party chair had a responsibility to stop the negative campaigning.

He told the reporters, who were suddenly glad they had sat through the Mad Cow presentation, "If we had strong leadership in the Democratic Party, it would be calling the other candidates and saying somebody has to win here." He continued, "If Ron Brown (the DNC chair during Bill Clinton's successful bid in 1992) were chairman, this wouldn't be happening."

But he didn't stop there. He also implied that his supporters might not support the Democratic nominee if it wasn't him. "If I don't win the nomination, where do you think those million and a half people, half a million on the Internet, where do you think they're going to go? I don't know where they're going to go. They're certainly not going to vote for a conventional Washington candidate."

His comments were a gift to the media, which could always count on him to give them something to write about, and to his opponents, who were counting on him to self-destruct.

□ □ □

Close to 400 caucus goers greeted Howard as he took his place behind a podium set up on a small stage in the Iowa State Center at

Iowa State University in Ames. He had just completed the ritual of getting his picture taken with a handful of key activists who had been lined up in a small conference room down the hall. It was another Commit for Change event and now came the time to persuade undecided Iowans to support him. Mad Cow was the issue of the day – at least for Howard – and he began his remarks by outlining the president's lack of leadership on the matter.

While Howard talked about Bovine Spongiform Encephalopathy, my cell phone buzzed. It was Terry McAuliffe. The comments Howard made to the media four hours earlier had made their way to Washington and the party chair was not pleased. He gave me a tongue lashing, one I promised to pass along to Howard. And although I told him that Howard would call him back, I wasn't sure that he would – or that he should. Both men were upset and any conversation between the two had the potential of making things worse.

Smiles, hugs, handshakes, autographs, and pictures followed Howard's speech. He was feeling good about the response he got, only to be told that McAuliffe had called, angry about his comments. Howard showed no sympathy for the party chair and adamantly refused to return his call.

□ □ □

Pouring a milk shake on a person's head was a tradition at Stella's Blue Sky Diner in Urbandale, Iowa. Howard was at Stella's to speak to the 150 supporters who packed into the family-owned restaurant. But as the saying goes, "When in Rome do as the Romans do."

The setting for the event – a diner replete with a juke box, lunch counter, and vinyl and chrome furnishings – energized the crowd even before Howard took the stage or, in this case, the chair he stood on to be seen above the crowd.

When he was done "having fun at the president's expense," he hopped off the chair and sat down. He put on a turquoise colored shirt with "Stella" embroidered on the back in pink letters. The shirt was like a shield, there to protect him from the any loose falling ice cream.

With a towel at the ready, the owner of the restaurant urged Howard to "trust us." A young restaurant worker named Kyle hopped on the chair behind him. He handed Howard a clear glass and instructed him to hold it steady on top of his head. As Kyle mixed the thick shake with a spoon he asked Howard, "Are you ready for this?" With a sly, slightly nervous grin on his face, he replied, "No." Any one of the other Democrats, and the national party chair for that matter, would have relished the opportunity to change places with Kyle.

From three feet above Howard's head, Kyle poured the milk shake into the glass. It cascaded down like a thick strawberry waterfall. The crowd cheered and applauded while Howard remained focused on staying still, knowing that the slightest movement would result in a milk shake shampoo.

It took only seconds for the ice cream drink to pass from one glass to the other. When the event was over Howard shook hands with Kyle and promptly downed the shake.

December 29, 2003

Howard was more willing to have ice cream poured over his head than he was to call Terry McAuliffe. When we headed to the airport in Des Moines to catch a flight to Green Bay, Wisconsin, he had not returned McAuliffe's phone call from the evening before. He knew he had to if there was going to be peace between the campaign and the national party, but he didn't want to. He didn't want to be chastised by the party chair and he wasn't in the mood for a confrontation.

After a little coaxing he placed the call. The conversation lasted just several minutes. It was pleasant enough, but McAuliffe spurned Howard's wishes that he insert himself in the presidential campaign.

One plane ride and two hours later, Howard was standing on a stage in front of more than 200 supporters at Green Bay's Southwestern High School, wearing a piece of yellow foam on his head. The hat, shaped to look like a wedge of cheese, was considered fashionable by the fans of the Green Bay Packers football team.

As the state's Democratic governor looked on from a few feet away (although he was smiling, his eyes were willing against what was clearly about to happen), Howard picked up the hat that been thrown to him from the crowd and with no prodding required promptly put it on his head.

December 30, 2003

The bus was waiting for us in the parking lot at the Holiday Inn in Florence, South Carolina. Howard and I and three other members of the campaign staff got on board and headed down the road to Horne's Country Buffet restaurant. We rode alone without the other 35 passengers including supporters and the media; they wouldn't join us until the next stop – a fact that made for a quiet and pleasant journey.

We read the news clips that had been faxed to us from Burlington. Newspapers from the *New York Times* to the *Des Moines Register* carried the story of our fundraising success. We were on track to raise more than $40 million dollars by the end of the year, an amount Joe boasted would be "more than any Democrat in history. I don't think anybody comes close to it."

When we arrived at Horne's, we were greeted by a restaurant filled with hungry Democrats, many of whom had already made their way through the breakfast buffet that included eggs, bacon, and biscuits lathered in gravy.

The group gathered around tables set up in a small function room off of the main restaurant and enjoyed their meal while they listened to Howard. He delivered a muted version of his stump speech, appropriate for his audience, which was made up of African American business leaders. He was projecting a serious image for a key constituency group.

After breakfast we boarded the bus along with 20 reporters and an equal number of staff and supporters and began the two-hour ride to Georgetown, South Carolina. Although the bus was full, it was a quiet ride that in many ways reflected the fact that a long year of campaigning was coming to an end and everyone was too tired to speak.

□ □ □

It was sunny and a little breezy when we arrived at the Kaminski House in Georgetown. The front lawn of the historic house would serve as the site for a campaign rally. More than 200 supporters were there to greet Howard when he stepped onto the stage that had been constructed next to the house. While he gave his speech in the shadow of an oversized American flag, I was a few feet away on the telephone with Burlington.

Despite the newspaper headlines touting our record-setting fundraising, we faced a cash shortage, a result of our decision to eschew federal matching funds. While we were successfully raising money, we were also spending it. By opting out of the federal program, we would not get the $19 million in matching funds in January, which left us to raise the money on our own – money that was important with the contests in Iowa, New Hampshire, and beyond looming large.

Our predicament meant that members of the staff faced having to work without pay for several weeks. The solution would not include the consultants, who worked under contract and according to federal campaign finance guidelines couldn't volunteer their services. Instead, the many young people who were making just a

311

few hundred dollars a week and were sleeping on the floor in a Burlington house nicknamed the "flop house" would be the ones asked to make the sacrifice.

When his speech was over, Howard walked along the rope line shaking hands, signing autographs, and posing for pictures. One gentleman passed him a check for $50, which I promptly snatched from his hand. Suddenly every penny mattered.

□ □ □

When Howard walked into the Drayton ballroom at the Charleston Place Hotel in Charleston, South Carolina, the hotel staff was attempting to take down the removable wall that separated two ballrooms. More than 500 people had packed into a room that seated less than half that number and if they were going to accommodate the unexpected crowd, the wall needed to come down. The event was Renaissance Weekend, the annual retreat for the elite, and the reason for the large crowd was Howard.

The response to his presence was a far cry from his first visit in 2001, when the idea that he would run for president was all but laughed at by the attendees. Now he was the front-runner, and the same people who had dismissed him with the roll of an eye were elbowing each other out of the way to hear him speak.

When his presentation, "A Really Immodest Proposal: Why I Should Be President," ended, the room took on the feel of a Dean rally. There was no "We Can" playing in the background, but the members of the upper class audience resembled Deaniacs as they pushed their way to the small stage, trapping Howard in the process and forcing us to escape out the service entrance.

December 31, 2003

Howard spent the last day of the year in the living room of his Burlington home worrying about the campaign.

We had set fundraising records, but we were facing cash flow problems. We boasted that we were building the "greatest grassroots campaign in the modern area," but beyond the Internet (where instead of ending the year with our stated public goal of 1 million e-mails we tallied just 550,000 – a fact we never discussed) he was concerned that no one had a handle on what actual voters on the ground were thinking. His unease led him to call governors, party officials, and local activists in Arizona, Michigan, New Mexico, South Carolina, Washington, and Wisconsin in order to get their read on how the campaign was doing.

And during a meeting known only to the five of us who sat in his living room, he pondered the future.

Howard, Bob Rogan, and I listened to the campaign's lawyers explain what we would need to do if Howard became the nominee. Lyn Utrecht and Eric Kleinfeld had served as counsel to Bill Clinton and Al Gore, making them well versed on the matter.

As I scribbled notes in a worn and ragged spiral notebook, they outlined a timeline for the general election, beginning as early as March 2 (after Super Tuesday) and running through Election Day. They explained how the convention was organized, described the vice presidential vetting process, and gave us the dates for the presidential debates that would occur in the fall in Florida, Missouri, and Arizona. And they counseled Howard on the best way to put together a campaign organization suited for a general election and how to select the staff needed to do the job.

Howard did more listening than talking, soaking up the information for decisions that he hoped (and feared) he'd have to make someday.

It felt odd to be having the conversation, and not just because we sat bundled in our winter coats because Howard had the thermostat set low. The last time Bob and I joined Howard in his living room was two years earlier. Back then, with a shrug of our shoulders and a smile on our faces, we said "why not" to putting a long shot campaign together.

We still had smiles on our faces, but now they were the product of disbelief and nervous energy.

Part V

—

2004

—JANUARY—

January 2, 2004

2004 always seemed far way, but with the flip of the calendar it had arrived. With 17 days to go before the Iowa caucuses and just over three weeks before the New Hampshire primary, Howard was still the candidate to beat, a fact that brought with it a sense of urgency.

Dick Gephardt was betting everything on the caucus state, and a failure to win there would spell the end of his campaign. John Kerry was focusing his resources on Iowa and New Hampshire, but continued to trail Howard in both states. Wes Clark and Joe Lieberman had abandoned Iowa, choosing to focus their attention on New Hampshire, hoping a strong showing there would help their chances in the states that held contests on February 3 (Arizona, Delaware, Missouri, New Mexico, North Dakota, Oklahoma, and South Carolina). And John Edwards was looking to finish in the top three in either Iowa or New Hampshire and then win South Carolina on February 3. Each candidate had a separate path to the nomination, but the same obstacle stood in their way: Howard.

□ □ □

The ground was covered with snow and the air was cold when we boarded the plane in Burlington that would take us to New Hampshire.

Hundreds of people came out to hear Howard speak at town hall-style meetings in Peterborough, Nashua, and Concord. With primary day looming large, his mission was to convert undecided voters, but it was a challenge because of the Dean supporters who packed the rooms, making the meetings feel more like rallies than the informational sessions they were intended to be.

The words he used were familiar to his supporters, but his tone – and look – was tailored to the undecided voters in the crowd.

There were no rolled up shirtsleeves, instead he stood on the stage looking serious in his business suit.

When he announced to the audience in Peterborough that the American flag was not the property of Rush Limbaugh or Jerry Falwell, he did so with conviction, but without the fiery passion that riled up the true believers and may have been off-putting to the undecided voters in the crowd.

When the speech was done, he stood on the stage and answered questions from those in the audience who raised their hands in response to his call for "questions, comments, and rude remarks."

He was attentive to his supporters as he shook hands, signed autographs, and posed for pictures, but he didn't hide his affection for the undecided voters. At the slightest hint that someone was leaning his way, he called out to a member of the staff, who would collect the person's contact information whether they wanted to give it or not. It felt a lot like the beginning of the campaign, when we added names to our database one by one.

□ □ □

Howard stood outside the Peterborough Diner talking to a voter who had stopped him on his way out of the popular lunch spot. We had just descended upon, or more aptly ambushed, the lunch crowd. The press entourage that accompanied us crammed into the empty spaces between the tables. The lunch patrons were polite and patient as Howard inched his way from table to table, holding out his hand and offering an introduction, "I'm Howard Dean."

Before leaving, Howard ordered his own lunch – a strawberry shake to go – which he sipped while shivering outside in the air cold enough to see his breath. The voter who stopped him on his way to the car seemed oblivious that he was without a coat and he wasn't about to lose a vote by complaining.

The scene at the morning town hall meeting in Peterborough was repeated in the afternoon in Nashua and Concord. With American flags serving as the backdrops – and props for him to point to – Howard stood before crowds that packed the VFW Hall and Elks Club, fishing for the undecided voters.

By dinnertime we were on a plane to Sioux City, Iowa. With no time off during the holidays, Howard was starting the year tired and it showed. During a conversation with the traveling media, he sat on a small couch with half a dozen reporters in front of him and two on each side. His suit coat fell open as he leaned back, propping his head up against the side of the airplane. The questions were coming from different corners, but he never moved. His head remained firmly planted against the wall. The only indication that he was directing his comments to a certain reporter was the shifting of his eyes.

There were still weeks to go, but the media were treating him like the nominee. Their questions focused on the general election. "What will it be like running against him [Bush]?" Howard's eyes moved and with a slight smile, the best he could muster, he responded, "I don't know. We're not there yet. We've got to run against him first."

By 8 p.m. he was standing in front of a crowd at Sioux City West High School. It was his first visit of the year to the caucus state. The Commit for Change event drew undecided voters and supporters (including a local man who had reached celebrity status for winning $200,000 on Jeopardy).

We had left New England behind for the Midwest, but our mission was the same. We had to convert the undecided voters. And with that in mind, Howard shook every hand in the room.

January 3, 2004

"In the Appropriations Bill that is before the Senate there are words, laws, and amendments that reduce help for small farms and that increase and continue subsidies for big corporations. This is an administration that is not friendly to small businesses of any kind and certainly isn't friendly to small farmers. I think we need a different approach."

Howard made his pitch to the more than 100 voters who had gathered at the VFW hall in Emmetsburg, Iowa. The banner hanging on the wall confirmed that it was a Commit for Change event. He began the year ahead of Dick Gephardt in the caucus state, but the time to convert undecided voters grew shorter with each passing day.

The group that sat in the metal folding chairs before him was different from the one he encountered in New Hampshire the day before. There was more listening, less cheering, and, by the reaction, more undecided voters. In fact, there was little reaction to his remarks that he tailored for the community of small family farmers.

After taking "questions, comments, and rude remarks," he held one of the 4" x 6" Commit for Change cards in the air and urged everyone in the room to fill one out. But if they weren't ready to commit to his campaign, he was happy to take their contact information so he could "pester" them in the weeks ahead. The event ended with handshakes, pictures, and autographs. Being undecided didn't make a voter any less interested in walking away with a souvenir.

□ □ □

It was a scene the media would have relished witnessing, but they were inside the truck stop far from the van where we were sitting in silence. Howard was angry and needed a few minutes to calm down before he went inside to cheerfully shake hands with the patrons.

For months his rivals and the media had been questioning his temperament. He had been described as angry and quick to fly off the handle, certainly not the kind of person whose finger should be on the nuclear bomb launch button. In fact, the day before, the *New York Times* ran an investigative piece detailing his explosive nature with first person accounts of him screaming at his son's high school hockey games and jokingly blowing up during a friendly card game with his friends.

Howard was not temperamental, but the charge had been repeated so often that it had taken on a life of its own. There was, however, no denying that as we sat in the parking lot he was angry. Moments earlier he had been on the phone with *Newsweek* columnist Howard Fineman, who was writing a piece about the comments he had made at the end of the year regarding the guilt or innocence of Osama bin Laden. After quickly dispensing with his question, Fineman changed the subject. Unbeknownst to Howard, another *Newsweek* reporter, Michael Isikoff, was writing a story about his personal finances, and Fineman used the opportunity to ask a few questions on behalf of his colleague. Howard was upset that no one in Burlington – including the staff member who asked him to call Fineman – told him about the story. He grew angrier when he learned from Fineman that the campaign had given Isikoff some of his personal financial records without his consent or knowledge.

Howard called communications director Tricia Enright for an explanation, but he was forced to leave a message on her voice mail.

When his face was no longer burning red, Howard whipped open the door of the van and made his way into the truck stop. The members of our traveling press corps were there, waiting and wondering what took us so long. As if nothing had happened, Howard happily chatted with the waitresses who stood behind the lunch counter. When it was time to leave he waved and smiled to his new friends and hopped back into the van where he promptly began where he left off – calling Tricia. She wouldn't take his call. Instead, another member of the staff got on the line and timidly asked if someone else could help him. He hung up unsatisfied – and with an hour to stew in the van as we drove to our next stop.

□ □ □

The worn wood façades of the buildings at the Fort Museum Opera House in Fort Dodge had the air of the Wild West, and an hour earlier Howard would have gladly donned a holster for a shootout. He was still upset about the call with Howard Fineman, not just because the magazine was writing a story he considered ridiculous, but because his own staff hadn't told him about it. He was upset but no longer angry with the staff (the same could not be said about *Newsweek*). By the time we arrived in Fort Dodge, he had yelled at Bob Rogan and press secretary Jay Carson and it was a cathartic experience that left him feeling better.

The Opera House was the setting for the third Commit for Change event of the day. It was a meeting for undecided voters, but they were outnumbered by the Dean supporters (including a black poodle sporting a Dean T-shirt) who greeted Howard with a standing ovation. And not everyone in the room was from Iowa. A dozen people wearing orange knit hats mingled in the crowd. The hats were distributed by the campaign to the out-of-state volunteers who were in Iowa to work on Howard's behalf.

It was more rally than town hall, but Howard remembered his mission. He outlined his belief that, contrary to the views of his rivals, the middle class did not see a tax cut. The hundreds who had gathered listened intently and nodded their heads in unison when he asked if they had seen an increase in their health care premiums or property taxes – a phenomenon he blamed on Bush favoring Washington special interests and corporations like Enron and its CEO Ken Lay.

Supporters and undecided voters alike enjoyed a joke he tried out in Iowa for the first time. They laughed and applauded when he referred to the fake prop turkey President Bush had presented to the troops in Iraq during a Thanksgiving photo opportunity. He joked, "That is not the only fake turkey in this administration."

Before he left the stage he held a Commit for Change card high in the air. He urged every Iowa voter in the room to fill one out.

He was well aware that applause meant little if the cards were left blank. As the campaign theme song played in a continuous loop, the supporters, including those from out-of-state wearing orange hats, gathered around to snap his photo, shake his hand, and get his autograph.

□ □ □

Howard sat in the van happily sipping the milk shake that a member of the Iowa staff had fetched for him as a surprise while he was on stage in Fort Dodge. We had a two-hour drive to our next stop and he used the time to make phone calls to supporters, potential donors, and his campaign staff.

The campaign had been calling supporters in our targeted states to find out if they were remaining solid or if there were any changes in their support. Howard called the campaign's national field director to get the results. When he asked for the information, she told him that she couldn't give it to him. When pressed, she hesitantly admitted that Joe had made it clear to everyone that they were not allowed to give Howard any information about campaign activities.

Once again fuming – and thankfully hidden from the media – he called Joe and left him a voice mail message sternly reminding him that, as the candidate, he was in charge of the campaign and he expected to get any and all information he asked for.

□ □ □

It was after 10 p.m. The air outside was below zero and even with the heater running the van felt cold. Our day began 15 hours earlier and we still had an hour long drive before we'd reach Des Moines, where we were spending the night.

While Howard was pleading his case to a group of the undecided voters at the fairgrounds in Boone, I had received a call from Steve McMahon. Mike Ford wanted to meet with Howard when he got back to the hotel. Steve and Mike had a new plan regarding who would run the campaign after a victory in New

323

Hampshire and they wanted to share it with him. Howard had no interest in hearing about it and listened as I, per his instructions, told Steve that he was too tired to meet.

Seconds later, Howard's cell phone rang. It was Steve. You could almost feel the steam rising in the cold van as Steve asked Howard to meet with Mike. We sat in silence as an unhappy Howard repeated what Steve had just heard from me.

January 4, 2004

It was snowing when we pulled up to the Iowa Public Television Studios in Johnston, 20 miles outside of Des Moines. The large fluffy flakes of falling snow were blowing so hard that it was difficult to see out of the car windows, but the loud cheers were an indication that something was going on.

Howard got out of the car and said hello to his supporters who stood bundled in winter coats, hats, gloves, and boots at the edge of the driveway. Not far away three tall construction cranes held blue banners that together spelled out "Win With Dean." They were the same banners that were unfurled at the Jefferson-Jackson Day dinner in November.

Supporters of John Edwards, Dick Gephardt, and John Kerry stood alongside. They had their own signs and the Kerry campaign sounded its own cheer, "JK all the way!" Although none boasted a display so elaborate as to necessitate the use of three cranes.

Everyone had gathered for a debate sponsored by the *Des Moines Register*. Rallying supporters and competing with the opposition before a debate seemed reasonable in the spring, summer, and fall, but set against freezing temperatures and flying snow it was down right ridiculous.

Howard hopped out and said hello to his supporters in recognition of their willingness to brave the harsh winter weather. Moments later he was back in the car and his supporters were left to wait to get a glimpse of the opposition and hope their presence would be intimidating.

The scene inside was as predictable as the one outside. Kerry, Edwards, and Gephardt, along with Dennis Kucinich, Joe Lieberman, and Carol Moseley Braun, joined Howard on stage. Lieberman wasn't competing in Iowa, but chose to attend the debate anyway so he could attack Howard.

Not surprisingly, Howard was the center of attention, with his opponents reciting the litany of attacks they had been making for months. He would cut Medicare and increase taxes for the middle class. They called on him to release his sealed gubernatorial documents. They asserted that his hesitancy to call Osama bin Laden guilty and his belief that the country was no safer with the capture of Saddam Hussein made him unfit to be commander-in-chief.

For his part, Howard used the opportunity to put his opponents on the spot. When it was his turn to pose a question, he asked his rivals to raise their hands if they would commit to supporting the nominee if it wasn't one of them. He smiled as all hands went up. It was a self-serving question from the candidate in the lead.

Howard's responses to the questions were important, but even more so was his demeanor. The press, pundits, and other candidates were anxious for him to lose his cool and show his alleged anger to the voting public. Doing so would be considered a win for his rivals. But it didn't happen. He remained calm or, as one newspaper reported, "At no point did the doctor bluster or betray any sign of irritation." In the end the press and the pundits declared the debate a draw.

January 5, 2004

The gentleman at the breakfast for undecided Democratic caucus goers was just the kind of voter Howard was looking for – one who wouldn't normally support a Democrat, but was making an exception to caucus for him.

Solid Dean supporters joined those who hadn't made up their minds at a campaign-sponsored breakfast at Tom's Restaurant in New Hampton, Iowa. Howard went from table to table at the family restaurant introducing himself to the more than 50 people who had turned out to meet him.

He was tired and it showed as he carried out the routine greeting. His suit was wrinkled and his eyes were puffy, but he lit up when the man on the other end of an outstretched hand announced that he was caucusing for the first time since 1980. Then he caucused for Republican Ronald Reagan, this time he would be supporting Howard.

Our next stop was at the Floyd County Museum in Charles City, Iowa. The Commit for Change event took place at the museum that housed artifacts from days gone by – wooden carriages, sleighs, dresses, and quilts.

Howard stood on a riser in a large garage. An old printing press that took up a quarter of the room served as his backdrop. The crowd sat on metal folding chairs, set up between the printing press and the half a dozen tractors that filled the rest of the room.

His voice echoed over the sound system as he made his case. By now he was mixing and matching his themes, and his speech was beginning to vary at each stop. He asserted that the president was supporting corporations and special interests over the needs of ordinary Americans. And he reverted back to an old favorite – the day the mother of his daughter's college roommate laughed when she learned he was going to run for president. The folksy tale was a hit with crowds, and because it stressed the importance of Iowans in the nominating process, seemed appropriate as the caucuses grew closer.

When the time came, he confidently answered questions from the audience, but out of sight behind the podium his nervous energy showed as he swung his legs and slipped his feet in and out of his shoes, each time revealing socks with threadbare heals.

When cued by "We Can" he happily signed autographs and posed for pictures, a ritual he had repeated for months, but now the price of an autograph or photo was the promise to fill out a caucus card. No one was denied a souvenir, but Howard was politely relentless. When one potential caucus goer collected his handshake and turned away, Howard grabbed the man's arm and pulled him back. He was set free only upon his assurance that he had filled out a caucus card.

By dinnertime, Howard was walking into a ballroom at the Ramada Inn in Grand Forks, North Dakota. The first 500 people to arrive filled the room to capacity, while another 200 stood in the hallway craning their necks to get a glimpse of him. North Dakota wasn't an obvious place to campaign, but it was one of seven states along with Arizona, New Mexico, and South Carolina to hold a contest on February 3.

While Howard stood on a small riser under the standard issue hotel ballroom chandeliers that dangled from the ceiling, telephone lines were buzzing in Vermont. Reporters with the Associated Press were calling Howard's friends, trying to confirm whether he and Judy were getting a divorce. We suspected the rumor was the work of the Kerry campaign, but had no proof. Lending fuel to the fire was the fact that, unlike other spouses, Judy had not been seen on the campaign trail since Howard's announcement in June.

There was no truth to the rumor, and when Howard called Judy to give her the heads up on their marital status the two of them had a good laugh.

January 6, 2004

It took us three hours to fly from North Dakota to Manchester, New Hampshire, and only 30 minutes to complete our one and only event.

The reason for the quick trip was for Howard to pick up the endorsement of Bill Bradley. The former Celtics basketball player, U.S. Senator and 2000 presidential candidate had called Howard four days earlier to offer his support.

At 6'5" Bradley towered over Howard as he declared that the "Dean campaign is one of the best things to happen to American democracy in decades." The hastily planned event attracted around 50 supporters to the Best Western hotel.

After quickly signing autographs, we headed to Iowa to repeat the endorsement event. Two planes were chartered for the three-hour trip, one for the press and another for Bradley and Howard. Bradley's height forced us to charter a larger plane, a perk rarely bestowed upon Howard.

It was cold and there was snow on the ground when we landed in Des Moines. The endorsement event took place in a large garage connected to our campaign headquarters. The space was not heated, so heat lamps were set up around the room. Coats, hats, and gloves also helped the crowd stay warm.

Cheers and whistles filled the room when Bradley announced that the "Dean campaign is one of the best things to happen to American democracy in decades." Howard smiled as if he was hearing it for the first time. Thirty minutes later Bradley was heading to the airport and Howard was on his way to a debate.

□ □ □

Iowa State University in Des Moines was the site for the debate sponsored by National Public Radio. The event was not televised nor was there a studio audience. This left Howard, Dick Gephardt, John Kerry, Dennis Kucinich, Joe Lieberman, and Carol Moseley Braun sitting around a table looking at each other. (John Edwards opted to attend a campaign event instead of the debate.)

Down the hall a half dozen Dean staffers, including Jeani Murray, Tricia Enright, and Joe Trippi, accompanied by the CNN camerawoman, sat in a small windowless conference room around a table cluttered with soda, chips, and sandwiches. We listened to the debate on a portable radio that was static free, thanks to the potato chip bag we slipped over the antenna.

There was no need for the candidates; we could have acted out the debate on our own. The two-hour interaction followed the same script as the *Des Moines Register* debate two days earlier. Dick Gephardt accused Howard of wanting to scale back Medicare. Joe Lieberman, who wasn't competing in Iowa, flew in from New Hampshire to take Howard on proclaiming, "I'm afraid Howard Dean has said a number of things that are polarizing. He has represented anger. Anger has fueled his campaign." John Kerry charged that Howard gave tax breaks to big corporations while governor and he attacked both Howard and Gephardt for wanting to roll back the Bush tax cuts, an action Kerry contended would hurt the middle class.

After the debate, Joe and Mike Ford pulled Howard aside. They had another plan regarding the future of the campaign. This time Joe would voluntarily give up control to Mike. The conversation lasted only a few seconds before Howard announced that he didn't want to discuss it.

January 9, 2004

The headlines told the story. *New York Times*: "Tape Shows Dean Maligning Iowa Caucuses." Iowa's *Quad City Times*: "Dean Fires Two Campaign Aides." *Des Moines Register*: "Kerry and Gephardt Campaigns Accuse Dean Staff of Dirty Tricks." Iowans awoke to the news of plots, schemes, and disparaging remarks. With Howard in the lead in Iowa (polls showed him at 30 percent, Gephardt at 23 percent, Kerry at 18 percent, and Edwards at 11 percent) and with just ten days to go, things were getting nasty in the caucus state.

We were in Portsmouth, New Hampshire, geographically far away, but still in the middle of the mess.

The night before, NBC News aired comments Howard made in 2000 during an appearance on the Canadian television program, *The Editors*. On the show he questioned the fairness of the Iowa caucus system, describing it as being "dominated by special interests in both parties." He went on to say, "The special interests don't represent the centrist tendencies of the American people. They represent the extremes. And then you get a president who is beholden to either one extreme or the other, and where the average person is in the middle."

The comments caught us by surprise. The campaign's research team had failed to find the tape of the show or the quote when they investigated Howard's past record and only learned of it when the campaign was approached by NBC. Howard didn't remember making the comments. It was before he decided to run for president and long before he knew anything about how the caucus system worked.

While the caucus comments were hitting the airwaves, the Gephardt and Kerry campaigns were accusing our campaign of unethical tactics in Iowa.

The Kerry campaign sent a formal letter of complaint to Jeani Murray – and the media alleging that two Dean workers came to its office posing as undecided caucus goers in an attempt to gather information on the Kerry campaign's efforts. The allegation turned out to be true and the two volunteers, who acted on their own, were asked to leave the campaign.

Meanwhile, Gephardt campaign manager Steve Murphy sent a letter to Joe Trippi – and the media – claiming that a Dean staffer had confessed that our campaign planned to send out-of-state volunteers posed as Iowans to the caucuses to vote for Howard. It was an allegation Joe vehemently denied.

Howard was dogged throughout New Hampshire by what was going on in Iowa. He called the claims by the Gephardt campaign, "ridiculous" and "unsubstantiated." And when asked about the comments aired on NBC, he tried to put the matter to rest by telling a reporter, "Four years ago, I didn't really understand the Iowa caucuses. I wouldn't be where I am without the Iowa caucuses."

□ □ □

"Ain't no stoppin' him now. He's on the move. Ain't no stoppin' him now. He's got the groove."

A band, made up of two singers, a drummer, and a saxophone player, belted out its own version of the hit R&B tune "Ain't No Stoppin' Us Now" as Howard made his way through the crowd after the town hall meeting in Portsmouth. The people who packed the New Hampshire Music Hall eager to shake his hand and snap his picture were oblivious to – or just didn't care about – the controversies brewing miles away in Iowa.

While Howard's rivals were reveling in his problems, he received a telephone call that would change the course of the day. Before he walked onto the stage in Portsmouth, Jeani Murray had called. Iowa Senator Tom Harkin was prepared to endorse him. It was an endorsement that was much sought after by all the Democrats because of the influence and network of supporters Harkin had throughout the state. Suddenly the Dean train was back on the tracks.

Howard didn't see the endorsement press conference that took place just a few hours after he learned the news from Jeani. He was in a small studio doing satellite interviews with television stations in Arizona, Michigan, New Mexico, Oklahoma, and South Carolina. But Gina Glantz (Bill Bradley's former campaign manager and SEIU senior advisor had joined the campaign at the end of 2003), Mike O'Mary, and I watched it on a big screen television in the studio's waiting area with ABC's George Stephanopoulos.

The man who once introduced Howard as "John Dean" stood on a stage in Des Moines surrounded by supporters and proclaimed, during the announcement carried live on CNN, that

Howard Dean "is our best shot to beat George W. Bush and to give Americans the opportunity to take our country back."

The press found the Harkin endorsement frustrating. On a day that Howard was being hit by his own words and his opponents, Harkin had changed the subject. During a news conference later in the day, the media asked Howard how it was that each time the campaign hit a bump a positive announcement seemed to follow. He just smiled and shrugged his shoulders.

January 11, 2004

Howard walked into the community center in Waterloo, Iowa, wearing an apron and rolling up his sleeves as he waved hello to the crowd. The forty-eight pancakes Yvonne the pancake lady had poured onto the griddle were sizzling, waiting for him to flip them over. It was Sunday morning and the room was packed. Howard dove into the task at hand, displaying his talents by throwing the pancakes into the red and blue streamers that hung from the ceiling.

The crowd pressed in for photos while the media did the same. Howard stacked pancakes onto the Styrofoam plates while the hungry breakfast goers smothered them with the Vermont maple syrup that was flown in special for the event. It was a picture perfect scene.

Several hours later he was standing on a stage at the Community Plaza in Oelwein, Iowa. The audience of mostly senior citizens sat in rows of metal folding chairs in a room painted pink and trimmed with floral wallpaper borders.

Howard stood in front of a backdrop of blue curtains, an American flag, and a Commit for Change banner. There were no pancakes to flip, just an audience with questions.

The days were getting longer, the attacks were never ending and Howard was tired. During the question period, he called on a gray-haired gentleman sitting in the middle of the crowd. The man didn't have a question; instead he used the occasion to take Howard to task for the way he talked about President Bush. The man, who later admitted to voting for Bush in the past, urged Howard to "please tone down the garbage, the mean-mouthing of tearing down your neighbor, and being so pompous."

Howard was quick to respond, "George Bush is not my neighbor." When the man tried to interrupt, Howard waved his finger at him and impatiently yelled, "You sit down. You've had your say, and now I'm going to have my say."

The campaign staff in the room held their breath while the media covering the event feverishly moved their fingers across their laptop keyboards, excited about the prospect of reporting on what the *New York Times* would describe as Howard's "much-talked-about-temper."

□ □ □

The final debate before the caucuses took place at the Polk County Convention Center in Des Moines. Wes Clark was the only candidate to skip the MSNBC sponsored Black and Brown Forum that focused attention on the concerns of African Americans and Hispanics.

With eight days to go, Howard was the target. A poll released earlier in the day showed him leading Dick Gephardt 25 percent to 23 percent with John Kerry and John Edwards trailing with 15 percent and 14 percent respectively.

From the start of the campaign, Howard was faced with the challenge of proving his ability to relate to African Americans, especially in the southern part of the country. And Al Sharpton used the debate to call that ability into question.

In a sharp exchange, he asked Howard how many African Americans he had on his Cabinet during his 11 ½ years as governor of Vermont. The former governor of the second whitest state in the nation was forced to admit that he had none. But he told Sharpton, "I will take a back seat to no one in my commitment to civil rights in the United States of America."

While Al Sharpton attacked Howard, the other African American in the race came to his defense. Carol Moseley Braun admonished Sharpton for his attack, "You can always blow up a racial debate and make people mad at each other . . . but what are you going to do to bring people together?"

When the debate was over, Moseley Braun pulled Howard aside and asked for a private meeting. He and Moseley Braun had a friendly relationship (as evidenced by her coming to his aid), so he agreed. Both candidates were staying at the Hotel Fort Des Moines so they made a plan to meet at the hotel.

By 10 p.m. Howard was in Moseley Braun's room. After meeting for close to 30 minutes he emerged. Mike O'Mary and I joined Howard in his room, where he announced that Moseley Braun was dropping out and planned to endorse him. Although not a requirement for the endorsement, she had asked for his help in retiring her campaign debt and finding a job for her top staff including her campaign manager. Howard called Joe, but after waiting for 30 minutes for him to call back to no avail, he lost his patience. He went to bed; he'd deal with it in the morning.

□ □ □

Despite the pancake breakfast, I hadn't eaten all day. So when I left Howard's room I went down to the hotel lobby to get my dinner of Fig Newtons out of the vending machine.

When the elevator door opened on the lobby level, Joe was standing there. He was visibly upset and said he needed to talk to me. I got the cookies out of the machine and we were waiting for the elevator to take us up to my room when Gina Glantz walked into the hotel.

Since nothing good ever came out of Joe and me being together, I invited Gina to join us. The three of us went to Gina's room. As soon as we entered, Joe plopped down on the couch and told us that he was leaving the campaign after New Hampshire, no matter the outcome. He couldn't resist adding that he knew that would make me happy.

I wasn't in the mood for a fight and was about to leave when he got to the point. He had just been out to dinner with a reporter who shared with him the results of a poll that showed Howard losing his lead in Iowa. It contradicted the Zogby poll released earlier in the day that showed him holding a slight lead over Dick Gephardt and topping John Kerry and John Edwards by 10 points. Joe wouldn't reveal who conducted the poll, but the results were bad enough to make him nervous.

It was always hard to know what numbers – if any – to believe (Howard always said that the only poll that counted was the one on Election Day), but it was the first time I had seen Joe show concern about Howard's chances.

We called Mike Ford, who was at the Des Moines headquarters, to tell him about the poll and see what he knew. Each night Dean supporters were surveyed to make sure they were remaining committed to Howard. Mike had just gotten that night's numbers, and from the results he concluded that nothing was wrong, our supporters were solid.

January 12, 2004

After starting the morning off flipping pancakes for voters in Pella, Iowa, we headed to a senior center in Sigourney.

Howard appreciated the opportunity to talk to true Iowa voters, but with seven days remaining before the caucuses, he was anxious and exhausted. He was constantly changing his speech, searching for the message that would convert the undecideds. And while he valued his supporters, he was frustrated that events planned for undecided voters turned into Dean rallies populated by the out-of-state volunteers in orange hats who had flocked to the state to work on his behalf.

When we arrived at the senior center, three dozen seniors were quietly eating their lunch and sipping milk and coffee. One minute they were enjoying their daily lunch, the next a mob of press and campaign staff had descended on their tiny senior center.

They seemed unfazed, as the photographers took pictures and reporters leaned in to catch their reaction as Howard said hello while making his way down the row of folding tables set up in the middle of the room. They were friendly and Howard was happy. He was on the hunt for caucus goers and, with no out-of-staters in sight, he had found some.

The seniors were receptive and their support along with the cozy feel of the room made Howard nostalgic. He wistfully recalled the many stops he made at senior centers when he campaigned for governor in Vermont. It was a story he told often during his early visits to the caucus state. But he was just as much defiant as he was warm and fuzzy.

When one woman expressed her frustration with Dick Gephardt's accusation that the campaign planned to send out-of-state residents to the caucuses, he smiled and issued a rallying cry to the seniors, "We've been attacked by the establishment news media and the establishment candidates from Washington. This is your year to fight back! Go caucus!"

While Howard was struggling to find the winning message, Joe and Mike were sure they knew what it was. In light of the poll numbers Joe had seen the night before, the two men determined that, although our internal numbers remained strong, Howard needed to dramatically change his message to Iowa voters and they faxed it to me at the senior center:

This is what it's like to take on the establishment.

- Today the establishment is desperate and they are coming at us with everything they have – all their power.

Barbarians at the gate.

- As far as the establishment is concerned, we are the barbarians at their gate.
- As far as we are concerned, they are the barbarians who have locked us, the American people, out for far too long.
- Don't let them stop us. It's up to you. You have the power to take the power away from the special interests, to rid our politics of the control of a rotted political class.

You have the power.

- Two hundred years ago, our ancestors fought in the snow coatless and shoeless to bring to this world modern self-government. It is now in our hands and Monday it is in the hands of Iowa. Next Monday, you can tell the large corporations, the legions of moneyed interest that infest the halls of government that it's time to go home, we are here to reclaim our government.

I couldn't imagine Howard calling the milk-sipping seniors "barbarians" and neither could he. He glanced at the talking points then handed them back to me.

January 14, 2004

We sat in the Iowa Public Television studio green room and watched the evening broadcast of ABC's *World News Tonight*. Howard was the top story. With a pained and concerned look on her face, anchor Elizabeth Vargas explained that allegations had been made that Howard knew that a Vermont state police officer on his governor's security detail had abused his wife, and instead of firing the trooper Howard had protected him.

The story first came to the forefront in 2000 when Howard was running for re-election and the trooper and his wife were in the middle of a bitter divorce. The trooper's wife made the accusation to the CBS affiliate in Burlington. After looking into the claim, the station deemed it to be unfounded. Someone unknown to us in

Vermont had been shopping the story to the national media for months, and while other national news organizations turned it down the gentleman peddling it had success when he contacted ABC.

ABC News investigative reporter Brian Ross, whose previous investigations included the 9/11 terrorists and Wal-Mart sweatshops, told the story in dramatic fashion. Ross recounted the accusations while a picture of Howard's raised ranch home in Burlington appeared on the screen.

Ross interviewed the attorney representing the trooper's wife, who spoke about the abuse but had no evidence that Howard knew anything. He interviewed the trooper himself, who said that Howard didn't know what was going on inside his marriage, and if he did know about the accusations he would have removed from the governor's detail – which he was when the divorce papers became public.

The interviews led up to Ross's conclusion that Howard knew nothing about the alleged abuse. With five days to go before the caucuses, ABC had made a sensational story out of something they admitted had no merit.

□ □ □

The energy in the room was electric even before the surprise was revealed. Rob Reiner led the crowd in a spirited cheer of "You say Howard, I say Dean!" Fellow actor and fictional president Martin Sheen joined the director and actor on stage. The two men, both early Dean supporters, were in Iowa to stump for Howard during the final days leading up to the caucuses.

Several hundred supporters packed the Tourism Building at the Iowa State Fairgrounds in Des Moines. Senator Tom Harkin was tasked with introducing Howard, and as soon as he said his name he turned like a game show hostess towards the large garage door behind him, which magically lifted open to reveal a tour bus.

The bus rolled slowly into the room and as it came out of the darkness Howard appeared standing in the front next to the driver. The crowd roared when it realized the bus was carrying their candidate. With a smile on his face Howard waved to the crowd. The bus driver sounded the horn and the crowd roared again.

Howard, wearing a red tie and pale blue dress shirt with the sleeves rolled up to his elbows, bounded out of the bus and onto the stage. He gave two victorious thumbs up to the crowd and a bear hug to Reiner, Sheen, and Harkin. The enthusiastic crowd waved campaign signs that read "Howard Dean. A New Day for Democrats."

The event was staged to kick off a bus tour that would take us to 16 Iowa towns. It was a joyous celebration that signified the end of our two-year campaign in the caucus state. Howard grabbed the microphone and through the excitement reminded his supporters why they were there, "If you want to change America, if you want to change Washington, and if you want to take the power back for ordinary people then I need your help. I need you to vote. I need you to go to caucus. I need you to drag your neighbors there. I need you to make not five, but ten phone calls. This is too important not to do this."

With that he gave a strong wave to the crowd as the chants of "We Want Dean!" drowned out the campaign song "We Can," which blasted over the sound system. Howard was mobbed by his supporters who crowded in for a handshake along with the 50-odd members of the media who crowded around to the capture the action.

When the rally was over a jubilant Rob Reiner followed Howard onto the bus. Between the loud cheers coming from the energetic crowd and the fancy bus it was impossible not to get caught up in the excitement of the moment.

Howard put his hands on Reiner's shoulders and exclaimed to one of his first public supporters, "Who could have thought that this is where we were going to end up two years ago."

A beaming Reiner responded, "We're going to do it. We're going to close this deal."

Moments later Sheen appeared. He was bouncing when he announced, "You have turned this place on fire. We're so jazzed up!" He drew a huge laugh from Howard, Reiner, and the staff on board when he declared, "You're everything they said you would be!"

"Okay, close the door," Howard told the driver when Reiner and Sheen left the bus. He had had as much excitement as he could take. He was tired and suddenly appeared like a balloon that was deflating. He sat down and didn't want to get up to wave to the people who had gathered in the parking lot to see him off. It was dark outside, so they couldn't see into the bus anyway, he rationalized. But when told they could see him, he got up and dutifully smiled and waved.

All the air rushed out of him when he was told that we had to stop at a nearby studio to film a television commercial. Taping the ad would mean he wouldn't get to his overnight stop until close to midnight. "Shit," was his response to the news.

January 15, 2004

"What do you think of the poll that shows Kerry leading?" It wasn't the question Howard wanted to hear as he hopped off the bus in Fort Dodge. It was the first day of our self described "People Powered Howard" bus tour through Iowa.

The glee of the evening before had come face-to-face with the reality of a political campaign. One day you can be up, the next you can be down. Howard began the year on top in Iowa, leading Dick Gephardt by just a few percentage points. John Kerry was in third place, trailing by as much as 10 points. But with four days to go before the caucuses Kerry's numbers had steadily grown and he found himself on top with 22 percent to Howard and Gephardt's 21 percent.

Howard did his best to avoid the reporters who stood in the below freezing temperatures at the foot of the bus waiting for him to exit. Walking alongside Tom Harkin he kept his gaze focused straight ahead and greeted the shouts from the media with, "Nice day in Iowa isn't it?"

Howard and Harkin entered the packed room at the Fort Dodge Opera House through a door behind the griddle. The event marked the debut of a new fashion style for Howard. Taking a cue from Harkin, who was dressed casually in a red fleece vest over a pale yellow shirt, Howard donned a blue sweater.

Yvonne, the pancake lady, who had been waiting patiently for them to arrive, greeted the two men wrapped in green aprons. She squirted batter onto the hot grill while Howard – spatula in hand – stood at attention.

Howard's arrival caused chaos in the room. Close to 50 reporters and photographers pressed in to snap a picture. Supporters and would-be supporters elbowed their way in line to get a pancake and catch a glimpse of Howard tossing them high in the air while flashbulbs flashed like strobe lights. When one supporter asked Howard to pose for a picture, he looked around and oblivious to the irony asked, "Does anyone have a camera?"

□ □ □

When the bus parked in front of the high school in Carroll, Iowa, Joe joined us on board. Minutes later Howard hopped off ready to deliver a new, succinct message to the voters inside the school's gym. But first he had to get by the members of our traveling press corps who were waiting for him at the foot of the bus.

Flanked on either side by Tom Harkin and Carol Moseley Braun, he smiled and replied, "It's a lovely sunny day in Iowa," when asked if he was concerned about the poll numbers. Although he didn't answer the question, he promised he would at a press conference after the rally.

Once inside it was about power and special interests. It was the message Howard and Joe discussed on the bus and Howard would stick to it.

"This campaign is about taking the power back from Washington insiders and special interests and that's what we're going to do," he told a reporter from ABC News who cornered him in the hallway before he went into the gym. When the reporter followed up with a question about the poll numbers that showed Kerry on the rise, he responded, this campaign is "really about whether you want to change who has the power in this country or not."

Even Stephen Colbert from the *Daily Show* on Comedy Central wasn't spared. When Colbert asked Howard what a cow says, he responded, "When a cow goes moo it's saying 'I want to belong to the family farmer not big corporations.'"

Howard, Harkin, and Moseley Braun walked into the gym to the cheers of the crowd. They stood on a small stage and waved. After enough time had passed to allow the press photographers to get a shot, a podium was hoisted onto the stage. Moseley Braun announced that she was ending her campaign and throwing her support behind Howard. After a hug between the two the podium was removed and Howard told the crowd, "This election is about power."

When the handshakes were completed, Howard left his supporters behind and faced the media. "What are you going to do over the next few days to reverse what's happening in the polls?"

Howard's reply: "First of all, not much is happening in the polls and second of all, polls really don't matter in the last few days. It's all organization."

□ □ □

After the event in Carroll, we began a seven-hour bus ride across Iowa. The bus was a big step up from our Winnebago Sports van. It had once been used by singing legend Aretha Franklin and was equipped for a rock star, with cream-colored leather seats and couches, mirrors on the ceiling, two flat screen satellite televisions, a small kitchen, and a bathroom with a shower.

There was no mistaking who was on board. "Howard Dean for America" and "You Have the Power" was written on the sides in red, white, and blue block letters. The back read "People Powered Road Trip. America's at the wheel."

Howard spent the time slouched back in one of leather chairs calling supporters, thanking them for their help and reminding them how important it was to get to the caucuses.

The staff sat glued to the televisions. Our schedule was such that we rarely had the opportunity to watch and we made up for lost time during the drive. We anxiously watched Larry King coax an endorsement out of Texas Governor Ann Richards. We talked to the television – "You can do it, Ann" – until the governor announced her support for Howard.

We made several quick stops on our way to our overnight destination. One was to a Dairy Queen. A member of the Iowa staff had arrived shortly before we did and warned the workers that we were on our way. Still, no amount of warning could prepare them for what would happen when we overwhelmed their tiny ice cream shop.

The media ran into the store and jockeyed for the perfect position. Some sat or stood on the half dozen booths, while others stood in back of the counter. Howard was the last to enter, pushing his way through the crowd and up to the counter. He approached the woman standing behind the cash register and inquired in front of the dozens of cameras pointed in her direction, "Can I ask you to do me a favor?"

The woman, dressed in a red T-shirt, looked puzzled and hesitantly responded, "Yeah."

"Will you go to your local caucus for me on Monday night?"

The room was quiet while everyone waited in anticipation for her answer (some in the room where obviously hoping that she would say no). Feeling the pressure, the woman responded, "Sure." Howard shook her hand while the cameras clicked and then she quickly scampered away.

The three workers made the 66 ice cream sundaes – half butterscotch, the rest chocolate – as fast as they could. As they slid the plastic covered dishes and red plastic spoons onto the counter, Howard handed them out to the press. He had a hard time persuading them to accept the frozen treat. It had nothing to do with not being hungry; it was just impossible to take a picture while holding an ice cream sundae. Howard finally appealed to common sense and asked, "You've got to have enough shots by now?"

When we walked outside we found two police cruisers parked next to our bus. Between our tour bus, the press bus, and three vans, we had blocked the road and made a traffic hazard. The officers didn't care that Howard was a presidential candidate, we were asked to move along.

January 16, 2004

"A year ago a week would go by and you wouldn't notice. Now time has come to a standstill."

Howard made the comment during an interview with a reporter from MSNBC as we made our way down the open road on our tour bus, raindrops pelting the windows.

And he was right. Our desire to reach the finish line made the days drag by. They seemed never ending and each was a repeat of the one before.

The last Friday morning before the caucuses began with a pancake flipping session in Ottumwa with Yvonne. In between two rallies, we stopped at a Maid-Rite sandwich shop in Montgomery where, like at the Dairy Queen the day before, we took up most of the space in the tiny shop. The sundaes Howard had held up for the news photographers were replaced with loose meat sandwiches.

Howard spent the hours on the bus working his cell phone while the rest of us ate microwave popcorn and watched the cable news channels that repeated the same news every 15 minutes. We buried our noses in the latest edition of *People* magazine. Under the guise of reading the feature story on Howard and Judy, we flipped through the celebrity dish and the "How I Lost 100 lbs" cover story that documented one man's quest to lose weight.

The monotony was broken when we invited the MSNBC reporter on board. The big news was the sweater Howard was wearing. He unveiled the new look the day before, and it had become a matter of great interest to the media, which speculated that it was part of a strategy meant to convey the image of a regular guy. Howard explained that there was no strategy behind his knitwear. Tom Harkin was dressed casually and he was just following his lead. It was an explanation that was greeted with a look of skepticism from the reporter.

The one thing that did change from day to day was the poll numbers. The results of the Zogby daily tracking poll showed John Kerry leading with 24 percent, Howard and Dick Gephardt tied with 19 percent, and John Edwards not far behind at 17 percent.

But we didn't let the numbers get us down. We were in a cocoon of leather furniture and screaming supporters and besides, according to our numbers, we had no reason to believe that we were in trouble. Howard had given up dodging questions about the polls, telling the reporter, "We're getting a lot of reports in and we're not seeing any kind of erosion."

January 17, 2004

The ice on the roads didn't keep people from turning out for the pancake breakfast in Mason City. It was the Saturday before the caucuses and it would be their final opportunity to see Howard.

Several hundred people sat in white plastic chairs arranged around the round tables at Music Man Square. It was our third visit to the site, named after the musical of the same name written by Mason City native Meredith Wilson. As had become the custom, the pancakes were flipped by Howard and Tom Harkin, with assistance from Yvonne, the pancake lady.

When we boarded the bus three days earlier, Howard left behind the tempered speech for the undecided voters and brought back the fiery rhetoric that energized the true believers. It was no longer time to convince, it was time to motivate.

If there were any undecided voters in the room, they didn't admit it. When Harkin bellowed over the microphone, "Are you ready to take back our government from the special interests?" the crowd that packed the room responded with a wild, "Yeah!"

They were out of their seats, cheering and waving signs when he announced that the "Dean Express rolls on and Monday night we're going to bring it all home!"

Like the Pied Piper, Howard was followed by a group of supporters as he left the museum to make his way to the bus. Much to their delight he stopped to pose with a ten-foot tall replica of a "Deanie Baby" bean bag toy that had positioned itself on the sidewalk. A cartoon-like picture of Howard, his shirt sleeves rolled up to his elbows, adorned the yards of light blue nylon fabric. The only sign of the human inside was the feet that hopped and danced on the sidewalk.

With a life-size bronze statute of the local hero, Meredith Wilson, in the background, Howard gave a thumbs up to the dozens of cameras eager to snap his picture with the toy look-alike.

□ □ □

With just two days left and a lot of ground to cover, we left our tour bus behind and boarded a plane for a 50-minute flight that would take us 200 miles to Council Bluffs near the Nebraska border.

Six hundred people filled the gymnasium at Woodrow Wilson High School. Like the pancake breakfast a few hours earlier, it was a raucous event. One third of the crowd was made up of the out-of-state volunteers who had flooded the state on Howard's behalf. Wearing orange knit hats distributed by the campaign, their presence did not go unnoticed, especially by the media, which had taken to noting that many of the people attending the events for Iowa voters were not from Iowa.

Howard and Harkin stood on a stage flanked by members of the America Federation of State, County and Municipal employees, the union members' green T-shirts serving as the colorful backdrop.

The sweater he was wearing may have made Howard look like the low key children's show host Mr. Rogers, but underneath he was the candidate with the rolled up shirt sleeves. The crowd cheered as he passionately talked about funding schools, roads, and bridge projects.

In a loud, deep voice he called out the names of the countries that provided health insurance for their citizens. "The Germans, the French, the Italians, the Irish . . . all have health insurance and so should weeeeee!" His voice was hoarse when he punched the air with his fist. The sound of cowbells rang through the gym.

As "We Can" played, he shook hands and posed for pictures. He signed posters, magazine covers, baseballs, and even an arm. He reached in six deep to shake the hands of the supporters who were not going to leave until they got a piece of him.

□ □ □

The ABC News bus was parked outside the high school. Inside the mobile studio was nightly news anchor Peter Jennings. With just days before the caucuses, high profile media types like Jennings had arrived in the state looking for one last chance to talk to the candidates.

Howard slid into the vinyl-covered booth across the table from Jennings in the small kitchen that had been transformed into a casual venue for an interview. The taped interview would air at the end of the day – a day that began with poll results that continued to show a tight race. A tracking poll released in the morning showed John Kerry at 23 percent, Howard at 22 percent, Dick Gephardt at 19 percent, and John Edwards at 18 percent.

After exchanging a few pleasantries, the cameras started rolling and Jennings, dressed in a blinding salmon colored shirt, posed a question to Howard, "Why are you wearing a sweater?"

□ □ □

It took us 20 minutes to fly to Sioux City, Iowa. Instead of following the media off the plane, Howard remained on board, leaving them to stand shivering on the cold tarmac wondering why there was a delay. We needed them out of the way so Howard could call his wife Judy.

He had been clear – to both the media and his staff – that he had no intention of dragging his family around the country. His son was in high school, his daughter in college, and Judy was a practicing physician. Some people thought he was crazy to think he could campaign for national office without involving his family, while others applauded Judy for her independence. She was seen as a crusader taking up the cause for women everywhere by not putting her life on hold for her husband. But Judy wasn't a crusader or trying to make a statement, she was just living her life the way she always had. She didn't campaign when he was governor, so why do so just because he was running for president.

But with the caucuses just days away, Howard's poll numbers fluctuating, and the media wondering why she wasn't campaigning, many on staff urged Howard to ask Judy to join him in Iowa. He resisted asking her until Tom Harkin and his wife intervened and convinced him that Judy's presence would be an asset. While the press waited, he sat on the plane and called Judy in Vermont.

□ □ □

The sound system made Howard's voice echo throughout the lobby of the Sioux City courthouse. Hundreds of supporters surrounded the stage while others looked down from the balcony above.

Howard walked into the rally buoyed by the news that Judy would be joining him the next day. She didn't hesitate when he asked, and because it was a Sunday there would be no problem with patients. She would fly to Iowa in the afternoon and return to Vermont in the evening.

After watching Howard sign autographs to the tune of "We Can" and "Love Train" we drove to the airport and hopped on a plane bound for Georgia, where the next morning we would meet with President Jimmy Carter.

Whether to make the trip had been a topic of debate within the campaign. Because the visit was just one day before the caucuses, there was concern that Howard should be in Iowa, not Georgia. If he left, would Iowans see it as a sign that he was taking them for granted? Or would a picture of Howard and Carter in the newspapers on Monday convince undecided voters to support him? After much discussion among the staff and input from Tom Harkin, we decided that the positives outweighed the possible negatives. Howard would go to Georgia.

□ □ □

It was after 10 p.m. when Howard, Mike O'Mary, Doug Thornell, and I arrived at the Windsor Hotel in Americus, Georgia, just outside of Plains. The hotel, built in 1892, was not only proud of its "Victorian elegance," but of its most famous neighbor, Jimmy Carter, whose photograph adorned the free postcards and brochures handed out at the hotel. Howard was escorted to the

Presidential Suite, which, according to the brochure was named, not surprisingly, in honor of the former president.

Howard was tired, but in a good mood. Judy would be in Iowa the next day, the crowds were great, and in a few short hours he was going to meet with the man he admired. But he did have one thing to worry about – the latest poll numbers.

I left him in his room sitting on the antique sofa that faced the fireplace contemplating the latest Zogby poll that showed Iowa was still anyone's race.

January 18, 2004

Chip Carter was standing with Bob Rogan on the sidewalk outside the hotel. I wheeled my suitcase to the van ready to introduce myself, but there was no need, he knew exactly who I was. The president's son was a Meetup regular and a fan of my postings on the campaign blog that detailed our travels around the country. Chip Carter was a Deaniac.

Howard appeared moments later with his suitcase slung over his shoulder. We all hopped into the van and made our way past fields, houses, and at least one statute of a giant peanut to the Carter residence down the road in Plains. When we arrived, we pulled into the driveway on the side of the brick house. It was modest and gave no hint that a former president called it home.

The Carters were welcoming and gracious. While Howard met with the former president in the living room, Chip gave Bob and me a tour of his father's woodworking shop located in a small building just outside the side door. It was spotless and filled with sophisticated equipment that revealed that its owner approached the task as more than just a hobby.

Bob ate scones in the kitchen while I pulled out my laptop and worked in the casual family room. The walls were crowded with family photographs depicting a lifetime of memories. Mrs. Carter came in to chat and pointed out the furniture in the room –

including a lounge chair – the president had made in the nearby workshop.

After a 45-minute meeting, the living room door opened and Howard and Carter walked through. The two men were smiling and relaxed, Carter in a white dress shirt and a bolo tie, Howard with his suit coat off. We chatted like old friends. Carter gave me a hug and thanked me "for taking care of Howard." Bob told the former president that he had been a volunteer for his campaign. To which Carter replied, "A lot of dregs worked on that campaign." When I burst out laughing, Carter realized what he had said and assured Bob, while flashing his famous grin, that he wasn't referring to him.

Howard and the Carters came out the front door and made their way down the brick walkway. Waiting for them at the end were two dozen members of the media and two Secret Service agents. Carter and Howard waved for the cameras and greeted the media with, "Good morning." As they walked to the white van that would take them to church, one reporter shouted a question to Howard, "What do you think of the poll numbers?" The reporter was referring to a poll published in the morning edition of the *Des Moines Register* that showed Howard in third place with 20 percent, John Edwards in second with 23 percent, and John Kerry in the lead with 26 percent. He ignored the question with a wave and a smile.

□ □ □

The Marantha Baptist Church was made of brick and topped with a white steeple. It made no special accommodation for the former president of the United States, except to open the church doors an hour and a half early to allow for the large crowds that appeared when the president was teaching a Bible class.

Howard and Mrs. Carter took their seats in a pew three rows from the front of the room. Carter waited out of sight, preparing for his lesson. Thirty people were arranged in two rows of folding chairs behind the altar. The absence of a banner was the only thing that differentiated it from a town hall meeting. In the back of the church the two dozen members of our media entourage clamored for a good spot to stand. It was quiet as the 300 congregants listened to a church elder tell the tale of Carter's history as a Sunday school teacher.

Carter entered through a side door. His entrance may have gone unnoticed if the dozens of congregants, cameras in hand, hadn't popped up to join the media in snapping pictures.

The former president spoke in soft, quiet tones. Before his lesson he inquired if there were any visitors in the crowd. "I'm from Michigan, Arkansas, Florida, Michigan, South Carolina, India, Germany . . . and Vermont." Carter gave Howard a thumbs up and asked him to stand. The crowd's loud applause made Howard smile in embarrassment.

When the lesson was over it was time to prepare for the church service – and the photo opportunity that went with it. Howard and Mrs. Carter moved to a pew on the other side of the church where they would eventually be joined by the former president. The media were moved to a holding room off the sanctuary where they would wait until Carter was seated.

While the switch was being made, Carter unexpectedly went into the press holding room to say hello. There was no plan for him to speak to the media, so they were happy to have the chance to ask him a few questions. But it took only one to derail our carefully planned visit to Plains.

Carter was asked when and why he decided to invite Howard to pray with him at his hometown church. He responded that he hadn't invited Howard to Plains.

Based on information they received from our campaign, the media were under the impression that Carter had been the one to initiate Howard's visit. In fact, Howard had told them as much himself. So the answer left the media angry, believing we had intentionally tried to deceive them. But Howard truly believed that the president had made the invitation. He knew he never called Carter to specifically ask if he could visit Plains.

Suddenly, what was supposed to be a nice photo opportunity the day before the Iowa caucuses was turning into a public relations disaster.

Doug Thornell stayed with the unhappy press corps while I ran outside and jumped into the minivan and started calling Vermont to find out who knew what. It took me almost an hour to find out that Joe had told the press that Carter had invited Howard to Plains.

It dated back to November, when Howard called Carter to talk to him about the Confederate flag problem. At the end of the conversation Howard mentioned to the president that perhaps he could come to Plains one day to see him. Carter said sure, but never followed up. It was our office that called the president and coordinated the visit to happen the Sunday before the caucuses.

When the service was over, Howard and the Carters went outside and stood on the front lawn greeting visitors. People looking for photographs surrounded Howard, some wearing Dean buttons.

Meanwhile, I looked for Chip and Tim Kraft, who managed Carter's campaign in Iowa in 1976 and was now helping Howard. I explained our predicament. The two men agreed to talk to the former president.

Downtown Plains, Georgia, looked like a movie set. The buildings boasted brick and wood facades and were filled with local businesses like The Peanut Patch and Main Street Antiques.

The main street had been transformed into the perfect backdrop for a campaign event. It was roped off and a small riser was set up beneath the large red, white, and blue sign that proudly proclaimed, "Plains, Georgia home of President Jimmy Carter our 39th President."

Howard and the Carters walked onto the stage to the cheers and applause of the dozens of onlookers who lined up against the rope. Carter acknowledged the barrier that kept the people back joking, "This is the farthest I've ever been away from folks in Plains."

Chip and Tim had talked to Carter and he started off his remarks with a gracious welcome that served as an attempt to temper the perception that he had nothing to do with Howard's visit:

> I want to say that I'm delighted to have Governor Howard Dean come and visit us. This is something I've been wanting to see for a long time for him, and, as a matter of fact, the other candidates, to come to Plains. We had earlier planned on his being here the first week in January, but there was a conflict with an afternoon debate in Iowa so we had to postpone until today. So it's a very wonderful blessing for me personally, for our church, and for Plains to have this distinguished guest here.

He did not endorse Howard – we didn't expect him to – but his words were encouraging. "I have been particularly grateful at the courage and outspoken posture and position that Governor Dean has taken from the very beginning."

Howard was used to being the one to dominate the stage, but despite his serene presence it was Carter who was the center of attention. Howard stood off to the side and listened, appearing humbled by the president's kind remarks.

For his part, Howard kept his remarks brief, expressing his admiration for the former president and recounting the story he had told many times in the early days of the campaign - how he got his start in politics licking envelopes for the then sitting president who was running for re-election. (He did, however, leave out the part that usually got the biggest laugh - voting with Carter, but partying with Kennedy). The event ended with no music, no hands held in the air, just a gracious handshake between the two men.

The wait to board the plane back to Iowa was tense. Our press entourage was still angry, believing that we had intentionally deceived them about who initiated the trip to Plains. And they were not buying our explanation of what really happened.

Howard tried to avoid the media mob by sitting in a small airport conference room instead of waiting with the press as he normally did. And his attempt to elude them was duly noted.

□ □ □

Judy Dean's plane landed at the airport in Davenport, Iowa, shortly after we returned from Plains. Out of sight of the media, she boarded our plane. Moments later she joined Howard for the orchestrated walk across the tarmac to the waiting tour bus. The media cameras were lined up at the bottom of the airplane stairs, where they could get the perfect shot of Judy making her first appearance on the campaign trail.

Our first stop was at a rally at West High School in Davenport. Judy hadn't just agreed to travel to Iowa, she also agreed to speak. During the flight from Vermont, she prepared her first ever public remarks with the help of Mark Squier and Sue Allen, Howard's former press secretary.

She used the short bus ride from the airport to the school to practice her speech in front of a live audience. Standing in the aisle under one of the ceiling mirrors she read from a sheet of paper. Mark, Sue, Joe Trippi, Steve McMahon, Jeani Murray, and I were a far cry from the hundreds that she would be speaking in front of, but we were well attuned to the rabid nature of Dean supporters and did our best to replicate their response. After every sentence we interrupted her with applause, cheers, and chants of "Judy! Judy! Judy!" She smiled broadly and laughed. Not being a student of Dean rallies, she couldn't believe that anyone would applaud and cheer for her.

Howard and Judy walked into the high school and greeted the local Democrats who had been lined up against the student lockers by the campaign. While Howard looked on Judy signed autographs. They said hello to the cheerleaders who waited eagerly in their white and red uniforms, then made their way down the locker-lined hall to the school's cafeteria.

Standing just outside the packed room, they planned their movements on the stage. Howard and Tom Harkin had their moves down pat – hands in the air and a wave to the crowd. But now Judy needed to be incorporated into the act.

The two expert politicians contemplated the possibilities. The person on the right would wave with his right hand and the one on the left with his left hand. But what about Judy who would be standing in between the two men? Should she wave with her right hand or her left? Howard worried that she would feel "very peculiar" trying to wave while standing in the middle.

Under the watchful eye of the C-SPAN camera that was broadcasting the scene live, Howard and Judy stood outside the open cafeteria doors, his arm around her shoulder, and listened to Harkin. Moments later Howard and the "next first lady of the United States" walked into the room and onto the stage. The crowd roared with delight upon seeing the elusive Mrs. Dean for the first time during the two-year campaign.

Judy stood in between the two men. Her sky blue sweater set and black slacks complemented Howard's sweater and Harkin's fleece vest. Harkin waved with his left hand, Howard with his right, while Judy ably waved to the crowd with her left hand.

They were still cheering when she walked up to the podium. Harkin stepped forward to adjust the microphone and then moved back. The floor was Judy's. She stood against the backdrop of supporters, who were arranged on three risers behind her, and underneath the red, white, and blue streamers that hung from the ceiling. She hadn't uttered a word when the 500 people gathered began to chant, "Judy! Judy! Judy!" She smiled in amazement and looked back at Howard.

When they quieted she began, "Thank you very much. For those of you who might be wondering my name is Judy Dean." The announcement, which came as no surprise, brought a cheer from the crowd. As she continued, the crowd interrupted her, just like during our practice session on the bus.

"I wanted to come here today and say thank you to the people of Iowa who have been so kind and so gracious to my husband, Howard Dean." The mention of Howard's name brought a roar from the crowd. "Howard has telephoned me many times from Iowa with stories of how the people in the state have opened up their homes and shown him kindness and given him hospitality. I haven't been here with Howard as much as I would like. We have a son in high school, a daughter in college, and I have a medical practice in Vermont with patients that depend on me daily." Her commitment to her patients was greeted with loud cheers and applause. "But I wanted to come today to say thank you to Iowa and to support my husband for president – Howard Dean."

With that the two-minute speech ended with cheers, applause, waving signs, and the ringing of cowbells. Judy walked back to Howard and he gave her a hug in recognition of a job well done.

□ □ □

Howard made phone calls to supporters during the hour-long bus ride from Davenport to Cedar Rapids. He sat at a table in the back of the bus covered with papers, peanuts, and empty soda cans and dialed through a list given to him by the Iowa staff.

He was upbeat as he encouraged his town and country chairs to the finish line, "This is a close race. We're down by one point tonight. If we get all our votes out we can win, so as many people as you can get to the polls the better off we are."

Between calls he cracked open peanut shells and kept an eye on the television that was tuned to a football game featuring the New England Patriots. It was a kick-off interception one staffer explained, answering his inquiry into what happened on the field just as he was hanging up with a supporter who, he announced, was "a little old lady who's not working her ass off at all."

□ □ □

Howard, Judy, and Tom Harkin walked in the darkness around dumpsters brimming with trash and made their way through the back entrance of Jefferson High School in Cedar Rapids.

There to greet them was a group of local supporters. The three of them made their way up the line, posing for pictures and in the process getting closer to the gymnasium where more than 1,200 people eagerly awaited their arrival.

Harkin worked up the crowd before introducing Howard and Judy, who walked on stage and joined him for the wave they had perfected at the first stop.

Harkin gave Judy tips on talking into the microphone before turning the stage over to her. She repeated word for word the speech she gave in Davenport and was greeted with the same reaction.

Howard took the microphone, and in contrast to Judy, who read her lines with controlled calm, spouted off his speech in rapid fashion, as if he were running late to his next appointment. In a deep voice he fired off the list of countries that had health insurance, the "British, French, Germans . . . even the Costa Ricans!" He was yelling and swinging his arms in the air by the time he haltingly announced "and – so – should – we!"

It was hard to know if he was yelling to be heard over the crowd or if his yelling made the crowd grow louder. In any case, by the time he reached the end of his speech he was hoarse. In a raspy tone, he issued a final call to the people of Cedar Rapids. "Tomorrow at 6:30 p.m. you have the power to take the White House back and that's exactly what we're going to do!" He followed it up with an Elvis-like, "Thank you very much" and rolled onto the tips of his toes and waved to the crowd.

Howard, Judy, and Harkin held their hands high in the air as "We Can" blared over the sound system. After a quick good-bye to Howard, Judy slipped off the stage. She had to catch a plane back to Vermont. She had patients to see in the morning.

The glow of the bright lights silhouetted Howard and Harkin who remained on stage, Harkin pumping his fists in the air, while Howard pointed at the crowd in his best "You have the power" fashion – with the emphasis on "YOU."

□ □ □

"You know how to do that rock star thing - hand, hand, hand. Just run it." Those were the instructions a member of the campaign staff gave Howard as he looked out the bus window at the crowd lined up in front of the University of Iowa in Iowa City. The orange knit hats gave away the fact that they were volunteers from out of state. He needed to move quickly without stopping if he was going to make it inside to where the caucus goers were waiting.

He hopped off the bus and did what he was told, rapidly making his way down the rope-lined sidewalk, using both hands to touch the outstretched hands of his supporters who shivered in the cold.

Inside, more than 1,200 people filled the student union hall to capacity. Four rows of supporters were lined up on risers on the stage. A red "Give 'em Hope, Howard" banner hung behind them. The crowd waved "Howard Dean: A New Day for Democrats" signs while the larger than life "Deanie Baby" bean bag blindly moved through the packed room trying not to get knocked over by the enthusiastic supporters.

It was after 10 p.m. when Howard answered Harkin's call for "the next president of the United States" and bounded up the stairs onto the stage. The two men exchanged a high five as the crowd went wild. Howard gave the crowd two thumbs up and punched the air with his fist. The roar of the crowd was deafening and he encouraged them by holding his microphone out in their direction.

He spoke in the same rapid-fire fashion he did in Cedar Rapids as he whipped up the crowd. "There's no shame in being a Democrat and supporting organized labor! There's no shame in being a Democrat and supporting the environment! There's no shame in being a Democrat and funding schools! There's no shame in being a Democrat and standing up for the oppressed!"

The room filled with chants of "We want Dean!" as he reminded his supporters that the next day would be a test of the campaign organization, one that many thought was nothing more than an Internet phenomenon. Tomorrow "we're going to find out if this [grassroots organization] works."

Howard's voice was deep and his delivery fast as he ended the final rally of the night, "Tomorrow at 6 p.m. we have the power to take the White House back and that's exactly what we're going to doooooooo!" He gave the air a right jab, held hands with Harkin, then pointed to the crowd and chanted, "You have the power!"

Howard made what seemed like a victory lap down the rope line. As "We Can" blared he shook hands, posed for pictures, and signed posters, magazine covers, and orange hats. In the crowd were several of the people we stayed with during the early days of the campaign, people who knew us when no one else did. They had come out to see Howard one last time, but hoped they'd see him again – as the Democratic Party nominee.

January 19, 2004

It could have been any day. The air outside was cold. Howard was dressed in a sweater. We sat on the bus eating Fig Newton cookies for breakfast. But it was no ordinary day. It was caucus day in Iowa.

After a series of live appearance on *Good Morning America*, the *Today Show*, CNN's *American Morning*, and *Fox and Friends*, Howard boarded the bus. Two years earlier we made our first visit to Iowa, now we were headed out for our last hours of campaigning in the caucus state.

Our first stop was at the Hamburg Inn in downtown Iowa City. The family-owned restaurant had held its own presidential preference contest, the coffee bean caucus. For days patrons were asked to put a coffee bean in the jar that represented their choice. Howard was the top bean getter.

We parked the bus on the street in front of the restaurant. When Howard hopped onto the sidewalk the bartender from a nearby bar, who had noticed our bus looming large outside his window, came out to see what was going on. "Good luck, buddy" he wished Howard before inviting the ginger ale drinker in for a morning beer. Howard jokingly replied that he might need one, but he had a busy day, so he had to decline the offer.

The clicks of the media cameras and flashes of the flashbulbs announced Howard's entrance to the cafe patrons who were busy eating eggs, bacon, and toast. The press photographers followed Howard around the restaurant as he walked from table to table alternating between, "Hi, I'm Howard Dean" and "Are you going to caucus tonight?"

□ □ □

When we arrived in Des Moines two hours later, Howard was sitting in the front of the bus behind the driver. His sweater was gone, replaced by a business coat and tie. It was appropriate attire for our next stop, an event to celebrate Martin Luther King Day.

His cell phone was up to his ear as we drove through the city's downtown and past the State House. "I don't know what's going to happen tonight, but I think it's going to be close. If our field guys do what they're supposed to we're going to win," he told a group of supporters in New Hampshire. He went on to assure them that, "Whatever happens we're going to go into New Hampshire and kick some more butt and we're going to have fewer players in, but one of the ones that leaves is not going to be us."

After a short drive through the city, the driver parked the bus on the street across from the State Historical Building where the King event was taking place.

Moments after the bus came to a stop, more than 25 press photographers and a dozen reporters surrounded us. They stationed themselves at the foot of the door, all jockeying to be the first one to snap a picture or ask a question. As soon as Howard stepped off the bus he was swallowed up by the crowd and became separated from the person who was going to show him the way to the event. The result was a mass of 50 people having no idea where they were going, all thinking they were following someone who did. It wasn't until we walked up a flight of stairs, down the same stairs, and through an empty alley did anyone realize that we were walking in circles.

When we finally arrived at the auditorium, Howard, with the media on his heels, made his way to the seat that had been reserved for him in the front row. Not wanting to lose sight of the candidate they were covering, the media entourage crowded into the aisles and between the seats blocking the view of the Des Moines residents who had turned out for the event.

The grumbling of the crowd was audible and their discontent was directed as much toward Howard as it was toward the press. The disruption was only occurring because of his presence. Caucus day was no time to alienate voters, so before the program began Howard got up and left.

Less than 15 minutes after leaving the bus he arrived back followed by the media. They surrounded the door as he tried to get on. One reporter asked him how he was feeling about the caucuses. Upset that he was forced to leave the event he responded, "I'm feeling great but you guys have got to behave yourselves out of respect for Dr. King." He quickly turned his back and with a disgusted look on his face walked on the bus leaving the stunned media behind.

□ □ □

The room was a sea of orange knit hats. The out-of-state volunteers chanted, "Dean! Dean! Dean!" as they waited for Howard to make his way into the room. He was visiting the empty storefront to thank the volunteers for their help before they ventured out into the cold to knock on doors and remind Iowans that it was caucus day.

A huge smile appeared on his face in reaction to the screams that welcomed him when he walked into the crowded room. He reached in with both hands to greet the people who had come from as far away as California, Oregon, Texas, Washington, and Wisconsin.

He hopped on a chair and fired them up. "You guys have built this campaign and now you're going to deliver! No matter what happens tonight we're going to New Hampshire . . . South Carolina, Arizona, New Mexico, and Texas! This is only the beginning!" With fists held high in the air the crowd roared, "Yeah!"

NBC News anchor Tom Brokaw and a cameraman were waiting for Howard when he emerged from the room of screaming people. Brokaw was looking for a quote for the evening news. He asked Howard why he should be the nominee. "We're the only people who can beat George Bush because we're the only people who have mobilized anybody new in the Democratic Party and we have the capacity to raise money that nobody else has," Howard said as he stood in the shadow of orange hats.

□ □ □

Howard took one last walk through the Des Moines headquarters, thanking the staff for their hard work. A year earlier it was an empty space, bare of furniture and staff. Now he walked through spaces crammed with desks, chairs, and recycled couches (aptly described as resembling a 'hamster cage' by Jeani Murray), shaking hands with workers who hadn't seen sunlight in days.

They looked weary and rumpled in sweatpants, jeans, and T-shirts, but their faces came alive when Howard appeared. For many it was the first time meeting the candidate for whom they had uprooted their lives. There were smiles, nervous giggles, and requests for photographs.

He ended his tour stepping over the empty cardboard boxes, torn posters, and pieces of wood that filled the space that weeks earlier had been the site of Bill Bradley's endorsement. Now, beyond the trash, more than 50 volunteers, each equipped with a telephone, sat at folding tables calling Iowans, reminding them of the caucuses that were just hours away. The volunteers greeted his arrival with cheers and applause and for a few moments they abandoned their phones to shake his hand.

One woman dressed in a Dean T-shirt and orange hat was overcome with emotion at the sight of him. She openly wept when she told him of her son-in-law who was in Baghdad and quietly asked him to, "Please win. Please make a change."

We left the headquarters not through the front door, but through the back. Howard wanted to escape the media hoard that had been following him, so we slipped out and hopped into a van that was waiting in the alley. Our bus was still parked out front leaving the impression for the waiting press that Howard was still inside the building.

□ □ □

After spending an hour tucked away at the Des Moines home of a supporter, it was time to go to the University of Iowa in Ames for our last rally in Iowa.

On our way to the event we made a quick ten-minute stop at the headquarters. Joe Trippi, Steve McMahon, Paul Maslin, Mike Ford, and several members of the senior staff were sitting in Jeani Murray's office. Standing in the corner against the wall was Peter Goldman of *Newsweek* magazine. The group was discussing where to focus the campaign's resources after the New Hampshire primary, which was a week away. Should we concentrate on Arizona and New Mexico that held their contests on February 3? Or Michigan on February 7? Or Wisconsin on February 17?

The only decision that was made was to hold off making a decision until after the caucus results were in. The strategy might change they told Howard if, on the off chance, he came in second instead of first in Iowa.

□ □ □

When we arrived at the University of Iowa the rock singer Joan Jett and comedian Janeane Garofalo had just finished entertaining the more than 750 supporters who were waiting anxiously for Howard to arrive. In just over an hour they would be making their way to their caucuses.

Howard was back in his sweater. He looked tired, but was upbeat as he stood in the hallway listening for Tom Harkin's cue to enter. With the words "Are you ready for the next president of the United States Howard Dean?" he burst through the set of double doors that led into the room and ran to the stage, thumbs up in the air like a runner approaching the finish line. The crowd roared and waved their blue "Dean's #1" foam fingers.

Supporters surrounded the small riser in the center of the room while others looked on from above, hanging over the three levels of open balconies that circled the room. Harkin and Howard pumped their fists in the air as the crowd chanted, "Dean! Dean! Dean!" Howard acknowledged their enthusiasm with, "You're unbelievable!"

His speech was part rallying cry and part strategy session. "One person can't do anything, but a half million can," he told the crowd in reference to the more than 500,000 people who had signed up online to support the campaign. "Tonight we're going to find out whether this all works or not, whether you can build a movement to try to take this country back on the Internet and with shoe leather and mouse pads. You're going to prove it to yourselves and to all of us."

And for the first time, he instructed his troops on what to do at the caucuses. "When you get to those caucuses you need to talk to people about switching their votes. Some of them are going to go in there not knowing who they're going to vote for. Some of them are going to go in there and their candidate's not going to have 15 percent. Tell them about what's happening in this movement to take America back."

His 18-minute speech was interrupted by cheers and chants from the excited crowd. It was shorter than usual because he feared talking too long would make his audience late for the caucuses. When they mingled around at the end hoping for a photo, handshake or autograph, Howard took to the microphone and asked everyone to leave – there would be time for that later. He bid the caucus goers good-bye, "We'll see you at the victory celebration in Des Moines tonight.

□ □ □

While the caucuses were taking place around the state, we waited for the results at the home of a supporter in Des Moines. The homeowners were attending their local caucus, so Howard, Gina Glantz, Mike O'Mary, Kelly McMahon, and I were left alone to wait.

The house was neat and comfortable. We sat in the kitchen at the white counter surrounded by matching white cabinets. The wood floor in the kitchen extended into the living room where a white wraparound sofa took up most of the room.

For the first time in two years there was nothing we could do but sit and wait. About a half hour after the 6:30 p.m. caucus start time, Howard decided to watch television. He was too anxious to do much else. He picked up the remote control and switched on the television in the living room.

The television was tuned to MSNBC. Howard was standing in front of the set, remote in hand, when the cable channel announced the results of a statewide entrance poll – results that showed him coming in a distant third behind John Kerry and John Edwards.

We were stunned. The caucuses weren't expected to be over until 9 p.m. at the earliest, so how could anyone have enough information to predict the outcome just 30 minutes after the meetings began.

For a spilt second, we thought that if we waited more numbers would come in and the results would change, but they wouldn't and we knew it. Unlike a ballot election where people cast votes all day, the caucuses took place at a set time. The doors of the statewide meetings closed in unison at 6:30 p.m. and no new voters were allowed in. The poll results were gleaned from a survey of voters as they arrived at their caucuses and asked who they were there to support. Despite all of our efforts, Dean voters did not show up.

Howard tried to change the channel to see what the other networks were reporting, but it wouldn't change. The television had multiple remote controls and we couldn't figure out how to use them. Frustrated, he went into the kitchen hoping he'd have better luck with the small television on the counter. But he didn't. We were stuck on MSNBC listening to the results we didn't want to hear.

I called Steve and asked him to come to the house right away and bring Joe and Paul with him. Howard wanted to see them. But Steve didn't want to come to the house; instead he asked us to meet him at the site of what was supposed to be a victory celebration.

We quickly packed up our things and left the house, leaving behind on the kitchen counter the uneaten chicken dish the homeowners had made for us. The car the campaign sent to pick us up was too small, forcing four of us to squeeze into the back seat. Howard was the last one in. He closed the door and announced, "It's over."

No one said a word during the 15-minute drive to the Val Air Ballroom, where soon supporters would gather to watch the results come in.

□ □ □

Our bus was the only vehicle parked in the lot behind the ballroom. Howard and I got on board and walked to the back where Steve and Joe were waiting. Joe was standing while Steve was sitting in a folding chair next to the table. The results of the entrance poll were flashing on the television screen. The caucuses weren't over yet, but Howard's chances of winning were.

It would be an understatement to say that Howard was upset. It had been three years since he first thought about running for president and, suddenly and unexpectedly, his campaign had been derailed. He looked at Steve and Joe and in a stern voice said, "It was the message. It was the message."

There was nothing we could say, so we didn't even try. Howard said nothing more before he turned and walked back to the front of the bus. It was time for him to do the live television interviews, including *Larry King Live*, which had been scheduled by the campaign. When he was booked on the shows the assumption was that he would be the winner, now a different story was unfolding.

When Howard was out of sight, Joe looked directly at me and yelled, "It wasn't the message. It was the messenger!" I was too angry to respond.

Howard completed the television interviews and got back on the bus to wait until it was time for him to speak to his supporters. Our emotions ran from confusion to shock to disbelief to denial.

We watched the Fox News channel and clung to the words of a Democratic strategist who argued that a third place finish was good for Howard. "He's been under attack these weeks. He has been the issue not just with the other candidates, but with the press, too.

368

But now he gets to be the insurgent. He gets to run against the field on a wide host of issues." We took the words as fact.

For his part, Howard was anxious and wanted to leave Iowa right away, but that wasn't possible. His supporters were attending the caucuses and wouldn't arrive for at least another hour.

While Howard waited on board, Joe, Steve, and Tricia Enright spun the press in the ballroom and Tom Harkin mingled with supporters, all in an effort to show that we weren't bothered by the results that proved the entrance polling right. With 18 percent of the caucus vote Howard was a distance third behind John Kerry with 38 percent and John Edwards 32 percent. Dick Gephardt found himself in fourth place with 11 percent.

A few minutes before Howard made his way into the ballroom to address his supporters, Joe and Tricia explained to him what they wanted him to do. No speech had been written in advance – not a victory speech and certainly not one for a third place finish. Howard would have to make it up as he went along.

The more than three thousand people who packed into the ballroom were diehard supporters, both Iowans who had caucused for Howard and out-of-state volunteers who had spent the day knocking on doors and making phone calls. They would be disappointed and it would be up to Harkin and Howard to soften the blow. The two men huddled on the bus underneath the ceiling mirror and listened as Joe and Tricia outlined their plan.

We went inside the ballroom where Howard stood behind the stage, shielded from his supporters by a blue curtain. The bright spotlights that illuminated the stage were blocked by the fabric, leaving him to wait in the dark.

He stood alone, stone-faced and silent, listening to his supporters chant, "USA! USA! USA!" and "Take our country back!" When Harkin introduced him, he rounded the curtain and bounded up the stairs, seeing for the first time the supporters he had been listening to. He shook hands and exchanged hugs with the three rows of supporters who were lined up on the stage. When he finished he turned towards the crowd and exchanged a high five with Harkin as the audience roared and waved small American flags given to them by the campaign.

He stripped off his suit coat revealing to those standing behind him one of the orange knit hats given to the out-of-state volunteers stuffed into his pant's back pocket. As Joe and Tricia had instructed, he made a show of tightly rolling up his shirtsleeves until they reached his elbows. He pulled the hat out of his pocket and held it in the air then threw it into the crowd like he was pitching at a baseball game. The crowd roared, furiously waving their flags as he jabbed the air with his fist and exchanged another high five with Harkin.

He put the microphone up to his lips and in a deep voice said, "Hello!" The crowd went wild chanting, "Dean! Dean! Dean!" He reached down and plucked a flag from the crowd and waved it high in the air. He completed the theatrical entrance in less than a minute.

He waited for the crowd to quiet and calmly began, "I was going to say that I'm sure there are some disappointed people here. But if you had told us one year ago we were going to come in third in Iowa we would have given anything for that."

The crowd accepted his explanation of why they shouldn't be disappointed and roared in defiance of anyone who would say the campaign had failed. They signaled that they weren't going to give up and, buoyed by their enthusiasm, neither was Howard. "We will not give up!" he roared.

In response the crowd yelled, "No!" The back and forth continued with Howard's voice rising and the crowd screaming louder.

"We will not give up in New Hampshire!"

"No!"

"We will not give up in South Carolina!"

"No!"

"Arizona!"

"No!"

"New Mexico!"

"No!"

"Oklahoma!"

"No!"

"North Dakota!"

"No!"

"Pennsylvania!"

"No!"

"Ohio!"

"No!"

"Michigan!"

"No!"

The audience exploded with cheers and flag waving when he announced, "We will not quit now or ever! We want our country back! Yeah!"

He gave the speech in rapid speed. Eleven minutes after he bounded onto the stage he was finished. He ended with two thumbs up and a point to the crowd. After another thumbs up and another point for good measure, he hopped off the stage and worked the rope line as the tune "You Ain't Seen Nothing Yet" played in the background.

As Howard posed for pictures and signed autographs my cell phone buzzed. "What's wrong with Howard? Is he having a breakdown?" the voice on the other end asked. It was one of Howard's college classmates and I was puzzled as to why he would think something was wrong. He explained that he had just watched Howard on television delivering his speech and he looked like a maniac. But I was there. He may have been excited, but he didn't seem crazy.

When the speech was over, Howard and I got back on the bus. Everyone else was still in the ballroom, except for Steve who was sitting in the back in the same chair we found him in when we first arrived.

Despite the support from the crowd, Howard was still upset. He had had enough and told Steve that Joe would be replaced as the campaign manager after New Hampshire and the consultants, including Steve himself, would be just that: consultants. They would no longer be spending all of their time in the campaign headquarters in Burlington.

After issuing the order, Howard, Steve, Mike O'Mary, Jeani Murray, and I got in a minivan and drove to the airport. We hopped out at the curb and said good-bye to Jeani. It would be awhile, however, before we bid good-bye to Iowa. The media had to file their stories on the night's events and since they were flying with us, we were forced to wait.

For close to 90 minutes Howard, Mike, Steve, and I sat around a large wooden table in a windowless conference room at the airport. The room was filled with tension and anger. Howard spent the time listing off the changes that would have to be made. He wasn't looking for our opinions or suggestions, so we sat and listened in silence.

Steve and I sat at opposite sides of the table, trying to avoid eye contact. Before we entered the room I had yelled at him. I believed that he and Mike Ford were partly responsible for the loss. They had spent more time protecting Joe and their own self-interests than looking out for Howard. (The idea of becoming the next James Carville was alluring.) And I had made sure that Steve knew how I felt.

□ □ □

The flight time from Des Moines to Portsmouth was two and a half hours, but the silence made it seem much longer.

More than 100 passengers made the flight. A soft murmur came from the back of the plane where the 75 members of the media chatted among themselves. Unlike the campaign staff, who were in shock, the media hadn't lost anything that night. To the contrary, they were covering the big story.

Waiting for each passenger was a brown paper bag filled with food. Each bag was stuffed with a turkey sandwich, one piece of lettuce, a slice of tomato, a dozen red grapes, and a bottle of water. The food had been out just long enough for it to become warm and mushy. In contrast, the flight attendants walked through the airplane offering champagne and shrimp, obviously ordered in anticipation of a win.

Joe, Steve, Paul, and I sat just rows apart in the front of the plane, but I didn't speak to them and they didn't speak to me. Howard sat in the front row ignoring the food and everyone on board.

January 20, 2004

Our plane landed in Portsmouth a little after 3 a.m. The calendar said it was a new day but, because we hadn't slept, for us it was still the day we lost the Iowa caucuses.

Howard was tired and wanted to go to the hotel. It had been a long night and he was scheduled to be on the network morning shows in three hours, but there were more than 400 people waiting for him in the airplane hangar. The crowd was there to welcome him to New Hampshire after what was supposed to be a victory in Iowa. There was no victory, but they rallied any way.

The outside temperature was below zero and although the hangar provided shelter over our heads, it didn't protect against the cold, forcing the supporters who packed the room to remain in their coats, hats, and gloves. They created their own heat by cheering and slapping together long plastic noisemakers –

appropriately called thunder sticks – that reverberated like thunder through the large space.

Howard listened in the doorway as Joan Jett and her band played a rendition of their 1982 number one single "I Love Rock 'n Roll" replacing the words "rock 'n roll" with Howard Dean.

Ignoring the cold, he appeared on the stage with his shirtsleeves rolled up. A handmade sign hanging above his head read "Welcome Home Howard!" He looked into the sea of blue campaign signs and white thunder sticks. "Whoa! You are unbelievable! We have eight days. We have eight days. This is fantastic. You have proven that we are the folks who can beat George Bush because you're all here at 3:30 in the morning. I can't imagine why else you'd be here other than to beat George Bush," he told his supporters who slammed their thunder sticks together in agreement.

Not long after, we got in a minivan and drove 15 minutes to the Sheraton Hotel in Portsmouth. It was a dark, cold, and silent ride. And our stay at the hotel was brief – only three hours – two spent resting and one filled with interviews on the early morning television shows.

By 7:30 a.m. we were back in the van and on our way to Manchester to the Homewood Suites Hotel where we would stay for a week, until Election Day.

□ □ □

It was 11 a.m. when Howard, Bob Rogan, Joe Trippi, Steve McMahon, Paul Maslin, and I, along with Mike Ford on the phone from Vermont, met in my room at the Homewood Suites. We were there to discuss what to do next.

The New Hampshire staff had delivered a large gift basket filled with chocolate cookies, brownies, and candy, presumably to celebrate our victory in Iowa. Now it was just something to munch on.

It was the first time we had been together as a group since the results in Iowa and they were the elephant in the room. We all knew what had happened, but we avoided acknowledging it. Some came to the meeting with trepidation and others with anger.

Steve and Joe looked nervous about what Howard might say. Steve knew that he wanted changes, but would he outline them at the meeting? My feelings from the night before hadn't subsided. I blamed Joe, Steve, and Mike for the loss and believed they owed Howard an apology or at the very least an acknowledgement of the role they played.

We sat facing each other in the small living area, the couch and chairs surrounding the coffee table where the gift basket was placed. There was an awkward silence; no one knew what to say.

Howard spoke first, saying he didn't want anyone to feel badly about the results; he took full responsibility. He was right. The buck did stop with him. But I still believed that Steve, Joe, and Mike shouldered some of the responsibility and, regardless of what Howard said, they owed him an apology. But one never came. And that was it; our conversation about what happened in Iowa ended and we would never talk about it again.

The discussion quickly turned to what states we should focus on after New Hampshire. Should we concentrate our resources in Arizona and New Mexico or Michigan and Wisconsin? Howard rebuffed any suggestion that he focus on just two of the four states. He would put his resources into all of them. Between his supporters who were working hard and the time he had spent in each state, he believed he had a chance of doing well in all of them.

The meeting was over soon after it began. There were no pleasantries when it broke up and no agreement to talk again. Howard did, however, leave Joe with one task – deal with the brewing controversy over the speech he delivered in Iowa the night before.

When we left Iowa none of us understood why Howard's speech would lead his college classmate to think that he was having a breakdown. But by the time our plane landed in New Hampshire, the speech had become big news, and just about everyone who had watched it on television had come to the same conclusion as his classmate that Howard was crazy.

We had yet to see what the speech looked like on television, but we were aware that the press had wasted no time in dubbing it the "Dean Scream" and coverage of it had eclipsed the news of his third place finish.

With nothing left to say, Joe and Paul drove back to Vermont while Bob, Steve, and I stayed in New Hampshire with Howard.

□ □ □

"I'm so happy to be here I could scream," a monotone yet grinning Howard announced to the crowd that had gathered in the ballroom at the Manchester Holiday Inn. It was impossible for him to ignore the media frenzy around his speech, so he took the opportunity to make his first public comment, acknowledging it the only way he could – with humor.

But beyond the opening joke, it was a subdued Howard Dean who stood before the crowd. His demeanor was due in part to a cold and lack of sleep, but it was also in response to the shift in the campaign. In just 12 hours everything had changed. He had lost his front-runner status to John Kerry and after a fourth place finish in Iowa, Dick Gephardt was out of the race.

Dressed in a dark suit and red tie, he stood at the podium in front of a blue curtain and six American flags arranged behind him along with a banner that read "Give 'em Hope, Howard!" (Although it seemed that Howard was the one who needed hope.)

The noontime crowd welcomed him with cheers and applause. His supporters were not short on enthusiasm, but there was no hooting, hollering or sign waving. Instead, there was a genuine feeling of respect and affection, along with an unspoken acknowledgement of the Iowa results reflected in their warm greeting.

Howard responded with a smile, then adopted a serious posture, placing his hands on either side of the podium. He had a prepared speech, one that was short on fiery rhetoric and long on policy. It may have sounded like it was written to counter the "scream" in Iowa, but it had been prepared days before the Iowa caucuses and timed to coincide with the State of the Union address that President Bush would deliver later in the evening.

Before he began reading, he put the script aside and reflected on his candidacy, not from the lofty perch of the front-runner, but as the long shot candidate who had entered the race to change the dialogue in Washington:

As soon as I got in the race I realized that the Democratic Party wasn't standing up to George Bush. I got in the race to see if I could get the Democrats to stand up for what we believe in again. . . . There was no reason not to stand up to the president. Not to stand up against the war. Not to stand up against No Child Left Behind. . . . The line I so frequently used was that Democrats around this country are almost as mad at the Democrats in Washington as they are at the Republicans. Well, the campaign has changed a lot and other Democrats are standing up, speaking their piece, criticizing the president and that's a good thing and I welcome that.

The media were out in force. More than 100 reporters and photographers packed into a ballroom at the Holiday Inn for Howard's first press conference since the Iowa results. It was hard to know if the swelled group had descended upon New Hampshire hoping to witness the end of a campaign or a comeback.

Howard stood at a podium in front of a banner that read "Join the Movement. Dean for America" as the media peppered him with questions, shouting over each other until the rest conceded the floor to the reporter who could yell the loudest. "How are you going to regroup?" "What kind of blow would it be to your campaign not to win in New Hampshire?" "Are you thinking about what appears to have gone wrong in Iowa?"

He didn't concede defeat in Iowa nor did he express concern about his prospects in New Hampshire. Instead he told the media, "I'll stand up for what I believe in whether it's popular or not."

January 21, 2004

It was before 8 a.m. and Steve McMahon and I were meeting with Howard in his hotel room. The senior staff and consultants were waiting in Burlington to brief him on a plan they believed could turn the campaign around in New Hampshire.

His 30-point lead over Kerry of a month earlier was now down to just two points and the full impact of what happened in Iowa had yet to be reflected in the poll results. We had to anticipate that things would get worse before they got better.

Howard's door was propped open and he was slumped in the straight-backed desk chair when we came in. He looked awful. He was sick with a cold, his face was ashen, and it was apparent that he hadn't slept much the night before.

Asking him how he was or even saying good morning (there was nothing good about it) seemed insincere, so we skipped the niceties and stuck to the business at hand. It was an especially awkward situation for Steve. Howard had informed him the day before that Joe would be replaced as campaign manager and his own role would change after New Hampshire.

We called the small group of senior policy advisors and consultants in Burlington. They wanted Howard to unveil a campaign finance reform plan later in the morning. They argued that it was an issue New Hampshire voters supported and would provide him with something concrete and non-controversial to talk about.

Howard wasn't sold on the notion that it was going to turn the campaign around, but there was no reason not to offer a plan, so he agreed to announce it.

□ □ □

The volunteers and staff who gathered at the Manchester headquarters were excited to see Howard. The Iowa results hadn't dampened their spirits; to the contrary, it had stiffened their resolve. He stood on a chair inside the warehouse-like office and spoke to the group over a sound system. He was there to thank them and inspire them – which he did despite his hoarse voice.

The press had been invited in to see that his supporters remained determined and to hear him pitch his campaign finance reform plan. The crowd's enthusiastic response proved the first point, but Howard bungled the second.

When he outlined his plan, he failed to mention the main point: limiting contributions to $250. The omission frustrated the staff in Burlington who saw the plan as critical to doing well in New Hampshire. They quickly issued a press release detailing what Howard had forgotten.

After the visit to the headquarters it was time to head home to Vermont. It would be a quick visit – we would return to New Hampshire early the next morning – but it was a necessary one. A week had passed since the last time Howard was in Vermont. He needed at least a few hours to see his family and recharge his batteries before beginning the final push in New Hampshire.

On our way to the airport we stopped at a Dunkin' Donuts in Manchester. Two dozen reporters and photographers followed Howard into the small shop, where we outnumbered the half dozen people who were inside enjoying donuts and coffee.

Like a bee to honey, Howard was drawn to the two people sitting at a table by the window. The innocent bystanders found themselves encircled by the hoard of cameras, note pads, and boom microphones.

Across the room, two men waited at the counter to place their orders. Standing in front of a maroon and orange sign advertising cappuccino lattes, they looked on annoyed as they tried to figure out who was causing the ruckus. One man asked, "Is that Dean?" The other, unable to hide his contempt responded, "I don't know who he is and I don't care."

□ □ □

When we arrived back in Vermont our day wasn't over. Howard spent two hours doing satellite interviews into Arizona, Maine, Michigan, Missouri, New Mexico, Oklahoma, South Carolina, and Washington State. He was looking beyond New Hampshire.

Meanwhile, I went to the campaign headquarters where Joe, Mike, Paul, and Steve were sitting in the office that Joe and I shared. We didn't speak to each other. I was there to pick up Bob Rogan. The two of us were going to the nearby office of a longtime supporter where, unbeknownst to those we left behind, we would have a conference call with Howard and New Hampshire state director Karen Hicks.

Karen outlined her plan for the next six days. The out-of-state volunteers would be there, but without the orange hats that overwhelmed Iowa caucus goers. There would be rallies, but also town hall meetings where Howard would take questions. And she wanted Judy to join Howard on the campaign trail.

Judy's involvement was important. ABC News had invited Howard, along with Judy, to appear on the show *Primetime Live*. The network was taking advantage of our situation and our need to turn the campaign around by offering the primetime slot to Howard in return for the first ever television interview with Judy.

We knew we had to do it. It would be a chance for Howard, with Judy's help, to show the nation that he wasn't the crazy person who they saw "screaming" in Iowa.

Howard put us on hold while he called Judy at work. The show aired on Thursday – or in this case tomorrow. They would have to tape the show the next day. Howard got back on the line. Judy agreed to do the interview and would campaign in New Hampshire over the weekend.

Bob and I went back to the headquarters and I shared the plan with Joe, Steve, Paul, and Mike.

January 22, 2004

At 7:15 a.m. I met Howard and Bob Rogan in the parking lot of a Burlington supermarket and the three of us headed down the highway to New Hampshire in a rented minivan. Things had changed overnight. John Kerry, feeling the momentum of his Iowa victory, had taken the lead in New Hampshire. Polls showed him at 27 percent to Howard's 24 percent. A volunteer had been recruited to drive Howard and me, but the thought of making Howard sit in a van for hours pretending that everything was okay didn't seem right, so Bob volunteered for the duty.

Ninety minutes later we were in Hanover, New Hampshire, a town just over Vermont's eastern border. Howard was sitting at the lunch counter at Lou's Diner. The long black wool coat he was wearing made it awkward to sit on the round, vinyl stool.

It was the breakfast hour and the diner was packed, but the wait staff was forced to concede its workspace to the dozen photographers and equal number of reporters who stood across the counter from Howard, their eyes – and cameras – trained on his every move.

He tried to ignore the scene by engaging the shy diners on either side of him in casual conversation. The patrons, sitting at the two dozen booths that filled the rest of the restaurant, looked on, glad that they hadn't made the mistake of sitting at the counter.

□ □ □

Howard walked onto the stage at the Opera House in Claremont, New Hampshire, to the sounds of "We Can" and the cheers of the standing-room-only crowd. The banner announced that the event was "Dean's New Hampshire Homecoming."

The event had the sounds of a rally, but the tone and appearance of a town hall meeting. Supporters without signs sat in metal folding chairs that had been arranged in a horseshoe on the stage.

Howard maintained the calm – some would say more presidential – demeanor he had adopted upon arriving in New Hampshire. The rolled up shirt sleeves, fiery rhetoric, fist pumps, and chants of "You have the power" were gone, replaced with a more businesslike suit coat and a new emphasis on an old argument for his candidacy. "I don't think we're going to beat George Bush with a Washington insider. I don't think we're going to beat George Bush with a group of folks that promise everything and can deliver nothing."

But he still had his sense of humor. With a grin on his face he announced to the crowd, "I'm a little hoarse, but it's not because of the Iowa screech. I actually have a cold."

He was also humble, embracing as virtues the aspects of his character that others deemed wrong, including the JC Penney suit he was forced to give up. "I can promise you that I may wear the wrong suits and I may say the wrong thing, but you are always going to know who I am and what I believe in."

□ □ □

We left our front-runner status in Iowa, but our rock star tour bus followed us to New Hampshire.

By afternoon, the bus arrived after making the 1,200-mile trek from the Midwest to New England, and we began our "Get on Board with Dean" bus tour. The campaign had signed a lease with the bus company that allowed us to use it until midnight on January 27 – primary day in New Hampshire. We had paid for it, so we were going to use it whether we liked it or not.

The bus was exciting the first time we hopped on board in Iowa, but the novelty had worn off with the caucus results. With Howard's name plastered on all four sides of the vehicle, it was impossible for us to move around unnoticed. Attention was one thing when you're ahead and something different when you're not.

The flat screen televisions that we once cherished now meant that we had to watch the Iowa speech over and over again. No matter what cable channel we turned to it was on, being analyzed and dissected every 15 minutes. It seemed the only time we were spared the pain was when the networks ran footage of the pop star Michael Jackson standing on the hood of his black SUV, waving to fans after a hearing on child molestation charges that had been brought against him.

Our first ride on the bus was back to Vermont to the Norwich Inn, where Howard met Judy for the interview with Diane Sawyer. The ABC crew had set up in the parlor. Howard and Judy sat across from Sawyer on an antique love seat covered in brushed velvet fabric. Judy wore a red sweater set, while Howard had changed into the green sweater that made its last appearance in Iowa.

Once they were situated the parlor doors closed and the interview began.

□ □ □

After Howard and Judy said good-bye to Diane Sawyer, then to each other, we boarded the bus and went back to where our day began, Lou's Diner in Hanover.

It was after hours and we were using the empty restaurant as the backdrop for a segment Howard was filming for the *Late Show with David Letterman*. For two days the Iowa speech had been fodder for Letterman and his NBC rival Jay Leno. The comedians made fun of it during their opening monologues and set up comedy sketches where, among other things, they blew up Howard's head and led a fake Howard away in a straitjacket.

When you can't beat them, you'd better join them and that's exactly what Howard did. The fact was the "scream" really wasn't a scream at all. It only appeared that way on television because Howard's microphone was hooked up incorrectly – but no one wanted to hear the technical explanation. So instead of trying to explain, Howard poked fun at himself.

He read the evening's Top Ten list – "The Top Ten Ways, I, Howard Dean, Can Turn Things Around" – from the cue cards put together by the *Late Show* staff.

Listening through his earpiece that was connected to the studio in New York, he read his lines after being prompted by the producer. Ever the perfectionist, he requested several takes and looked to the handful of us gathered in the diner – including actor/director Rob Reiner – for advice. He was animated as he read through the list, whipping his coat off at "show a little more skin" and shrugging with a grin when he said, "I don't know. Maybe less red-faced rants."

□ □ □

It was the only debate before the New Hampshire primary and the first time Howard would encounter his rivals since his third place finish in Iowa and the "scream heard 'round the world."

There was no debate prep. We arrived at St. Anselm's college in Manchester just 30 minutes before the debate, sponsored by Fox News, would go live on the air. The nationally televised event would be the first of three television appearances Howard would make that night.

Our holding room was a music classroom. Once Howard made his way onto the stage, Joe Trippi sat down at the piano. In his rumpled trench coat and with a Diet Pepsi bottle resting on top of the black baby grand, he ran his fingers over the keys. Bob Rogan, Steve McMahon, Tricia Enright, and I sat at the student desks. There was tension among us and under other circumstances there would have been harsh words, but we barely spoke to each other.

We had to be on our best behavior because Rob Reiner was watching the debate with us.

We were minding our manners and so too were the seven candidates on stage. Much had changed since the last debate in Iowa almost two weeks earlier. Then, Dick Gephardt and Howard were battling for first place. Now Gephardt was gone and Howard was clinging to his second place position behind John Kerry in New Hampshire.

The Democrats stayed away from attacking each other, instead focusing their attention on President Bush. Howard was subdued or, as one paper put it, "serene" as he told the viewing audience, "I am not a perfect person."

□ □ □

When the debate was over, Howard joined us in the classroom to watch *Primetime Live*. We were too nervous to sit, so we all stood around the television to watch what the show's announcer said "could be the most important interview in Howard's career."

There were 42 questions during the interview. Only two were on policy issues. The rest had Diane Sawyer probing about the Iowa concession speech and why Judy was suddenly appearing on the campaign trail.

After making Howard and Judy watch a clip of the Iowa speech on a small television monitor set up on an antique end table, Sawyer, playing a therapist, sought to understand Howard's deepest thoughts. "What do you see when you look at this?" she asked with a pained and confused look on her face.

Thirteen times she asked why Judy was now on the campaign trail after Howard vowed he wouldn't drag her around like a "prop." As a clip of Bill and Hillary Clinton's 1992 appearance on the CBS show *60 Minutes* appeared on the screen, Sawyer asked, "I've actually heard somebody say that this is like Bill and Hillary Clinton. This is the stand-by-your-man interview." (The Clinton's did the interview on the heels of the allegations that Clinton had

had an extramarital affair.) Howard and Judy laughed at the comparison and Judy took the question. "No," she answered. "I think we are who we are and I came out today because Howard asked me to."

We clicked off the television when the announcer previewed the next segment about "a young American exchange student brutally murdered in an overseas motel."

There were smiles all around and a handshake between Howard and Reiner. The interview was a success, but we could only hope that it was enough to move New Hampshire voters.

January 23, 2004

Howard started the morning off at the Lions Club in Londonderry. Two hundred people had come out to the event that was billed as a town hall meeting. He stood on the stage surrounded by Dean signs and leftover Christmas wreaths that still hung on the walls.

He was reflective, less fiery, as he told the group that stared at him from their metal folding chairs, "What drives me is social justice. I lead with my heart instead of my head." As the ceiling fan whirled above, he stressed his message. "The problem with this country is we seem to have leaders who want to say whatever it takes. George Bush is the worst example."

□ □ □

"In medical terms is your campaign out of the woods?" the reporter asked.

The more than 75 members of the news media sitting in the function room at Martha's Exchange, a restaurant in Nashua, were eager to take Howard's temperature. The first poll taken after the Iowa caucuses showed John Kerry increasing his lead with 30 percent to Howard's 22 percent.

Howard wasn't measuring his success in poll numbers; instead, he focused on the feeling he was getting from the voters – and it was positive. He seemed to be successfully addressing the Iowa speech with humor, large crowds were showing up at his events and his supporters were out in force. He answered the question telling the media assembled, "I feel pretty good about the direction we're going in. . . . We've turned a corner and we're going to come back up and then the question is can we close the gap between now and then."

□ □ □

The crowds made the third place finish in Iowa feel like it was just a bad dream, not reality.

More than 200 hundred people stood in front of a 27" screen television set up in the Keene High School cafeteria. They were watching and listening to a young woman in the nearby auditorium sing the national anthem. They were forced into the overflow room by the hundreds of people who packed the school's auditorium. There, Howard stood on the stage, blinded by the bright lights and barely able to see the full house in front of him.

As the ceiling fans moved air around the stuffy room, Howard spoke to the crowd. They cheered and applauded as he made his appeal for votes. Gone was the Iowa message that a good showing would be proof that a grassroots movement could work. Instead, it was replaced with a simple plea, "If you want to change this country, I need you to vote and America needs you to vote." He ended with "Thank you very much" and a wave.

While roars came from the auditorium, the people in the cafeteria sat mostly silent. The speech had a different feel when it was filtered over a small television screen.

When the speech was over, Rob Reiner, who had been watching from the wings, emerged and gave Howard a hug. The two men walked down the stairs and worked the rope line, shaking hands, signing autographs, and posing for pictures. All the while the upbeat song "Walking on Sunshine" played in the background.

They couldn't hear the music, but when they got word that their patience would be rewarded by a visit from Howard, the crowd in the cafeteria walked on their own kind of sunshine. They pressed against the rope that had been set up to maintain order in the room and roared when Howard walked in. There was no stage; instead he gingerly stepped onto an unsteady metal folding chair that had been set up next to a Snapple vending machine.

Without the aid of a sound system and with a voice made hoarse by a cold, he repeated his speech for his loyal supporters.

January 24, 2004

We left the hotel and headed to Somersworth where Howard would kick-off a door-to-door get-out- the-vote canvassing drive.

When Howard hopped off the bus at the local high school, his supporters were out in force. Despite the cold, they were on the sidewalk holding signs and chanting, "D-E-A-N. Let's take our country back again!" He thanked them and smiled broadly when one supporter yelled, "We love you Howard!"

A goat dressed in a red coat greeted him when he walked through the front door of the high school. There was no explanation as to why the goat was there, but it did have a Dean bumper sticker affixed to its winter wear. The show of support prompted the photographers to ask Howard to pose for a picture. He knelt down next to the animal and gently patted its head. The goat, ever the professional, turned to face the cameras.

The gym was filled with hundreds of people ready to meet Howard before hitting the streets on his behalf. He gave them a quick pep talk, then took his place alongside a dozen campaign staffers behind a folding table, where his supporters lined up to get their assignments. He had no idea what he was supposed to do, so he smiled awkwardly as he relied on the young woman next to him to carry out the task. Once the assignments were handed out,

Howard set out on one of his own – he would go door-to-door, too.

The sunshine masked the cold; we could see our breath as we walked down the street. The houses we visited had been pre-selected by the campaign. The occupants were chosen because they were undecided voters, but also because they were polite and wouldn't embarrass Howard in front of the media by slamming the door in his face.

Our first stop was by coincidence at a white house. Howard knocked on the bright red door and waited as it was tentatively opened by the homeowner, who knew that he might stop by but was unaware of the entourage that would accompany him.

Four dozen members of the media stood behind Howard. Along with reporters armed with notepads, there were still photographers, video cameras, and fluffy boom microphones, all ready to capture the moment the door opened.

The homeowner opened the door just wide enough for Howard to slip inside, leaving the media shivering outside without a picture or story. The spectacle prompted nearby neighbors to come out to find out what was going on at the house next door. Were we from Publishers Clearinghouse, there to present an oversized check?

By the next house we had reached a compromise. The staff brought out a yellow rope that, much like the tape used by police at crime scenes, kept the media at a distance that wouldn't intimidate the homeowners. In exchange for being penned in, one photographer and a print reporter were allowed to stand with Howard at the door, and if the homeowner agreed, they could go inside and report to the group what took place.

Four houses later we hopped back into the bus and the press into the four vans that took up most of the residential street and headed to Portsmouth.

□ □ □

The sun glistened on the water next to the Wentworth by the Sea Hotel in New Castle. The oceanfront hotel was the site of our only rally of the day. The more than 500 people who filled the ballroom were matched by the crowd in the overflow room. Many were New Hampshire supporters, while others had come from neighboring Vermont and New York to help on the final weekend before Election Day.

Howard bounded into the room as "We Can" blared. Lights beamed toward the stage, while the chandeliers that hung from the ceiling were dim, making it hard for him to see his audience. But what he couldn't see he could hear and he acknowledged the roar of the crowd with a wave and a thumbs up.

He introduced his mother to the crowd, but didn't acknowledge his daughter, who sat in the front of the room. She preferred to remain anonymous.

He sipped warm water for his ailing throat as he spoke to the crowd that sat at attention in the maroon hotel ballroom chairs. They cheered at his final words, "You have the power to take this country back and that's exactly what we're going to do!"

January 25, 2004

"My name is Judy Dean." There were cheers from the crowd of Dean supporters when Judy announced what they already knew.

Dressed in a black pant suit and light blue turtle neck sweater, Judy, who Howard had described just moments earlier as his "secret weapon," stood on the small stage that had been set up in the middle of the room. As Howard looked on, she read the brief remarks that had been tailored for the "Women for Dean" event:

> I wanted to come here today not only to show support for Howard and to thank all of you in person for the hard work and support you have given him, but also to share my personal appreciation for all the sacrifices you have made. Whether it is our careers, raising our children

or being there for the people we love, we all struggle and juggle to do it all and I'm here to tell you that Howard gets it.

With that she turned and smiled at a beaming Howard as the crowd cheered.

□ □ □

It was a 90-minute drive from Hanover to Plymouth. It was only six o'clock when we ventured out, but it was winter in New England so it was dark. It was a quiet ride. We sat with the lights dimmed watching television.

Our final destination was Plymouth State University, where Howard would meet with voters at a town hall meeting.

Walking into the school gym was a shock to our systems. The energy in the room was electric and felt more like a basketball game than a political town hall meeting. The people who packed into the bleachers were cheering and waving signs (one read "Scream for Dean") long before Howard walked into the room. A large American flag covered the entire length of one of the walls and a seven foot tall Uncle Sam on stilts entertained the crowd.

A group of 25 elementary school-age kids preformed a patriotic pageant. It wasn't your average school production, where every kid is given a role regardless of their talent level. Dressed in blue jeans and red, white, and blue T-shirts emblazoned with the American flag, they performed a musical and spoken word rendition of the national anthem like they were on a Broadway stage. Under different circumstances we may have been able to appreciate the show, but we were tired, sick, and with every note our time of arrival back at our hotel got closer to midnight.

Fifteen minutes after the show began, Howard and Judy walked hand-in-hand onto the stage to the cheers of the crowd. It was hard to know who they were more excited to see, Howard or Judy.

Judy took her place in front of the podium and began with her traditional opening, "My name is Judy Dean." After thanking the young singers for their "amazing performance," she launched into her two-minute introduction of Howard. When she was finished, the crowd stood up and cheered, "Judy! Judy! Judy!" She waved then went back to the podium. Showing her newfound ease with public speaking, she laughed with delight and added, "I'm not used to this, but you guys are great."

January 26, 2004

In 24 hours New Hampshire voters would be going to the polls. We had been working hard to regain the momentum we had lost after the third place finish in Iowa and the speech the media allowed no one to forget. And it appeared that we were successful. A Zogby tracking poll conducted the day before showed Howard at 28 percent, just three points behind Kerry who was in the lead with 31 percent.

Howard's goal was a close second place finish in New Hampshire. A strong finish would prove his viability and help him going into the contests on February 3.

He set out on the final day with no regrets, just the wish that he had a few more days before the voting began. With a little extra time, he surmised, he might be able to win the state.

He started the morning off in his room at the Homewood Suites doing eleven seven-minute radio interviews before we boarded the bus and headed to a "meet the candidate" breakfast in Nashua. By the time we arrived there was no food in sight, just an enthusiastic group of supporters.

They welcomed Howard and cheered for Judy when she introduced herself, "As you probably know my name is Judy Dean." They applauded when she explained that her commitment to her son and her patients made it hard for her to campaign, and they cheered again when they learned she had cancelled her appointments for the day to support Howard.

The next stop was the Palace Theater back in Manchester, where more than 800 people packed the seats on the floor and in the balcony. Howard and Judy watched from the wings as Martin Sheen spoke to the audience. Dressed in brown slacks, a light blue shirt, and a dark blue fleece vest, he looked more New Hampshire than Hollywood.

Howard and Judy walked onto the stage to the actor's introduction and the three of them clasped hands and held them high in the air as the crowd roared.

Judy stood behind the podium and with a smile on her face addressed the crowd. For a political novice, she had quickly taken to campaigning and no longer needed to refer to her notes when introducing her husband.

Howard gave his speech and then answered questions from the audience under the watchful eye of one of his rivals, who stood in the aisle not far from the stage. It was Chris P. Carrot, a six-foot tall orange foam vegetable that was running on the People for the Ethical Treatment of Animals ticket.

As Chris P. stared him down from the front of the room, a young man in the back began shouting. As the crowd chanted "We want Dean! We want Dean!" to drown out the noise, the comedian Al Franken quickly dispensed with the man by pushing him out the door.

More than 1,000 people came out to see Howard at the University of New Hampshire in Durham. Judy made the introduction and then headed back to Vermont – she had patients to see the next day.

The crowd was armed with the thunder sticks that greeted us in the airport hangar a week earlier. The slapping of the plastic noisemakers turned the event into a raucous rally.

Howard, feeding off the enthusiasm of his supporters, was upbeat and animated, but at the same time composed and cautious. In a voice still raspy because of a cold, he delighted the crowd by listing off the names of the countries that provided health care for their citizens. The crowd joined in, but he was able to avoid repeating his Iowa over-exuberant recitation of the states he wanted to win.

He ended the speech with the familiar line, "You have the power to take back the White House in 2004 and that's exactly what we're going to do!" He hopped off the stage and walked the rope line to the Sheryl Crowe tune "A Change Will Do You Good" (which itself was a welcome change from "We Can").

He signed autographs, shook hands, and posed for pictures, then worked his way out the gymnasium door and down the line of supporters who couldn't fit into the gym, including Chris P. Carrot who had been joined by his friend, Corn on the Cob.

□ □ □

"I'm so happy to be here I could scream," Howard deadpanned to the audience at Phillips Exeter Academy in Exeter. The town hall at the private school attracted more than 1,000 people. It was Howard's last event in the Granite State and for many it was their last chance to hear him speak. Close to 300 people didn't arrive in time to get a seat inside. But no worries; they ignored the cold and lined up on the sidewalk for a quick handshake as he passed by.

After his speech to the packed audience, Howard grabbed a brownie off the platter of desserts supplied by the school and we boarded our bus headed for Derry, New Hampshire. By the time he had finished eating a jar of peanuts, we were arriving at the local campaign office. It was nearing 10 p.m., but the office was bustling.

Dozens of supporters roamed around the room, handmade signs were plastered on the walls, day-old bagels sat abandoned on plates, and for unexplained reasons cases of Yo Baby yogurt for infants filled the commercial size refrigerator.

Volunteers had spent the day leaving videotapes of the *Primetime Live* interview on doorsteps. Hundreds of tapes had yet to be distributed, but that didn't seem to faze the volunteers who stood ready to begin knocking on doors early the next morning.

Howard's first order of business was a television interview with a local reporter. The camera was set up in the middle of the busy room and the volunteers served as the backdrop. The reporter asked Howard what he was going to do if he lost New Hampshire. With a grin he responded, "I'll be in South Carolina the next morning." The no retreat answer brought a cheer from the crowd.

After posing for pictures, signing autographs, and shaking every hand in the room Howard hopped on the bus and we headed back to the hotel in Manchester.

January 27, 2004

For us Election Day began early. Howard joined the staff and reporters in the hotel lobby at 5:30 a.m. He grabbed a quick orange juice at the salad-bar-turned-breakfast-buffet before heading out the door. There would be no rallies or town hall meetings; instead it was time to get out the vote.

Our first stop was at the Merrimack Restaurant in Manchester, a place we had visited for the first time two years earlier. It was dark outside, but inside red, white, and blue bunting dangled from the ceiling. Howard posed for pictures with the half dozen patrons who braved the early hour, then slipped into a dark red vinyl booth that had been converted into a radio studio. He was going to catch the people who were listening to the radio over Corn Flakes or in their car driving to work.

By the time we arrived at the campaign headquarters a few hours later, the first exit poll numbers were in. Kerry was leading 37 percent to Howard's 24 percent. If the numbers held it would be a decisive win for Kerry and a disappointing second place for Howard. It hurt, but there was no time to dwell on it. Getting people out to vote was more important now than ever.

Dozens of volunteers sat at long wooden tables set up around the room. Armed with telephones, they dialed through the list of identified Dean supporters, reminding them to vote. Meanwhile, just a few feet away, Howard sat in a small conference room and began another round of radio interviews. Water bottles covered the folding table and a mattress was propped up against the brick wall. As press photographers and reporters looked on, Howard multitasked, keeping one eye on the morning news clips while making his case to the voters over the airwaves. "I don't think we're going to beat George Bush with a candidate from inside the Beltway."

After the media were ushered out of the room, Howard focused on another task, plotting out his schedule for the days after New Hampshire. Win or lose, the campaign was moving forward and as he promised the television reporter the night before, he'd be going to South Carolina.

Howard took a break from radio interviews to visit two polling places. The stops were more photo opportunity than practical as he could reach more people over the radio than standing in a parking lot, but they gave him the chance to thank his supporters, some of whom had traveled from California and Florida to hold signs in front of an elementary school and community center in Manchester.

The volunteers cheered when they saw him emerge from the van. He shook their hands then asked, "Okay, who wants coffee?" He then grabbed a Box 'o Joe from Dunkin Donuts and filled paper cups with the steaming hot beverage, making sure to ask each person, "cream or sugar?"

□ □ □

Joe and I were in the lobby of the Hawthorne Suites when the polls closed. The cheery waiting area had taken on a funeral parlor feel. The flat screen television over the fireplace announced the end to voting and although no votes had been counted, John Kerry had been declared the winner by the media. Without saying the words, we both knew that the results most likely ended Howard's chances of becoming the nominee. We had barely spoken to each other since the Iowa caucuses a week earlier, but for a moment we put Howard's feelings above our own and calmly discussed who should go up to his room. When I arrived, he was sitting in front of the television watching the news.

We didn't discuss the results. Instead, we took the elevator down to the lobby, walked out the front door, and hopped into the van that would take us to the election night party at Manchester's Southern New Hampshire University. A vegetable platter and crackers and cheese were waiting for us when we arrived at the gymnasium complex. But we didn't stop to sit on the comfy couches or watch the big screen television in the holding room. Instead, Howard had interviews to do with the national networks and cable stations.

We were escorted to a room where the cameras were set up. The gray unpolished cinderblock walls, dim lights, and exposed electrical wires hinted that the room's true purpose was a storage area. The only pop of color in the space came from the blue curtain that was set up behind Howard's chair.

A few feet away across the hall, Howard's supporters packed into the school's gymnasium. They stood on bleachers and on the floor, silently watching the television sets that beamed in a smiling John Kerry celebrating his win.

The doors that led into the gym were closed, shielding Howard from his supporters who waited inside for his arrival. Joe, Steve, and Paul stood back, creating a physical distance that removed them from the action, making them observers instead of participants.

When the time came, the doors flew open and Howard bounded onto the stage as "We Can" played. With his appearance, the room was transformed and took on the feel of the Val Air Ballroom in Iowa a week earlier. Howard fell short of victory, but you'd never know it by the enthusiasm of the crowd. For five minutes, they cheered, applauded, and stomped their feet on the ground chanting louder when he tried to interrupt.

He had made his first appearance in New Hampshire in a JC Penney suit, but for his last he wore the dark blue Paul Stuart suit he bought in New York. He hadn't taken the coat off since he flew in from Iowa and it remained on his back when he took to the stage.

He did not want to repeat what happened during the speech on caucus night in Iowa, so while he was upbeat, he was also conscious that his audience extended beyond the hundreds of supporters in the gym. He was being seen in living rooms across the country and closely watched by the media.

This time he came with talking points. A note from the staff written on the cover sheet explained that the first few points had been drafted in the "event of a good result." He had accomplished what he wanted – a second place finish. But his 26 percent to Kerry's 39 percent was not as close as he hoped it would be.

He was not able to say, "Tonight in New Hampshire we had a battle between the pundits, the pollsters, and the people. And the people won. We are alive and kicking. In fact, we are better than ever." Nor did he say, "Tonight was a comeback." Instead he read from the notes scribbled in his own hand, "The people of New Hampshire have allowed our campaign to regain its momentum."

□ □ □

By 11 p.m. we were headed back to Vermont. The lease on the bus was set to expire at midnight, so Howard, Bob, and I rode back in a van. Before leaving the high school, Howard had asked Joe, Steve, and Paul if they wanted to ride with us, but they declined.

It was dark and cold as we made the two and a half-hour trip from Manchester to Burlington. The ride was long and depressing. Howard and Bob reclined in the seats in the second row, while I stretched out on the fabric-covered bench behind them. We were tired, but there was work to be done.

With the New Hampshire primary behind him, Howard knew for the sake of the campaign he had to make the changes he talked about in Iowa. Because of the caucus results, donors and supporters were beginning to question the campaign's strategy, criticizing the television advertising, and wondering where $40 million went.

He knew that in order to reassure his supporters and donors that he understood the problems and was serious about turning things around, he had to act fast – he had to name a new campaign manager the next day. But as we drove up the interstate highway that connected Vermont and New Hampshire, he didn't have a replacement for Joe lined up. He had spent the week since the caucuses focusing on salvaging New Hampshire, not recruiting new staff.

He did, however, know who he wanted for the job: Roy Neel. Roy had served as chief of staff to Vice President Al Gore. Howard and Roy met for the first time during a fundraising trip we made to Tennessee in November. If the campaign was going to remain viable, the new manager had to be respected and seen as credible, and Roy fit the bill.

Howard hadn't talked to Roy and it was after 11 p.m. when he placed a call to Tennessee. Roy wasn't home. Howard had no time to waste, so along with his phone number, he left a detailed message asking Roy if he would run the campaign.

The three of us sat in the van hoping to hear back from Roy and wondering what we were going to do if he declined to take the job. No phone call came and we dropped Howard off at his house without a solution to our problem.

January 28, 2004

It was early in the morning and I was at home when my cell phone rang. It was Roy Neel. He had tried to reach Howard, but his line was busy. Roy was willing to help and ready to take on the job of campaign manager. He understood the urgency of our situation and would be on a plane to Vermont right away. Now all Howard had to do was talk to Joe.

□ □ □

Howard and Joe met in a conference room at a downtown Burlington law firm.

After losing Iowa and New Hampshire, it shouldn't have come as a surprise that a change would be made, and despite the fact that Howard had made his intentions clear to Steve, Joe said he didn't see it coming.

When their private meeting was over, Steve McMahon, Mark Squier, Paul Maslin, Bob Rogan, and I joined them. We sat around the same large conference table we used to prepare for our very first debate in May, and Howard announced to the group what Bob and I already knew: Roy Neel had agreed to come on board as campaign manager.

He also explained that he had asked Joe to stay on to oversee the Internet component, an offer Joe had declined.

The change was accepted as inevitable by all in the room except Steve, who asked Howard to reconsider. But before Howard could respond, Joe stepped in and said that leaving was what he wanted to do.

Steve then urged Joe to stay on and asked Howard to give him, Mark, and Paul time to discuss the idea with Joe. Howard gave them one hour; after that he was scheduled to meet with the entire staff to explain the changes to them.

□ □ □

The small conference room in the campaign headquarters was packed. The staff was forced to stand shoulder to shoulder and some stood in the hallway, craning their necks to see and hear Howard.

Joe did not join Howard for the announcement. He sat in his office instead. Howard explained that Roy was coming on board and he had asked Joe to stay on. What he couldn't tell them was whether Joe was staying or not because he didn't know himself. He hadn't been told the outcome of the meeting at the law firm.

Joe eventually joined the meeting and cleared up the question. He told the group that he was leaving, but the campaign would move forward. The reaction among the staff was mixed. Many in the room said nothing, while those who worked closely with Joe were visibly upset.

When the meeting broke up, Joe went around the office hugging and saying good-bye to the staff as tears streamed down his cheeks. But there were no tears for me. Instead he stepped close and said, "I'm going to get you and I'm going to get Howard. I know things."

A short time later, Joe and his wife Kathy left the headquarters, followed by a handful of staff members. When they got outside they were met by Candy Crowley of CNN. It appeared that Joe's leaving was breaking news.

I had no idea that CNN was out front until a member of the staff came in with a message from Joe. He was sure that I had alerted the cable network to embarrass him and if I did anything like that again it would be, in his words, all-out war. Joe's suspicions were misplaced. I hadn't called CNN nor did I know who did. (Although it seemed safe to assume that the CNN camerawoman who followed Joe's every move had something to do with Crowley's appearance on the scene.)

Howard would tell reporters during a conference call later in the evening, "Roy brings enormous experience both in management and national politics. I felt we've needed a strong organizational force in the office."

January 29, 2004

"It's a kind of mea culpa, and I'm as guilty as anybody else," Diane Sawyer told the audience of *Good Morning America*. Sawyer was acknowledging what everyone in the room at the Val Air Ballroom in Iowa on caucus night already knew: Howard's "scream" wasn't a scream at all.

"Listen to how it was in the room. The so-called scream couldn't really be heard," Sawyer continued, explaining that the handheld microphone Howard used blocked out the sound of the 3,000 supporters who packed the room. Because of the microphone, television viewers only heard Howard, not the crowd.

Sawyer's revelation came a week after she interviewed Howard and Judy on *Primetime Live*. During the interview, Sawyer replayed and dissected the speech, even getting Judy to admit that Howard looked "kind of silly."

But Sawyer's mea culpa came too late. Howard's sanity and temperament had been called into question. The speech had been played nearly 700 times by the networks, more when cable and Internet coverage was included. Sawyer's piece prompted the heads of ABC, CBS, CNN, FOX, and NBC to admit that they probably overplayed the clip of the speech.

Could he have placed first in New Hampshire instead of second if the speech hadn't been overplayed? It was impossible to know. But one thing was for sure: Howard's disappointing third place finish in Iowa came before he made the speech, a fact that changed the campaign

Joe Trippi was gone. Joe Costello and Mike Ford followed. The grassroots revolt that Howard worried would result from Joe's departure didn't happen. Steve McMahon and Paul Maslin remained with the campaign, but no longer worked in Burlington full time. And Roy Neel was on his way to Vermont. It was a new day and a fresh start and the beginning of what Howard described as a "leaner, meaner" campaign.

He had spent the day before in Vermont, explaining the management changes to his staff and reassuring his donors and supporters that he was committed to fixing the problems in the campaign.

He couldn't afford to lose the support of his money raisers. Despite collecting a record-setting $41 million, the campaign was short on cash, forcing the staff to go without pay for two weeks and making it impossible for us to run television ads – ads that had become a sore point for the donors who didn't like them and questioned their effectiveness.

To address these concerns, Howard insisted on the formation of a new creative team. Steve McMahon and Mark Squier would be assisted by our entertainment industry supporters, including Rob Reiner. (During a meeting with Howard and the senior staff, Mark Squier offered his firm's resignation. If hiring a new firm would quiet the disgruntled donors he wanted Howard to have that option. Steve balked at the idea and Howard didn't accept the offer.)

With the changes made, Howard set out to make good on the promise he made to the reporter in New Hampshire the day before the primary – we were off to South Carolina.

□ □ □

Howard may have been down, but he wasn't counting himself out. Only two states had voted and there were 18 contests in February and almost 800 delegates in play leading up to Super Tuesday on March 2, when 1,159 delegates were up for grabs in 10 states.

On our way to South Carolina we made a stop at a rally at Michigan State University in Lansing. Michigan wasn't exactly on the way to South Carolina, but it was a caucus state. We had made an effort there, hiring a state director and opening an office. Howard believed that, with a little work, he could reach the 15 percent threshold necessary to pick up some delegates.

The more than 800 people who greeted us in Lansing were unfazed by the setbacks the campaign had suffered. They filled the auditorium at Michigan State University to capacity and spilled into the hallway. They were there to cheer Howard on during his first public appearance since his second place finish in New Hampshire.

Dozens of eager members of the American Federation of State, County and Municipal Employees and the Service Employees International Union surrounded Howard on the stage. They donned green and purple T-shirts. He opted for his suit coat.

There was no mention of the losses in Iowa and New Hampshire or the changes in the campaign organization. Nothing could change the past. The focus was on the future.

"The style of Washington politicians is to promise you everything and hope you don't remember when they get in there. They're promising middle class tax cuts, health insurance for everybody, free college in some cases, some of them promised the war in Iraq, too," Howard told his cheering supporters.

Never mentioning Kerry by name, he continued, "We cannot go on in this country electing politicians in either party who keep promising everything and delivering nothing. The whole thing here is do we want business as usual in Washington or a government that's going to stand up for ordinary people?"

□ □ □

From Lansing we flew to Greenville, South Carolina, for an NBC-sponsored debate. It was the first and only meeting of the candidates before the February 3 contests in Arizona, Delaware, Missouri, New Mexico, North Dakota, Oklahoma, and South Carolina.

Wes Clark, John Edwards, John Kerry, Dennis Kucinich, Joe Lieberman, Al Sharpton, and Howard stood on the stage at the Peace Center for the Performing Arts. A random drawing put Howard between Kerry and Kucinich.

Polls showed Edwards and Kerry in a virtual dead heat in the state that was the first in the South to hold a contest. Edwards was at 25 percent, Kerry 24 percent, and Howard trailed in third place with 9 percent. A year earlier, he had hoped that the South Carolina election results would prove that he could appeal to Southern black voters.

Tom Brokaw served as the moderator.

The seven Democrats may have been competing against each other, but they directed most of their criticism at President Bush and Vice President Cheney. Providing fodder was the recent testimony of chief United Nations weapons inspector David Kay. Kay told a congressional panel that the administration was wrong about the existence of weapons of mass destruction in Iraq.

Announcing that he wanted to make the debate "a little less mellow," Howard shifted his attention to Kerry.

"Now, Senator Kerry is the front-runner, and I mean him no insult, but in 19 years in the Senate, Senator Kerry sponsored 11 bills that had anything to do with health care, and not one of them passed. If you want a president who is going to get results, I suggest that you look at somebody who did get results in my state."

In the end, news accounts described Howard as "subdued but seeming a bit prickly over his campaign's sinking fortunes."

□ □ □

It took us two hours to drive south from Greenville to Columbia. We checked into the Clarion Hotel just in time to watch an interview with Joe Trippi on the cable news channel MSNBC. The telephone interview took place as Joe was driving from Vermont to his home in Maryland. As the network showed a map of his route, he tearfully told how hard it was to leave the campaign. (Days later MSNBC would announce that Joe had joined the station as a political analyst).

January 30, 2004

From South Carolina we flew to St. Louis, Missouri. The home state of former candidate Dick Gephardt wasn't on our priority list, but it had delegates up for grabs on February 3 and was an easy stop to make on our way to New Mexico. (We were stopping in states as if we were in a car pulling off interstate exits.)

Howard was on the hunt for delegates, and despite the losses in Iowa and New Hampshire he was ahead in the delegate count. The support he received from the so-called superdelegates (elected officials and state party leaders) put his total at 114 to John Kerry's 103.

The "Stand Up for Education" town hall meeting took place at the Missouri History Museum in St. Louis. More than 800 people filled the museum's theater to capacity and packed into an overflow room two floors down. The audience was filled with die-hard supporters who roared and jumped to their feet when Howard announced, "The power to change this country is in your hands, not mine, and it's in your hands in Missouri in a few days."

"Governor Dean, what I do want to say is that no matter what happens all of the candidates are better candidates because of you." The woman who offered him encouragement had hopped onto the elevator that we were taking down to the overflow room. Howard grinned, looked straight ahead and in a matter of fact manner responded, "Ah, that's true."

After the visit to the overflow room (where he was greeted by a twenty-something waving a "Dean Rocks My Socks Off" sign), we boarded our plane and headed to Albuquerque, New Mexico.

□ □ □

The journalists traveling with us weren't interested in breaking any news and Howard wasn't interested in making any. Instead, we sat back, munched on snacks, and engaged in casual conversation during the three-hour flight.

Without a notebook or camera in sight, one reporter asked Howard about the speculation that John Kerry had recently had the wrinkle-removing agent Botox injected into his forehead.

"Governor/Doctor Dean do you think John Kerry has used Botox?" Howard laughed and, aware of his propensity to speak first and think later, quickly put his hand over his mouth (speak no evil). "But you saw him up close (at the debate)," the reporter asked trying again for an answer. Howard confirmed that he had seen Kerry close up and couldn't resist adding, "And don't think I didn't look either!"

◻ ◻ ◻

Over the next four days, our flight plan would take us on two identical loops around the country with stops in Arizona, Michigan, New Mexico, Washington, and Wisconsin. We had checked Michigan off the list the day before and now we were in New Mexico, where 26 delegates were up for grabs on February 3.

The hundreds of people who gathered in the exhibition hall at the fairgrounds in Albuquerque greeted Howard with cheers and whistles. And having embraced the Iowa concession speech that had reached cult status, four supporters held individual signs that together read "I Scream, You Scream, We All Scream For Howard Dean!"

Hispanics accounted for close to half of the Democratic voters in New Mexico, which prompted Howard to begin his speech in Spanish. He paused to allow the crowd to cheer for his attempt, but save for the three people who hooted, the audience was silent. It turned out there were very few Spanish speakers in the crowd. He laughed and offered a translation, "I want your vote tonight!"

From New Mexico we flew to Tucson, Arizona. Howard curled up in one of the leather seats and, with his seat belt strapped around his wrinkled suit, planted his head firmly against the window and took a nap.

January 31, 2004

John Kerry was in Missouri and Michigan. John Edwards spent the day in South Carolina and New Mexico. Wes Clark took the day off. And we made visits to Arizona and Washington State.

It's hard to say what was motivating Howard's supporters. Were they ignoring the losses in Iowa and New Hampshire? Were they invigorated by his return to long shot status? In any case, they came out in record numbers.

Our first event of the day was a 9 a.m. rally in Tucson. The Saturday morning event brought more than 2,000 people to the outdoor venue at Reid Park. Under a blue sky, they cheered and waved homemade signs with the message that was popping up everywhere, "I Scream, You Scream, We All Scream For Howard Dean!"

Howard was flanked on stage by two dozen supporters and a giant American flag. Looking presidential in his suit coat, he continued to cast himself as the Washington outsider and John Kerry in the role of the ultimate insider. A story in the morning edition of the *Washington Post* named Kerry the biggest recipient of lobbyist money in the U.S. Senate, and Howard used the information to pound on the newly-crowned front-runner.

John Kerry is a "special interest clone" he announced to the screaming crowd. "John Kerry has taken more special interest lobbyist money than any other senator in the last 15 years. We are not going to beat George Bush by nominating somebody who's a handmaiden of special interests. . . . We are not going to beat George Bush with somebody who has his hands as deeply in the lobbyists' pockets as George Bush. . . . We're not going to take our country back by nominating just another inside the beltway guy who's played the game for 15 years."

His speech, with its fiery rhetoric and attacks on John Kerry, indicated no retreat. And when he left the stage to the rock tune "You Ain't Seen Nothing Yet" you believed it.

After a three and a half-hour flight we landed at our next stop: Seattle.

We were back for a rally at the Seattle Town Hall, the site of our first rally in May. Then a record 1,500 people filled the former sanctuary to capacity to get a glimpse of the candidate who was an asterisk in the polls. Since then Howard had gone from front-runner back to long shot, but the crowd had nearly doubled in size.

Every seat in the hall was filled, while another 1,000 people packed the basement and lined the streets around the hall for blocks.

He surprised his supporters by walking up the stairs in the center of the hall. He was coming up from the basement as if he was rising from the ashes. The response to the grand entrance was deafening, the crowd exploding in chants of "Dean! Dean! Dean!"

The event was billed as a town hall meeting to discuss health care, and members of the largest health care union in the country, the Service Employees International Union, dressed in their purple T-shirts, sat behind Howard on the stage.

"We need action not rhetoric from the United States senator," he proclaimed as he told the crowd that the senator from Massachusetts had introduced 11 health care bills, yet not one had passed.

"I'm not here to say anything mean about him [John Kerry]," he continued, not fooling the crowd that knew something negative was sure to follow. "But I saw this morning in the *Washington Post* that he accepted more special interest and lobbyist money than any other senator in the last 15 years. We are not going to beat George Bush with the lesser of two evils. We have to change the Democratic Party."

His supporters hopped to their feet and cheered. He encouraged them to yell louder by pointing his handheld microphone in their direction.

The crowd's enthusiasm brought a moment of reflection from Howard. When the noise died down, he paused and with a smile on his face, calmly announced, "We're going to win sooner or later, but I'd rather win sooner than later." The proclamation brought a cheer from the understanding crowd.

When the event was over, we made our way to a minivan that was waiting outside. We walked through the crowd of people who had surrounded the van and drove by the hundreds of others who still lined the streets. Not deterred by the rain that blanketed the city, they had waited for hours to get a glimpse of Howard as he drove by.

"This place is mobbed," he noted as he waved good-bye to the crowd from inside the dry van. Three and a half hours later we arrived in Milwaukee.

—FEBRUARY—

February 1, 2004

Howard began the day on NBC's *Meet the Press*. It was his first time on the Sunday morning show since he appeared the day before his official announcement in June 2003. The show's producers had invited him to be a guest the Sunday before the New Hampshire primary, but we declined the invitation. After Iowa we couldn't risk a "gaffe" just two days before New Hampshire voters went to the polls. But now we had nothing to lose and Howard needed the exposure.

Tim Russert flew to Milwaukee to interview Howard face-to-face in the studio at a local NBC affiliate.

"What happened? How did you blow $40 million?"

"We took a gamble and it didn't pay off," Howard told Russert, summing up his dwindling war chest and the losses in Iowa and New Hampshire. As for the future, "We probably won't win someplace by February 3, with the possible exception of New Mexico, and we're going to continue on. We're going to continue on through February 17, and we're going to continue on through March 2, and we're going to win."

At a morning news conference after *Meet the Press*, Howard picked up the endorsement of Milwaukee's African American mayor.

Close to 75 members of the local and national news media sat in the chairs the campaign had arranged in rows in front of a the podium in a ballroom at the Hilton hotel. With laptops open and cameras at the ready, they were less interested in the endorsement and more interested in how Howard thought he was going to win the nomination.

"The reason I think I can win is because I have a record as opposed to rhetoric," he explained. "Washington is about the only place in the world where people think if you sit on a committee that qualifies you as an experienced person. . . . I do not think you can run for president against the special interests and be the senator who's taken the most special interest money in the last 15 years. Therefore, I think I'm the most electable of all the Democrats."

The mayor of Milwaukee was willing to endorse Howard, but others weren't so quick to do so. Many labor unions had decided to hold off endorsing any candidate until after the New Hampshire primary. Before Iowa and New Hampshire, many of the unions were torn between Howard and Dick Gephardt, but now Gephardt was out and Howard had fallen, making John Kerry the heir apparent.

In between meetings and during drives in the car, Howard called labor leader after labor leader asking for support and encouraging members of the unions that had endorsed him – AFSCME, SEIU, and UPAT – to redouble their efforts in the states that would soon hold caucuses and primaries. The campaign staff instructed him to be "upbeat" and stress the need for the campaign to "build on the success in New Hampshire." And if necessary, remind the union leaders that when Howard expressed his support for fair trade, Kerry accused him of "pandering to labor."

It was Sunday morning, which not only meant *Meet the Press*, but church as well. With the mayor of Milwaukee in tow, we headed to mass at the Holy Redeemer Institutional Church of God in Christ in Milwaukee.

We certainly needed to pray for our situation, but we wouldn't have visited the church if its congregation wasn't predominantly African American. The campaign staff reminded Howard that the purpose of his visit was to "lock up and solidify the African American support" in Milwaukee. A note on the schedule also informed us that the bishop's family was "wealthy" and owned more than 300 Burger Kings and Pizza Huts around the country.

□ □ □

When our plane landed in Michigan, it marked the beginning of the second loop of our cross-country tour.

The town hall meeting in the Detroit suburb of Roseville had the trappings of a big rally. Risers were constructed to form the stage in the gymnasium at a local senior center. A blue curtain and American flags served as the backdrop. A giant banner that read "Michigan for Dean" hung from the wall and arranged behind the podium were members of the American Federation of State, County and Municipal employees union wearing their green T-shirts.

More than 500 people filled the bleachers and the metal folding chairs that had been set up on the floor. But the size of the crowd paled in comparison to the thousands that we saw the day before in Tucson and Seattle. And the press, looking for signs of a campaign nearing its end, concluded that Howard's support was dwindling.

His supporters, however, were excited to see him. They chanted, "We want Dean!" as he took his place behind the podium. He smiled and responded, "All right, you got him! Now make sure you keep him on February 7!"

There were only a few stragglers left in the gym when Howard made his way down the hall to a small conference room.

It was Super Bowl Sunday and as football fans gathered around television sets to cheer on the New England Patriots and Carolina Panthers, Deaniacs across the country gathered around speakerphones for "Super Goal 2004." The 75 house parties featured a conference call with Howard and would raise close to $30,000.

The campaign described the motivation behind the special event:

> No one expected the Patriots to even get to the Super Bowl. But they did. Many people hadn't even heard of the Carolina Panthers, let alone thought they'd make it to the Super Bowl. But they did. No one expected in January 2003 that we'd even be considered a viable campaign. When we shocked the political world by raising the most money in the second quarter of 2003, everyone wrote it off as a fluke. When we broke fundraising records in the third quarter, everyone began to attack us. Now, people say that there's no hope that we can win back the White House. But we will.

In the conference room, three dozen Dean fans were ready to take part in the call and watch the game on a big screen television. As they munched on pretzels and potato chips, Howard dialed into the conference call.

Things went as planned until an image of the country singer Willie Nelson appeared on the television screen. Howard, unable to show the restraint he had on the airplane two days earlier, remarked to the crowd that the 71-year-old singer could take a cue from John Kerry and use a little Botox.

We were on an airplane when the game kicked off. By the time we arrived in Santa Fe, New Mexico, the game was not only history, but would land forever in the history books. When we touched down, cell phones and Blackberries buzzed with the news of Janet Jackson's wardrobe malfunction. The R-rated moment made Howard's Botox comment seem tame.

February 2, 2004

We were supposed to be in Vermont taking the day off, but Howard didn't want to lose a single day of campaigning with the contests in Arizona, Michigan, New Mexico, and Washington just around the corner. So three days earlier, somewhere midair between Tucson and Seattle, he rearranged the schedule in order to make the second loop around the country. (The change came as a surprise to the staff in Burlington, as well as to the flight crew and press, who now felt like hostages on a plane at the mercy of their candidate captor.)

The new schedule meant that we'd start the day in Santa Fe, make a stop in Arizona, before ending the day in Spokane, Washington.

Despite the eager supporters who came out to the rally in a hotel ballroom in Santa Fe or the volunteers who packed into the headquarters in Tucson, the mood of the day barely resembled the heady days of the campaign.

Howard was facing the realities of a lagging campaign. He could no longer boast that he was ahead in the delegate count. Kerry had picked up the support of a dozen superdelegates, putting his total at 115 to Howard's 114. And with seven states holding primaries and caucuses the next day, Kerry's lead was guaranteed to grow.

Howard began the day sitting in a hotel room in Santa Fe reviewing a list of the members of his staff who would need to be cut from the payroll if we were going to be able to run the "leaner, meaner" campaign he had promised. Some worked in the Burlington headquarters, but most were field operatives from Iowa and New Hampshire. It was hard for him to let the young people who had dedicated their lives to him go, but he had no choice.

He then had to explain to his once enthusiastic donors in New York why they should help him raise money for a fundraising event scheduled in the city on February 19 – the day after the Wisconsin primary. The more than 50 people who took part in the conference call wanted answers before they would donate to a campaign that had squandered the money they had already contributed. What was his strategy to win the nomination? Why, with the exception of Arizona and New Mexico, was he skipping the contests on February 3? And why did he believe he could win the nomination by focusing on Maine, Michigan, Washington, and Wisconsin?

And he began to contemplate the future of a campaign with limited funds. It would look like the early days with a small staff, a reliance on volunteers, and flights on commercial airplanes.

February 3, 2004

It was another Election Day, the first since New Hampshire. Two hundred and sixty-nine delegates were up for grabs in seven states: Arizona, Delaware, Missouri, New Mexico, North Dakota, Oklahoma, and South Carolina. Aware that he wasn't going to fare well, Howard had kept expectations low. "We probably won't win someplace by February 3, with the possible exception of New Mexico," he had told Tim Russert two days earlier.

Looking to the future, we spent the day in Washington State. Howard believed the state, which held its caucuses along with Michigan on February 7, could change the dynamics of the race. He told reporters during an early morning visit to a hospital in Spokane, "We need to win Washington State. Washington State will be the turning point, if we win, of this campaign."

On the surface, he had reason to feel good. He was attracting large crowds at rallies and, as he walked down city streets, he was greeted with handshakes and calls of "good luck" from business owners and shoppers.

After a morning town hall meeting in Spokane, where he spoke to more than 500 supporters, we flew to Seattle.

We stopped at the city's famous fish market, where Howard attempted to catch a fish, not with a rod and reel, but with his hands.

Catching fish was an attraction in Seattle, but also serious business for the fishmongers who carried out the task. A fish that was thrown was on its way to be wrapped in paper for a paying customer. But for Howard the task was a photo opportunity.

Standing behind a counter stacked high with ice and fish and wearing a white apron, he held both hands high in the air like a wide receiver waiting for the pass from the quarterback. The first time the flying fish sailed in his direction, it slipped through his hands. He tried again. When he successfully made the catch, he twirled around and held his prize up by the tail to prove to the watching press and onlookers that he had, in deed, made the catch. (Whether Washington would be his second chance to stop the nomination from slipping through his hands had yet to be determined.)

"Thanks guys. That definitely made my day," he told the fishmongers who tried unsuccessfully to get him to buy a $200 fish. Spend hundreds of dollars on a fish? Our excuse for not making the purchase: We had no way of getting the fish back to Vermont.

After a woman in the crowd wiped fish scales off his face, he stood in front of the mounds of fish and declared to the media, "I intend to win the nomination."

From Seattle we piled into our minivan and set out on the 45-minute drive to Tacoma. Howard was in a buoyant mood after the fish toss (which he deemed "well worth it"). And as we drove by Seahawks Stadium, home to Seattle's NFL football team, he pondered the future. He mused about the possibility of holding a counter nominating convention for Deaniacs. Looking out the window at the 67,000-seat stadium, he proposed, "If we don't win this thing [the nomination] we ought to do a big rally in Seattle and fill that damn thing."

By the time we reached Tacoma the results of the day's contests were coming in. They were results that Howard couldn't ignore, but he wasn't going to concede defeat. He told the crowd of more than 600 who packed the Pantages Theater in downtown Tacoma, "Well, the votes are starting to come in and we're going to have a tough night tonight. But you know what? Here's why we're going to keep going and going and going and going and going and going, just like the Energizer bunny. We're going to pick up some delegates tonight, and this is all about who gets the most delegates in Boston in July, and it's going to be us."

After the rally we drove back to Seattle. By 8:30 p.m. we were hunkered down in our rooms at the Westin Hotel. Meanwhile, John Kerry was down the road at the Sheraton rallying with 4,000 supporters, reveling in his victories. He picked up 186 delegates with wins in Arizona, Delaware, Missouri, New Mexico, and North Dakota. Howard's third place finishes in Arizona and New Mexico netted him 10 delegates. John Edwards placed first in South Carolina, followed by John Kerry. Howard ended up in 5th place, yielding no delegates.

February 4, 2004

It was a new day and a new race. Overnight John Kerry had established a commanding lead in the delegate count. Joe Lieberman, failing to win even one delegate, had ended his campaign – a move many thought Howard should follow.

But he never entertained thoughts of quitting. He was intent on making it to March 2 – Super Tuesday – when 10 states held contests and 1,159 delegates were up for grabs.

We began the morning where we ended the night before, in Seattle. After an hour of interviews with radio stations in Maine, Michigan, Washington, and Wisconsin, Howard took the elevator down to a ballroom at the Westin Hotel where 200 people were waiting. It was 8 a.m. and instead of waking up to a rally he opted for a serious speech.

From behind a podium, he addressed his supporters, who sat politely at round tables covered with white linen tablecloths scattered with the remains of their breakfast.

"The last twelve months, and the last few weeks, have been quite a ride for our campaign and for American democracy. Voters across this country are beginning to have their say. We're still in the early stages of this contest," he reminded his supporters. "Let's take the American dream back at 10 o'clock on Saturday in the Washington State caucuses."

From Seattle we headed east to Madison, Wisconsin. The endless campaigning had taken its toll. Our plane had turned into a flying infirmary – the candidate, the staff, and the press were all felled by runny noses, sore throats, coughs, and fevers. The doctor on board wasn't able to provide a cure and with a schedule that didn't allow a trip to a drug store, we were left to suffer.

□ □ □

The scene in the Majestic Theater in Madison contradicted the state of our campaign. We had lost nine straight contests, yet hundreds of jubilant Dean supporters filled the theater to capacity. Our theme song "We Can" blared from the speakers even though there was little evidence that we could. And while Howard trailed Kerry by almost 30 points in the state, mirrored disco balls whirled from the ceiling highlighting the blue, purple, and yellow lights that formed patterns on the wall.

The event was a party to celebrate the anniversary of the formation of Dean Meetup groups, the get-togethers that served as the basis of our grassroots effort. It had been one year since more than 400 people met for the first time in 11 locations around the country to talk about an unknown Howard Dean. Since then more than 100,000 Dean supporters – far more than any other campaign – had been brought together by the online social networking site.

The raucous crowd of 500 greeted Howard as if he was the front-runner. They roared seemingly oblivious to the fact that the highly touted online community had yet to produce even one first place finish.

Howard gave them a reason to feel successful. "We've had a great effect on the Democratic Party, all of us. Finally they've found a little spine," he announced to the cheers of the crowd.

And he continued to keep hope alive and his supporters energized, telling them, and himself, that just one win could change everything. With a parting thumbs up he exclaimed, "On February 17th you have the power to take back the White House and that is exactly what we're going to do!"

From Madison we flew to Michigan. It was 11:30 p.m. when we touched down in Flint. Our arrival marked our third state and third time zone of the day.

February 5, 2004

It was just 7 a.m. but it wasn't too early for a campaign controversy.

I was standing in the lobby of the Marriot Hotel in Flint waiting for my turn to check out, when a reporter from CBS News asked me how I felt about Howard's decision to drop out of the race if he didn't win the Wisconsin primary. I asked him where he got that idea, because no such decision had been made. He showed me a fundraising e-mail that had been sent out under Howard's name just after 1:30 a.m. In the e-mail Howard told his supporters that he needed $700,000 to run ads in Wisconsin, and he asked them to contribute to the cause.

"The entire race comes down to this: We must win Wisconsin. We will get a boost this weekend in Washington, Michigan, and Maine, but our true test will be the Wisconsin primary. A win there will carry us to the big states of March 2 and narrow the field to two candidates. Anything less will put us out of the race."

I went to Howard's room to see what was going on. He didn't know about the e-mail. It had been sent out without his knowledge or approval.

An hour later, Howard was standing on a small stage set up in the corner of the food court in the student center at the University of Michigan's Flint campus. The blue campaign banner that hung from above announced to those passing by that it was a Dean event.

He didn't have to answer questions about the e-mail from the 175 people who sat in the metal folding chairs or stood around the fringes of the food court – most didn't know about it yet.

However, he couldn't avoid the members of the media who were confused by the missive from the self described "Energizer bunny," who had vowed just two days earlier to "keep going and going and going" and had steadfastly refused to talk about ending his campaign.

After his remarks to his supporters, he was ushered into a small conference room where the media were waiting. Members of our traveling press corps, along with representatives from the local media outlets, peppered Howard with questions about the e-mail. Why the sudden shift in strategy? Was it just a fundraising ploy?

How could he explain that he had no plans to leave the race when his name was on the e-mail? How could he admit that he had not seen the e-mail without making his already shaky campaign look disorganized? His only option was to answer the questions without confirming or denying that he would drop out. "We're going to win Wisconsin," was his reply.

□ □ □

"Why is he so special?" the four-year-old asked his teacher as Howard walked around the child care center in Royal Oak, Michigan. The young boy was one of the two dozen kids ranging in age from two to four who were trying to figure out why the man in the suit was so interested in their art projects, and why the people with the cameras were so interested in him.

The kids weren't the only ones wondering why Howard was there. Only a handful of people at the child care center were of voting age, leading the press to question our choice of venue.

We had barely gotten into the van after our morning appointments when Howard announced that we were canceling the remaining events in Michigan and flying to Wisconsin.

The media speculated that the move was in response to the Wisconsin e-mail, when in fact it had to do with two lackluster and sparsely attended town hall meetings in the morning (not to mention the visit to the child care center) and a forum later in the day where the only other candidate scheduled to attend was Al Sharpton. Howard didn't want to appear one-on-one with a "second tier" candidate.

He also felt he had done everything he could in Michigan. With the caucuses just two days away, polls showed him with 10 percent of the vote and Kerry with 47 percent. He needed to reach the 15 percent threshold to pick up any delegates, and visits to child care centers or town hall meetings with the faithful were not going to advance his cause. In the end, it would be his organization not his presence that would make the difference.

I called Vermont and told them of our plans and the news was not received kindly. One staffer went so far as to order us not to leave. From their perch in Burlington, they saw Michigan as the place where we could pick up extra delegates and leaving would only hurt our chances.

Once the staff in Burlington accepted the fact that with or without their blessing we were leaving, Howard called the Wisconsin state director and delivered the news that we were headed in his direction.

On our way to the airport we stopped by the campaign headquarters in Detroit. Howard wanted to thank the staff and volunteers for their hard work and encourage them to keep up the fight. After a group picture we left Michigan and never looked back.

By the time we arrived in Wisconsin the campaign was scrambling to explain that the e-mail that read, "The entire race has come down to this: We must win Wisconsin. . . . Anything less will put us out of the race" didn't really mean that the campaign would end if Howard didn't take first place.

Shortly after he saw the e-mail, Howard had made it clear to the staff in Burlington that, regardless of the results in Wisconsin, he had no plans to drop out.

While in Michigan he had done his best to avoid answering questions about the e-mail, but after abruptly changing his schedule to travel to Wisconsin he couldn't avoid the press inquiries any longer. And it was up to everyone in the campaign to pull back on the e-mail without looking like we were doing so. But our attempts were reminiscent of Bill Clinton's "it depends on what the definition of 'is' is."

When asked by a reporter if "win" meant a first place finish Howard responded, "I'm not going to get into the semantics." And answering a similar question during a conference call with reporters, Roy Neel replied, "I don't think that e-mail says that if he doesn't win Wisconsin he's out of the race. The e-mail said if we did poorly in Wisconsin, we may be out of the race."

The e-mail and apparent backpedaling left many people wondering what we were doing, but Howard tried to turn the e-mail to his advantage. He was intent on making the Wisconsin primary a two-person race between John Kerry and himself.

Meeting with a group of reporters in a hotel ballroom upon his arrival in Wisconsin, he set the stage for the campaign he planned to wage:

Our decision to fight here and to win here was made because we believe that people are voting for Sen. Kerry without knowing anything about him. This is going to be a fully contested, fully fought out primary, the first one since Iowa and New Hampshire, and we're going to make every attempt we possibly can to make sure people know exactly whom they're voting for. . . . There's a really clear difference in our record here and a real clear difference in our characters here and we're going to have a fight, and it's going to be in Wisconsin, and we're going to win.

February 7, 2004

While caucus goers were meeting in Michigan and Washington State, we were in Vermont. Howard had no public events, just one meeting in the campaign office. Gerry McEntee, the president of the American Federation of State, County and Municipal Employees, had flown up from Washington, D.C. Three months earlier, the union had joined the Service Employees International Union to announce its support of Howard at a press conference filled with flourish and fanfare. McEntee was now in Vermont to unceremoniously pull his union's support of Howard. McEntee would later describe the man he once wholeheartedly endorsed as "nuts."

By the end of the night the caucus results were in. John Kerry came in first in both Michigan and Washington. Howard finished second with enough votes to capture delegates in both states. The day's results made the total delegate count 411 for Kerry and 175 for Howard. John Edwards had 116 and Wes Clark followed with 82.

February 8, 2004

It was caucus day in Maine. Unlike other states, Maine allowed candidates to speak at the caucus meetings. Seeing an opportunity to sway undecided voters, Howard changed the schedule. The day we had originally planned to spend in Wisconsin would be spent in Maine instead.

We flew to Bangor, accompanied by 22 members of the media, arriving just in time for Howard to appear on the CBS Sunday morning show, *Face the Nation*. The interview took place via satellite from a small room at the Holiday Inn hotel.

A cameraman from the local CBS affiliate was sent to broadcast Howard's side of the interview. The curtains in the Shamrock conference room were closed tight and, except for a studio light, a camera, a few cables and a lone hotel chair, the room was bare.

Howard liked to sit behind a table or desk during television interviews (it helped with his posture), so the two of us dragged a desk from an adjoining guest room into the room turned television studio.

The local cameraman produced some make-up for Howard to apply to his face to stop shine from the light. There was no make-up artist around, so when the cameraman announced that it would be up to me to carry out the task, I decided that the natural look would have to do.

Howard listened through an earpiece as the show's host, Bob Schieffer, summed up the state of the campaign, "You had another bad day yesterday, to put it bluntly. You were overwhelmingly beaten in Washington State, where you once had an enormous lead. You got beat in Michigan, where I think you once had a lead. And the big union, the State, County and Municipal Employees, who had endorsed you, withdrew their endorsement. It seems to me that a lot of Democrats are going to be asking, 'Why are you still in this and why are you going to stay around?' So I guess that's my question, Governor. Why?"

"Well, we have, if you look at the charts, we have the second number of highest delegates after Senator Kerry. I think we had a good day yesterday. We picked up delegates in both states. Nobody else did that other than Senator Kerry. So it seems to me that we're doing okay," Howard explained to the television audience.

Kerry led by 236 delegates.

□ □ □

The temperature outside was below zero and the wind made it feel even colder, but that didn't stop Howard's supporters from staging an outdoor rally. The campaign anticipated that 250 people would attend the event at Bangor's Paul Bunyan Park, but just two dozen braved the harsh winter weather.

Bundled in coats, hats, mittens, and scarves and holding Dean signs, they clapped and cheered as Howard gave his speech from a small riser that had been set up in the snow. The supporters – like Howard – were on their way to the caucus taking place at nearby Bangor High School.

"We need a doer not a talker in the White House," he told the crowd, his breath visible in the cold air. The rally lasted four minutes and ended with hurried handshakes and chants of "D-E-A-N. Let's take our country back again!"

The caucus had yet to begin when Howard traded the frigid temperatures for the warmth of the Bangor school gym. We were there too early for him to speak, so he had to settle for handshakes and small talk with the caucus goers as they filed through the front door.

There was a minor media scrum when Howard came face-to-face with Robert F. Kennedy, Jr. Sporting a John Kerry button on his lapel, he was there to speak on behalf of his uncle's senate colleague. Howard wished Kennedy "good luck in there" and then jokingly added, "I've got all the votes though."

□ □ □

Howard's campaign signs weren't the only ones dotting the walls of the Auburn Middle School cafeteria, and the reaction to his arrival was mixed. Two-thirds of the people in the room either stood or applauded politely when he was introduced. The rest remained firmly planted in their seats with their arms crossed defiantly over their chests.

Howard liked to ask Democrats to close their eyes and imagine a debate between one of his opponents and President Bush. In Howard's dream, the Republican president turns to the Democratic nominee (one who isn't Howard) and poses the question: "You supported me on the war in Iraq, on No Child Left Behind, and on the tax cuts, so why don't you support me now for president?"

Howard didn't use a specific name, instead he asked the Democrats in Auburn to picture Bush asking the question to a "Washington insider," a term he was using to describe John Kerry.

I was standing too far away to see many of the faces in crowd, but the chilly feeling in the air made it clear that not everyone complied with his request.

□ □ □

The caucus in Portland seemed more like a Dean rally than a multi-candidate caucus.

The Dean supporters in the crowd were eager for Howard's arrival. They weren't aware that he was standing in the back of the gymnasium when they began waving their Dean signs high in the air in anticipation.

The floor and bleachers of the high school gym were packed with hundreds of Portland voters and they welcomed Howard like he was a rock star. As he made his way to the podium, the people sitting in the lower rows of the bleachers reached out for a handshake and one woman urged, "Don't drop out. We're going to win."

By the time he walked across the blue tarp that protected the wooden floor and up to the small riser, the crowd had worked itself into a frenzy. And Howard was enjoying it. He faced a sea of blue campaign signs and feeling at ease announced, "We're going to have a little fun at the president's expense!" To which the crowd erupted in cheers.

They enthusiastically joined in when he listed off the countries that provided health care for their citizens. They roared when he said that the American flag was no longer the exclusive property of Rush Limbaugh. They actually closed their eyes and imagined a presidential debate when he asked them to. And they went wild when he ended his speech with, "Together we have the power to take back the White House in 2004 and that's exactly what we're going to doooooooo!"

After his speech, he was mobbed by his supporters and was forced to flee out a back door with the press running to catch up. With only the light from a television camera illuminating the path, we walked through the snow and around the building in search of our car.

The cold temperatures forced Howard to walk quickly as he fielded questions from the local press. He maintained that he was pleased with his showing in the primaries that took place the day before. "We did well this weekend. We came in; we got some delegates and came in second in Michigan, second in Washington." And he added, "We've got to keep going because we've eventually got to win the convention."

When asked if he really thought that he could get enough delegates to stop John Kerry, he replied, "We're still second in delegates right now. We're maybe a couple hundred behind. We think we can do it."

After one last stop at a caucus in Westbrook, where Howard followed Dennis Kucinich, we boarded a plane for a three-hour flight to Wisconsin.

When we arrived in Madison just after 10:30 p.m., we were greeted by close to 75 supporters and staff. When Howard entered the small terminal at the private airfield, they chanted, "Dean is the voice. Kerry is the echo."

Back in Maine the results were in. With 45 percent of the vote, John Kerry came in first. Howard came in second with 26 percent.

The results allowed Kerry to pick up 19 delegates while Howard added 11 to his total.

February 9, 2004

"Remarks to the Madison Community" was how the staff described the morning event on Howard's schedule. The speech that he would give would "frame the Wisconsin contest."

The event also introduced a new slogan, "Real Choice, Real Change." It was meant as a contrast to John Kerry's "The Real Deal," which the campaign staff described as "meaningless."

When Howard took the stage in a ballroom at a downtown Madison hotel, he came with a prepared text. "Real Choice, Real Change" was written in blue letters on a bright yellow banner that hung from the wall and behind him four rows of Wisconsin voters stood at attention. Many were wearing the purple T-shirts issued by the Service Employees International Union, noticeably absent were the green T-shirts of AFSCME. The union and the campaign had issued a joint press release just hours earlier announcing the split.

"I'm going to give a speech that's sort of a for-the-record speech," he told the audience, "but I think it's important that I get every word right." His need to read garnered a laugh from his supporters who were well aware of their candidate's propensity to speak first and think later. With a little over a week left before the Wisconsin primary we needed to act deliberately.

At the end of the previous year, before any votes were cast, we were betting that strong finishes in Iowa and New Hampshire would carry us to victory in subsequent contests and then on to the convention. But now with Kerry winning 10 of the 12 contests and Howard coming up empty, we were fighting against the very momentum we had embraced and our time was running short.

After his third place finish in Iowa, Howard told New Hampshire voters, "New Hampshire has a habit of reversing

Iowans." Now he was making the same argument to the people of Wisconsin – only he was asking them to reverse the voters in 12 states.

"Let me get right to the point, Wisconsin," he read from the text. "Over the next eight days the power to take this country back lies in the hands of Wisconsin voters. The media claims that this contest is already over. They say that Wisconsin's voice doesn't count, that your vote doesn't count. They expect you to rubber-stamp everyone else's choice. You don't have to listen to them. Wisconsin, you have the power to keep this debate alive. You have the power to choose the strongest candidate to beat George W. Bush. You have a real choice. Let's hear Wisconsin's voice for real change, America."

Twenty-three minutes later the speech ended almost exactly like it began. "In Wisconsin you have eight days to go. You have the power to keep this debate alive."

And with a "Thank you very much!" the speech was over and Howard was left to smile and blush as the crowd cheered, "We want Dean!"

The scene at our next stop, a meeting room at the University of Wisconsin-Green Bay, was more collegiate than presidential. There was no yellow banner, instead "Real Choice, Real Change" was scrawled in red spray paint on a white bed sheet that dangled from the ceiling. In the back of the room the traveling press corps (who had deemed themselves "fun personified") tapped on their laptops while balancing yellow foam cheesehead hats (made fashionable by Green Bay Packer fans) on their heads. And in the front, Howard outlined his foreign policy experience to more than 250 people who had turned out to hear him speak. "I've been to over 50 countries; more than George W. Bush has been to."

It was the second event of the day and he kept to the script when he proclaimed to the people in Green Bay what he had told his audience in Madison in the morning. "Wisconsin, you have the power to keep this debate alive. I'm relying on Wisconsin because Wisconsin usually brings the nation to its senses."

□ □ □

"I've changed my mind. We're in!" Howard declared to a surprised television reporter during an interview moments after his speech in Green Bay. The reporter expected the standard answer, "We're going to win Wisconsin," in response to his question about the e-mail that announced the end of the campaign without a first place finish in the state.

But Howard was done pretending that he planned to get out of the race. He had spent the day being deliberate, reading from a prepared text so he would "say the right thing." But in a split second, what many believed was the right thing – dropping out – was replaced with his true intentions. He would be in the race after Wisconsin and whether that meant Super Tuesday on March 2 or beyond, he had yet to determine.

The camera was still rolling when Howard broke into a grin. I'm not sure if his smile reflected the relief he felt with getting the news off his chest or if he was simply enjoying the look of shock on the faces of the members of the news media and his own staff.

Knowing the speed at which news traveled, I slipped out of the room to call Roy and Bob. We were surprised, but we shouldn't have been. We knew that he didn't agree with the e-mail and we knew that it was impossible for him not to say what he was thinking. Still, we didn't expect him to blurt it out during an interview with a local reporter.

I wondered if Howard had suffered from a moment of temporary insanity, but when I asked him after the interview if he knew what he said, he smiled, clearly aware and clearly happy.

□ □ □

The University of Wisconsin in Steven's Point was the site of our final rally of the day.

430

Howard's announcement that Wisconsin would not be the end of his campaign had set off a flurry of activity, and the media sat in the back of the room wearing their foam cheesehead hats, wondering if more news would be made.

But Howard read from the speech that was set on the podium in front of him. "Wisconsin, you have the power to keep this debate alive. You have the power to choose the strongest candidate to beat George W. Bush. You have a real choice. Let's hear your voice for real change in America," he told the close to 500 people who gathered in the school's alumni room.

After reminding the crowd that "on February 17, a week from tomorrow, Wisconsin has an extraordinary opportunity," he walked down the rope line, shaking hands and signing autographs to the beat of "We Can." When every hand had been touched he headed to an overflow on the floor below.

By the time he arrived in the room packed with the 500 people who couldn't see the main event he was tired of reading the speech, so he greeted the news that they had heard it over a loud speaker with relief. He was free to be spontaneous.

"If I win the Wisconsin primary I will jog around the State House in Madison singing 'On Wisconsin,'" he announced to the crowd.

And if pledging to jog while singing the state song wasn't enough, he added, "If I win the Wisconsin primary I will make my victory speech with a cheesehead on." The crowd roared when he asked, "What about that?"

□ □ □

Howard's announcement that the campaign would go on generated both excitement and a great deal of anxiety. The press had a field day with the news. Howard's online supporters were happy with the prospect of soldiering on. But many of his high profile supporters and some on the campaign staff were disheartened.

As John Kerry won more states and more delegates, many of Howard's supporters believed it was time to unite around Kerry. However, they did not want to hurt or embarrass Howard by pulling their support like AFSCME had done, so they were willing to hold off and let him exit gracefully after the Wisconsin primary on February 17.

By 9:30 p.m. we arrived at our hotel in Superior. It had been a long day – 14 hours with a live interview on the 11 p.m. local news still to go – and Howard had received a steady stream of phone calls from people (including Al Gore, Tom Harkin, and SEIU president Andy Stern) urging him to change his mind about staying in.

But he couldn't be swayed – nor did he want to be. He stopped answering his telephone, letting the calls go to his voice mail instead.

February 10, 2004

"Well at least it's not math class," the seventh grader said to his friend as he and his classmates were ushered into the auditorium at a middle school in Superior. The kids had found the upside of trading an hour with numbers for time with Howard Dean.

While voters were going to the polls in Tennessee and Virginia (two states that we were forgoing), Howard was in Wisconsin talking education. The school was the setting for our first event of the day, a "Real Choice, Real Change" town hall meeting.

The campaign had made 11,000 phone calls to local residents to invite them to the public event. It was an effort that resulted in an audience that totaled slightly more than 200, including the seventh graders whose attendance was mandatory.

Our next stop was at the Longfellow Middle School in La Cross where Howard turned teacher.

His 90 minute stint included a visit to an eighth grade history class where he described the role drunken British soldiers played in

Vermont becoming a state, and a stop in a sixth grade geography class where he quizzed the kids. Pointing to a large map of the world, he asked, "Which coastal city is warmer, New York or London?" The answer: London because of the Gulf Stream. (One boy was brave enough to take a guess; the same could not be said for the press and staff in the room, who were visibly relieved that the question had not been posed to them.)

Another class showed him the duck migration project they were working on and he quizzed another on the pros and cons of drinking river water versus toilet water. "Don't go home and say that Howard Dean came to our classroom and advised us to drink water out of the toilet," he joked to the science class, after explaining that the purification process made toilet water the cleaner option. ("Assuming you flush it," he clarified.)

The tour was capped off by a visit to a sixth grade music class. Accompanied by their teacher on the piano, the 45 jeans and T-shirt-clad students kept their eyes trained on their music sheets. "Oh, the world is full of people just like you and me," they belted out for Howard. "If we just do our part hand in hand, heart to heart we will make a better world for you and meeeeeeee!" The big finish ended on a high note (too high for some).

They performed like any school music class, where trying is prized above talent, prompting one member of the media to whisper to his colleagues, "It sounds like they need a little work."

The song was specifically selected for Howard because, the teacher explained, "You're trying to make a better world for all of us." Howard thanked the students and then urged the three adults in the room to "vote next Tuesday!"

By the time we arrived at the United Community Center in Milwaukee, the members of the media were overheard asking each other, "What's the point of this?" It was the third event of the day and the third time our audience was comprised predominately of people under the age of 18.

Kids who ranged in age from five to 16 took part in the center's after-school program. Some worked on computers, others played pool and they all listened to the music that rocked the room.

The media dragged behind Howard as he told a fourth grader, "We're going to have to send George Bush back to Texas." And they watched him play ping-pong with a teenager who had to be reminded by a teacher to "take it easy" after he almost hit Howard in the head with the ball.

□ □ □

The Irish Cultural Center in Milwaukee was the setting for the final event of the day. The home base for Irish and Celtic organizations in Wisconsin was housed in a 110-year-old former Congregational church.

The serene setting of the sanctuary was transformed for the event that the campaign billed as a rally. A large "Real Choice, Real Change" banner hung from the wall, music blared from the sound system, supporters were lined up on the stage, and the audience in the pews held blue campaign signs high in the air.

The 200 people who came out for the event cheered when Howard began his remarks by thanking the members of the United Painters and Allied Trades Union and the Service Employees International Union for "sticking with us." It was a dig at AFSCME, which had defected days earlier.

The press watched from the balcony as his supporters yelled, "No!" when he asked, "Is Wisconsin going to be a rubber stamp for the media and the pollsters?" Howard smiled when he announced, "This has been a terrific campaign and when we win on Tuesday it will be a terrific administration!" And the crowd roared when he vowed, "We will continue to fight for a better America and to fight and to fight and we will never ever quit – ever!"

Howard was in a jovial mood when he announced, "We're going to Daytona!" There would have been grumbling if he was breaking the news of another scheduling change to the media or our flight crew, but he wasn't. Instead he was mocking the speech he made in Iowa.

Waiting for him in a small room off the sanctuary at the cultural center was a camera crew and three dozen staff members and supporters. They were ready to film a promotional video for NASCAR (National Association of Stock Car Racing) featuring Howard. The video wasn't exactly like the speech. Howard kept his suit coat on and announced that his delivery would be "lower key."

He did embrace the spirit of the task, however. Looking into the camera and surrounded by supporters, he read from the cue cards, "We're going to Talladega! And we're going to the Bristol Motor Speedway! And we're going to Sears Point! And we're going to the Poconos! And we're going to rent a bus and floor it to Boston! Who's coming with me?" he asked.

"We are!" the group surrounding him cheered.

□ □ □

When Howard got in the car, he was handed a breaking news story. By the time we reached the hotel just minutes later he was ready to leave the Democratic Party.

The story contained the names of the individuals who had made contributions to Americans for Jobs, Health Care and Progressive Values – the group that had run ads against him (most notably the ad featuring Osama bin Laden) in Iowa, New Hampshire, and South Carolina.

The group wasn't required to make its donors public when it aired the ads in December. At the time, Howard suspected that multi-millionaire producer Steve Bing had funded the group, but the just-released list absolved Bing. The money came from associates of Wes Clark, Dick Gephardt, and John Kerry. Even one of Howard's own donors contributed to the fund. S. Daniel Abraham, the founder of the Slim-Fast diet empire, contributed a whopping $100,000 to run the ads against Howard.

But the most controversial name on the list was that of former New Jersey U.S. Senator Robert Torricelli, who gave the group $50,000. Torricelli, a Kerry supporter who had raised money for the senator's presidential campaign, had a history of ethics problems that culminated in him having to abandon his bid for re-election in 2002.

Howard was angry. He could not believe that Democrats would form what he called a "secret organization" to run negatives ads against one of their own.

As the elevator took us from the lobby to our rooms, Howard stared at the list and pondered aloud the possibility of leaving the Democratic Party and becoming an Independent. I hoped he was joking, but he wasn't.

When the ding of the elevator bell announced that we had reached our destination, Howard asked for Al Gore's phone number. He wanted to talk to the former vice president about what he should do. I handed him the number and went to my room, leaving him to make the call.

While Howard was contemplating leaving the party, the results of the Tennessee and Virginia primaries were coming in. I sat in my room and watched the television coverage of John Kerry celebrating his two first place finishes at a "rollicking rally" in Virginia, and the contrasting coverage of a somber Wes Clark preparing to leave the race.

The retired army general had one victory under his belt (Oklahoma) and was fourth in the overall delegate count. Recognizing that winning the nomination was mathematically impossible he announced that he would end his campaign at a press conference in his native Arkansas the next day

Howard finished fourth in both Tennessee and Virginia behind John Edwards and Clark respectively

February 11, 2004

How many Democrats were left in the race – four or five? John Edwards, John Kerry, Dennis Kucinich, and Al Sharpton all called themselves Democrats, but did Howard? I didn't know the answer.

I went to his room at 7 a.m. He was on the telephone doing a series of live interviews with Wisconsin radio stations. As I listened, I learned that his talk with Al Gore the night before had convinced him not to leave the party, but his anger towards his fellow Democrats hadn't subsided. It was stronger than ever and directed at just one of his rivals: John Kerry

The radio listeners couldn't see the smile on his face as he laid out his suspicions that the Kerry campaign knew that Americans for Jobs, Health Care and Progressive Values planned to run the ads long before they aired.

There wasn't a shred of evidence to support the claim, but Howard loved a good fight and he was enjoying the one he was starting with Kerry. And his rhetoric escalated as the day wore on.

By the time the national media got their chance to ask him about the donor list during an afternoon news conference, he was calling Kerry's ethics, among other things, into question.

"I am deeply disappointed in Senator Kerry's behavior," he told the reporters gathered in a conference room at the Milwaukee Area Technical College. "I have not heard of a case where other candidates have had their supporters contribute to a secret political action group to run ads, unattributed ads, attacking another candidate. I have not heard of that happening before on the Democratic side."

Calling Kerry "more like President Bush than we ever imagined," he continued, "we now see that Senator Kerry is not only supporting the Bush agenda on the war, the Bush agenda on No Child Left Behind, but Senator Kerry apparently also supports the kind of politically corrupt fundraising mechanisms that George Bush has also employed."

When asked if Kerry would make a better candidate than the Republican president he responded, "I intend to support the Democratic nominee under any circumstances. I'm just deeply disappointed that once again we may have to settle for the lesser of two evils."

His contention that Kerry was "the lesser of two evils" prompted him to all but endorse John Edwards. He told the Milwaukee Journal Sentinel editorial board, "I think Sen. Edwards is a stronger candidate in the general election than Sen. Kerry is. Because I don't think he's as deep into the Washington culture of kind of back-door fundraising." When Edwards heard the news he called Howard a "very wise man."

February 12, 2004

We were headed back to Wisconsin. We had flown to Vermont the night before so Howard could attend his son's high school hockey game. It was the first of two games we would return to Vermont to see. Despite the state of the campaign, Howard was intent on putting his family first.

With us were the 11 members of the media who had flown to Vermont to attend the hockey game with Howard. They had never met Howard's son or set foot in Burlington High School, but they would cheer the team on nonetheless if it meant being there if Howard made news.

Judy Dean and Roy Neel were also on board. Judy was making the trip to reprise her role as a supportive spouse and Roy was venturing out to assure the Deaniacs that he appreciated their grassroots efforts.

Our first event of the day was a visit to a health care clinic in Oshkosh. Howard and Judy walked through the tiny hallways with one of the clinic's administrators. They didn't see any patients.

Instead they walked into empty exam rooms along with the members of the media who squeezed in for a look. The closest they came to a person in need was a training mannequin that was laid out on a gurney covered from the waist down with a sheet, a blood pressure cuff (that the Drs. Dean knew as a sphygmomanometer) wrapped around its arm.

The image of Howard looking at the body made the press corps giggle and wonder if the body in need of resuscitation represented the candidate himself, who was fighting to stay alive in the race. A newly released poll of Wisconsin voters showed Howard in third place, 33 points behind John Kerry and even trailing Wes Clark, who had announced that he would end his campaign.

□ □ □

We were walking through the back hallways of the Grand Opera House in Oshkosh making our way to the main theater where Dean supporters were ready to rally, when we received word that the Drudge Report had posted a statement online announcing that it had news to report on one of the Democratic candidates for president. The conservative website said nothing more than the "dramatic" news would be posted within the hour.

We couldn't think of any news about Howard or the campaign that would be considered dramatic or worthy of a mysterious special announcement. It was more likely that the news had to do with John Kerry. Rumors were swirling that Kerry had engaged in an inappropriate relationship with a 27-year-old freelance journalist. A lack of evidence made the allegation nothing more than idle gossip, but did the Drudge Report know more? It wasn't outside the realm of possibility given that Drudge was the first to break the Bill Clinton-Monica Lewinsky affair in January 1998.

We didn't wish a scandal on anyone. However, we couldn't help but wonder what the rumors would mean for the race if proven to be true.

As Judy was on stage introducing Howard to the crowd as the "best candidate," the headline appeared on the Drudge Report: "Campaign Drama Rocks Democrats: Kerry fights off media probe of recent alleged infidelity, rivals predict ruin." Drudge went on to report that "the Kerry commotion is why Howard Dean turned increasingly aggressive against Kerry in recent days, and is the key reason why Dean reversed his decision not to drop out of the race after Wisconsin, top campaign sources tell the Drudge Report."

The contention that Howard had become aggressive or was motivated to stay in the race because of the rumors about Kerry was a complete fabrication – either by Drudge or by "top campaign sources" who were out of the loop. Howard wouldn't talk about the gossip and forbade anyone on the campaign from pushing the story in the media.

□ □ □

Eau Claire, Wisconsin, was our final destination, but first we had to make a quick trip to nearby Minnesota. We crossed over Wisconsin's western border to attend a fundraising reception at the Minnesota Convention Center in Minneapolis.

Three hundred Deaniacs mingled around the small ballroom sampling the punch and cookies that were carefully arranged on the tables that lined the side wall. Meanwhile, one escalator ride up, hundreds of people filed through the mammoth exhibition hall planning their vacations and inspecting the dozens of recreational vehicles on display at the annual camper show.

The Minnesota caucuses were more than two weeks away and it was questionable whether Howard would still be in the race, but that didn't stop him from keeping hope alive for the faithful who came out to see him. "I need your help winning the Minnesota caucuses on March 2nd. I know we can do that," he told his supporters.

When his speech was over, he worked the rope line, shaking hands and signing autographs for the kids and adults of all ages who gathered around him or were passed in his direction. A one-year-old baby made his way to Howard, thanks to the strangers who passed him from his parents to the front of the room. When the baby, who was proudly wearing a "Drool for Dean" bib, landed in Howard's arms for a photo op, the tiny supporter burst into tears to the cheers of the crowd.

February 13, 2004

The sky was blue, the sun was shining, and the air was crisp – below zero to be exact. Howard was dressed in blue jeans, boots, and an orange down winter jacket that spit feathers. It was the coat he wore when he started the campaign, but was forced to abandon in favor of a more dignified wool variety when he became the front-runner.

Our media entourage, dressed in similar attire, followed him as he toured the family farm in Eau Claire guided by the farm's owner. Not having mastered the task of taking notes or snapping pictures while wearing gloves, they struggled to document the event with frozen fingers.

We made our way to the milking barn passing a dozen black cats that huddled against the wall in an effort to shield themselves from the wind that whipped through the yard. It was Friday the 13th and the cats were an ominous sight.

After Howard explained the hazards of manure pits to the "city slicker" press corps (he ruined his loafers when he stepped in one when he was lieutenant governor), we headed to a press conference in a barn that housed tractors and bales of hay. He wanted to talk milk pricing and trade policy, the media wanted to talk about the future of the campaign.

"What was it like coming out of the losses in Iowa and New Hampshire and what is it like now?" asked a reporter from MSNBC.

"You know, you've got to put one foot in front of the other every single day," Howard responded. "That's all it is. That's what it was when I was the front-runner and now that I'm not I've still got to do the same thing, just work every day."

When they continued to press him about the presumed demise of his campaign, a frustrated Howard cautioned them, "I think it's a little too early to be writing postmortems yet."

When the press conference was over, we hopped into a minivan. A local volunteer was behind the wheel ready to take us to our next event. The man was excited to have Howard sitting in his car (it would probably be awhile before he vacuumed the backseat). He pulled out a photograph and asked Howard if he'd be willing to sign it. In the picture, a beaming Howard, with his shirt sleeves rolled up to his elbows, was standing in front of 5,000 screaming supporters at a rally in Madison that took place at the beginning of October. Howard stared at the photograph and wistfully recalled the event before picking up a black felt tip pen and signing it, a ritual he had carried out thousands of times before.

□ □ □

"You gave me hope again," a young twenty-something woman told Howard as he made his way through the dimly lit hallway behind the stage at the State Theater in Eau Claire. It was hard to tell if she was reminiscing about a soon to end campaign or giving him a reason to continue on.

Moments later the curtain opened revealing Howard to the 800 people who filled the auditorium that served as a vaudeville theater in the 1920s. Three rows of supporters stood behind him, while a giant America flag dangled from the back wall. For thirty minutes he pled his case to an audience that needed no convincing.

"Let me ask for your help again on Tuesday," he said, making a final appeal to the crowd. "Wisconsin has a long history of being independent and liking independent-minded candidates. Let me ask for your help for the rest of America so that we really can change

America and not just substitute one inside Washington politician for another. You have the power to take the White House back and that's exactly what we're going to do!"

After a sweeping hand wave and a "Thank you very much," he hopped off the stage and worked the rope line to the tune "A Little More Satisfaction."

□ □ □

Howard stood in the back of the plane wearing his orange winter coat, holding a video camera. An MSNBC producer had asked him to take on the role of cameraman for a piece he was doing for the cable network.

"Welcome to the 'You Have the Power Show.' I'm Howard Dean," he announced to the members of our traveling press corps who had gathered in front of him, many pointing their cameras in his direction to capture him filming them.

The mood was jovial and the media took the opportunity to reveal that they had named the new airplane. They made a game of naming the planes that we traveled on. One was called Pearl Jam after the rock band that once rode on the aircraft. When they learned from the flight crew that the country singer Kenny Rogers had flown on our newly acquired DC-9 they decided to dub the plane Gambler I after a song by Rogers of the same name.

Howard couldn't recall the song, so the reporters and photographers, who had obviously done their homework, belted out the country tune.

On a warm summer's evenin' on a train bound for nowhere
I met up with the gambler, we were both too tired to sleep
So we took turns a starin' out the window at the darkness
Til boredom overtook us, and he began to speak

He said, "Son, I've made a life out of readin' people's faces
And knowin' what their cards were by the way they held their eyes
So if you don't mind my sayin', I can see you're out of aces
For a taste of your whiskey I'll give you some advice"

So I handed him my bottle and he drank down my last swallow
Then he bummed a cigarette and asked me for a light
And the night got deathly quiet and his face lost all expression
Said, "If you're gonna play the game, boy, ya gotta learn to play it right"

You got to know when to hold 'em, know when to fold 'em
Know when to walk away and know when to run
You never count your money when you're sittin' at the table
There'll be time enough for countin' when the dealing's done

"All my decisions are one decision. We're holdin' 'em!" Howard exclaimed when they were finished. His camera was still pointed in their direction and theirs in his when he mocked his Iowa speech roaring, "And then we're going to California, Minnesota, New York, and then Rhode Island and Massachusetts!"

□ □ □

After stopping at the Wonderful World Coffee Shop in Sheboygan, where we watched Howard order hot chocolate with whipped cream on top and wondered aloud why we were at a place that's name was the antithesis of the campaign, we headed to the American Serbian Hall in Milwaukee.

Hundreds of people sat at the tables that filled the banquet room. They were there for the regular Friday night Fish Fry. As a tune by the Canadian born singer Celine Dion played in the background, Howard walked from table to table, shaking hands with the locals as they dined on fried cod, French fries, and Cole slaw. (The cod was even better when topped with Serb sauce – a mixture of peppers, onions and tomatoes – more than one diner informed him). With a smile on his face, he extended his hand and introduced himself, "Hi, I'm Howard Dean."

Publicly, he remained firm that the campaign would continue on after Wisconsin – and he did so privately as well. In fact, much to the frustration of many on the staff, he avoided talking about the future of the campaign at all.

444

It would have been easy if the campaign had been a patient. Dr. Dean would have looked at the facts – no wins, few delegates, and no money – and would have diagnosed the end. But in this case he was the family member who needed to come to terms with the fact that it was time to pull the plug.

He ran for president because he wanted to change the dialogue in Washington and he had succeeded. And along the way he had attracted hundreds of thousands of followers, found himself the leader in the polls, and raised more money than any of his rivals. How could he leave it all behind?

He was beginning to realize that he didn't have to, that the end of his campaign for the presidency didn't have to mean the end of his campaign for a different Democratic Party or a different Washington, D.C. He had active supporters in every state and more than 500,000 e-mail addresses. As a group they would still have the power to influence the election.

While Howard cheerfully solicited votes, I picked French fries off the plates left behind by the dinner guests and called David Halperin in Burlington. David, a former speechwriter for President Bill Clinton, had taken on the task of drafting speeches after Howard refused to read those written by Joe Costello. Howard wanted David to secretly begin putting together a speech that would end his campaign for the presidency. He was far from embracing the idea of leaving the race and if and when he would actually read what David wrote had yet to be determined, but he had found his safety net.

February 14, 2004

It was Valentine's Day, but the press showed Howard no love. The day before, he had cautioned them against writing postmortems, but they did anyway. The morning papers told the tale of a campaign on the decline.

Despite Howard's protestations to the contrary, a *Boston Globe* headline read, "Dean Bid Shows Signs of Ending." The accompanying story reported that no campaign events had been scheduled after the Wisconsin primary and that the campaign's contract with the charter airplane company ended the day after the primary. Both were true.

The New York Times described Howard taking his own pictures with supporters by holding the camera in front of their faces. It was something he had done when he was the front-runner, but now the action was used as evidence that the campaign was losing its luster. And the Associated Press called him "a political also-ran."

The members of our media entourage made no secret of the fact that they were sure the end was near. One reporter sat in the back of one of Howard's events searching for vacations destinations on the Internet. Wanting to go somewhere "hot, relaxing, and apolitical," he was drawn to the Sandals Royal Bahamian resort, which boasted an "all-inclusive Caribbean vacation."

In contrast, the Kerry campaign was soaring. "More Are Falling In Line Behind Kerry," boasted the headline in the *Los Angeles Times*. "Expecting to lock up the Democratic nomination shortly, Kerry plans to spend much of the next month traveling coast-to-coast, aggressively wooing the donors who sat on the sidelines in 2003," wrote the *Washington Post*. And the *Boston Globe* reported on a new poll that showed Kerry 40 points ahead of Howard in Wisconsin. (Kerry 53 percent. Howard 11 percent.)

But as Kerry solidified his status as the front-runner, the whispers that he had had an affair were growing louder and spreading rapidly on the Internet. Kerry had avoided addressing the matter, but he was finally forced to answer the accusation. "I just deny it categorically. It's rumor. It's untrue. Period." he told reporters in Wisconsin.

We had two events to attend before we hopped on a plane and headed back to Vermont for another hockey game. The first was a breakfast with African American leaders in the banquet hall at the Holy Redeemer Church in Milwaukee. The dozens of guests sat at the white linen covered tables set up in the church's banquet hall and looked on as Howard was serenaded by a singer who was accompanied by a gentleman playing a Wurlitzer piano.

The second event was a town hall meeting in Racine. Several hundred people gathered in the town's Festival Hall, well short of the 500 the campaign had hoped for, a fact that didn't go unnoticed by the media that was keeping track of the numbers.

By 12:30 p.m. we were on a charter plane on our way to Vermont. A flight attendant wandered through the small plane offering us salads and a selection of peanut butter, Oreo, and raspberry brownies. In the back of the plane, four members of the traveling press corps joined Howard in a raucous card game, which saw the candidate gloating when the reporter from CBS News folded first.

As day turned to night, the results of the caucuses in Nevada and Washington, D.C. were in and they brought John Kerry's total wins to 14 out of the 16 contests held to date. He took Nevada with 63 percent to Howard's second place 17 percent. Kerry came out on top in the nation's capital with 47 percent of the vote, ahead of Al Sharpton with 20 percent and Howard with 18 percent. It was a disappointing finish. One week before his loss in Iowa, Howard had won the non-binding primary vote in the capital city.

February 15, 2004

It was the Sunday before the Wisconsin primary and we began the morning at the private air terminal in Burlington. Howard was in the airport's small conference room looking into a television camera. Before we boarded the plane, he had to appear on the Fox Channel's Sunday morning news program.

The media reports of the day before that he had no public events scheduled after Wednesday and the claims from unidentified campaign workers that they were leaving Burlington on Tuesday night only heightened the speculation that the campaign was nearing its end.

Howard spent his 15 minutes of national television airtime addressing the rumors. He confirmed for the show's host Chris Wallace that there were no events planned after Tuesday and no charter airplanes reserved, but that only meant that he was going to "re-assess" the campaign. "We're going to keep going no matter what," he told Wallace.

As for the top aides who planned on leaving the campaign, "Nobody's told me that," he responded. It was a truthful answer. If people were jumping ship, they hadn't mentioned it to him.

□ □ □

Our first stop in Wisconsin was at a church service at the Christian Faith Fellowship Church in Milwaukee.

I sat in the section of the church reserved for families (the seats were close to the door and allowed for a quick escape for fidgety kids and campaign workers). I was joined by scheduling director Todd Dennett. The two of us were obvious strangers in the African American congregation and, although it was common practice for us to leave before the service was over, knowing that our departure would not go unnoticed and would only confirm that we were there for politics not preaching still brought about pangs of guilt.

Howard sat on the pulpit between two of the church's pastors. He smiled as the choir's soloist, standing just a few feet away, microphone in hand, sang a hymn accompanied by a jazz band.

He was given five minutes to speak before the sermon began. And he did what he had hoped to do during the early morning interview on Fox News Sunday, tout his record as governor.

When his speech was over the congregation applauded and Howard walked off the pulpit and out the door. We were in a hurry to get off the church grounds before the arrival of John Kerry, who was rumored to have plans to attend the same service.

By the afternoon the rumors regarding the campaign's future were running wild, fueled by "top advisors," "top campaign aides," and "senior campaign officials" – all nameless – claiming to have knowledge of what Howard planned to do after Wisconsin.

The Associated Press quoted anonymous inside campaign sources who confidently peddled conflicting stories. Some said he would drop out entirely, while others contended that he would only suspend his campaign. He would convert his grassroots network and help elect John Kerry, some sources told the press. Others said that he wouldn't.

The truth was, Howard wasn't seeking advice from anyone, including the many on staff who desperately wanted him to end the campaign. Some of the unnamed sources were using the media to put pressure on him to get out, while in most cases it was simply a matter of not wanting to admit to the media that he was not confiding in them.

In an attempt to put the rumors to rest, Howard did his own interview. "We are not bowing out. Anybody who says anything to the contrary has misspoken," he told a reporter with the Associated Press.

The interview came not long after he participated in a forum on health care, which itself highlighted the state of the campaign. John Edwards and John Kerry opted to skip the event, leaving Howard and Dennis Kucinich the only candidates there. Appearing with a "second tier" candidate was a situation he would have taken great pains to avoid when he was the front-runner, but now he needed the exposure. It also provided a chance to switch the subject from the state of his campaign to his ideas on health care reform. His traveling press corps was a captive audience, which made a story on his health care plan possible, but at the same time a story on his participation with Kucinich was almost assured.

The final debate before the Wisconsin primary took place at Marquette University in Milwaukee. Unlike during the forum earlier in the day, Edwards and Kerry joined Howard and Kucinich on stage.

The debate, broadcast live on MSNBC, was uneventful. Media reports described Howard as "subdued" and his approach "genteel." And they seemed disappointed by the fact that he and Edwards "sidestepped" attacking Kerry. Instead, all four men leveled their criticism at Bush.

For Howard, the debate provided an opportunity to talk policy. But the reprieve from answering questions about the fate of his campaign didn't last much beyond the 90-minute debate.

□ □ □

"If Howard Dean does not win the Wisconsin primary, I will reach out to John Kerry unless he reaches out to me first."

It was 8 p.m. and Howard had barely walked into his room at the Hilton hotel in Milwaukee when he was confronted by comments Steve Grossman made to the *New York Times.* The fact that Steve planned to support Kerry was a surprise to all of us, one that we learned about only after the article appeared on the online version of the paper.

Having his campaign chairman announce two days before the Wisconsin primary that he planned to support another candidate did not send an optimistic message to the voters of Wisconsin.

Steve went on to tell the paper, "I will make it clear that I will do anything and everything I can to help him [Kerry] become the next president and I will do anything and everything I can to build bridges with the Dean organization." He didn't anticipate that he was going to have to repair his own bridges first.

The New York Times posted the story on its website before contacting Howard for his reaction. After reading it, he offered a comment through his press secretary.

Technically, Steve had not yet left the campaign (he would make the move after the Wisconsin primary he told the reporter), but in Howard's mind he had. The response he gave to the paper was short and simple, "We'll miss him and we wish him well."

The defection of one of our first public supporters was a blow. The timing was anything but helpful, but for Howard the biggest disappointment was hearing the news from the media. Steve didn't call him before the story appeared and no call came after. Likewise, Howard made no attempt to reach out to Steve. His comment to the media would suffice.

□ □ □

The debate should have been Howard's last event of the night and as far as the rest of the campaign staff knew it was. But he had scheduled a meeting of his own – a secret one with John Edwards. He had pulled Edwards aside at the debate and asked for the meeting.

Howard had publicly asserted that Edwards would make a better candidate against George Bush than John Kerry. It was time to talk directly to his rival.

After issuing his statement about Steve Grossman, we slipped out of the hotel. Howard enjoyed the convert nature of the meeting. Not wanting anyone to find out about it, he insisted on walking to Edwards' hotel; driving would mean enlisting the help of a driver and a car. Mike O'Mary and I went with him. Edwards' hotel was more than 10 blocks away. It was dark, the air was frigid, and the wind was whipping, all of which turned the walk into a jog.

Howard met with Edwards and his wife Elizabeth in a private dining room on the second floor of the hotel's restaurant, while Mike and I sat in the bar with two members of the Edwards staff. For all of the campaign events we had attended together, it was the first time we were meeting and for the first time we were on the same side.

Howard and Edwards emerged 30 minutes later. Howard hadn't confirmed the inevitable (that he would soon be dropping out) or committed to endorsing the former North Carolina senator, but he had no plans to meet with Kerry.

Surprised that we had arrived on foot, Edwards offered to have a member of his staff drive us back to our hotel. When we reached our destination, the Edwards staffer asked if he could have his picture taken with Howard. Mike snapped the picture of the two men. Standing just a few feet away watching the activity (but not knowing where we had been or who was standing next to Howard) was Steve Elmendorph, a former aide to Dick Gephardt and now an adviser to John Kerry.

February 16, 2004

The day began with another round of Steve Grossman stories. The morning newspapers and early morning television shows announced his defection to anyone who was not glued to their computer the night before.

Polls continued to show Howard trailing John Kerry (23 percent to 47 percent) in Wisconsin and the press dogged him. A local television reporter barely let him finish his breakfast at a local Howard Johnson's before asking, "Is Wisconsin it for you?"

"No, Wisconsin is not it," was Howard's response. "We're gonna go on from here, and we're going to do well."

It wasn't a good way to start the day before the primary.

□ □ □

The scene at the University of Wisconsin in La Crosse was reminiscent of previous rallies. Three rows of supporters stood on the stage in front of a large American flag that hung behind them. Blue campaign posters were taped to the white cinderblock walls. And Howard, suit coat on and microphone in hand, addressed his supporters who stared up at him from the floor below.

(It was Howard's second visit to La Crosse in less than a week. During his first visit he extolled the virtues of toilet water versus lake water to a group of middle school students.)

The campaign had anticipated a crowd of 500, but only half that number had gathered in the school's Valhalla Room. (John Edwards had stood in the same room three days earlier and Dennis Kucinich would greet his supporters there after Howard left.) The institutional style carpet that peaked through the open spaces accentuated the sparse crowd.

The true believers stood close to the stage, while the curiosity seekers mingled around in the back of the room, coming and going through the two back exits.

Although we were on a college campus, people who had received degrees decades earlier peppered the crowd. They cheered and clapped, but missing was the unbridled enthusiasm that occurred at most Dean rallies.

Howard looked toward the future taking a line he first used during a speech to the Vermont Legislature years earlier, "We've got to stop thinking in two and four and six year terms in this country. We need to think in 100 year terms."

His supporters were thinking about the future as well, the future that began on Wednesday after the Wisconsin primary. "If you have no chance of winning the nomination will you still take delegates and go to the convention?" one man asked when Howard opened the floor to "questions, comments, and rude remarks."

"First of all, I'm pretty optimistic," he responded. "We've picked up a lot of ground in a short period of time, but whatever happens tomorrow we are going on. This has come too far. Now, we're staying in and we need all of you to stay in no matter what, past the convention, past the election to make sure we hold their (the Democrats) feet to the fire."

"If you don't win will you encourage your people to support the nominee?" another supporter asked.

"This whole campaign is all about the power of the people. It's not a from-the-top-down campaign that tells you what to do. You're telling us what to do," Howard replied as the crowd clapped in agreement. "So I'm never going to be able to deliver 700,000 people to whoever the nominee is and I wouldn't want to have that power," he continued. And he wasn't ready to talk about another nominee, telling the crowd, "If you do the right thing tomorrow and make sure I win in Wisconsin we have a really good chance at having a fundamental change in this country."

When the crowd ran out of questions Howard hopped down and signed autographs and posed for pictures as the Sheryl Crow tune "A Change Will Do You Good" blared from the loud speakers. Meanwhile, on the stage the campaign staff discussed the next pressing issue: lunch. We reminded each other that sandwiches were waiting for us behind the stage.

When the event was over, we hopped into the minivan and headed to the airport to fly to our next stop: Wausau. We ate our long anticipated lunch on the road. For Howard it was a turkey sandwich he pulled out of a brown paper bag. "The crowd turned out to be good," mused the Wisconsin state director as he peeled the plastic wrap off a giant brownie.

□ □ □

"Is there any press out there?" Howard asked as he stood in the kitchen surrounded by stainless steel appliances and pots and pans at a labor hall in Wausau. Five cameras was the answer that came from an upbeat campaign worker. Since only three cameras were traveling with us, the other two must be from the local stations we surmised. The news meant that the event would get local coverage.

When the swinging doors that looked like they came right out of a Wild West bar opened, Howard walked into the meeting room, greeted by a cheering crowd. He shook hands with his supporters until he reached a small rectangular piece of gray carpet that had been placed in the center of the room. The carpet remnant would serve as a stage.

Meanwhile, the staff was in another room preparing for the interviews he was scheduled to do with the local media. One by one a member of the staff peeled the protective backing off bumper stickers and carefully placed the stickers in rows on a large piece of white paper that had been taped to the cinderblock wall. We didn't have a banner, so the makeshift sign would have to do. "We're running out of money, shouldn't we be conserving these?" a staffer joked. "Howard's going to peel them off afterwards," another said in response.

One hour later Howard was facing the media. The banner, made of the meticulously placed bumper stickers, was behind him, but he was standing too far away for it to be captured by the media cameras.

The press didn't care about the backdrop anyway. "Your campaign chairman stepped down today. How was that and what's next?" one Wisconsin reporter asked. Howard responded with what had become his mantra, "What's next is that we hope to win Wisconsin tomorrow. We've done really well here, we're working really hard and I think we're going to do well enough to keep going. We're going to go right through Super Tuesday and then we'll re-evaluate after Super Tuesday."

We are the "Howard Dean of radio stations" the two on-air personalities from Z104 radio in Madison told their listening audience. The two had left the studio and ventured out to the labor hall to cover the town hall meeting. When they requested an interview with Howard, he was reluctant. Were they mocking him? "I don't know what that means," he told the radiomen. Their response, "It means we're cool" brought relief and a smile to Howard's face.

□ □ □

The Orpheum Theatre in Madison was built as a Vaudeville house and would later host stars like Frank Sinatra and Liberace. And it was where Howard would rally his supporters one last time before Wisconsin voters went to the polls the next day.

The 1,500 people who filled the theater cheered and chanted, "D-E-A-N! We want our country back again!" with the enthusiasm of fans at a football game. The marching band music that blared through the sound system was so loud that it was easy to imagine that a live band was behind the heavy gold curtain waiting to strut its stuff. Close to 100 supporters milled around on the stage waiting to do duty as Howard's backdrop.

Howard smiled as he watched from the darkness of the wings. It had been weeks since he had seen such a large crowd and enthusiastic demonstration of support. The scene was reminiscent of the days when he was the front-runner.

When he appeared on stage, he had removed the suit coat he was wearing just seconds earlier and had rolled up the sleeves of his white shirt. The crowd wanted a rally and he was going to give them one. The last time he rolled up his sleeves was in Iowa on caucus night, and no one could forget how that turned out. But he knew that this would likely be his last rally, so he decided to throw caution to the wind and embrace the moment.

Within seconds he was surrounded by the people on the stage, who instead of forming neat rows swarmed around him like an unruly mob.

"All right Wisconsin!" he yelled at the top of his lungs. The speech was an enthusiastic give and take between Howard and his supporters.

"What we lack in Washington are leaders who are as good as the American people," brought cheers from the crowd. A loud "Yeah!" followed, "We are going to beat George Bush!"

His supporters cheered in agreement when he reminded them that "Wisconsin is the state where you don't have to be a rubber stamp for the media and the pollsters." And when he changed his tone and softly and slowly announced, "The power to change this country is in – your – hands – not – mine," the crowd erupted in chants of "We want Dean!"

The 40-minute speech ended in the traditional manner, "Tomorrow we have the power to take the White House back and that's exactly what we're going to do!" Punching the air with his fist he exclaimed, "Thank you very much!" in a voice made hoarse by the fiery speech.

As a recording of the University of Wisconsin marching band performing the school's fight song and official state song "On Wisconsin" played, Howard shook hands with the supporters who surrounded him during his speech, then hopped down to work the rope line.

Squeezed by his supporters and the media, he worked his way down the line using both hands to touch the dozens of hands that were stretched in his direction. He stopped for photographs and put his signature on the posters, bumper stickers, and pieces of paper held in front of him. He posed for pictures with members of the SEIU and hugged two supporters from New Jersey who had flown in from their vacation in Egypt to be there.

His followers called him "President Dean" and encouraged him with pleas of "Give 'em hell, Howard" and "Keep going Howard." And as he made his way out a side entrance he passed by a woman who called out, "Don't ever quit!"

There was no hint that he was trailing Kerry in the state by 25 points.

February 17, 2004

"The glory days of Howard Dean's campaign are over. . . . The signs of the Dean Death Watch are all around. On Sunday, campaign chairman Steve Grossman said he would leave the campaign if Dean didn't win on Tuesday in Wisconsin. . . . Lower-level Dean staffers are talking openly about their career and vacation plans after the campaign ends. Reporters are repeatedly questioning Dean on when he will get out of the race," read the story on *Time* magazine's website.

"Dean's campaign has melted down since his shocking third place finish in the Iowa caucuses four weeks ago. But now it is in a state of chaos and confusion such as few supposedly serious presidential campaigns have ever seen in U.S. history," the United Press International reported.

Those were just two of the news reports that greeted us as Election Day dawned in Wisconsin.

For Howard, the day started at 6 a.m. with two and a half hours of live radio interviews. It was his last chance to make a pitch to voters.

By 1 p.m. we were standing in the hotel lobby with three dozen members of our traveling media entourage; it was time to leave Milwaukee and head to Madison. But first, they wanted to give Howard a gift.

The reporter from the *Los Angeles Times* was selected to speak on behalf of her peers. She held a white long sleeved T-shirt in front of Howard and read aloud the words printed on the shirt. "We have the power. Dean Press Corps 2004" was emblazoned on the back in blue and gold, the campaign colors. She turned the shirt around to reveal the words "Establishment Media."

"Governor, since you gave us the name (establishment media) we thought it was only appropriate that our campaign T-shirts reflect that and that you also get your own personal establishment media shirt," she told him.

Howard had dubbed the national press the "establishment media" after months of what he believed was inaccurate, uninformed, often biased, and relentless coverage that began in March of 2003 when the *Los Angeles Times'* Ron Brownstein misstated his position on the war, continued with the *New York*

Times story on his draft status, and picked up steam after he was deemed the front-runner by the media, no less.

"And indeed you do have the power," Howard said as he pulled the T-shirt over his dress shirt.

□ □ □

Howard held a tall mug of root beer in the air. As he complimented the taste, photographers scrambled hoping to catch him with a frothy root beer mustache.

We were at Sprecher Brewery in Milwaukee, makers of beer and soda. Why were we there on what was probably the most important Election Day of the campaign? Two reasons: Howard liked root beer and we didn't have anything else to do. What the voters were going to do was out of our hands, now all we could do was make it through the day. Hence, the time-consuming visit to the local brewery.

With the "establishment media" in tow, we walked around the brewery with the owner, Randal Sprecher. We watched as the soda-filled glass bottles moved down a conveyor belt and dropped into cardboard cartons, which were shut tight with the help of a blast of air that lifted up the sides of each box. Howard sipped from his tall mug as the process was repeated over and over to the beat of clinking bottles.

We toured the aging room, a refrigerated warehouse filled with hundreds of silver colored kegs, and ended in the gift shop where beer, soda, and a cuddly stuffed version of the company's mascot, Rooty the Root Beer Griffin, were up for sale. And thanks to Randal Sprecher, we didn't leave empty handed. Cases of soda were loaded into our van and the press bus. Five cases – three filled with root beer and two with cream soda – were destined for Howard's house.

After the brewery visit we left Milwaukee and began the 90-minute drive to Madison. During the trip we received the results of exit polling that a group of news organizations was conducting throughout the state. The survey, done as voters were leaving the polls, showed John Kerry favored by 41 percent of the voters, followed by John Edwards at 31 percent, and Howard a distant third with 17 percent.

Howard was sitting in the back seat of the van. He looked at the numbers that were written on a small white index card, but didn't say a word.

□ □ □

It was after 4 p.m. when we arrived at the Concourse Hotel in downtown Madison, where we would wait for the Wisconsin results to come in and our supporters would gather later in the evening. The gathering was not called a celebration or rally. Instead it was noted as "remarks to supporters" on Howard's schedule.

We had five hours before he would address the crowd. Howard and I, along with Mike O'Mary and two members of the Wisconsin staff, passed the time in a small two-room suite the campaign had rented on the top floor of the hotel.

The wait was long. For the first time in more than two years we had nothing to worry about or look forward to. There had always been another day – a schedule to follow, a plane to catch, an interview to do or a speech to give. But there was nothing scheduled for the next day or any day after that. We did the only thing we could do – order room service and watch television as the election results came in.

We ventured out of the room once to visit the Madison campus of the University of Wisconsin. Howard went to rally his student supporters who were standing outside the campus polling place.

The dozens of students who stood in the cold and darkness cheered when he emerged from the van. When they saw their candidate, one student led the others in chanting, "When I say Howard, you say Dean!"

Howard moved quickly through the crowd shaking hands with the young people as they chanted in rapid fashion, "Win with

Dean," "D-E-A-N! We want our country back again!" and "Let's go vote for Dean!"

Our visit lasted only minutes. The college students were excited to see Howard and clearly believed that their votes were going to help him in Wisconsin, but the exit polls hadn't changed over the course of the day, making a first place finish out of our reach. It seemed wrong to be there knowing that Howard had no chance of overcoming Kerry.

When we arrived back at the hotel, Howard and I sat in the suite and called Bob and Roy in Vermont. The polls had yet to close, but Howard was ready to talk about the future of the campaign and, despite all of the speculation and hand-wringing by some of his staff and supporters, he knew what he needed to do. The only question that had to be answered was when he would announce that he was leaving the race.

We were set to fly back to Vermont later in the evening after he spoke to his Wisconsin supporters. He could make the announcement from Burlington the next day or wait a day to give himself more time to prepare what he was going to say.

Howard saw no point in waiting. He didn't look forward to the prospect of spending an entire day fielding calls for him to drop out from nervous supporters, advisors, and staff. He would tell the staff in the morning and make the public announcement in the afternoon.

The decision to end the campaign was made as quickly as the one he made three years earlier to get into the race.

Howard was not one for reflection, but for a few minutes that evening he was. After the call ended, we talked about all that had happened over the last three years. We talked about Iowa. The caucuses were supposed to be the turning point for the campaign and they were. Only the third place finish we dreamed of three years earlier was supposed to catapult the campaign to success, not derail it.

He expressed no regrets nor did he dwell on the things he could have, should have or would have done differently. That wasn't his way. He was at peace with the decision and smiled when he thought of the amazing journey he had been on and the one that was to come.

I was just relieved that the decision had finally been made. I had been sick for weeks. I was desperate for sleep. And for the first time in my life I craved a green vegetable. I had eaten enough Krispy Kreme donuts, cookies, and candy to last a lifetime.

□ □ □

Shortly before 9 p.m. we took the elevator from our top floor suite to the basement of the hotel, where supporters were waiting in a small ballroom. Howard's brother, Jim, campaign pollster Paul Maslin, Texas Congresswoman Shelia Jackson Lee, and Wisconsin Attorney General Peg Lautenschlager took the ride with us. The elevator door opened onto a small hallway outside the ground floor ballroom.

Blue campaign posters were taped to the ballroom's gold wallpaper. Round chandeliers hung from the ceiling and two dozen supporters, including members of the Painters Union and SEIU, were lined up in formation on the stage. The media were set up on risers in the back of the room.

Howard watched through the open ballroom door as he was introduced. When "We Can" began to play he walked up the stairs and onto the stage. He held both thumbs in the air then pointed to his supporters who, like the crowd in Iowa on caucus night, waved small American flags as they chanted, "Dean! Dean! Dean!"

He took his place behind the podium where he set the text of his speech. He pulled the microphone out of its stand, but that was as casual as he would get. "You all make me so happy I could scream," he announced, proving that even in defeat he hadn't lost his sense of humor.

Conventional wisdom had him dropping out – he had finished a distant third in Wisconsin with 18 percent of the vote to John Kerry's 40 percent and John Edwards' 34 percent – but he had proven himself nothing short of unpredictable. And he gave a speech that kept hope alive for the diehard Deaniacs and gave the staff and supporters who wanted him to end the campaign heartburn.

In what had become an all too familiar refrain, he told the 500 people who packed the room, "Some of you are disappointed because we didn't do as well as we hoped we would do in Wisconsin."

When he expressed a similar sentiment in Iowa and New Hampshire, the campaign continued to fight on and his words indicated no retreat now:

> We – are – not – done! We have a long way to go. In order to change America we have to fundamentally change Washington, both Democrats and Republicans. We are going to fight for a fair America. We have only begun our work.

The crowed greeted the speech with cheers and chants of "Dean! Dean! Dean!" and "We want Dean!"

Sixteen minutes after the speech began it was over. There was no "You have the power." Instead, Howard told the crowd, "We together have only begun our work. We will change the Democratic Party. We will change America and we will change the White House. Thank you very much. Keep up the fight for a better America. Thank you very much for your help. Fight on. Keep up the fight for a better America. Never give up! Never give up! Never give up!"

And with that he walked off the stage and into the crowd. As he signed autographs and shook hands with his supporters, "We Can" played in the background for what no one in the room knew would be the very last time.

Howard exited the room and walked across the hallway that was crowded with reporters and media cameras. "Governor, are you staying in this campaign?" one reporter shouted. Without stopping his stride, he responded, "Well, we'll . . . ." He quickly thought better of answering the question and waved both hands in the air as he pushed his way through the crowd and onto the elevator.

□ □ □

By 11:30 p.m. we were boarding the plane headed for Vermont. Joining us on the media-dubbed Gambler I were 31 journalists. Representatives from ABC, CBS, CNN, FOX, and MSNBC, along with their print colleagues from the Associated Press, *Los Angeles Times*, *New York Times*, *Newsweek*, *Time*, and the *Washington Post*, were just some to make the trip to Burlington.

The scene on the plane was reminiscent of the last days of high school, when yearbooks are passed around for classmates to scribble messages to their soon departing friends.

In our case, foam cheesehead hats substituted for books. Reporters signed each other's hats and passed them to Howard, who used a black marker to write his name on the yellow foam wedges in his illegible doctor's scrawl.

The reporters on the plane did not know that he was planning to end his campaign in a little more than 12 hours, but there was a profound sense that everyone knew it would be our last flight together, despite Howard's announcement that we were headed to Hawaii, which held its primary on February 24.

Howard spent the flight in the back of the plane eating, sleeping, and chatting with the reporters who wandered back from their seats. No one asked about the campaign or his future plans, instead they talked about his son's hockey team.

□ □ □

There was a celebration on the airport tarmac in Burlington. It was close to 1:45 a.m. and the staff from the campaign headquarters was there to surprise Howard when he arrived home. They weren't aware that he would be ending the campaign in a matter of hours and they were in a buoyant mood, mostly due to the fact that they had come from a Mardi Gras celebration in downtown Burlington, where they had consumed just enough alcohol that even a third place finish in Wisconsin didn't bother them.

Howard stood by the airplane's door and looked down at the tarmac as his staff filed out of the small airport and gathered at the bottom of the stairs, waiting to greet him when he exited the plane. But he wasn't ready to get off. First, he needed to find the soda he got at Sprecher's. He knew if he didn't take it with him it would get mixed up with the luggage and be lost forever.

When the soda was located, he descended the stairs and waded into the crowd. He appreciated his staff being there, but he was tired and anxious to get home. He said a quick thank you, and then hurried through the tiny airport followed by a cart carrying five cases of soda.

We loaded the boxes into the back seat of my car and drove off, leaving the staff and the press waving good-bye from the curb. I drove Howard home like I had done every time we returned from a trip.

It was icy, cold and, because it was 2 a.m., quiet as we put the cases of soda on the front steps of his house. I reminded him that Bob, Roy, and I would be over at 9 a.m. to discuss what he was going to tell the staff and his supporters. I said good-bye and got in my car to drive home, but not before Howard asked if I wanted to take some soda with me.

February 18, 2004

We were numb. The cloudless, sunny sky belied the frigid temperatures outside. It was, after all, February in Vermont. But the numbness we felt had nothing to do with the weather. Instead, we didn't know how we were supposed to feel now that the campaign was ending.

At 9 a.m. Bob, Roy, and I arrived at Howard's Burlington home. We were there to help him prepare the speech he would give later in the afternoon. But he didn't need our assistance; he knew what the message would be. It wasn't long before we hopped into Bob's car and headed to the campaign headquarters. Howard needed to tell the staff that the campaign was over.

It was no secret that he would be making a speech at an event scheduled for 1pm at a nearby Burlington hotel – the staff and the press had been told the news after Howard and I pulled out of the airport parking lot just hours earlier. There had been no confirmation of what Howard was going to say, but the usually bustling office was quiet and the sadness that hung in the air made it clear that the staff already knew.

A dozen members of the senior staff from the policy, political, scheduling, and fundraising teams were gathered in the office that Joe and I once shared. Howard sat in a chair against the wall facing the staff. The room was silent. No one knew what to say to the presidential candidate who was about to end his two-year long quest for the White House. (There was no pithy Hallmark greeting for the occasion.)

The silence was broken when Howard announced that the campaign was over. The news came as a surprise to no one, but no amount of awareness could stop the tears from following. It began with Howard who thanked the staff for their hard work and continued with the staff who applauded him for being a candidate they could believe in.

The message was repeated to the dozens of staff members who jammed into the conference room, many were the young twenty-somethings who had left their lives behind to join the campaign. The last time Howard gathered the staff together was after the New Hampshire primary when he explained the changes in the organization and Joe announced that he was leaving. Back then there was little reaction from the staff. This time they gave Howard a round of applause.

□ □ □

When it was time for Howard to make his way to the Sheraton hotel for the official announcement the headquarters was empty. The staff had already left for the event. Judy met us at the office and joined Howard, Bob, and me for the five minute drive to the hotel.

We entered the hotel through a back entrance and took an elevator to the kitchen that adjoined the ballroom. Visits to hotel kitchens used to include handshakes, autographs, and photo ops, but not this time. The five members of the hotel staff who were there to greet us were excited to see Howard, but they said nothing, sensing the somberness of the occasion.

Hundreds of people waited in the ballroom and spilled out into the hallway. Campaign staffers mingled with the Vermonters who knew Howard long before he became a presidential candidate.

Meanwhile, Howard, Judy, Bob, Roy, and I waited in the kitchen under the watchful eye of the hotel staff and the three press photographers who were there to document the end. The camera shutters clicked as Howard peeked into the ballroom and mused, "It's a good crowd for such short notice."

When the time came the kitchen doors swung open and Howard and Judy walked onto the stage, Judy wearing the same sky blue sweater set and black pants she wore for her first appearance in Iowa.

Howard and Judy held their hands high in the air as the crowd greeted them with applause, whistles, and cheers of "Howard! Howard! Howard!"

Despite his losses he was still a celebrity in the United States and around the world as was evidenced by the television cameras in the back of the room that were beaming his remarks live to a nationwide audience.

When the room was quiet Howard looked down at the text he had placed on the podium. "Thank you very much. My thanks to all of you who got this crowd together in about three hours notice. I appreciate that very much," he said softly.

He continued, thanking his supporters in the room, in Vermont, and around the country. He singled out the SEIU and Painters Union for standing with him "when others abandoned us." (He hadn't forgotten what AFSCME had done.)

He acknowledged the big donors who "did not do what the establishment of the Democratic Party did. They followed their hearts and stood up for what was right." He thanked the 300,000 small contributors who "decided they wanted their country back." And he thanked Judy for "promoting the debate that's needed to happen in this country for a long time about whether a woman needs to gaze adoringly at her husband."

Ten minutes into the speech he got down to business.

"I am no longer actively pursuing the presidency." He chose the words deliberately with the help of the campaign attorney. The words gave him leeway with campaign finances and meant that while he wasn't going to do anything to promote his candidacy, he wasn't going to discourage his supporters from carrying on. He wasn't releasing his delegates from their commitment to him and he wouldn't stop his supporters from voting for him in the caucuses and primaries yet to be held.

The room went silent. The crowd didn't care about legalese or nuances; they knew the meaning of his words. The campaign was over.

But their disappointment was short lived. "We will, however, continue to build a new organization using our enormous grassroots network to continue the effort to transform the Democratic Party and to change our country." The pronouncement was music to the ears of the once and always Deaniacs who cheered. The campaign may have been over, but their work together wasn't.

For 20 minutes he rallied the troops:

> We are not going away. We are staying together unified, all of us. Dean for America will be converted into a new grassroots organization. We need everybody to stay involved. We are determined to keep this entire organization as vibrant as it has been through this campaign. There are a lot of ways to make change. We are leaving one track, but we are going on another track. We will take back America for ordinary people again. . . . This is the end of phase one of this fight, but the fight will go on and we will be together in that fight. We will continue to bring our message of hope and change to the American people. We will speak out, we will fight on.

"You have the Power." Howard closed his remarks with the words he had recited so often that his supporters knew them by heart. Only now no one had the power to make him president. But all was not lost. They still had the power to make a difference. It was a message Howard needed to hear just as much as his supporters:

> Abraham Lincoln said that a government of the people, by the people and for the people shall not perish from this earth. You have the power to take back the Democratic Party and make us stand up for what's right again. You have the power to take our country back so that the flag of the United States of America no longer is the exclusive property of John Ashcroft, Dick Cheney and Rush Limbaugh – it belongs to all of us again. And together we have the power to take back the White House in 2004 and that is exactly what we're going to do!

His voice was full of passion when he thanked the crowd and waved his hand in the air in a gesture of appreciation. It wasn't good bye. It was see you soon.

As the crowd cheered Howard gave Judy a kiss then shook hands with the supporters who stood behind him on the stage. He hopped off the riser and with Judy worked his last rope line. He moved quickly – spending a short five minutes shaking hands and signing campaign posters for his teary-eyed supporters as the aptly named tune "I'm a Believer" by the 1960s group the Monkees played in the background.

When he reached the end of the line he took Judy's hand and walked into the kitchen where Roy, Bob, and I were waiting. We walked to the elevator, Howard acknowledging the hotel staff with a nod and a thank you. The photographers followed, but stopped short of getting on board. Instead they aimed their cameras in our direction. Click. Click. Click. We watched as the photographers snapped one last picture of Howard before the elevator doors closed and the cameras disappeared.

—EPILOGUE—

In a matter of days the staff was gone, leaving the once bustling national campaign headquarters virtually empty. Office supplies and equipment were piled high on tables in tag sale fashion waiting to be picked over by local teachers. The phones stopped ringing. The e-mails stopped coming. And the former front-runner was at home attending to long overdue home improvement projects.

They say the higher you fly, the harder you fall. Our fall was painful. Despite this, or perhaps because of it, Howard refused to be counted out.

He won the Vermont primary and endorsed John Kerry. And he continued to set out on his own path.

One month after leaving the race he fulfilled his promise to his supporters by forming a new group. Fund for a Healthy America, which started more than two years earlier with only a chairman and a treasurer, was renamed Democracy for America, an organization with over 600,000 followers.

One year later he became chair of the Democratic National Committee, beating out six candidates to head the party that at first ignored his candidacy and then feared that he would win.

Howard told a group of New Hampshire Democrats in 2002 that he would win the nomination because he was "persistent."

And that he was.

—ACKNOWLEDGMENTS—

This book could not have been written without the support of my family, who put up with me before, during, and, most of all, after the campaign. Kevin O'Connor and Sue Allen, who thought it was a story worth telling. Jilisa Snyder and Tim LaRosa, who made it possible for me to write it. And, of course, Howard Dean, who let me be part of a 14-year adventure that no one imagined would include a run for the White House.

—NOTES—

PART II: 2001

September

5 "President Dean? Not That Crazy an Idea.": *Rutland (VT) Herald*, September 7, 2001.

5 "should he run for president . . .": *Boston Globe* editorial, September 6, 2001.

December

30 "extreme skepticism accompanied by eye rolling": Eleanor Clift, "Howard Who?" *Newsweek*, January 4, 2002.

PART III: 2002

January

"Compared with the burgeoning and well-oiled machines . . .": Robert Dreyfuss, "The Darkest Horse," *American Prospect*, July 15, 2002.

"The speech offered a tantalizing glimpse . . .": Editorial, "Making a Difference," *Barre-Montpelier (VT) Times Argus*, January 9, 2002.

June

20 "Invisible Man. The Most Intriguing Presidential Candidate You've Never Seen": Jonathan Cohn, *The New Republic*, July 1, 2002.

July

1 "Paltry": Tracy Schamler, "Campaign Fund Still Modest," *Rutland (VT) Herald*, July 16, 2002.

August

5 The nationwide survey . . . : Zogby International, July 30-August 2, 2002.

23 a nationwide poll . . . : Zogby International, July 30-August 2, 2002.

September

18 "The big winner . . .": Howard Fineman, "Living Politics: Who's For Real in Democrats' Race," *Newsweek*, September 18, 2002.

October

17 "paltry": Tracy Schmaler, "Campaign Fund Still Modest," *Rutland (VT) Herald*, July 16, 2002.
17 "dwarfed": Associated Press, "Dean Reports Campaign Cash," *Brattleboro (VT) Reformer*, October 17, 2002.

November

13 "terribly flawed": Greg Toppo, "Dean Urges Rejection of Federal Dollars," *Burlington (VT) Free Press*, April 19, 2002.

December

16 "Governor Dean has been here . . .": Rod Bosbart, "Gore Decides Against '04 Bid," *The Gazette*, December 16, 2002.
31 "eye rolling": Eleanor Clift, "Howard Who?" *Newsweek*, January 4, 2002.

PART IV: 2003

January

11 Nationally, Howard was dead last . . . : Zogby International, January 4-6, 2003.
11 But he fared better in New Hampshire . . . : American Research Group, January 7-10, 2003.
18 82 percent of Iowa voters . . . : Iowa poll: Zogby International, January 17-19, 2003.

March

1 "Charitable descriptions liken Mr. Trippi . . .": Jodi Wilgoren, "Dean's Manager: Inside Savvy and Outsider Edge," *New York Times*, December 13, 2003.
20 Brownstein wrote that Howard was "backing away from earlier

plans . . .": Ron Brownstein, "Democratic Hopefuls Rally Behind Bush," *Los Angeles Times*, March 21, 2003.

20 "I'm not going to back off my criticism . . .": Nedra Pickler, "Dean Says He'll Lighten Up Criticism of Bush During War," *Brattleboro (VT) Reformer*, March 21, 2003.

April

1 "paltry": Tracy Schmaler, "Campaign Fund Still Modest," *Rutland (VT) Herald*, July 16, 2002.

4 "Kerry, Dean tied in New Hampshire Poll": Holly Ramer, "Kerry, Dean Tied in New Hampshire," *Brattleboro (VT) Reformer*, April 4, 2003.

12 "He's no longer in power": David Espo, "U.S. Gains More Control," *Brattleboro (VT) Reformer*, April 12-13, 2003.

12 "U.S. Gains More Control": David Espo, "U.S. Gains More Control," *Brattleboro (VT) Reformer*, April 12-13, 2003.

15 "U.S.: Fighting Is Over": *Brattleboro (VT) Reformer*, April 15, 2003.

15 "Dean Faces Post-War Tightrope": *Brattleboro (VT) Reformer*, April 15, 2003.

15 "I would anticipate . . .": David Espo, "Powell Warns Syrians to Halt Aid to Regime," *Brattleboro (VT) Reformer*, April 15, 2003.

28 "We [the United States] have to take a different approach . . .": Karen Tumulty, "The Dems Get Ready For Prime Time," Time.com, April 28, 2003.

28 "serious questions about his capacity . . .": Dan Balz "Kerry Campaign Blasts Dean's Credentials," *Washington Post*, April 29, 2003.

May

3 "Dr. Dean scowled . . .": Adam Nagourney, Democrats First Presidential Debate Shows Party Fissures," *New York Times*, May 4, 2003.

16 "What activists like Dean . . .": Ross Sneyd, "Dean's Supporters Defend His Record," *Brattleboro (VT) Reformer*, May 16, 2003.

26 Howard was in fourth place in Iowa: Zogby International, April 25-27, 2003.

26 and slightly behind Kerry in New Hampshire: Zogby International, June 4-7, 2003.

June

22 "faltering": Walter Shapiro, "Democratic Race Still Tight Enough to Turn on Accident of Timing," *USA Today*, June 24, 2003.
22 "shifting" and "evasive": "On Howard Dean's Terms," The Note, June 23, 2003.
24 *Late Night with David Letterman*, "Top Ten Signs You're In Love With Democratic Presidential Candidate Howard Dean," June 24, 2003.
27 Howard received 44 percent or 139,360 votes . . . : MoveOn.org, June 24-25, 2003.
27 "We're ecstatic about the 44 percent . . .": Michelle Goldberg, "Most Likely to Succeed," Salon.com, June 28, 2003.

July

13 "His features collapse . . .": Howard Fineman, "Feeling Dean's Pain," *Newsweek*, July 21, 2003.
13 "Not knowing everything . . .": Howard Fineman, "Feeling Dean's Pain," *Newsweek*, July 21, 2003.

August

3 "The Dean Factor . . .": *Time*, August 11, 2003.
3 "Howard Dean: Destiny or Disaster": Jonathan Alter, "Howard Dean: Destiny or Disaster. Inside the Democrats Dilemma," *Newsweek*, August 11, 2002.
3 "Washington Democrats have a failed strategy . . ." Jonathan Alter, "The Left's Mr. Right," *Newsweek*, August 11, 2003.
3 "A Dean nomination could again mean . . .": Jonathan Alter, "The Left's Mr. Right," *Newsweek*, August 11, 2003.
3 "Dean may not be a maverick . . .": John Cloud, "The Cool Passion Of Dr. Dean," *Time*, August 11, 2003.
3 "The poll showed him favored by 23 percent . . .": Jonathan Roos, "Dean Leads Democrats, But Many Undecided," *Des Moines Register*, August 3, 2003.
16 backing "away from his pledge to adhere to spending limits . . .": Ron Fournier," Dean Waffles on Spending Limits Now," *Brattleboro (VT) Reformer*, August 16-17, 2003.
20 "Poll: Dean Grabs Lead in New Hampshire": *Brattleboro (VT) Reformer*, August 20, 2003.
30 "Dean Surges Ahead in New Hampshire": *Brattleboro (VT) Reformer*, August 29, 2003.

September

8 "It's hard to say . . .": Associated Press, "Lieberman Questions Dean on Middle East," September 8, 2003.

12 "Howard Dean actually agreed . . .": Associated Press, "Gephardt Compares Dean to Gingrich," *Brattleboro (VT) Reformer*, September 13, 2003.

20 "Dean's imploding" and "his bubble is bursting a bit": Michael Janofsky, "Kerry Says Dean Is Imploding," *The New York Times*, September 20, 2003.

25 "Un-Dean": Howard Fineman, "The Race Is On For The Un-Dean," *Newsweek*, September 16, 2003.

25 "Dr. Dean's face reddened . . .": Adam Nagourney, "Some Sharp Exchanges in Democrats' Debate," *The New York Times*, September 26, 2003.

October

4 "high-energy rap session": James S. Tyree, "Supporters 'Raise the Roots' for Howard Dean," *Norman (OK) Transcript*, October 2, 2003.

November

11 "his Washington team . . .": Associated Press, "Two More Officials Leave Kerry Camp," *Brattleboro (VT) Reformer*, November 12, 2003.

23 "sleaze": David Yepsen, "Win on Merits, Not Slime Ads," *Des Moines Register*, November 23, 2003.

24 "Trippi blamed Kate O'Connor . . .": Paul Maslin, "The Front-Runner's Fall: The Dean implosion up close, from the vantage point of the candidate's pollster," *The Atlantic Monthly*, May 2004.

24 "sometimes raucous . . .": Adam Nagourney, "Rivals Attack Dean at Debate, Focusing on Medicare," *New York Times*, November 25, 2003.

24 "appearing exasperated": Adam Nagourney, "Rivals Attack Dean at Debate, Focusing on Medicare," *New York Times*, November 25, 2003.

24 "arching his eyebrows": Patrick Healy and Glen Johnson, "Rivals Launch Attack on Dean at Debate," *The Boston Globe*, November 25, 2003.

24 "stayed above the fray": David Yepsen, "Debate-winner Dean is Back on Top in Iowa," *Des Moines Register*, November 25, 2003.

24 "respect and courtesy": David Yepsen, "Debate-winner Dean is Back on Top in Iowa," *Des Moines Register*, November 25, 2003.

December

9 Polls showed Howard leading his rivals nationally, in Iowa, and in New Hampshire . . . : Nationally: Gallup poll, December 5-7, 2003. (Dean 25%; Clark 17%). Iowa: Zogby International, December 1-2, 2003. (Dean: 26%; Gephardt: 22%; Kerry: 9%). New Hampshire: Zogby International, December 1-3, 2003. (Dean: 42%; Kerry: 12%).

11 "trusted inner circle": Paul Farhi, "Trusted But Tiny Inner Circle Surrounds Dean," *Washington Post*, December 2, 2003.

12 which prompted Dick Gephardt to launch a new round of attacks accusing him of "gross hypocrisy," "attacking President Bush's . . ." while he "turned Vermont into a tax shelter . . .": Brian Blomquist, "Gephardt Slams Dean Enron Deal," *New York Post*, December 13, 2003

27 "withering attack": David M. Halbfinger, "Kerry Paints Stark Contrast Between Dean and Himself," *New York Times*, December 28, 2003.

30 "more than any Democrat in history . . .": Glen Justice, "Dean Raises $14 Million and Sets Record, Aides Say," *New York Times*, December 29, 2003.

31 "greatest grassroots campaign . . .": Ian Bishop, "Dean's the Man for Raising Funds," *Brattleboro (VT) Reformer*, August 1, 2003.

PART V: 2004

January

4 "At no point did the doctor bluster . . .": David Yepsen, "Lights, cameras – and a lot of sweat," *Des Moines Register*, January 5, 2004.

9 With Howard in the lead in Iowa . . . : Los Angeles Times/Chicago Tribune, mid-date January 7, 2004.

9 "dominated by special interests in both parties": Mark Murray and the NBC Investigative Unit, "NBC: Old TV Shows Answer Some Questions," NBC News, January 8, 2004.

9 "The special interests don't represent . . .": Mark Murray and the NBC Investigative Unit, "NBC: Old TV Shows Answer Some Questions," NBC News, January 8, 2004.

11 Howard's "much-talked-about-temper": Jodi Wilgoren, "One Church, One Microphone, Two Hopefuls," *New York Times*, January 12, 2004.

11 A poll released earlier in the day . . . : Zogby International, January 8-10, 2004.

15 Kerry's numbers had steadily grown . . . : Zogby International, January 12-14, 2004.

16 The results of the Zogby daily tracking poll . . . : Zogby International, January 13-15, 2004.

17 A tracking poll released in the morning . . . : Zogby International, January 14-16, 2004.

18 The reporter was referring to a poll published in the morning . . . : Jonathan Roos, "Iowa Poll Finds Surge by Kerry, Edwards," *Des Moines Register*, January 18, 2004.

22 Polls showed him at 27 percent . . . : Zogby International, January 19-21, 2004.

26 A Zogby tracking poll conducted the day before . . . : Zogby International, January 23-25, 2004.

29 Polls showed Edwards and Kerry in a virtual dead heat . . . : Zogby International, January 27-29, 2004.

February

7 "nuts": Adam Nagourney, "The 2004 Campaign: The Former Governor: A Top Labor Supporter Says Dean Ignored His Entreaties to Quit Race," *New York Times*, February 20, 2004.

10 "rollicking rally": Robin Toner, "Clark Ends Presidential Run; Edwards Finishes Second," *The New York Times*, February 11, 2004.

11 "very wise man": Kristen S. Charnberg and Rick Pearson, "Dean Jabs At Kerry, Favors Edwards," *Chicago Tribune*, February 12, 2004

12 A newly released poll of Wisconsin voters . . . : Milwaukee Journal Sentinel/WTMJ-TV, February 4-7, 2004. (Kerry 45%; Clark 13%; Dean 12%).

12 "the Kerry commotion is why Howard Dean . . .": "Campaign Drama Rocks Democrats: Kerry fights off media probe of recent alleged infidelity, rivals predict ruin," Drudge Report, February 12, 2004.

14 taking his own pictures with supporters . . . : Jodi Wilgoren, "As Fortune Changes, So Has Dean's Campaign," *New York Times*, February 14, 2004.

14 "a political also-ran": Ross Sneyd, "Dean Sharpens Stop Kerry Rhetoric," February 14, 2004.

14 "Expecting to lock up the Democratic nomination . . .": Ceci Connolly, "Kerry Spurs Ambitious Fundraising," *Washington Post*, February 14, 2004.

14 And the *Boston Globe* reported on a new poll . . . : "Glen Johnson, "Dean Bid Shows Signs of Ending," *Boston Globe*, February 14, 2004. (Kerry 53%; Edwards 16%; Dean 11%)

14 "I just deny it categorically . . .": Helen Kennedy and Maggie Haberman, "Stay It Ain't So," *New York Daily News*, February 14, 2004.

15 "subdued": G. Robert Hillman and David Jackson, "Kerry Goes After Bush in Democratic Debate," *Dallas Morning News*, February 15, 2004.

15 "sidestepped": Adam Nagourney, "In Wisconsin Forum, Kerry's Rivals Pull Their Punches," *New York Times*, February 16, 2004.

15 "If Howard Dean does not win . . .": Jodi Wilgoren, "Top Dean Aide Discusses Plans to Back Kerry," *New York Times*, February 15, 2004.

15 "I will make it clear . . .": Jodi Wilgoren, "Top Dean Aide Discusses Plans to Back Kerry," *New York Times*, February 15, 2004.

16 Polls continued to show Howard trailing . . . : Zogby International, February 13-15, 2004.

17 "The glory days of Howard Dean's campaign are over . . .": Perry Bacon, "The Dean Campaign Winds Down," Time.com, February 17, 2004.

17 "Dean's campaign has melted down . . .": UPI, "Dean's Lament: Woulda, Coulda, Shoulda," February 17, 2004.